VENERATE THE PLOUGH

LAND USE IN
EARLY NEW JERSEY

A Historical Geography

LAND USE IN EARLY NEW JERSEY

A Historical Geography

PETER O. WACKER

PAUL G. E. CLEMENS

NEW JERSEY HISTORICAL SOCIETY
NEWARK
1995

This publication is supported in part by a grant from the Charles Edison Fund.

Published by the New Jersey Historical Society, 230 Broadway, Newark, New Jersey 07104

Cover: Thomas Russell, "View from Kingston, New Jersey," page 12 of sketchbook.
Courtesy Historical Society of Pennsylvania, Philadelphia.

Half-title: Illustration from *Columbian Magazine or Monthly Miscellany* 1 (1787),
opposite page 77 (October 1786 issue).
Courtesy Special Collections and University Archives,
Rutgers University Libraries, New Brunswick, N.J.

Chapter heading illustrations: Carl R. Woodward New Jersey Agricultural History Collection,
Special Collections and University Archives, Rutgers University Libraries.

ISBN 0-911020-30-6

Library of Congress Cataloging-in-Publication Data

Wacker, Peter O., 1936-
Land use in early New Jersey : a historical geography / Peter O. Wacker, Paul G. E. Clemens.
p.   cm.
Includes bibliographical references and index.
ISBN 9110203060
1. Land use, Rural—New Jersey—History-18th century.
2. Agriculture-Economic aspects—New Jersey—History—18th century.
3. New Jersey—Historical geography. I. Clemens, Paul G. E., 1947-. II. Title.
HD266.N5W33 1994
333.76′ 13′ 0974909033—dc20   95-5542
                                                                          CIP

For Jill

◆

JMJK

C

SECC

pour

une bonne mère,

une bonne amie,

une bonne collègue

CONTENTS

LIST OF ILLUSTRATIONS

Maps

1. New Jersey Physiographic Regions
2. New Jersey Settlement, 1665–1765
3. Drainage and Bodies of Water
4. Population Density, 1784
5. Population Density, 1810
6. New Jersey Township Boundaries, 1784
7. Initial European Settlements
8. County Boundaries, 1772–1820
9. Von Thünen's Hypothetical Land Use Zones
10. Unimproved Land Utilized Primarily for Livestock, 1726–82
11. Improved Land, 1784
12. Mean Farm Acreages, ca. 1780
13. Farms of 25–49 Acres, ca. 1780
14. Farms of 50–99 Acres, ca. 1780
15. Farms of More than 200 Acres, ca. 1780
16. Landless Persons, ca. 1780
17. Paled Gardens, 1747–79
18. Natural Productive Capacity of Soils
19. Banked Meadows, 1734–82
20. Meadows, 1724–50
21. Average January Temperature
22. Average July Temperature
23. Average Days of Frost-Free Season
24. Average Days of Vegetative Growing Season
25. New Jersey Revolutionary Battles and Skirmishes, 1776–83
26. New Jersey Revolutionary War Damage Claims Locations
27. Distribution of Wheat, 1730–82
28. Distribution of Rye, 1757–82
29. Distribution of Indian Corn, 1752–82
30. Distribution of Flax and Hemp, 1732–82
31. Distribution of Orchards, 1724–50
32. Distribution of English Grasses or Meadow, 1729–82
33. Cattle per Taxable Inhabitant, ca. 1780
34. Cattle per Hundred Acres, by Township, 1784
35. Dairy in Cellar, Dairy Room, Milk Cellar, Milk Room, 1746–82
36. Dairies, Dairy Houses, Milk Houses, Spring Houses, 1746–82
37. Hogs per Taxable Inhabitant, ca. 1780
38. Smokehouses, 1746–82
39. Horses per Taxable Inhabitant, ca. 1780
40. Horses per Hundred Acres, by Township, 1784
41. Distribution of Covering Horses, ca. 1784

Figures

LIST OF TABLES

Appendix

PREFACE

This book began as a sequel to my earlier work, *Land and People: A Cultural Geography of Preindustrial New Jersey*. The work was to focus on New Jersey's early cultural landscapes, components of which have lasted to the present day. Agricultural landscapes would, of course, comprise an important portion of such a study. In the course of my research on agriculture, so much data was uncovered dealing with land use in general that I decided a book-length publication was in order. Casual conversations with Donald Skemer, then director of publications at the New Jersey Historical Society, resulted in an application to the Charles Edison Fund for a grant in support of publication. Dr. Skemer also suggested that Paul Clemens be invited to add two historical essays covering the same subject.

Readers may consult *Land and People* for a more extensive discussion of settlement history and the circumstances of land division in the state. However, the maps of farm sizes in this volume supersede the maps in the earlier volume, based as they are on original tax lists and not on newspaper advertisements.

In addition to the generous support of the Charles Edison Fund, I wish also to acknowledge much-needed support for portions of other projects that have found their way into this study. I thank especially the New Jersey Historical Commission and the Rutgers University Research Council.

I also want to express my thanks to Robert Burnett, who began the editing of this book, and to Kathryn Grover, who skillfully completed it. Several scholars knowledgeable on various aspects of land use in early New Jersey were asked to read either portions of or the entire original manuscript and made valuable suggestions. I thank especially David Fowler, Theodore Kury, Phyllis Mount, and Lorraine Williams. Of course, any errors of fact or interpretation are my responsibility.

A large part of this work involved the production of original maps. Frank Kelland of Montclair State University produced the original versions of a number of the maps in this book as parts of earlier projects. Michael Siegel, director of the Rutgers University Cartographic Laboratory, has been responsible for most of the other maps and the final design of all of the maps and graphs. Cartographers are an extremely valuable adjunct to research, and I am grateful for their contributions. I am also indebted to Betty Ann Abbetemarco and Elaine Gordon of the secretarial staff of the department of geography at Rutgers University for their general helpfulness and kindness.

Any scholar involved in historical research is helped immeasurably by the staffs of research facilities. Over the years, many people have helped me on this study. I thank them here, and I extend my sincere apologies to anyone I may have forgotten. First and foremost, my thanks go to the staff of the Special Collections Division of the Alexander Library at Rutgers University in New Brunswick. Donald Sinclair, now "retired," was chiefly responsible for building the magnificent collection there, which now bears his name. I am one among many scholars who still seek

Don's advice and help with sources. Ronald Becker has ably filled Don's position and he, too, has been of great help. Other staff members who have graciously assisted me over the years include Clark Beck, Thomas Frusciano, Bonita Grant, Albert King, Vincent Larkin, Janice Levin, Janet Riemer, Ruth Simmons, and Edward Skipworth. I also want to thank the director of the Alexander Library, Ryoko Toyama, for providing study space.

The other major respository of nonofficial early manuscripts concerning New Jersey is at the New Jersey Historical Society in Newark. Here Barbara Irwin and Rosalind Libby, former directors of the library, are to be thanked, along with Nancy Blankenhorn, Carl Lane, and Elsa Meyers.

For New Jersey's official records, the Division of Archives housed in the State Library in Trenton is the main repository. William Wright, the director for many years, has been of great aid to me, as has his successor, Carl Niederer, and his staff, Bette Epstein and Daniel Jones. Formerly in that division but in recent years a member of the state library staff specializing in genealogy is Rebecca Colesar, who continues to assist in my research.

The staffs of several other regional libraries provided valuable help. I thank especially Edith Hoelle, Gloucester County Historical Society; Roxanne K. Carkhuff, Hunterdon County Historical Society; Joseph Hammon, The Historical Society of Monmouth County; Lois Densky-Wolff, Joint Free Public Library of Morristown and Morris County; and Clara M. Kirner, Savitz Library, Rowan College. Staff at the New-York Historical Society and the Historical Society of Pennsylvania have also been kind and helpful in my occasional visits there.

Peter O. Wacker
New Brunswick, New Jersey

My initial attempt to make sense of farm accounts and agricultural diaries was aided substantially by comments from Stephen Innes, Rhys Isaac, and Michael Zuckerman. Thomas Slaughter read the manuscript with considerable skepticism and forced me to reconsider many aspects of the argument. Lorena S. Walsh shared with me her own yet unpublished work on Chesapeake plantation management and provided me with both methodological suggestions for working with probate inventories and cautionary advice about efforts to relate behavior and consciousness. Kathleen Jones, bringing to the manuscript the perspective of a historian of the twentieth century, contributed immeasurably to my attempt to frame questions broadly, tell the story engagingly, and analyze problems clearly. Jennifer Jones forced me to go back, when the manuscript seemed complete, and rework aspects that yet required restatement. I owe a special debt to Lucy Simler, whose previous collaboration with me in our studies of Chester County, Pennsylvania, helped make this work possible, and to Lois Green Carr, who for more than two decades has taught me what it means to be an historian of early America. The National Endowment for the Humanities, the American Association of State and Local History, and the Rutgers University Research Council all provided grant support at crucial stages of my work. Finally, there is the enormous debt that I owe to my editor. Without the effort of Kathryn Grover this work, in its current form, might not even have been imagined, let alone brought to conclusion.

Paul G. E. Clemens
Metuchen, New Jersey

ABBREVIATIONS

Short Titles

Docs. Rel. N.J., 1st ser.

William A. Whitehead et al., eds., *Archives of the State of New Jersey: Documents Relating to the Colonial, Revolutionary and Post-Revolutionary History of the State of New Jersey,* 1st ser., 42 vols. (Newark, Trenton, Paterson, N.J., 1880–1949).

Docs. Rel. N.J., 2d ser.

William S. Stryker et al., eds., *Archives of the State of New Jersey: Documents Relating to the Revolutionary History of the State of New Jersey,* 2d ser., 5 vols. (Various Places, 1901–1917).

N.J. Laws

Bernard P. Bush, comp., *Laws of the Royal Colony of New Jersey,* 3d ser., 5 vols. (Trenton, N.J., 1977–86).

N.J.S.L.

New Jersey Session Laws is the uniform subject heading for acts of the colonial and state assemblies of New Jersey. The acts of a given legislative session were printed in pamphlet form by various printers; they then were privately bound and variously titled by different entities, including libraries and law firms. The title, for example, of the 1813 session laws in the library at NjHi is *Acts of the 37th General Assembly;* for 1818, *Acts of the 42nd General Assembly.*

S.S.   Second Sitting
Priv. & Temp.   Private and Temporary Acts

Proc. N.J.H.S.

Proceedings of the New Jersey Historical Society, 1st and 2d ser. (Newark, N.J., 1845–).

N.J.H.

New Jersey History, journal of the New Jersey Historical Society (Newark, N.J.)

Major Repositories

NjHi   New Jersey Historical Society, Newark
NjR   Alexander Library, Rutgers University, New Brunswick
NJSA   New Jersey State Archives, Trenton

First Month, January, 1819.

FOREWORD

Rural Culture and the Farm Economy in Late Eighteenth-Century New Jersey

PAUL G. E. CLEMENS

On April 30, 1797, Erkuries Beatty entered in his diary a brief description of the past week's activities on his Princeton, New Jersey, farm:

> Sunday—Have been so busy with my Barn and other things that I let my Book [diary] get back and have forgot the state of the weather, but this I am certain we have had a great deal of Rain — sowed clover seed on oats ground — grafted about thirty apple trees last week — chiefly the August apple and barn apple. . . . in my hay orchard — also some yellow pippins from my own orchard and sundry other fruit got of Abraham Sthyker — Isaac finished working the Corn ground this week besides waiting on the Carpenters and helping them — raining — the Carpenters not ready to raise on Tuesday but Mr. Reid and Isaac invited hands for Wednesday and on that day we got it [the barn] up very well without any accident and the Cow shed too except one Bent —We had 32 people at the raising and gave them all supper, at least twice as many people as we wanted, but I was happy I had so many friends to help me. — Thursday and Friday the carpenters finished the cow shed[,] . . . that is raised the other Bent Spirt the Rafters on & — I made a lean-too to the Barn North to Stow way Straw &c — also . . . put the Rafters on my Sheep House — so all in readiness Now to weatherboard & the Carpenters all went off early Saturday morning —[1]

Erkuries Beatty left generous documentation of a spirited life, but if he was no ordinary farmer his farm diary nonetheless speaks to one of the central questions that has perplexed historians of late colonial America. The April 30 entry acknowledges Beatty's dependence on his neighbors (collectively they raised his barn) as well as his reciprocal obligation to them (needed or not, they all were fed supper), while at the same time it testifies to the commercial character of his farm: he hired skilled laborers (carpenters) and showed interest in improvement (grafting apple trees and sowing clover). Beatty thus reponded both to community and to market, and for historians the question has been the relative importance of each, community and market, in the lives of ordinary farm families in early America. Community, defined as a set of face-to-face relationships governed by customary practices and neighborly sociability, allowed individual farm families to supply most of their material needs and wants through the local exchange of produce, crafts, and labor. Such needs, some have argued, were relatively well defined and essentially unchanging; the goal was not to accumulate but to conserve and endure, not to transform but merely to pass intact to the next generation the same way of life. This world has been defined as a subsistence economy, or, alternatively, as a collection of self-sufficient communities in which the "use value" of goods, rather than their market or "exchange value," determined economic relationships.[2]

Market, in contrast, defined a world more distant, more impersonal, and less predictable, a world where prices, set by the supply of and demand for agricultural products across the Atlantic, controlled the economic fortunes of local residents in seemingly isolated early American towns and counties. In early America, this argument runs, production was meant for sale, labor was purchased, and economic resources were risked (and wasted) for profit. People sought to improve their situation and accumulate material possessions; they calculated, improved, and speculated. Market society in sum encompassed not simply different patterns of behavior but a different sort of imagination.[3]

The debate about market and community in early America began with a questioning of the assumptions historians had made in interpreting the behavior of farm families. The critique focused on the assumption that every type of economic activity was equally evidence of "liberal," market-oriented, or capitalist values. When early American householders eagerly bought and sold land, was their intent speculative and their goal profit and accumulation? Or were these transactions the least risky, most likely way to protect the family by assuring that the next generation could live as comfortably as the present one? The first explanation emphasizes market values, the second community values. While most historians would deny that early Americans thought in terms that so sharply contrasted these values, they have nonetheless found it worthwhile to attempt to elicit values (about which little is directly known) from behavior (about which evidence is relatively abundant).[4]

Also clearly at stake in the debate over community and market in early America is the question of how "disruptive" the elaboration of market relationships was of "traditional" ways of life. Some argue that from the outset English settlers were individualistic, profit-seeking, and self-interested (and thus that market involvement was neither new nor unsettling), others that communal values were antithetical to market values and that early Americans consciously resisted market involvement. The late eighteenth century, according to those who characterize the market as intrusive, marked a critical watershed, a point in time when regional, national, and international markets seriously undercut traditional patterns of household economy and community life. The more systematic use of dependent labor, and, in particular, wage labor; the mounting accumulation of consumer amenities in rural households; and the growing investment in financial securities— mortgages, bonds, bank and government notes, and turnpike stock—all were indexes of new forms of behavior, and all had disruptive potential.[5]

Posed in these terms, questions about market relationships in early America have provided crucial and controversial ways of thinking about the American Revolution, which historians have viewed as a critical transition point in the development of a modern economy. By studying the impact of transatlantic markets on economic security in rural America, and, more recently, by investigating the spread of a "consumer culture" in British North America, historians have found that unease with market involvement created some of the sources for the mid-eighteenth-century ideological opposition to British imperial policy. Market entanglement led to anxieties and frustrations that were projected outward onto the British and that resonated powerfully in both the formal, ideological objection to British policy and in the informal stories colonists told themselves to make sense of the economic and political shocks they experienced in the mid-eighteenth century.[6]

Finally, the debate has major implications for our understanding of the nineteenth century. If "community" predominated over "market" in the eighteenth century, then "market" helps explain the transition to a more competitive, individualistic, diverse, and unequal society in the nineteenth century. A "simple" eighteenth century becomes the template against which change is measured in the next century. But if the eighteenth century was not so simple—which is where the debate began, with an effort to complicate the "common sense" reading of economic behavior—working out nineteenth-century patterns becomes that much more difficult. Moreover, such a reading also makes it increasingly difficult to blame (or credit) the market alone for the state of nineteenth-century society.[7]

While the relationship of community and market in early America remains a contested subject, the debate has nonetheless suggested several general conclusions that help frame the investigation of rural life in late colonial New Jersey. To find a clear case of a sustained subsistence economy in early America, one would have to look at the combination of hunting, gathering, fishing, and horticulture among Native American peoples. The difference between Euro-Americans and Native Americans was a matter of kind, not degree; relative to these first agriculturalists, European settlers were dependent on and committed to a market economy. Family farming, however, was not market-driven in the same way, for example, that nineteenth-century manufacturing would be. Households put basic security—which meant food production—first, not profit maximization, and depended more on household labor than they did on wage labor. Within this context, most farm owners in New England and the Mid-Atlantic participated comfortably in an economy in which commodity prices and (extrafamilial) labor costs were determined by the market, even if they protested angrily when they were pinched by the consequences of market involvement. For most, the primary locus of such market involvement was local: families secured their wants and needs through frequent local exchanges with similarly situated neighbors, but over time those local exchanges were increasingly governed by supply and demand conditions in broadening regional markets linked, through coastal ports, to the Atlantic economy. Moreover, involvement in the market was gendered; wives and husbands both participated in networks of exchange, and both had responsibilities for production and consumption, but those networks and responsibilities were as often distinct as overlapping. If we created a two-dimensional continuum of market involvement, running from precontact Native American horticulturalists to nineteenth-century, profit-maximizing factory owners, and from the early to the late eighteenth century, early American farmers would fall somewhere in the middle, with the extent of their involvement with the market increasing over time.[8]

Thus framed, the intriguing question is not the "either/or" proposition about market and community but understanding the way market relationships are embedded in community life. This book explores market involvement in rural New Jersey from settlement times to 1820, with primary focus on the eighteenth century. Starting with the assumption that Euro-Americans brought with them a commitment to market agriculture, Peter Wacker analyzes how regional geographical settings and the cultural background of settler populations shaped, contained, and facilitated market involvement. What emerges from his research is a highly nuanced, comparative study of what market involvement meant in different regions of New Jersey to particular peoples. This essay comes at some of the same questions from a somewhat different perspective, that of three relatively prosperous farm residents in the late eighteenth and early nineteenth century: Erkuries Beatty of Princeton, his neighbor and contemporary, James Ten Eyck of North Branch, and Betsey Crane, a farm wife who lived near New Providence in the Passaic Valley. A close reading of the three texts they left teases out particular ways that market and community, economics and culture, intersected, at least among the landed households in the immediate hinterlands of urban marketplaces. The effort will not be to prove that one set of ideas (or pattern of behavior) or the other dominated rural life, but rather to use the ideas of market and community to explore the meaning of the account books and diaries left behind by people as comfortably situated but essentially obscure as Erkuries Beatty.

This essay will also attempt to come to terms with two distinctive types of sources: Beatty and Crane left farm diaries, exceptionally rare documents in a society in which members of farm families seldom took the time to reflect in writing on their daily labors. Ten Eyck left a farm ledger, a more commonplace record of economic activity, as well as a series of cash books, that together chart several decades of planting and harvesting, buying and selling in the Raritan Valley. Both farm diaries and account books provide concrete, detailed evidence of everyday rural life, but each also provides a different picture of the sum and purpose of farm activities. Neither record gives a complete picture; each is the creation of a single individual in one place at a unique point in time, and each is the product of the special purposes for which it was kept. In contrast, Wacker's analysis deals systematically with numerous sources. In place of Ten Eyck's account book, Wacker explores dozens; in place of the listings for Ten Eyck and Beatty in local tax lists, Wacker scrutinizes all the remaining tax lists for evidence of agricultural practices. In place of what was unique, he describes what was general and then analyzes regional and cultural variations. Wacker moves out of the rich agricultural heartland of New Jersey, where this chapter focuses, to the marginal farming areas, and he explores the circumstances of smallholders, tenants, and agricultural laborers as well as the situation of more substantial householders. By combining findings about these general trends and their broad variations with the particular records of the rural past left by Beatty, Crane, and Ten Eyck, a better sense should emerge of what notions shaped the agricultural lives of New Jersey farm families.[9]

The agricultural hinterlands of New York City and Philadelphia, an area that included Beatty's Castle Hope Farm in Princeton Township, presented a distinctive environment for the development of rural husbandry. This region was plagued by neither the rocky soil nor harsh climate that circumscribed New England farming, and, while slavery was not unknown, the systematic exploitation of bound labor for profit never played the same role in the agricultural economy of the region as it did in the Chesapeake and Carolinas. Within this context of free labor and bountiful nature, what balance was struck, by farmers such as Beatty, between older patterns of extensive cultivation and the search enlightened agricultural writers of the period urged upon farmers for ways to improve the farm and increase yields? What, if anything, did improvement mean to Beatty—rationalization? experimentation? accumulation? What reliance did Beatty place in neighbors and kin? How, at least as he recorded it, did he balance or conflate the demands of community and market?

Erkuries Beatty was born in 1759 in Bucks County, Pennsylvania, the son of a Presbyterian preacher. His father, Charles Clinton Beatty, had left Ireland as a child in 1729 and come to Cape Cod, Massachusetts, with his mother and uncle. The family later moved to New York. Charles initially made his way as a peddlar. His path crossed that of William Tennant, then engaged in the revitalization of the Presbyterian faith in the Delaware Valley; Charles stayed with Tennant to prepare for the ministry, and in 1743, when Tennant retired, Charles was called to Tennant's former position at the Forks of the Neshaminy, Pennsylvania. In 1746, Charles married Ann Reading, the daughter of John Reading, who would serve as a governor of colonial New Jersey; in 1758, he was chaplain to a contingent of Pennsylvania troops sent to the frontier; and in 1768, he published an account of his observations of the life of backcountry Indians. He died in 1772 while on a trip to the West Indies to raise money for the College of New Jersey, leaving behind his wife, ten children, and a large estate. He had bequeathed Erkuries influential friends, a genteel upbringing, and ample property.[10]

A boy of seventeen in the summer of 1776, Erkuries fought on the patriot side at the battles of Long Island and White Plains and initiated a military career that would last until 1793. Whatever the factors that led him to enlist, the decision must have seemed self-evident. Presbyterian support for the cause of independence was strong, and three of Erkuries's brothers and his cousin, George Clinton, served as officers in the Revolutionary army. Erkuries was wounded at Germantown in 1777 and fought under General Sullivan in 1779 against British and Indian forces in New York. On the 1779 expedition, Erkuries began the first of several journals he kept throughout his life, recording the tedium of long, weary marches as well as the systematic destruction of Indian villages ("we stayed there about 8 hours and killed some five horses and a number of hogs & plundered their houses and set fire to them and marched on about 4 o'clock") and developing a talent for observation that remained with him in later years.[11]

Beatty's letters and his journal entries reveal a man at ease with the conventions and opinions of his class. Like so many families in New Jersey and Pennsylvania, the Beattys had friends and kin who did not support the patriot cause during the Revolutionary War, and Erkuries could comfortably break the monotony of camp life by spending a winter afternoon in Princeton "agreeably romping" with "two bouncing female cousins and a house full of smaller ones," who, he wrote his brother, Reading, "were exceedingly clever and sociable" but had to be discreetly steered off the subject of Toryism. When he billeted in the house of a "rigid old Quaker and of course a damn'd Tory," he wrote in another letter, he avoided political arguments by engaging in religious haggling until his host simply ignored him.[12]

Away from his fellow officers, Beatty seemed reasonably comfortable drinking in Philadelphia taverns, but his willingness to mix with those of a different station and situation did not extend to frontier settlers. The best he could say of Pittsburgh, he wrote in his journal in 1786, was that it was "a very dissipated place as usual, chiefly owing I believe to the number of strangers continually passing and repassing, yet the lower class of people in this place scarcely does anything but drink whiskey." Of the Indians, whom he had fought during the Revolution and marched against again in the 1780s, he had even less good to say. Describing the bartering of government goods for Indian land, he wrote to his brother with obvious contempt for the Indians who, the treaty concluded, now went "shining about with their gold lace hats and jackets which about as much becomes them as a jewel does a hog's nose." "We like fools," he continued, "giving them rum, and so it has been all the treaty, our house continually full of these devils till we are heartily sick of them."[13]

Such anecdotes, with their mixture of scorn, ethnocentrism, and humor, serve a purpose in coming to terms with Beatty as an essayist. A narrative art that flourished among the Chesapeake gentry, agricultural diaries were only rarely kept in the middle colonies and New England. Beatty was, then, not simply unusual but in fact must be judged as something of an outsider, a soldier turned farmer at the midpoint of his life. As an officer, he betrayed in his earlier writing concerns and sympathies appropriate to his rank and status that would carry over to his farming. His very willingness to write suggests the symbolic importance to Beatty of diary keeping as a confirmation of his place among the literate Whig elite of the new republic, while the writing itself, with its detailed characterizations, suggests that Beatty more often saw than understood, more often observed than tried to explain, what he noted in his letters and journals. Neither reserved nor austere, Beatty felt comfortably removed from the concerns of ordinary people, and the judgmental quality of his jottings carried over to his relations with farm workers. At the same time, his penchant for description served him well in efficiently summarizing the operation of his farm, and it makes the occasional flashes of reflection and speculation all the more unusual and significant. Not surprisingly, Beatty tired quickly of agricultural diary keeping (if not of farming itself), which suggests that for an individual with his adventurous past, the routines of day-to-day farm life soon seemed to leave him little to write about.

Beatty's letters provide clues about his decision in 1793 to leave the army. Perhaps it was a sense that his opportunity to seize the main chance was passing him by, for in 1784 he had written his brother to ask why he should not "do as the rest of the world generally does, [and] make money by any means." It is as likely that he left because of a bitterness common to Revolutionary officers adjusting to peacetime politics, a bitterness that surfaced graphically in a 1786 letter in which he questioned why he had ever entered "such a rascally service, when cringing sycophants in the midst of plenty, kick the worn out soldier out the door, because he does not debase his feelings with the most rascally servility to upstarts of a day." But what may have sealed his decision to leave the army was the taunt of a female acquaintance that "when talking on love [said] that I had got too old to feel in any great degree that powerful passion or create it in the breast of a young Lady." Beatty had long liked the company of women, but at thirty-five military service had not yet provided him the opportunity to marry.[14]

In 1794, his military career over, Beatty bought Castle Hope farm near Princeton; he held the property until 1816, and twice, in 1797–98 and again in

1799–1800, he recorded in some detail the pattern of farm work on the property. The diary reveals little about Castle Hope itself, but a 1776 entry in the *Pennsylvania Journal* described the farm as including a dwelling and separate kitchen, barn, stable, coach house, and other buildings on 160 acres (Beatty bought 143) with ample woodlands and several orchards. In 1797, the year he began his diary, Beatty was taxed for 120 improved acres in West Windsor Township as well as for four horses and nine cattle; in adjoining Somerset County, he owned 21 unimproved acres and a lot. Beatty was fairly representative of the middling grain and livestock farmers of the Middle Atlantic states.[15]

Beatty's initial jottings reflect what is apparent throughout his diary: market relationships were woven into the very texture of his agricultural world, but his life was paced by seasonal rhythms and his outlook shaped by the immediate problems of dealing with the weather and environment. There is little evidence that risk taking or the calculation of profit and loss weighed heavily on his mind; rather he structured his days around customary farm tasks, the responsibilities of town and church, and opportunities for neighborliness.

That Beatty began his diary in April could (other than by mere coincidence) be interpreted in two ways. April, of course, brought spring and with it the customary beginnings of the agricultural year (until 1753, the calendar year had begun in late March). By organizing his note taking from April to March, he acknowledged his inevitable acceptance of a structuring of time imposed by the seasons. On March 31, 1800, he wrote appropriately, "So ends this agricultural year." The seasonal pattern of farming could, however, readily incorporate market arrangements. Late March and early April were also times when Beatty and other Middle Atlantic farmers most often rented cottages, leased plots of land, hired laborers, and took on apprentices—that is, spring not only began a new crop cycle, it also began a new set of economic relationships. Moreover, interspersed among the numerous references to the seasons are measurements of accomplishment by the hours of a clock: "Benjamin and me finished ploughing in seed by 9 o'clock;" or, as he recorded on August 19th, "too wet to harrow early in the morning, began about 9 o'clock and finished before 12 a little." Such statements suggest a determination to impose control on activity previously governed by nature and custom and the possibility that he found reassurance in precision.

Beatty's awareness of the market is clear in his April 1797 notes on the current market price for several of his crops—wheat at £0.11.6 (zero pounds, eleven shillings, and six pence) a bushel, rye at 0.6.0, potatoes at 0.4.6, and so on. Yet he did not list prices again until April 1798, and on only two other occasions in 1797 or 1798, when he had taken crops to the Trenton market, did he record price figures. In April 1798 and again in April 1800, he speculated on the possible consequences that fear of a war with France might have on the prices of his crops, but in neither case did he record having taken any action to adjust to the market situation. Price was thus for Beatty essentially just another observation, a notation that signified the economic significance of the annual crop cycle but that did not guide what ought to be planted for maximum benefit in the coming year. Beatty, of course, did not purposely set out to avoid making rational, market decisions; there was simply not much he could do in the short run to adjust to changing prices. At the same time, there is almost no indication that he planned in any way to alter crops or types

Table 1
Monthly Activity on Erkuries Beatty's Farm, 1797–1798

| | | *Spring Months* | |
	April	*May*	*June*
Planting	timothy	clover	pumpkins
	barley	corn	cabbage
	oats	beans	
	potatoes	onions	
	cabbage	parsnips	
	flax	pumpkins	
		cabbage	
		beets	
		carrots	
Tending	plowing	plow fallow	plow buckwheat, potatoes,
	plaster of paris	furrow corn	corn, fallow
	on fields	haul manure and	harrow corn
		ashes	
Harvesting			clover (hay)
Other Work	build barn	build stone fence	inoculate cherry trees
	haul rails	wash and shear sheep	
	graft apple trees	care for swine	
	fencing		
Produce		wool	1.5 tons hay
(in bushels or noted)			28 oats
Laborers	Isaac	Isaac	Isaac
(days worked)	TR (3)	TC	MJ (1)
		BA (1w)	BA (1)
		JP (1)	JP (1)
		KM (1w)	
		JR (1)	
Trips	Mapletown (1)	Cranbury (1)	Allentown (1)
(in days)	New Brunswick(1)	Kingston (1)	Princeton (1)
	Princeton (2)	church (3)	Rocky Hill (1)
	church (1)	mill (1)	Trenton (2)
	mill (1)	meeting (3)	meeting (3)

of husbandry in terms of economic opportunity. Linked to an agricultural regime that required little adjustment, Beatty's world encompassed the market without being fully or directly its product.

Following Beatty at Castle Hope beyond these initial entries, through 1797/98, elucidates four aspects of the relationship of the market to farm life—how he managed his farm, how hard he worked, the use he made of dependent labor, and how he tried, if at all, to improve his property (table 1). On any farm, spring meant planting and sowing. On Beatty's farm as on others throughout the Middle Atlantic, what distinguished the planting season was, first, the great variety of crops begun (timothy, barley, corn, and oats; several vegetables; and flax) and, second, the fact that there was no specialization: the twelve acres he devoted to corn were the largest allotment for a particular crop. Returning from a walk about his newly sowed fields on a Sunday in mid-May, Beatty reflected that his "barley and oats look tolerable and the young clover first sown [is] coming up; my flax I'm afraid [is] too thin again, and oh! my poor cattle, I am afraid they must starve to death." By mid-May, Beatty had virtually completed his sowing, and now, although the corn

Table 1 (cont.)
Monthly Activity on Erkuries Beatty's Farm, 1797-98

	July	August	September
		Summer Months	
	July	*August*	*September*
Planting	turnips	cabbage	rye
		timothy	wheat
Tending	corn	potatoes	dung
	buckwheat	clear ground	
		dung fallow	
Harvesting	wheat	rye	hay
	barley	apples	buckwheat
	rye		
	oats		
	flax		
	potatoes		
	pumpkins		
Other Work		fencing	make cider
		ditching	haul logs
		haul stone	fencing
		breed horses	thresh flax
		clean chaise	
Laborers	Isaac	Isaac	Isaac
(days worked)	Benjamin	Benjamin	Benjamin
	JP (1w)		KM (2)
	MW (1)		
	JS (1)		
	DR (1)		
Produce	35 wheat		2 bar. & 1 hhd cider
(in bushels or noted)	100 rye		3.5 flax
	250 oats		.5 ton hay
	colt		9 pigs
Trips	Bridgetown (1)	Milltown (1)	Princeton (3)
(in days)	Elizabeth (1)	New Brunswick (1)	Trenton (3)
	church (1)	Newtown (1)	church (2)
	court (1)	Trenton (2)	mill (1)
		meeting (3)	neighbors (1)
		weavers (1)	funeral (1)
			militia (2)

had to be plowed and harrowed periodically, the fate of the crop depended as much on rain and sunshine as on human endeavor.

On July 5, Beatty jotted in the margin of his diary "harvest begins," although on June 27, he had already started mowing hay. On July 6, Beatty wrote, "cut Virginia wheat today [and it is] very poor but a good deal of timothy which obliged us to let it lie in swath, but it will make fine fodder." On the 10th, he was "cutting rye and stacking it. Finished orchard and ½ woodland. Much better bound than last harvest but not extraordinary cutting or raking. . . . Perhaps may have 100 bushels." Winter rye, like summer corn, was one of Beatty's principal crops. The two winter grains accounted for, the barley and oats still had to be cut and the flax pulled before the month was out. The worst and weariest work of farming was thus bunched into two spurts of activity, spring planting and summer harvest. During the remainder of the year, Beatty directed his attention to tending the crops, collecting firewood, fencing his fields, and caring for the livestock—all according to a

Table 1 (cont.)
Monthly Activity on Erkuries Beatty's Farm, 1797-98

	October	Fall Months November	December
Planting	rye		
Tending			
Harvesting	buckwheat apples potatoes	corn flax	
Other Work	fencing make cider kill sheep haul wood	haul wood kill hogs and cow	thresh oats and rye salt meat haul wood fencing break flax clean wheat and barley
Laborers (days worked)	Isaac Benjamin JR (1) TR (1) KM (4)	Isaac JR (1) TR (1)	Isaac JP (1w) BS (1)
Produce (in bushels or noted)	38 buckwheat 34 potatoes 1.5 b. cider 1 hhd cider	308 corn 20 turnips 954 lbs. hog fat 338 lbs. meat	40 oats 30 wheat
Trips (in days)	Cranbury (1) Griggstown (1) Kingston (1) Princeton (1) Trenton (2) court (3) election (1) mill (1)	Trenton (1w) mill (1)	Morristown (3) Trenton (4) meeting (4) mill (3) visits (2)

seasonal pattern common to virtually every farm in the Mid-Atlantic.

Like most landowners, he shared this work with hired help and contracted for farm laborers in several different ways. Isaac Skillman worked at Castle Hope for the entire year; he was probably Beatty's cottager. If so, he lived on the property and undoubtedly received a yearly wage, against which rent, provisions, days lost from work, and other expenses were charged. In August, with the heaviest work behind him, Beatty made a bargain with Benjamin Sunderland's father for the boy's services, and when the one-month trial period ended, the boy agreed to stay through January 1798 (he actually left in November 1797, receiving ten dollars for the two additional months of work). He made a similar bargain in May with Tom Clendemin to work at five dollars for the month, but he did not renew the agreement when the crop was in. When Beatty needed more help than Isaac and Benjamin could provide, he hired one or more of about a dozen neighbors (probably all older boys or young men) for a day to a week. Thus on May 10 his diary read, "Isaac, James Parker, Benjamin Applegate, and Tom planted all our corn today." Parker seems to have worked only that day; Applegate was kept for the week. In late June, as the harvest began, Beatty recorded that "I finished harrowing corn by dinner time. M. Jobs, James Parker, Benjamin Applegate and Isaac mow-

Table 1 (cont.)
Monthly Activity on Erkuries Beatty's Farm, 1797-1798

	January	Winter Months *February*	*March*
Planting			clover
Tending			
Harvesting			
Other Work	clean flax hunting cut wood thresh oats and rye	clean flax haul wood fencing	make beehive graft fruit trees haul stone thresh corn
Laborers (days worked)	Isaac TR (1) AC (task)	Isaac	Isaac
Produce (in bushels or noted)	287 oats 25 rye		150 corn
Trips (in days)	Hillsborough (1) New Brunswick (1) Princeton (1) mill (3) visit (5)	Princeton (1) Trenton (4) mill (3) visit (1)	Philadelphia (5) Princeton (2) Trenton (3)

Source: Erkuries Beatty, Castle Hope farm journal, 1797–1800, MS. 897, New-York Historical Society, New York City.

ing lower meadow." On June 10 he had four hands cutting and stacking rye; on July 17, "James Parker came by," and he and Isaac cut oats; and on October 3 Isaac, Benjamin, Kyle M., and Beatty raked up buckwheat; then the three hands and another hired worker spent the afternoon threshing. Finally, there were several occasions when skilled workers were hired for specific tasks—the carpenters to construct the barn, William Witherly to make shoes, and Amy Cownoun to spin flax. Strikingly, this mention of Cownoun is one of only two instances when Beatty paid women for their labor; he also briefly engaged Mary Robinson to keep house in 1800 before his new wife joined him on the farm. It may well be that Beatty did not hire women workers because some of the work that women were paid to do was labor generally supervised by a farm wife, and Beatty did not have a wife during much of the period when he kept a diary.

When the agricultural year ended, Beatty rented his farm to Isaac Skillman, his former worker; Skillman left in March 1800, and Beatty, "glad I'm clear of him," took over management of the farm and bought slaves. Slavery was by no means uncommon in late eighteenth-century New Jersey, and even farmers of such modest accomplishment as Beatty found it profitable to own several slaves. Beatty noted briefly in his diary: "I having got married have again taken the farm into my own hands for which purpose I have purchased Black people, Bristol and Mary, his wife, with their child Joseph." He paid $160 for the family, agreeing to set the adults free in ten years and the child at age twenty-five; he also purchased for $200 a fourteen-year-old black boy named Abram whom he was to set free at age twenty-eight. Yet even with slaves to help him, Beatty still used wage laborers at crucial times in the crop cycle. The June mowing again saw James Parker and Jonathan Robinson, now working with Bristol and Abram, in Beatty's fields.

In sum, Beatty's ability to maintain Castle Hope depended on his access to both short- and long-term wage laborers as he needed them; because such a labor market existed, he could produce far more than he needed for mere subsistence. Beatty's laborers came from the surplus of young, underemployed farm boys who had the physical ability to do farm work but not yet the age or property to farm for themselves; from the growing number of landless workers, black as well as white, for whom physical health, farming skills, and, if they were fortunate, some knowledge of a craft acquired through apprenticeship were their only inheritance; on rare occasion, from the daughters or wives of his male workers or neighbors; and from slaves. The expectations and opportunities that families held out to their children shaped not only the lives of the young but the market for agricultural labor as well. Market relations—the buying and selling of labor—were thus embedded in customary and slowly evolving patterns of family relations as well as in a system of racial subordination that affected both free blacks and slaves, a system we can only dimly perceive in Beatty's diary.[16]

Beatty's hiring of wage laborers as the need arose was critical to the running of Castle Hope because work on the farm, while often tedious, was neither continuous nor unusually exhausting. In late June, presented with "noble hay weather indeed," Isaac Skillman had the hired hands at work until nightfall raking and loading hay. On July 27, getting the oats in, Beatty commented that he had "worked hard today"; the next day his hands were sore, and he looked on as Skillman and Benjamin worked. In August, with little but plowing and fencing to do until the crops could be harvested, "Isaac and Benjamin went hunting early in the morning and did not return 'till 10 o'clock with two squirrels." For days like August 21, when Beatty declared that he had done a "good days work and tired I am," there were always days like August 26, when he "did little or nothing." To balance October 30, when Skillman and Sunderland as well as Beatty "all hauled corn until night and we was tired," there was the first of March, before spring planting, when Beatty wrote, "I do not know what Isaac did but not much." Each of these entries speaks both to the need for and liabilities of long-term wage contracts. Without the guarantee of regular workers like Isaac, Beatty could be caught short at harvest time, but keeping on full-time hands also meant paying wages when there was little to do. For Beatty, the calculation may have involved weighing risks and costs; more likely, he hired Skillman because he had a cottage to rent, and when there was little work to do, he let Isaac do it and took time off himself.

Beatty, like many New Jersey landowners, used slave as well as free labor; more generally, he found in the increasing number of free, poor blacks a convenient source of short-term workers. The 1745 colonial census listed 4,606 slaves in a population of 61,403 (blacks were approximately 7.5 percent of the total population); the 1790 federal census counted 2,762 free blacks and 11,423 slaves in a population of 184,139 (7.7 percent); and the 1810 census listed 7,843 free blacks and 10,851 slaves in a population of 245,562 (7.6 percent). Most of Beatty's time was spent in Hunterdon, Somerset, and Middlesex counties where, at the turn of the century, blacks constituted respectively about 8, 15, and 9 percent of the population.[17]

Beatty's crankiness about ordinary people and his sense of paternal distance from his workers is even more pronounced in his second year of journal keeping when he dealt with slave laborers. As with Isaac and other hired help, Beatty more often than not used his diary simply to describe what Bristol and Abram (Mary was seldom mentioned) were doing, and commonly the slaves had spent the day in the field working with either Beatty himself or a white wage laborer. On occasion, he jotted down a note of exasperation in his diary: "O the lazy Negroes!," he wrote in October after his hands had harrowed over the wheat, "I never can touch it [the wheat] again and expect it will be ruined. . . . Rained all day and I scolded everybody this morning dreadfully." (He made similar, but not racial, remarks about Isaac's work habits.) To comments about how little his slaves (as well as his white workers) had done while he was off the farm, Beatty added paternal notes—on September 25, that "our Black people at [the College of New Jersey] Commencement" in Princeton; on December 8, that "all hands at [the Presbyterian] meeting;" on Christmas, that "the Black people keeping holiday"; and at New Years, that the "Negroes [were] frolicking"—comments, however brief, that were more evocative and condescending than his statements about white workers.

Beatty enjoyed riding about. He was off the farm frequently, as much as one day in three, and his outings generally mixed practical concerns with sociability. There were market trips to Trenton in December carting wheat, to New Brunswick by sled in January with barley, and to a local mill with some regularity. In September he went to commencement at the College of New Jersey, where he observed a "great many people there, were of all sorts, sizes, descriptions, and colors"; in March he took a week-long trip to Philadelphia to "walk about the city" and perhaps meet storekeepers and old friends; and in December, he spent three days going and returning from Morristown, where he tried but "did no business." In November, he spent a week in Trenton getting a commission as justice of the peace and the week immediately after was home sick in bed. Additionally, he never worked Sundays (although his farmhands did so occasionally), and perhaps once a month he went to a local Presbyterian church and jotted in his diary that he had heard "a backwoods preacher," "a good sermon from these words: 'think of these things,'" or "W. Scott preach, whom I never heard before: middling well."

There is more than one possible interpretation for the pattern of work on Beatty's farm. The pattern itself is clear enough: hard, continuous labor was the exception, even during the supposedly busy months of spring and summer. Beatty may, of course, have been an exceptionally bad farmer, unhappy with his calling, and lacking the temperament to keep either himself or his hired workers at their assigned tasks. But in 1797, he had maintained the farm for three years, and he continued to live there for almost two more decades—strongly suggesting he knew what he was doing and liked it. Somewhat more plausibly, Beatty may have come to Castle Hope as a "gentleman farmer," a northern counterpart of the aristocratic planter of the Chesapeake, as concerned with leisure as with work. In fact, Beatty had little in common with the new nation's landed gentry: he worked in the fields alongside his hired hands, and during his military career his companions had been men who moved readily into politics, law, and commerce where they flourished or failed on their entrepreneurial skills. But Beatty could live rather comfortably without pushing himself or Skillman too hard and with the common wisdom that even if he did, the additional work would have yielded little additional income. On a farm where fertilizer was already in use, improving yields meant significantly increasing the labor input at Castle Hope on specified days, and this Beatty did with hired labor; making the farm more productive did not depend on the systematic intensification of his own or his hands' labor. Both nature and technology conspired to keep farming what it had so long been, the most dependable but least adventuresome way to make a living in early America.

Within these limits, there was still much a householder could do to improve a farm. A short list, drawn from the late colonial period, might have included adjusting the crop mix, substituting livestock for grains, managing the soil better, experimenting with new varieties of plants or animals, purchasing better tools, using more dependent laborers, or introducing accounting methods. Beatty's diary certainly cannot speak to the situation in New Jersey in general, but it does permit a view of how concerned one well-educated, comfortably situated farmer was with improvement, to what purpose, and with what results. In general, Beatty took cautious, practical steps that, with one exception, probably did not affect greatly the way he farmed. What comes across most clearly is the way collective memory of trial and error governed most decisions on a farm. When he discovered, for example, in October 1800 that his potatoes were not as good as he had hoped they would be, he jotted down a reminder ("mind this in the future") to plant them next spring just after the moon changed in May. A bit more suggestive of a systematic approach to farming was an early diary entry: "May 10th [1797] . . . planted all our corn today—perhaps 12 acres as it took nearly a bushel and half of corn and they allow 10 acres for a bushel—half a bushel [was] of the extra ordinary kind got of Rule Cown—over planted; sort of yellow and yields abundantly." Like most farmers, he was concerned with seeding ratios because he had to gauge the amount to hold out of one year's harvest for the next year's planting, but Beatty had gone a step further and bought seeds, presumably from a local farmer with a reputation for good corn. In July, he noted with discouragement the results of another attempt to plant a new variety of seed: "took up wheat and hauled in a poor crop, 2 bushels sowing, will have perhaps 8 or 9 bushels.—Done with Virginia Wheat." He, like other area farmers, had found it required thicker sowing than common wheat, that it could not stand Jersey winters well, and that it had been badly damaged by pests; when he took it to market in Trenton, he felt "quite ashamed" at its poor condition and could sell it at no better than £0.10.6 a bushel.

Beatty's commitment to improvement extended to his farm tools. In August 1800, he hired a carpenter so that together they might build a "clover machine." He noted in his diary that it was "lined with short iron which costs about half [as much as the carpenter's] besides my own work and I hope it will answer a valuable purpose." Apparently the machine was already in local use, because a neighbor had had one built and then, by bungling, had broken it. Beatty's success, or failure, is not recorded.

Beatty went to some lengths to maintain the fertility of his farmland. In April he used plaster of paris on a small patch, and in May his hands carted loads of ashes and dung from Kingston to Castle Hope for the corn. (Beatty penned his swine, but he apparently did not have enough cattle to provide his own dung.) In September he used dung to prepare for the fall rye planting. Corn, in particular, exhausts soil nutrients, and dunging the fields certainly helped correct the situation. Moreover, it involved cost and a choice, as Beatty might have addressed the problem by rotating his fields and using extended fallow periods, which he often did as well. Of his various efforts to improve his farming, this was the simplest and most common, as well as the one that probably helped the most. In 1800, he went a step further: he covered one-and-one-quarter acres of wheat land with sixteen loads of dung: "a strong [solution] of Cow dung was prepared several days, then strained off and the wheat soaked in it twenty-four hours, then taken out and as much plaster of Paris put to it as would stick." So coated, the wheat was sown, but again the diary does not record the result of the experiment.

Other than dunging the fields, Beatty's most consistent efforts went into his orchards. From his neighbors, Beatty purchased new varieties of fruit trees, and he worked at improving his own grafting methods. In mid-March, he summed up his recent efforts: "plumb graft on wild plum bears soonest and best flavor but subject to overgrown stock. Apricot second best on plum. Grafting solution plaster rather than dry resin, beeswax, tallow." There is nothing to indicate that the fruits he raised found their way to the market, and although he took his apples to a neighbor's mill neither cider sales nor prices are listed in the diary.

On March 31, 1800, Beatty closed the third year of his diary by noting: "It is doubtful whether I [will] go any further with my remarks." He did not. Perhaps the same lethargy that had led him to turn his farm over to Isaac the previous year took its toll of his diary writing as well. Or perhaps his marriage redirected his energies or imposed an order on the household that mere diary writing could not. Beatty's diary is drab, but its drabness conveys an important message. Plodding through the seasonal routines of rural husbandry and noting his activity, he was unable to impose his descriptive imagination on the process. Rather, farming had imposed itself, somewhat uncomfortably, on him. As he was caught up in the repeated tasks of the crop cycle, he, like his contemporaries, needed only the knowledge that an oral culture passed from parents to children and from neighbor to neighbor, while he found little toward which his literary talents could easily be directed.

James Ten Eyck lived in North Branch, Somerset County, New Jersey, not far from Erkuries Beatty's home. Both farmed in the late eighteenth and early nineteenth centuries, both occasionally traveled to Trenton to conduct public business, and both went to New Brunswick one or twice a year to market crops. But where Beatty left behind a descriptive agricultural diary, Ten Eyck's papers contain a ledger, several cash books, and numerous deeds, leases, wills, and inventories. If he had left a diary, our view of him would be different—more nuanced, perhaps, and surely more focused on kin and community. Examining Ten Eyck's farm life, then, involves not simply selecting a second example, but in fact viewing the past through a different prism.[18]

How different? Farm ledgers (or account books) are perhaps the most numerous of all the voluntary (that is, excluding the documents created because the law required or recommended they be kept) records of the early American agricultural past. To state as much is to recognize that such accounts spoke to a deep-felt need or fulfilled a significant function in the lives of rural people. Ledgers listed debits and credits for goods and services gotten and given, dated and grouped under the name of the person with whom the transactions took place. Beyond this, enormous variation existed in how ledger entries were made: debits and credits could be entered in a single column by date or placed in parallel columns (and dated); balances might be calculated regularly or not at all; exchanges might be entered in farm produce or every transaction converted to coin; dating might be haphazard or done with enough precision to calculate interest on late payments. This variation suggests that ledgers served a range of purposes, from a convenient way of recording exchanges that followed a pattern determined by seasonal needs (a bushel of hay after the summer harvest for a load of firewood during the winter) to a crude measurement of how profitably the farm was operating. Whatever the specific reason a farmer recorded his dealings in a ledger, however, a common concern to order, if not control, what seemed otherwise chaotic structured the endeavor and in fact connected the lives of rural ledger keepers and agricultural diarists.[19]

Cash books were far less common. Primarily kept by retail merchants, they were used to list in chronological order every sale, purchase, or other transaction into which the recorder entered. By itself, the cash book served little purpose except to provide a running record of economic activity, essentially a commercial diary. But used in conjunction with a ledger, cash books allowed a systematic ordering of business affairs. Each transaction was first recorded in the cash book, then, at the convenience of the farmer or merchant, transferred to an account book under the name of a particular individual. It was this double-entry system of economic record keeping that James Ten Eyck used, and it gives us a particularly detailed picture of his economic world.

The Ten Eyck family was originally Dutch and initially settled in New Amsterdam in the mid-seventeenth century. A century and a half after settlement, Ten Eycks still gave their children Dutch surnames, stored hay in "barracks" rather than in barns, and used a "Dutch fan" for cleaning wheat. Coenraedt Ten Eyck, who left Holland for the New World, became a prominent Manhattan tanner, left ten children, and lived to see his eldest son move to Albany. In 1725, Matthias Ten Eyck of the northern branch of the family sold to Jacob Ten Eyck a stock of household goods and farm utensils and a slave for a farm on the north branch of the Raritan River in what would become Somerset County, New Jersey. This Jacob (1693–1753) was James Ten Eyck's grandfather, and, like him, both his father, also Jacob (1733–94), and grandfather were prosperous farmers. His father saw active duty throughout the Revolutionary War as a captain in the Somerset militia and as paymaster for local troops; before his death in 1794, he had accepted appointment as overseer of the poor and leased the county the land for its first workhouse, acted as tax collector, and served as a justice of the peace in the early 1790s. The surviving 1770s tax lists include three Ten Eycks in Bridgewater Township (which includes the North Branch farm), all comfortably situated but none among the wealthiest inhabitants. In 1791, shortly before his death, Jacob was taxed on three hundred acres of land, eight horses, fifteen cows, and a slave.[20]

James's father secured his children's future by successful management of the family land. Through a fortuitous marriage to Margaret Hageman, whose brother made Jacob heir and executor of a considerable estate, and by purchase of new lands in both Somerset and Hunterdon counties, Jacob accumulated property that he could then rent and develop. A 1766 developmental lease to George Shaver of Woodbridge of a 120-acre tract in Bridgewater was typical: Shaver was to have the land for eight years and to pay only two pounds annually in rent, but he was also "from time to time during the said term, [to] clear twenty-six acres of upland, and three acres of meadow, and plant 50 apple trees, also take care of said Jacob Ten Eyck's cattle which shall be sent there to pasture." In another arrangement in 1773, Jacob leased 318 acres of his deceased brother-in-law's land for sixteen years to Jacob Nuff of Hunterdon County in return for one-third of the spring and winter grain, but he reserved the right to "come on the land to farm it" and in such event to split the common grain crop with Nuff. Such long-term leases improved the acreage and brought in small rents but generally were timed so the land could be switched to short-term leases or transferred when a family's children came of age.

Jacob died intestate in 1794 leaving his wife, Margaret, and six children, two sons and four daughters. At his father's death, James Ten Eyck was twenty-one years old. Like his father, he had mastered the complex art of surveying (and thus had some commitment to precision and calculation) and had served in the Somerset militia on its march to western Pennsylvania to quash the Whiskey Rebellion. His father left sixteen acres in winter grains; twenty-five cattle, six horses, and sixteen sheep; and nine slaves. The estate was appraised at £834.1.7. An additional £292.3.2 in bonds, bills, and notes were listed in the first account, but this rather considerable accumulation of assets had to be split six ways after Margaret had claimed her widow's third of the property. As it turned out, James did not do badly in the division. He and his older brother, Jacob, took over management of most of their mother's and sisters' inheritance, and they bought out the others' share of the home farm. Each received twenty-nine acres of lowland, thirty-eight acres of "interval," fifty-five acres of upland, and twenty-five acres of woodland; James acquired the house and barn. In 1802, after the division of the estate, James was taxed on 150 acres in Bridgewater Township, as well as on four horses, nine cattle, and a slave.[21]

During his first years on the North Branch homestead, James Ten Eyck left little record of systematic farming. His early ledger entries recorded payments made to him for pasturing cattle and horses, for allowing his father's prized mare to be used for breeding, for interest on loans or outstanding balances, and for a considerable amount of weaving (presumably by the slaves). From March to July, Ten Eyck hired the same workers his father had used to trim apple trees, plant corn, and harvest the hay crop, but over the course of a year he paid wages for no more than fifteen to twenty days of work. If he was marketing a significant quantity of grain, the account book does not record it; more likely, heavily involved as executor in disentangling his father's complex affairs, Ten Eyck simply kept the farm running without yet working to improve it. In 1798 he married Esther Hankinson and thereby got help, and in 1799 the first of nine children, Margaret, was born.

If James Ten Eyck at twenty-one prematurely assumed responsibility for his father's farm, he and Esther had it operating regularly as the nineteenth century began. In 1802, for the first and only time, he listed in his cash book the results of the annual harvest: 3 loads of flax, 16 bushels of flax seed, 2 bushels of oats, 50 bushels of winter grain (18 of wheat, 32 of rye), 77 loads of hay, 146 loads of buckwheat, 180 bushels of corn, 50 bushels of potatoes, and 4 loads of pumpkins. Not included in this account were 282 bushels of apples he delivered in September to a cider mill in return for 57 gallons of whiskey; the thousand pounds of pork he sold in December; and the shoats, cows, chickens, and turkeys he sold during the

Table 2
The Use of Wage Labor by James Ten Eyck, 1797, 1802, 1807

	Days Worked by Wage Laborers during Agricultural Year		
	1797	1802	1807
April	1	56.75	6
May	1	3	13
June	4	1	19.25
July	25	25.5	23
August	8	32	44
September	-	1	17.5
October	2.5	3	13.5
November	-	18	5.5
December	-	13.5	-
January	-	5	2.5
February	-	3	-
March	1	-	2
Total:	42.5	161.75	146.25
Total Wages ($):	41.59	77.41	108.55
Hours Worked:			
White Men	42.5	95.25	93.75
White Women	-	22	5.5
White Children	-	31.5	35.5
Black Men	-	13	11.5

Source: James Ten Eyck farm ledgers, Ten Eyck Collection, MS. 532, Rutgers University Library, New Brunswick, N.J.

winter and fall. He sold hay, corn, wheat, and buckwheat flour in bulk to local residents; the other crops were consumed at home or sold a bushel at a time to neighboring householders and farm laborers. For the year, his cash book records approximately $484 in sales, while his crop, conservatively, was worth no less than $529. Operating a considerably larger farm than Beatty, the Ten Eycks had become prosperous farmers.[22]

1802 also marked the year he began cash book entries, transferring each entry to his ledger (and noting the page in the cash book where the entry originated). In his loose papers are the results of an unsophisticated attempt to use his cash book to calculate his monthly net return. In January 1803, for example, he totaled $37.60 paid out, but $53.39 received, for a "gain" of $15.79. Not surprisingly, there is no indication that his calculations modified his behavior in subsequent months or years. Given the high fixed costs of farming and the limits that land and weather placed on the size of the crop, Ten Eyck had little room to maneuver. Having reached his harvest potential, which he probably had by 1802, he was left with choices of changing his crop mix or land use, and when he did (he seems to have decreased the amount of wheat and buckwheat relative to other crops), it was presumably based more on a knowledge of prices and yields than on his cash book calculations.

The cash book does demonstrate how sensitive he was to market fluctuations in the prices of his crops. The price that he received for rye, corn, and oats changed monthly and sometimes even weekly. To be sure, sales were often actually exchanges—of weaving for corn, apples for whiskey, leather for shoes—conducted face-to-face with a neighbor rather than at a mill or store, but the standard of value was the market. Thus the market could shape, without wholly controlling, what was after all in the short run a seasonal pattern of activity. What was sold and to whom depended on the fortunes of the seasons and the experiences of earlier years, and even Ten Eyck's attempts to systematize his record keeping and balance his books monthly did little to upset the basic planting routines of farm life.

Careful record keeping, in contrast, did net Ten Eyck something with individual farmers because he, like his father, charged interest on outstanding balances. In June of 1791, for example, Ten Eyck wove twenty-nine ells of cloth for Ebenezer Berry at 7 pence an ell, for a debt of £0.17.1. Four years later, he entered 0.4.9 in interest in his ledger, corresponding to an interest rate of seven percent. No additional interest was charged even though the debt was not settled until August 1797. Calculating interest was Ten Eyck's rule, not the exception, when dealing with neighbors and even family members, but interest also reflected an understanding that balances would not always be cleared quickly or fully, that the tidiness of the ledger book did not fully reflect the happenstance and circumstance of the face-to-face negotiations that were recorded in its pages; and when the debt was small, repayment occurred within the year, and the debtor was one of Ten Eyck's laborers, he charged no interest at all.

Ten Eyck, like Beatty, made modest efforts to improve his farm, although his ledger is a far less adequate mirror than Beatty's diary of such activity. The repair of a barn in 1795 at £0.11.1, paid to Philip Dumont and an apprentice carpenter, as well as the building of a new barn in 1803 for $416.55 were recorded in detail, from the $7.67 paid in 1803 for nails to the cost of hauling boards from the Delaware River to the wages for skilled workers. Also duly noted in each case was the allotment of whiskey and gin used to reward neighbors who had helped raise the structure. In 1808 in the cash book, a credit is entered under Clarkson Van Nostrand's name for "mending clover machine," the first specific indication that improved tools (and a new vocabulary) were part of James' daily life, although, more generally, his commitment to improved grain and livestock husbandry is evident from his diversified farming.

Perhaps the clearest indication of Ten Eyck's approach to farming is to be found in how he managed labor. As he freed himself from the responsibilities of his father's estate and began with Esther to raise their family, he gradually stepped up the use of hired laborers (table 2). At first, he hired almost exclusively for the July and August harvest and employed the same local workers—Luke Coovert, Philip Mullener, and John Stull—that his father had. Between 1797 and 1802, he almost doubled the wages he paid annually, began systematic hiring of white women and children as well as free blacks, and increased the days worked by hired hands by a factor of four. All this served several purposes: it allowed Ten Eyck to extend the harvest and increase production (the number of hours worked in August increased), to improve the farm (a building project in April), and to get additional help in early winter for husking corn and cutting firewood before the snow and cold of January and February virtually brought farm life to a standstill. At the same time, Esther used local girls and women to help with the household responsibilities of washing, spinning toe yarn, cleaning, and possibly gardening. In 1807, the number of days worked by wage laborers was actually less than in 1802, but, in fact, the number of days of field work increased substantially (the difference attributable to the unusual amount of carpentry work done in April 1803). Both in

August and September, James not only hired workers but contracted with neighbors to supply several hands and then paid the neighbor for both his own labor and that of the hands.

The use of contract labor was innovative; the use of family labor was more commonplace, and, over the long run, more significant. James did not simply hire men to do field work; he just as often hired their wives and children to help on the farm and often employed the same families his father had. Between 1797 and 1807, four families—the Van Nostrands, Tunisons, Cooverts, and Clickingers—supplied most of the farm labor. In 1807, for example, James paid daily wages to John Van Nostrand, his wife, their son John, and their daughters Isabele, Poll, and Nancy. Another son, Clarkson, was frequently hired by the year. Men and boys did field work or drove produce to New Brunswick and Raritan Landing; women and girls did housework, piecework (spinning flax or wool or making cloth), and, in summer, helped with the harvest. The Ten Eycks paid a "family wage," graduating payment by age and sex. In 1802, for example, when John Tunison made £0.5.0 daily for field work (before the harvest) and 0.8.0 daily for cradling at harvest time, his wife, Peggy, was paid 0.3.3 daily for raking and 0.4.9 for binding. His daughter Phebe received a daily wage of 0.1.0 for carrying sheaves of grain from the field.[23]

Table 3 summarizes the economic relationship between the Ten Eycks and the Van Nostrands during a typical agricultural year. Three of John Van Nostrand's children, his sons John and Clarkson and his daughter Isabele, did most of the work. John himself only agreed to work in the summer for harvest wages. Payment was seldom made in cash, although the Ten Eycks occasionally covered the Van Nostrands' debts by paying money to third parties (usually, Ten Eyck marked cash payments as loans in his ledger, suggesting that payment in kind was the agreed-upon procedure). Grain payments were not a mere exchange of food for work as each family needed one or the other; rather, payment was made when the work was done, and the amount paid was regulated by the market. Thus corn was worth £0.4.9 a bushel in April of 1803, 0.4.0 in May, 0.4.6 in June, 0.5.0 in July, and so on. In 1807 and 1808, in addition to working for the Ten Eycks, Van Nostrand also rented from James and, during the summers, pastured his swine on the Ten Eycks' property. Van Nostrand may have become Ten Eyck's cottager (renting a house and lot while agreeing to do wage work for a specific number of days), or he may simply have leased a field for his own purposes. In either case, the debt was paid by additional field work by his sons and piecework by his daughters.

The most fundamental fact about the relationship between such landed and laboring families was that it was mutually beneficial. The immediate advantage to James Ten Eyck of paying a "family wage" to the Van Nostrands, the Tunisons, and other neighbors was clear: James got inexpensive harvest help during the busy summer months and a reliable supply of labor the rest of the year. In turn, by helping support the Van Nostrands as a family, James increased the likelihood they would be there in the future to help him. Less directly, employing family labor meant that parental authority supplemented the wage relation in assuring that those he hired worked as he wanted them to work.

The benefits that the laboring families extracted from the relationship hinged on the fact that as agricultural workers they were already reasonably well-situated members of a rural community. None were truly poor, and none depended solely

Table 3
James Ten Eyck's Account with John Van Nostrand, an Agricultural Worker, March 1803 to April 1804

d: day(s); w: week(s); m: month(s); y: year(s); b: bushel(s).

Credits to Van Nostrand		Payments by Ten Eyck	
April		April	
1w son plowing	$ 1.13	5b rye 5/0, 2b corn 4/9	4.29
5d son plowing	.94		
		May	
May		1b corn 4/0	.50
3m daughter work	8.75		
3d son plowing	.56	June	
3d son planting corn	.56	7b rye 5/0, 1b corn 4/6	4.94
		pair of shoes for son	1.13
June			
2d son to Delaware River	.50	July	
1w son harrowing	1.50	cash paid Daniel Woodard	.20
4d plowing	2.00	6yds lining 3/0	2.25
		1b and a peck corn 5/0	.96
July		2b rye 5/0	1.25
5.5d son in corn	1.39		
8d son at harvest and 6.5d at harvest	7.75	August	
3w daughter work @ 5/0	1.87	8b rye 5/0, 2b corn 5/4, 1b wheat 10/0	7.59
		Cash lent by Esther	1.00
August		6 loads hay and hauling	22.00
5d in hay	2.50	9yds lining 3/0	3.39
1m son work	4.00		
9d son work @ 2/6	1.70	September	
		Wool hat for son	1.25
September		Pair of shoes for daughter	1.00
3.5d son thrashing flax	.69	4b rye 5/0, 1b wheat 10/0, 2b buckwheat 3/6	4.66
1y other son working	40.00		
13d son in corn	3.25	October	
		Cash	1.00
October		Pair of shoes	.87
6d son at corn	1.50	10b corn 5/0, 4b corn 5/4,	
		2b rye 5/0, 5b rye 5/6,	
November		.5b buckwheat 3/6	14.29
16d son at corn	4.00		
		November	
December			
Paid my tax	9.16	7b corn 5/0, 4b rye 5/0, 1lb wheat 10/0	8.13
		Cash paid for family	1.00
February			
21 yards fish net	2.66	January	
		2b corn 5/0, 4b rye 5/0	3.75
		February	
		2b corn 5/0, 4b rye 5/0	3.75
		March	
		2b oats 3/0, 2b corn 5/0, 4b rye 5/3	4.69
Total:	96.41		93.89

Note: prices and wages were given in pounds, shillings, and pence in the ledger and converted by Ten Eyck to dollars and cents at the rate of 8 shillings to the dollar. Prices are per bushel; wages are per day, week, or month.

Source: James Ten Eyck farm ledgers, Ten Eyck Collection, MS. 532, Rutgers University Library, New Brunswick, N.J.

on wage labor for their livelihood. All could trace their roots back several generations in Somerset County, and people like John Van Nostrand and John Tunison were probably the sons of landowners and were themselves smallholders, tenants, or cottagers. Van Nostrand died in 1817 with an estate of only $518 and no land, but he may have passed the bulk of his possessions on to his sons, John and Clarkson, before he made his will. George Clickinger, who with his son had done carpentry work for the Ten Eycks, died in 1804 with a (moveable) estate worth no more than $100 but with $200 in land (which was sold to cover his debts). These men were marginal farmers and artisans to whom the extra wages earned by their wives and children mattered substantially and for whom employment meant an assurance that they could get the grain, pasture rights, and clothing with which Ten Eyck supplied them.

Not surprisingly, Ten Eyck's cash books and ledgers document far more fully than Beatty's diary how thoroughly commercial agriculture prevailed in central New Jersey. In particular, Ten Eyck's use of wage labor, his charging of interest, and his pricing of produce speak to a concern for profit that is far more difficult to detect in Beatty's writings. Beatty's diary, however, suggests that the routines of agricultural life readily incorporated commercial activity without becoming fully subject to the dictates of the market. What was routine and traditional mattered as much as what was unpredictable and new. Neither source can stand alone in reading the meaning of day-to-day life on New Jersey farms.

Seen from a different perspective both sets of records ignore much that was ordinary, but vital, to late eighteenth-century farming. If James Ten Eyck's wife played a major role in managing the farm, his ledger and cash books indicate it only indirectly, and in Beatty's case even his diary records almost nothing of his wife's activities after he married. Both Esther Hankinson Ten Eyck and Susanna Ewing Ferguson Beatty were virtually invisible in the written records left by their husbands of farm activities, although both undoubtedly cleaned, cooked, washed, processed foods, and did garden work. Such invisibility may reflect the autonomy that women had in dealing with particular aspects of production, consumption, and household maintenance, but it may also reflect the growing devaluation of all labor, especially women's, that was not directed toward market production. Yet if diary writing and account keeping were ways of ordering rural life, women had as great a role as men in this ordering process and as least as much responsibility for mediating between the market and the household.[24]

The diary of farm woman Betsey Mulford Crane, drawn from a somewhat later period (the early 1820s), permits the exploration of rural life from this angle. Crane lived on the main road that ran from Morris County through New Providence Township along the Passaic River to Summit. In 1792, she had married John Crane and begun a household on his 40-acre farm in New Providence; thus they began farming at about the same time as the Beattys and Ten Eycks. John belonged to a family that could trace itself back to the original English settlers of Elizabethtown, and by the early nineteenth century there were more than a dozen families with the surname of Crane in the adjoining townships of Westfield, Springfield, and New Providence and perhaps half that many Mulfords. Betsey and her husband had ten children, two of whom had died and two of whom were married by the time she began the diary in 1824; left at home were daughters of twenty-one, sixteen, eleven, and eight years of age and sons of nineteen and fourteen.[25]

Crane was forty-nine in 1824, and she continued to jot short, daily entries in her book until two months before her death in March 1828. Like Beatty, Crane's first entry was made in mid-March, as spring began the new agricultural year. More than Beatty, she used clock time systematically, particularly in recording the weather, but she kept track of the day's activities by reference to the sun. And uniquely among the three, her writing was sprinkled with colloquialisms (as in April 1824, when she wrote: "Planted radish seed, the sign in the leg, old of the moon," and her occasional remarks that her sons held "poss" that day). The following entries, taken from her diary in 1824, give some sense of Betsey Crane's abbreviated descriptions of the day's activity on her farm:

October 27: I went to Granny Potter's quilting. Three of the young cattle came home. Vester sold 12 ducks to W. Hand.

October 28: Clear and pleasant. Father and Daniel took up a part of the flax. Vester and Pace went to Newark and got 5 gallons of molasses each. Debby came home from Long Hill where she had been to make Ann Crane a bonnet.

October 29: Clear and cold. Rained a little last night. Father up to Mr. Townley's vendue selling wood. Debby finished her blue frock.

October 30: Snow squall and cold; no frost until night before last to kill the blossoms. Meeting today; five persons dipped in the river at the mouth of Salt Brook. All gone to Meeting tonight. Father and the boys making cider today.

October 31: Clear and pleasant. Meeting two days; a great many there. Mr. Best preached from these words, "So run that ye may obtain." I wore a new pair of calf-skin shoes.

November 1: Clear and pleasant. Debby making Aunt Debby's gown; Aunt Debby here.

November 2: Cloudy and a little rain. Vester to Newark today and got 1½ tea, 7 pounds of sugar and a handkerchief. Debby got out Mrs. Ludlow's piece and finished Aunt Debby's gown. Father worked on the road. Election at Little's.

Despite the cursive nature of her statements, Crane depicted a more varied, complex set of activities than Beatty had in his diary. Her world was filled with travel, meetings, visits with friends, buying and selling, housework and farm work; she reported it all, never systematically and seldom focusing on a specific activity or person. The diary leaves little in the way of clues about why she kept it. Religious events are mentioned, but this was not a diary used to reflect on her own spiritual progress (John and Betsey were married in a Presbyterian church and probably became Methodists in 1806). Nor was it kept, as Beatty may have intended, as the equivalent of a travel journal, for Crane seldom took the time to describe anything except the weather and occasionally her health. More likely, she wrote it because of her age, the age of her children, and the conventions of the time. She was older and clearly less active than her daughters, and her children were old enough to care for themselves or, at least, not to need looking after. Thus she had the time to write, and by the 1820s it had become more common for women to keep diaries (although for a farm wife, the practice was still unusual).

Not surprisingly, one of the central themes of Crane's diary was work, and three points stand out in how and what she wrote about it. Comments on the day's work filled almost every page of the diary, but, like Beatty's, her journal was not a systematic record of work and productivity. Her husband was a farmer and a carpenter, and their farm had grown to perhaps eighty acres by the time Betsey began keeping her diary. On some occasions, she would note how many bushels had been put in the barn or taken to the mill, but there was no attempt to be thorough or complete. Thus on July 22, at the height of the harvest season, she noted that "father [her husband] and the boys [her two sons] have got all the rye, wheat and grass cut in the orchard," and three weeks later, she wrote that "father finished getting in oats and hay; there were 1350 sheaves; it grew in the corner lot." On February 24, 1825, she wrote, "Jo Smith here breaking flax; Father dressed 43 pounds"; two days later, she commented, perhaps with pride, perhaps in weariness, "we have spun a hundred weight of flax." One can reconstruct from her diary a fairly detailed picture of how the Crane farm operated and what was produced (the standard grains—corn, oats, rye, wheat, and buckwheat—as well as cider, wool, and flax) without developing any sense of whether the year was going well or poorly, let alone profitably.

Second, again as in Beatty's case, Crane paid far more attention to seasonal work directed at least in part toward the market than to the equally time-consuming, repetitive tasks required to run a household. Crane, unlike Beatty, recorded women's work as well as men's, but she too focused on labor that produced goods for use or sale beyond the home. From this perspective, the production of clothing for personal use shared with the cultivation of grain for sale a "public" quality, a significance beyond immediate home consumption; in contrast, she seldom mentioned such tasks as washing and cleaning, and she never noted cooking in the diary. For women, perhaps as much as for men, the cash economy measured the value of work and made a significant portion of the household labor invisible.

At the same time, productive work was a responsibility of the entire Crane household, with tasks separated for males and females. Sylvester and Daniel, ages twenty and fourteen in March 1824 (when the diary began), and Deborah and Mary, ages twenty-two and seventeen, not only worked around the home but were regularly sent to other communities on family business and, in the case of all but Daniel, often hired themselves out to neighbors to earn extra money. In some cases, male and female labor was entirely distinct: the boys worked with their father at carpentry, herding cattle, plowing, and delivering the *Elizabeth Town Gazette*, while the girls helped their mother with carding, spinning, sowing, and making clothing. Deborah occasionally hired out (going, for example, to John Little's, a general merchant, for three days in April to weave), but more often she did piecework at home; her younger sister, Mary, frequently earned wages doing washing for neighbors. In other cases, male and female work was synchronized if still distinct. Thus in April the men sowed flax and in July they pulled it; they thrashed it in September and broke it in December and January. The women then spent the winter and early spring spinning the flax into linen yarn. In recording all of this, Crane was as sensitive to the work of her husband and sons as to that of her daughters; tasks that were separated in fact by sex were equally part of common effort to make rural life viable and comfortable. Crane's perspective was thus considerably broader than Beatty's: she wrote about household work as a whole, not simply her own work or that of her daughters. Like Beatty, however, she focused on "productive" or "public" activity, labor or the products of labor that had significance beyond the household. Ultimately, she thought in terms that made much of women's labor not merely distinct from but less visible than that of men.

Work paid for the family's frequent trips to local stores. Over the course of the year, there were some two dozen trips to "Little's," a nearby crossroads store where they sold grain as well as bought hats, shoes, and other goods. They went perhaps half that often to "Britten's" and to one or two other merchants, and they bought goods from peddlars. This pattern of regular buying from local stores differed from Beatty's activities (who seems to have done most of his buying on occasional market trips to town) and Ten Eyck's (who bought chiefly from neighbors), and it probably reflects the growth by the 1820s of retail trading in the New Jersey hinterlands of major Atlantic ports. A list of the family purchases during May and June 1824 summarizes effectively the type of goods the Cranes bought:

calico	lime	fine-tooth combs	sugar
kersey	rye flour	shoes	molasses
muslin	wheat flour	dinner pot	indigo
check	seed corn	blue china teacups	tea
canvas		kittens	bread

A few durable goods, material from which to make clothing, and many purchases of small quantities of sugar, tea, and spices characterized the list virtually every month. They thus acquired not so much practical necessities as small luxuries (the china teacups were a birthday present) and conveniences. The Cranes were hardly "dependent" on the market, but they fashioned their standard of living—defined themselves, that is—in terms of material possessions, as much through store-bought goods as through household production, while they used market trips to enrich social relations.

As with Beatty, everyday life for Betsey Crane was filled with more than work. We can think of her world as encompassed geographically by three concentric circles, the tightest including her and her extended family, a second, larger one encircling several communities along the Passaic River, and the third circle extending well into East New Jersey. In each case, the circles were defined by both the demands of the market and the strength of personal relationships. Her most immediate world was built around kin and neighbors. In the course of a year (April 1824–March 1825), Crane made some eighty visits (excluding trips to church); she went occasionally to Little's to buy household goods and visited her brother and her uncle once or twice, but, these trips excepted, virtually all her visiting was with other women. Her daughter Orpha (then married), various aunts, and Mrs. Baily ("she is very lonesome," Crane wrote) made her welcome at least once a month, and, in turn, one or more of her friends and the friends of her older children visited the Crane household on more than half the days Crane remained at home.

Visiting—to share work, while buying goods, at church, or simply as a matter of sociability—mattered to Crane, and her diary was more than anything else a record of the comings and goings of a circle of female kin and neighbors.[26]

The diary also told a story of the numerous collective gatherings the Crane family attended. On September 11, for example, she wrote, "I went to Camp Meeting this morning at Wolf Hill"; the next day, she continued, "I went again to Camp Meeting through the mud. It was thought there was 4,000 people. Mr. Rusling preached in the morning; Manning Force in the forenoon, too. Mr. Rusling in the afternoon and evening." On September 14, she noted, "Meeting broke up this morning. I came home and all the rest cleared out. Jacob Bonnel's wife hung herself"—a jarring entry that elicited no further comment from her and reminds readers of how much in Crane's everyday life may have gone unrecorded. While we expect to read of revival meetings in the diary of a religious woman during the 1820s, it is more surprising to find how often more humdrum occasions brought folk along the Passaic River together. Take, for another example, the month of July. On the 2d they went to a "vendue" (the sale for probate purposes of a deceased person's estate) at Mrs. Bailey's; on the 3d "all hands [which excluded her, but probably not her daughters] cherrying," Crane wrote, "in the morning to Long Hill"; and on the 5th she noted "a great time at Elam Genung's. A Liberty Pole Raised and the place called Union Village." Three days later, she, her daughter, and her aunt were again off on a cherrying expedition; on the 20th, she recorded that "all hands gone to Jonathan Bailey's mowing frolic"; shortly thereafter, neighbors came to the Crane house to help with the harvest: "We had a flax frolic; 33 ate supper. They pulled 2 acres of flax down in the corner lot." By the 28th, the "mowing frolic" had moved to another neighbor's. Read against the terse entries of James Ten Eyck's account and cash books, Crane's diary hums with the activities of a vibrant rural community.[27]

Crane's year, then, was punctuated with these collective endeavors and occasions. Some were commercial (the redistribution of goods at death sales), many were religious (prayer meetings, Sunday services, and revivals), some were occasioned by the extraordinary demands for labor (at the harvest or for barn and house raisings), and some provided companionship as the seasonal tasks in a rural society were performed ("cutting apple frolics" and quilting and husking bees). Militia training days, dances, weddings, and other festivals filled out the calendar. In a society that made regular use of wage laborers, it is striking how often neighbors came together to work and celebrate. The interdependence of neighbors persisted, perhaps actually strengthened, as market relationships—cash sales and wage labor—figured more prominently in the rural economy. Buying and selling were neither impersonal nor at odds with neighborly sociability, and we can speculate that in many instances frolics, bees, and even vendues may have been gently subversive of contractual relationships and market sales.

Finally, there was a broader geographic context to the Cranes' life (a context that reflects the fact that Crane wrote in the 1820s). Visitors from as far west as Ohio (where relatives lived) and as far south as Maryland stopped at their home, while family members went regularly to Newark (seventeen times, in fact, in 1824), Chatham, Elizabethtown, Springfield, and Scotch Plains. In part, the Cranes' livelihood depended on these trips: John and his two sons cut firewood along the Passaic and hauled it to Newark, often by sled during the winter snows, for sale. As a carpenter, John built coffins, which had to be delivered throughout the region, and he and his sons were also responsible for distributing the Elizabethtown newspaper to local towns. While work seems to have occasioned much of the travel, and John and his older son did most of it, both Betsey and her adolescent children traveled as well. Fourteen-year-old Daniel went regularly to Chatham on family business and carried the *Elizabeth Town Gazette* to Springfield on his own; Betsey went to a carding mill in Chatham and to a store in Scotch Plains, as well as to visit friends; and her daughters rode to Newark in September of 1824 to witness Lafayette's tour of the city.

The pattern in all of this seems clear: the closer to home, the more Betsey shared experiences with other women; the further from home, the more she wrote about men and market responsibilities. Yet the division between male and female activity was not sharp, nor was the distinction between local, community activity and distant, market activity. Both Betsey and her daughters went to stores and mills and on occasion traveled to eastern Jersey towns; John Crane and his sons visited neighbors from time to time, and the Crane children often went together to see friends and attend social events. It is even more difficult to disentangle the way Crane wove together community and market in her diary. If the huskings, bees, frolics, quiltings, and raisings involved any wage labor, nothing in her writing indicated it; moreover, even if payment were involved, the way the community pooled its labor resources was still a striking aspect of rural life. In sum, Crane's attempt to order her world, if we can fairly describe her diary and the activities it lists this way, was intimate and personal, not so much separate as distinct from the other documents we have considered.

Betsey Crane's diary provides a different view of rural New Jersey than the records left behind by Erkuries Beatty and James Ten Eyck in three respects. Although she came to live on the Crane property at about the same time Ten Eyck and Beatty took over their farms, her diary dates from almost a generation later. The diary, moreover, described a different type of farming, with less emphasis on grain cultivation and more on flax growing and secondary employment (artisanal work, or what is often termed biemployment in an agricultural community). And, of course, Crane's diary was kept by a woman. Thus the diary cannot speak directly to the question of how rural life was transformed during the Revolutionary era, but it can at least suggest that the strength of community in the organization of day-to-day activity had not waned with time (perhaps it had even grown), that the household economy was nonetheless tied up with market transactions for women as well as for men, and that, while there was clearly a gendered appreciation of day-to-day life on a farm, separating men's from women's activity is as problematic as separating market from community. Both exercises distort as well as describe the life experience of rural folk.

The Beatty and Crane diaries and the Ten Eyck account books do not allow us to analyze change over the course of time. All they can illuminate concretely is specific, albeit significant, aspects of rural life of landed households in the more prosperous farming regions of New Jersey. It is hard to find in these sources deep anxieties about the market in general or indications in particular that such anxieties were projected into political discourse. What these sources disclose about the culture of the market in early America lies elsewhere. The rural world of Erkuries Beatty, James Ten Eyck, and Betsey Crane seems to have been one of relative stability. Beatty, Ten Eyck, and Crane shared with their contemporaries, especially those of the "better sort," membership in a cultural elite that was redefining itself and its relationship to both the natural order and ordinary people. The sources speak not to the political stresses of the Revolutionary age per se but to a more general attempt to cope with change harmoniously. Beatty's diary and Ten Eyck's ledger and cash book suggest three elements of this outlook—a sense of order and control imposed through written observation, a search for predictability and rationality implicit in their attempt to reduce the world to numerical certainty and explicit in their fondness for experimentation, and a substitution of paternal authority for compulsive obedience.

Each of these elements of their outlook requires examination. The "crisis" of late eighteenth-century America was not so much a fundamental disruption of economic and private life as it was a challenge to traditional forms of authority. Americans perceived how things had changed, and some were profoundly disturbed by what they saw. Ten Eyck and Beatty, locally prominent farmers and marginal members of an elite, must have recognized the unsettling implications of republican ideology, the overthrow of monarchical power, and the growing emphasis on affectionate family relations, just as they must have realized that the increasing importance to the agricultural economy of wage contracts, cottage laborers, and the burgeoning Philadelphia and New York City markets were altering rural ways. How consciously and deeply troubled agricultural inhabitants were, even as they embraced these changes, is not something about which they wrote explicitly. But in Beatty's diary and Ten Eyck's account and cash books lie indications of how each man came to terms with new forms of authority. Crane's diary offers a glimpse of how readily a farm woman, writing a generation later, could encompass both the relationship to kin and community and to commonplace commercial activity.[28]

Crucially, both Beatty and Ten Eyck wrote in what was still, in some measure, an oral culture. Writing not only identified them as socially significant (in republican society, other signs of status were suspect), but it also gave them a way to structure, order, and ultimately control their environment and relationships. That in Beatty's case this effort failed (when the routines of farming overwhelmed his need to write) is all the more significant. The continuities of rural life exercised a powerful hold on the way people thought, reaffirmed the customary sense of order even as that order was changing, and made change in rural society surely less serious than it was in urban places, where the everyday bustle and commotion of commercial enterprise seemed to define the very essence of life. By the time Crane began to write, diary keeping, especially among women, was more common, and its purpose was no longer to record personal religious progress but now to identify and reaffirm the continuities and connections that provided order and meaning to everyday life. In this sense, Crane's diary served the same moral purpose as Beatty's.

Even more clearly, the effort to calculate and improvise, whatever the practical benefits, served the dual purpose of identifying and empowering the authors. The attempt to make life rational and predictable with numbers, equations, and precisely engineered drawings placed Beatty and Ten Eyck not only with Virginia gentry and the master artisans of Philadelphia but with European intellectuals as well. At the same time, it gave them a new power seemingly to control, even to master, what ordinary folk had to leave to God and nature, and it reassured them of their status in a republican social order. This concern with mastery was not present in Crane's writing, even though the notions of an ordered household and a well-regulated domestic economy were part of the ideology of the era.[29] Crane created certainty through personal relationships, more often with women than with men.

Finally, farmers like Ten Eyck and Beatty found in cottage labor and the "family wage" system a new way to maintain a sense of control while using wage labor for profit more systematically. The account books and diaries tell us unfortunately little about the nature of the relationship between householders and workers, but they do make clear that the (increasing) use of wage labor did not represent a simple transition from personal, paternal control over family labor and indentured servants to impersonal competition for the services of hired help. In farm areas, wage labor was regulated by community relationships, complemented family labor, and did not eliminate collective community endeavor. If a lack of deference among workers and competition for laborers now characterized the labor market (issues on which these sources are silent), surely householders were able in large measure to compensate for such uncertainty through the connections that linked multiple members of a working family to the household of people like the Beattys, Ten Eycks, and Cranes.

If these speculations are correct, then, both farm life and farm values proved remarkably adept at adjusting to the economic currents that threatened to disrupt rural society. The process of adjustment was as much a matter of culture as political ideology. As others have argued, national elites transformed traditional republican political notions in the post-Revolutionary War era into liberal values that legitimated the use of private property to pursue self-interest. These records suggest that the rural parallel to such a reworking of political language was the imposition of specific conceptions of order—for men, through precise observation and statistical accounting; for women, through extended bonds of personal friendship—on everyday life.

Three lives alone, of course, cannot render a definite judgment on this supposition. One would want to know, at a minimum, if keeping diaries and account books did in fact become more common in the late eighteenth century, and whether the variety of such efforts at record keeping negates an attempt to find in them a common meaning. Whatever the verdict of future research, Beatty's, Ten Eyck's, and Crane's accounts point to the complexity of the way individual rural inhabitants lived through the Revolutionary era and the years of the early republic; if they embraced liberal values as they pursued commercial agriculture, they also sought to conserve, to order, and to control. The discovery that James Ten Eyck charged a neighbor interest for the advance of a bushel of winter grain is an indication that personal and market relationships had changed from the early colonial period, but this fact cannot reveal how Ten Eyck felt or thought about charging interest. If the task is to describe economic relationships and to measure their changing nature, how Ten Eyck felt is essentially irrelevant; if, however, the task is to probe the cultural consequences of patterns of behavior, recovering the outlook of farmers like Erkuries Beatty, James Ten Eyck, and Betsey Crane is the principal historical problem.

These diaries and account books give us little sense of regional variation in market agriculture; Peter Wacker's reconstruction of the economic geography of eighteenth-century New Jersey from a multiplicity of these and other primary sources offers extensive insight into this aspect of rural life. Together, these analyses make clear that the fit between market and community was surely a matter of location—of soil type and quality and of access to urban centers—and a matter of the particular histories of specific places—the cultural backgrounds and aspirations of the settlers, the growth of population, and other such factors. Used carefully, farm diaries and account books may have more to tell us than the price of corn; they may allow us recapture some sense of how rural people in early America coped with the ongoing changes in their material lives. They suggest that the response of rural landowners to concerns with public and private authority and economic competition may have had a broader cultural context than has been previously recognized.[30] That such prosperous, Middle Atlantic farmers found in farm life a sense of order and control, enriched by the natural rhythms of the agricultural year and deeply embedded in personal relationships, made their rural world a fundamentally ambiguous place where market and community coexisted without one ever entirely encompassing the other.

Notes

1. Erkuries Beatty, Castle Hope farm journal, 1797-1800, MS. 897, New-York Historical Society, New York City. Beatty titled the journal "Agricultural Remarks for the Years 1797-1798 & 1799." The statement on sowing clover is in the margin of the diary, as is the notation "raining." Indecipherable words have been replaced with ellipsis points. The exact spelling of "Sthyker" is not clear.

2. Daniel Vickers, "Competency and Competition: Economic Culture in Early America," *William and Mary Quarterly*, 3d ser., 47 (1990): 3–29 (hereinafter cited as *WMQ*) analyzes the debate over the place of the market in early American life. For important early statements that emphasize either community or kinship values over market values, see Michael Merrill, "Cash is Good to Eat: Self-Sufficiency and Exchange in the Rural Economy of the United States," *Radical History Review* 4 (1977): 42–69; and James A. Henretta, "Families and Farms: Mentalité in Pre–Industrial America," *WMQ*, 3d ser., 35 (1978): 3–32. For a response, see James T. Lemon, "Comment on James A. Henretta's 'Families and Farms: Mentalité in Pre-Industrial America,'" with a reply by Henretta, *WMQ*, 3d ser., 37 (1980): 688–700. The debate has focused primarily on New England, secondarily on the Mid-Atlantic.

3. The most thorough analysis of the strength of market relationships in early American rural communities is to be found in Winifred Barr Rothenberg, *From Market-Places to a Market Economy: The Transformation of Rural Massachusetts* (Chicago, Ill., 1992). For the Mid-Atlantic, see Paul G. E. Clemens and Lucy Simler, "Rural Labor and the Farm Household in Chester County, Pennsylvania, 1750–1820," in *Work and Labor in Early America*, ed. Stephen Innes (Chapel Hill, N.C., 1988), 106–43.

4. Henretta, "Families and Farms," first raised the question of how historians of early American society determined values from the study of behavior.

5. See, in particular, Allan Kulikoff, "The Transition to Capitalism in Rural America," *WMQ*, 3d ser., 46 (1989): 120–44. For two other excellent studies that deal with the "transition question," see Robert A. Gross, "Culture and Cultivation: Agriculture and Society in Thoreau's Concord, 1800–1860," *Journal of American History* 69 (March 1982): 42–61, and Christopher Clark, *The Roots*

of Rural Capitalism: Western Massachusetts, 1780–1860 (Ithaca, N.Y., 1990).

6. For recent studies that link political culture and the market during the Revolutionary era, see T. H. Breen, "Narrative of Commercial Life: Consumption, Ideology, and Community on the Eve of the American Revolution," *WMQ*, 3d ser., 50 (1993): 471–501, and James A. Henretta, "The War for Independence and American Economic Development," in *The Economy of Early America: The Revolutionary Period, 1763–1790*, ed. Ronald Hoffman et al. (Charlottesville, Va., 1988), 45–87.

The notion that American revolutionaries expressed their frustrations with the social order through their ideological opposition to British imperial policy was eloquently expressed in Gordon Wood's *Creation of the American Republic, 1776–1787* (New York, 1969). Wood argued that when "the political language of the eighteenth century is translated into modern terms the obsession with luxury, vice, and corruption becomes an obsession with America's social development, the way in which the society was moving and maturing" (113). This same theme became part of Robert Gross's detailed community study of the causes and consequences of the American Revolution in Concord, Massachusetts, *The Minutemen and Their World* (New York, 1976), 68–108.

7. For two sophisticated analyses of the pattern and pace of change from the eighteenth to the nineteenth centuries, see Clark, *Roots of Rural Capitalism*, and Mary P. Ryan, *Cradle of the Middle Class: The Family in Oneida County, New York, 1790–1865* (New York and Cambridge, Eng., 1981), esp. 18–59.

8. No one study supports all of these generalizations, but I have begun with these assumptions based on the analysis in Vickers, "Competency and Competition"; Bettye Hobbs Pruitt, "Self-Sufficiency and the Agricultural Economy of Eighteenth-Century Massachusetts," *WMQ*, 3d ser., 41 (1984): 333–64; Carole Shammas, "How Self-Sufficient was Early America?" *Journal of Interdisciplinary History* 13 (1982): 247–72; Jeanne Boydston, *Home and Work: Housework, Wages, and the Ideology of Labor in the Early Republic* (New York, 1990); and Laurel Thatcher Ulrich, *A Midwife's Tale: The Life of Martha Ballard, Based on Her Diary, 1785–1812* (New York, 1990). Native American peoples, of course, practiced a great variety of subsistence strategies, but the comparison of these strategies with the farming of Euro-Americans and African Americans helps put the notion of a subsistence agriculture in perspective. For an excellent overview of horticulture, hunting, and gathering among Native American peoples in the Northeast, see the various studies in *Northeast*, ed. Bruce G. Trigger (Washington, D.C., 1978), vol. 15 of *Handbook of North American Indians*, ed. William C. Sturtevant (Washington, D.C., 1978–).

9. Agricultural diaries are rare. While this essay focuses exclusively on Beatty's diary, several similar journals have been looked at as well: (1) Benjamin Hawley's diary of activities on his Chester County, Pennsylvania, farm during the 1760s, in typescript at the Chester County Historical Society, West Chester, Pennsylvania; (2) Gardner Island, New York, Farm Register, 1790–1809, New York Public Library, New York City; (3) James Pitcher, New Rochelle, New York, Farm Ledger, 1766–82, New-York Historical Society; (4) James Parker, Shipley Farm Account (typescript), 1774–81, Rutgers University Library, New Brunswick, New Jersey; (5) James Wilson, Somerset County, Maryland, Account Book [Journal], 1770–96, Maryland Historical Society, Baltimore. Wilson, a small slave-owner, was a grain and dairy farmer as well as a tobacco planter. Also of use on New Jersey is Carl Raymond Woodward, *Ploughs and Politicks: Charles Read of New Jersey and his Notes on Agriculture, 1715–1774* (New Brunswick, N.J., 1941). For a recent discussion of rural New England based on farm diaries, see the Annual Proceedings of the Dublin Seminar for New England Folklife, 1986: *The Farm* 11 (1988).

10. Beatty's life has been thoroughly discussed in Harry B. Weiss and Grace M. Ziegler, *Colonel Erkuries Beatty, 1759–1823, Pennsylvania Revolutionary Soldier, New Jersey Judge, Senator, Farmer, and Prominent Citizen of Princeton* (Trenton, N.J., 1958). Their careful research, while directed to different questions than this essay, has greatly aided my work. See also, in Richard A. Harrison, *Princetonians, 1769–1775: A Biographical Dictionary* (Princeton, N.J., 1980), the essays on John Beatty (3–8) and Charles Clinton Beatty (449–52).

11. "Journal of Lieut. Erkuries Beatty in the Expedition against the Six Nations under Gen. Sullivan, 1779," *Pennsylvania Archives*, 2d ser., 15 (1890): 219–53, quote at 223. It is, of course, possible that Beatty kept a journal, now lost, before 1779.

12. Joseph M. Beatty, "Letters of the Four Beatty Brothers of the Continental Army, 1774–1794,"

Pennsylvania Magazine of History and Biography 44 (1920): 193-263, quotes at 214, 223.

13. "Diary of his Western Tour by Major Erkuries Beatty, Paymaster, U.S.A., 1786-1787," *Magazine of American History* 1 (1877): 175–79, 235–43, 309–15, 380–84, 432–38, quote at 314. Also cited in Weiss and Ziegler, *Colonel Erkuries Beatty,* 71, and in "Letters of the Four Beatty Brothers," 253.

14. "Letters from the Four Beatty Brothers," 250, 258–59, 261.

15. The farm description is given in Weiss and Ziegler, *Colonel Erkuries Beatty,* 28. For tax information, see New Jersey Tax Ratables, Box 70 (West Windsor, 1797, 1802, 1809, 1810, 1817); Box 107 (Montgomery, 1793, 1794, 1796, 1802, 1806); Box 108 (Western Precinct, 1797), New Jersey State Archives (hereafter cited as NJSA), Trenton.

16. On rural labor, see Clemens and Simler, "Rural Labor and the Farm Household" and Gloria L. Main, "Gender, Work, and Wages in Colonial New England," *WMQ*, 3d ser., 51 (1994): 39–66.

17. Peter Wacker, *Land and People: A Cultural Geography of Preindustrial New Jersey: Origins and Settlement Patterns* (New Brunswick, N.J., 1975), 415–17. On slavery in the economy of East Jersey, see Jean R. Soderlund, *Quakers and Slavery: A Divided Spirit* (Princeton, N.J., 1985).

18. Unless otherwise noted, the discussion of James Ten Ecyk draws on the Ten Ecyk Collection, MS. 532, Rutgers University Library, New Brunswick, N.J. The collection includes deeds, inventories, wills, administrative accounts, music and lesson books, surveying maps, and letters, as well as farm ledgers for Jacob (father) and James (son), and James's cash books. It also includes public documents drawn up by the Ten Ecyks—a Bridgewater tax list, poorhouse records, and justice of the peace dockets.

19. While diaries are rare, account books are common, especially for the period after 1760. Both the Rutgers University Library and the New Jersey Historical Society, Newark, have extensive collections. Winifred B. Rothenberg's essays have demonstrated the use economic historians can make of account books. See, in particular, "The Market and Massachusetts Farmers, 1750–1855," *Journal of Economic History* 41 (1981): 283–314, and "The Emergence of a Capital Market in Rural Massachusetts, 1730–1838," ibid. 45 (1985): 781–808. There is also an excellent discussion of account books in Clark, *Roots of Rural Capitalism,* 28–38.

The argument in this essay depends, in part, on the question whether account book keeping became more common in the middle and late eighteenth century. The argument depends, as well, on taking account books more seriously as a form of writing and understanding distinctions among them in cultural as well as economic terms. Within this context, this essay is meant to be suggestive rather than definitive. My discussion of account books has been greatly aided by reading Lorena S. Walsh's unpublished manuscript on Chesapeake plantation management and Rhys Isaac's unpublished essay on Langdon Carter's personal and farm diary. See also Rhys Isaac, "Communication and Control: Authority Metaphors and Power Contests on Colonel Landon Carter's Virginia Plantation, 1752–1178," in *Rites of Power: Symbolism, Ritual, and Politics since the Middle Ages,* ed. Sean Wilentz (Philadelphia, 1985), 275–302.

20. The Ten Ecyk Collection contains handwritten genealogical information about one New Jersey branch of the family. See also Henry Waterman George, "The Ten Ecyk Family in New York," *New York Genealogical and Biographical Record* 63 (1932): 152–65.

21. New Jersey Tax Ratables, Box 104 (Bridgewater, 1791, 1796, 1802), NJSA. James originally had three hundred acres, but he presumably lost half of this in the estate division. Through 1820, neither his holdings of land or farm animals changed substantially, and he remained a slaveowner.

22. The crop estimate is based on the itemized harvest report for September 1802; it includes apples and pork as well as grains and vegetables. Some 53 percent (by value) of the sales were grains, 42 percent were meat and livestock, 5 percent were miscellaneous products (wood, cider, butter, cloth, etc.). The approximate value of the total output of the twelve Tunisons on the 1farm was $688. This combines the value of the grain harvest with the sale of all non-grain products. On New Jersey agriculture, see Herbert G. Schmidt, *Rural Hunterdon: An Agricultural History* (New Brunswick, N.J., 1945), and *Agriculture in New Jersey: A Three-Hundred-Year History* (New Brunswick, N.J., 1945).

23. Each of Ten Ecyk's male, adult workers appears on the 1802 Bridgewater tax list. John Van Nostrand and John Tunison were householders without land (probably cottagers) and with no other taxable property but a cow. George Clickinger and Hendrick Coovert owned houses and lots (of less

than ten acres), and Coovert was taxed for a tan yard. While none owned a farm, all but George Clickinger had landed relatives. There were, for example, 802 tax list, and most were landed householders. See also George Clickenger account and vendue, 1804, folder 35, Ten Ecyk Collection.

24. For excellent recent studies of women in early America, see Ulrich, *Good Wives: Images and Reality in the Lives of Women in Northern New England, 1650–1750* (New York, 1982), and Joy Day Buel and Richard Buel, Jr., *The Way of Duty: A Woman and Her Family in Revolutionary America* (New York, 1984). Barbara E. Lacey, in "The World of Hannah Heaton: The Autobiography of an Eighteenth-Century Connecticut Farm Woman," *WMQ*, 3d ser., 45 (1988): 280–304, presents a strikingly different picture of a farm woman, and of the relationship of private and public life, than the one drawn here from Crane's diary. In *Home and Work*, Jeanne Boydston uses the diary that Mary Cooper kept from 1763 to 1773 at her Oyster Bay, Long Island, farm to detail the extensive work of a farm wife; see esp. 11–18.

25. Betsey Crane Diary, Rutgers University Library. A typescript copy prepared by Mabel Day Parker and Stephen S. Day contains marginal notes about the diary entries and some biographical information. Biographical information is in Ellery Bucknell Crane, *Genealogy of the Crane Family*, vol. 2, *Descendants of Benjamin Crane* (Worcester, Mass., 1900), 467–69, 476, 486; John Griffin Wood, ed., "The Daniel Mulford Letters, 1803–1811," *The Genealogical Magazine of New Jersey* 12 (1937): 39–40, 57–59, 91–95 (Mulford was Betsey's brother); John Griffin Wood, ed., "Genealogical and Biographical Notes from Daniel Mulford's Diary, 1801–1807," *The Genealogical Magazine of New Jersey* 11 (1936): 89; "Records of the Presbyterian Church at New Providence, New Jersey, Kept by Rev. Jonathan Elmer, 1763–1793," *The Genealogical Magazine of New Jersey* 19 (1944): 39; New Jersey Tax Ratables, Box 41 (New Providence), Box 43 (Springfield), Box 44 (Westfield), NJSA; New Jersey Probate Records, Lib. 20, p. 12 (Joseph Crane will, 1776), NJSA. The discussion of Crane is based on the diary, with the additional sources used only to supply biographical information.

26. Crane, *Genealogy of the Crane Family*, provides ample evidence of Betsey's strong kinship ties; she had relatives in both Ohio and Georgia.

27. See Ulrich, *Midwife's Tale*, 102–33, 286–308, for the way another female diarist recorded local tragedies.

28. While the interpretation that follows is my own, I have found particularly helpful Jay Fliegelman's discussion of authority in early America in *Prodigals and Pilgrims: The American Revolution against Patriarchal Authority, 1750–1800* (New York, 1982) and Drew R. McCoy's exploration of political discourse in *The Elusive Republic: Political Economy in Jeffersonian America* (Chapel Hill, N.C., 1980).

29. In *Home and Work*, Jeanne Boydston explores the growing emphasis prescriptive literature gave to well-ordered, efficiently run households.

30. Some of these themes are developed in Christopher Grasso, "The Experimental Philosophy of Farming: Jared Eliot and the Cultivation of Connecticut," *WMQ*, 3d ser., 50 (1993): 502–28.

Second Month, February, 1819.

INTRODUCTION

In the eighteenth century, the middle colonies of New York, New Jersey, Pennsylvania, and Delaware were referred to as the "bread colonies" because of their reputation as great producers of wheat.[1] Agriculture dominated economic life in early New Jersey; agricultural land uses not only covered wide areas of the colony, but agriculture also provided the wherewithal for other landscape transformations. Despite the prominence of this activity, however, only general studies of the history of New Jersey agriculture have been published to date.[2] None have analyzed available data in a systematic manner, have endeavored to place New Jersey's experience in a comparative context, or have presented a basic spatial (geographical) study of the entire state over a long period of time. This work attempts at least partially to fill those gaps.

As a cultural geographer who has used New Jersey as a form of "laboratory" to determine how culture (way of life) may influence landscape transformation, I became convinced early in my research that the broader topic of land use in the period of settled field agriculture—roughly, from the earliest use of New Jersey by Europeans in the first few decades of the seventeenth century to about 1822—would be more appropriate than a narrower analysis of agricultural practice.[3] A symbiotic relationship often existed between agriculture and other means of exploiting the environment. For example, residents of the southeastern portion of the colony (the Outer Coastal Plain) were generally only part-time farmers or cattlemen and full-time woodsmen, lumbermen, or fishermen. Even in the well-settled areas, trapping, fishing, and hunting were critical adjuncts to the pursuit of agriculture well into the nineteenth century.

This study hypothesizes that several circumstances in early New Jersey affected the ways in which land was used in these years. Although the colony is often compared to and grouped with other middle Atlantic colonies, it stood apart from its neighbors in numerous respects. Its geography and its population were (and are) highly diverse, its method of land allocation was unique, and its situation with respect to large ports and urban populations placed special emphasis on producing agricultural and forest products for market. All of these factors affected physical and cultural environments through time.

Geological evidence has documented the existence of very different parent materials for New Jersey soils, which, with vegetative cover, differ greatly between the shore of the Delaware River and the shore of the Atlantic. Settlers were aware of these variations. For example, Peter Kalm, who was a disciple of the Swedish botanist Linnaeus, came to New Jersey in 1748 and was fascinated by the accounts of large shells being unearthed as wells were dug on the New Jersey side of the Delaware River and by the red soils prevalent in the central part of the colony. Kalm was surely one of the more learned observers of the settlement landscape, but even he had no real knowledge of landform evolution or of physiographic regionalization. He and his contemporaries knew that soils and vegetation varied widely between New Jersey's saltwater and freshwater coastlines, but they did not know why. Also, European perceptions of soils may have differed appreciably. Peter Lindestrom, who prepared a report on the lower Delaware between 1654 and 1656, thought the very productive sandy soils of the Inner Coastal Plain relatively infertile. Almost a century later, Peter Kalm thought the same thing but marveled at how well corn grew there. These Swedes were probably likening these soils to the generally poor sandy soils of northern Europe.[4]

The geography of surface expression in New Jersey divides physiographically in a northeast-southwest direction (map 1).[5] The largest division, to the southeast, is the Coastal Plain, divided further into an inner and an outer portion. Next, to the northwest, is the Piedmont, followed by the Highlands and the Ridge and Valley section. "Piedmont" and "Highlands" are New Jersey localisms but are in wide common use.

The coastal plains share much the same geological history but differ greatly in the type of material outcropping at the surface. The Outer Coastal Plain is very sandy with poor, droughty soils. Slightly better soils are present on terraces dating to the Pleistocene Era (the Ice Age) in places such as Cape May in the extreme south. The Inner Coastal Plain contains much more clay and, although the soils are sandy, they are generally very productive.

The entire coastal plain has a very gentle relief. The highest elevations rise about four hundred feet above sea level, and many very low places, especially in the Outer Coastal Plain where poor drainage has produced extensive swamps, exist as well. Early Dutch and Swedish observers noted the region's abundant small streams, which were navigable to relatively small craft and provided suitable mill seats despite the gentle relief. Along the Atlantic, sand beaches fringe the Coastal Plain. Barrier islands, not physically joined to the mainland, exist in places and are backed by bays, lagoons, and salt marshes joined to the sea by tidal inlets. Tidal marshes without sand beaches also front Delaware Bay and exist along the Delaware to the north.

The boundary of the Piedmont with the Inner Coastal Plain is easily discerned from the nature of the soils, which, as Kalm noted, are red and are based on shales and sandstones. Most of the Piedmont is a relatively low plateau from one to four hundred feet above sea level; in places, knobs and ridges rise several hundred feet further above the general surface. These upland surfaces emerged from ancient volcanic activity and are often too rocky or steep to support agriculture.

Tidal marshes exist where the Piedmont meets salt water at sea level. Pleistocene glacial activity created an especially extensive area of salt marsh in the lower Hackensack Valley and altered the course of the Passaic River to create a large lake between the fishhook-shaped Watchung ridges and the Highlands. Today, a collection of swamps and poorly drained places, the best known of which is the Great

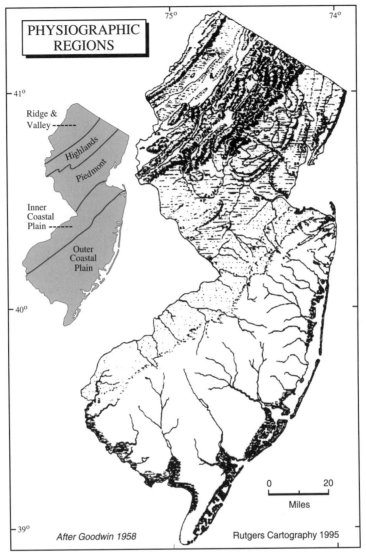

75° 74°

41°

Ridge &
Valley

Highlands

Piedmont

Inner
Coastal
Plain

Outer
Coastal
Plain

40°

0   20

Miles

39°   After Goodwin 1958   Rutgers Cartography 1995

MAP 1

Swamp, are the lake's legacy. Smaller swamps existed elsewhere in the Piedmont north of the terminal moraine.

Several rivers offer access to the Piedmont. Seagoing vessels can navigate the Delaware to Trenton and the Raritan to New Brunswick. On a flood tide, such craft could move slightly upstream on the Raritan to take in half a cargo at Raritan Landing. In flood times, smaller boats moved bulk cargoes downstream from above the fall line on both rivers. Small seagoing craft also navigated the Passaic and Hackensack rivers, but their hinterlands were much less important than those of the Delaware and Raritan. Thus the Piedmont was somewhat less accessible than the Coastal Plain.

The Highlands border the Piedmont to the north and west. An extension of New England's hard crystalline rocks, the Highlands are indeed "high," whether viewed from the Piedmont to the south or from the Ridge and Valley section's Kittatinny Valley to the north. Its uplands are generally called "mountains" and stand at four to six hundred feet above valley surfaces. The two largest valleys are those of the Musconetcong and South Branch of the Raritan rivers (Long Valley). These are structural valleys—that is, they follow basic surface fractures and were not created by erosion alone—and are underlain by limestones and shales. The continental glacier profoundly altered the surface of the Highlands and created vastly different agricultural potential northeast and southwest of the terminal moraine at Hackettstown. Valleys such as that of the Musconetcong were filled with glacial debris; drainage was also deranged to create many lakes and swamps north of the terminal moraine. The relatively few east-to-west passes and the distance from navigable water made the Highlands more remote than the Piedmont or the Coastal Plain.

To the northwest of the Highlands, the broad Kittatinny Valley begins an alternating Valley and Ridge system. Relatively soft limestones and shales form the lowland surfaces; sandstones and conglomerates lie at higher elevations. West of the Kittatinny Valley is the Kittatinny Ridge, a prominent feature penetrated by a wind gap (Culver's Gap) and the well-known Delaware Water Gap. Glacial activity also deranged drainage in the Ridge and Valley section; many lakes and swamps exist in this area, the least accessible part of New Jersey.

In 1973, an extensive study of the plant cover of New Jersey by Robichaud and Buell[6] revealed that vegetation has varied historically according to the presence or absence of water rather than according to climatic conditions, which do not vary greatly enough within the state to affect the distributions of most plant species. In simplified terms, Robichaud and Buell identified marshes, bogs, swamps, and floodplains in both northern and southern New Jersey; mesic, or well-drained, uplands in northern New Jersey; ridge tops, slopes, and rock outcroppings in higher elevations in northern New Jersey; and coastal plans and sand dunes in southern New Jersey.

A series of palynological studies[7] carried out by Emily Russell in northern New Jersey reveal more accurately the vegetation present at the time of first European settlement there. The region appears to have been largely covered by an oak forest, dominated by white and then red and black oaks, which was broken by swamps and meadows and occasional Indian clearings. Russell found little direct evidence of Indian burning, but the presence of charcoal in the record suggested nonetheless that Indian-set fires might occasionally have gotten out of hand. Chestnut was the second most important genus and may have been more prevalent on rockier areas settled later than it was on the better soils. Hickory was also present in this region, though its prevalence is unclear; it was probably a common tree associated with the oaks on better, well-drained lands. Similarly, birch, which formed 2 to 10 percent of the pollen record, was probably associated with oaks; some may have been an early succession in the Indian clearings. Hemlock, 6 to 8 percent of the pollen record, was probably part of swamp or lowland vegetation in the Highlands and Ridge and Valley sections. Maple, elm, and ash occurred at very low levels in pollen deposited during presettlement days. Another change in vegetation appears to have been the elimination of alder, widely found as brush in swamps; settlers cleared much of it as they prepared to drain low-lying areas.

The historical record is not always in full agreement with modern botanical and palynological studies. Hickory, for example, comprised 10 to 22 percent of the trees noted in early surveyors' records in north Jersey, but it was only 4 to 6 percent of the presettlement pollen record. Evidence also varies on the effects of clearance and burning by the Lenape. The palynological work was conducted in the north, where a more broken terrain may have discouraged burning.[8] But on the Inner Coastal Plain, where a more gentle terrain exists, the historical record asserts that Native Americans deliberately burned large sections of land. Samuel Smith, whose family had been among the pioneers of southwestern New Jersey, described the practice in his 1765 history of the colony:

> The Indians, before the European settlements, used every year regularly to burn the woods, the better to kill deer; the manner was to surround a swamp or cripple with fire, then drive the deer out, who not daring over the bounds, were easily kil-l'd with bows and arrows; this practice kept the woods clean.[9]

Historical records suggest that most of New Jersey was wooded in some degree. Oak and chestnut[10] prevailed from the Piedmont north, pine and oak on the better-drained coastal plain, broadleaf species (especially oak) along the lower Delaware, on Cape May, and on Atlantic coastal terraces, and almost pure stands of white cedar in the many swamps of the coastal plain.[11] White cedar was much more characteristic of southern New Jersey, but large stands existed at the time of first European settlement at such places as Secaucus in the Hackensack tidal marsh, where they were a remnant of a much wider distribution.[12]

Robichaud and Buell determined that three distinct forest types characterized the well-drained upland habitats of northern New Jersey—mixed oak, sugar maple-mixed hardwoods, and hemlock-mixed hardwoods. Later research based on pollen analysis has suggested that the dominance of the sugar maple in parts of the Piedmont, Highlands, and Ridge and Valley sections is recent; a mixed oak forest was probably widespread here at the time of the first European settlement.[13] A chestnut oak forest predominated in the drier habitats of northern New Jersey, generally steep slopes and ridges in the Highlands and Ridge and Valley sections. Still drier locations harbored a pitch pine-scrub oak forest in which pitch pine was dominant and scrub oak was dominant in the understory. These drier sections of the Highlands may in fact have been richer in earlier times. In 1799, Julian Niemcewicz, a good and reliable observer, reported the presence of "tremendous trees" near Mt. Hope. "Oaks, elms and mostly various varieties of nut trees comprise the woods of these places,"[14] he wrote, and estimated that centuries must have passed before rotting leaves and fallen vegetation had formed enough soil for tree growth on this rocky terrain.

Still, undisturbed vegetative conditions may have been rare; human intervention may have altered forest growth long before Europeans came to New Jersey. In some areas wood-free meadows, brushlands, and dense coppice woods were the rule. There were also open areas in the upland forests of northern New Jersey. Presumably the plants that are now classified as successional vegetation—annual herbs such as ragweed, foxtail grass, wild radish, and yellow rocket and perennial herbs such as aster, goldenrod, and little bluestem grass—also pioneered cleared areas in the seventeenth century. Woody invaders (plants encouraged by disturbances such as clearing) included especially the red cedar.

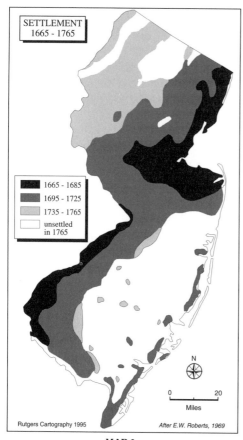

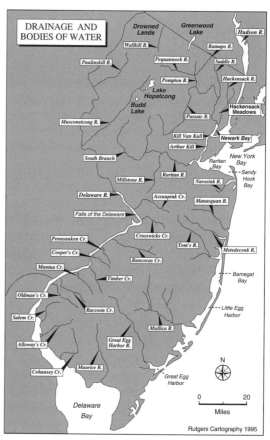

MAP 2

MAP 3

Sand dune habitats feature dunegrass nearest the salt water, then beach heather, then a shrub thicket from one to fifteen feet high including such species as low-growing red cedar and American holly, and finally dune woodland communities with full-sized red cedar, American holly, and other trees. Both shrub and woodland habitats had blueberry, bayberry, and beach plum bushes as well as such vines as Virginia creeper and poison ivy. Kalm commented that poison ivy grew "abundantly in this country,"[15] which suggests that this noxious plant was distributed far more widely by the middle of the eighteenth century.

The vegetative growing season is considerably longer in the south and east than in the north and west, and settlement was naturally oriented at first to the more accessible and fertile soils and milder climates. An isochronic map depicts settlement progression from the 1660s to the 1760s (map 2). The lower Delaware, Raritan, Passaic, Hackensack, and Hudson river valleys were settled first; the southeast, although readily accessible to seagoing vessels through several rivers (map 3), had very poor, droughty soils. Because the head of deepwater navigation on the Delaware was at Trenton, the northwest was more remote, and its topography consisted, in places, of glaciated bare rock.

Population densities also differed markedly. By 1784 (map 4), there were great contrasts between north and south.[16] Population in the glaciated Highlands and Valley and Ridge to the north and west and in the Outer Coastal Plain to the south and east was especially sparse. By 1810 (map 5), those townships lying to the south

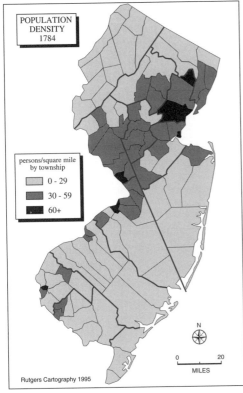

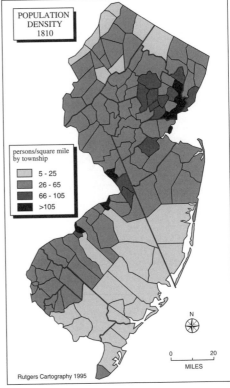

MAP 4

MAP 5

and east (Outer Coastal Plain) still had very few people, while the areas oriented toward Philadelphia and especially New York were beginning to fill in. This population distribution was reflected politically by the subdivision of townships, such as Newark and Elizabeth in Essex County (map 6); New Jersey tax data, most complete between the Revolutionary War years and 1784, were collected and presented by township from the earliest years of settlement.

Not only was the physical environment diverse and the progress of settlement slow in sections, but the history of land allocation in New Jersey was even more complex than what obtained, for example, in neighboring Pennsylvania.[17] New Jersey had been part of the Dutch West India Company's colony of New Netherland, and Dutch, Swedes, Finns, and New Englanders all attempted to settle themselves in the area before the Dutch established the first permanent community at Bergen, now part of Jersey City (map 7). The colony of New Sweden fell to the Dutch in 1655[18], and New Netherland fell to the English in 1664 when New Amsterdam capitulated to a fleet sent by the Duke of York, who granted the New Jersey portion to proprietors Lord John Berkeley and Sir George Carteret. However, the grant had uncertain boundaries with New York to the north and was ambiguous about whether the Arthur Kill, between Newark Bay and Raritan Bay, was a branch of the Hudson.[19]

Named for the ancestral home of Carteret, New Jersey was divided into an East and a West province, each governed by its own council of proprietors. English authorities reconfirmed the land titles of the Dutch settlers of Bergen and encouraged New Englanders to settle in the northeastern part of the colony. In 1674,

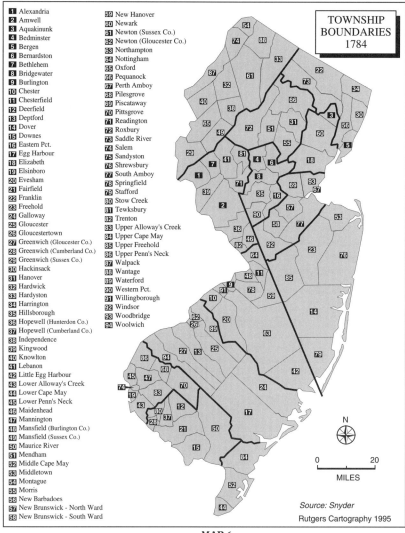

MAP 6

Berkeley sold his half of the colony, with its boundary and title issues still unresolved. This southwestern half came to be owned in common by a group of Quakers, largely from England, who established their capital at Burlington in 1678.

The boundary question between the two colonies was settled in an operational sense in 1688. West Jersey's eastern boundary was set at the eastern boundary of the counties of Burlington, Hunterdon, Morris, and Sussex. These counties, along with Gloucester, Salem, Cumberland, and Cape May counties, became West Jersey; Monmouth, Middlesex, Essex, Somerset, and Bergen counties comprised East Jersey. The proprietors relinquished the reins of government in 1702 when New Jersey became a single royal colony, but ownership of unallocated land remained (and remains to this day) theirs. This intricate pattern of land allocation was vastly complicated by continuing uncertainty about boundaries, inaccurate surveying, poor record keeping, and a very great deal of chicanery on all sides.

Moreover, the settlement history and cultural groupings in New Jersey were more diverse than in most other colonies.[20] The Dutch were earliest on the scene,

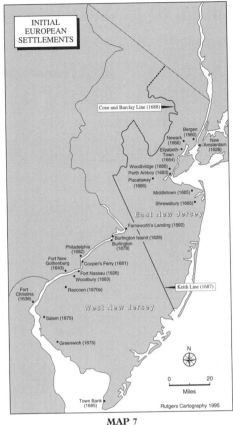

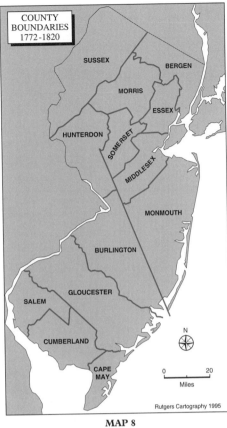

MAP 7

MAP 8

but their numbers were not augmented by other Dutch settlers for about two decades; thus their presence in New Jersey was largely a function of English government and land ownership. From about 1680 on, and especially in the 1720s and 1730s, the Dutch—many of them Protestants who had emigrated from other parts of Europe, especially France—began to settle in significant numbers in northeastern New Jersey and in the Raritan Valley of central New Jersey (see map 3). With them came many Africans, almost all of them slaves.

After the demise of New Netherland in 1664, New Englanders began to flock to the area north of the Raritan Valley and south of where the Dutch had established themselves. Elizabeth-Town was the first of their settlements, followed rapidly by Middletown, Shrewsbury, Woodbridge, Piscataway, and Newark. Other early New England settlements were at Town Bank on Cape May and in the vicinity of the Cohansey Creek in the south. Swedes and Finns had settled in the Delaware Valley by 1638, where they established Fort Christina (now Wilmington, Delaware). Only a few years before the English assumed control of the region, the Swedes and Finns had created their first permanent settlements in the southern part of West New Jersey, yet English Quakers dominated the early years of that province. Quakers established themselves first at Greenwich, Salem, and Burlington in the 1670s and in other parts of the province in the 1680s. Burlington was the capital of the colony and, like Salem and Greenwich, was planned to be a port. In the 1680s as well, East New Jersey also changed when a group of Scots bought the other half of New Jersey from Carteret's widow and made Perth Amboy their capital and chief port.

Hundreds of Scots subsequently came to the Raritan Valley, making it the most culturally heterogeneous area in New Jersey.

Two other cultural groups, Scots-Irish Presbyterians from northern Ireland and German-speaking peoples from central Europe, settled New Jersey in large numbers in the eighteenth century. The Germans came largely by way of Pennsylvania and settled northwestern New Jersey, north of Assunpink Creek near Trenton. Scots-Irish and English Pennsylvanians joined in this movement into the northwestern sections. Scots-Irish also settled widely in West Jersey south of Trenton and in the Raritan Valley. And well before the Revolution, increasing numbers of southern, Roman Catholic Irish were settling in the state; township tax lists generally document their presence as landless laborers.

The distributions of these cultural groupings can generally be understood using a map of New Jersey counties as they existed for the censuses of 1772–1820 (map 8). Because the next boundary change occurred when Warren County was set off from Sussex in 1824, this map also shows county tax data for the entire period of this study.[21] Beginning in the north, Bergen County was overwhelmingly Dutch, along with the northern part of Essex and Morris counties. In general, the African population was to be found, as slaves, along with the Dutch. Most of the rest of these two counties were settled by New Englanders, as was Middlesex north of the Raritan River. Except in its northern sections, heavily populated by Scots and Scots-Irish, Somerset County was largely Dutch. A mixture of Dutch, New Englanders, Scots, and Scots-Irish inhabited southern Middlesex and northern Monmouth counties; Hunterdon was settled by people from southern and eastern New Jersey (the area nearest southern Somerset being Dutch), but the largest single cultural grouping was probably Pennsylvanian, many of them Germans. Sussex County had fewer settlers from south Jersey, more from the east and from Pennsylvania. Burlington was especially English Quaker along with northern Gloucester and Salem counties. Southern Gloucester had an important minority of Swedes and Finns, who could also be found in eastern Cumberland. The rest of Cumberland County was populated by Quakers and New Englanders, as was Cape May.

New Jersey's strategic position on the seaboard and between the colonies' two major port cities also had direct bearing on its land use throughout this period. Philadelphia led New York in both population and in the volume of its port activity through about the time of the Revolution, after which New York forged ahead. After about the middle of the eighteenth century, New Jersey had very little direct export or import trade but rather used Philadelphia and New York as entrepôts; before the Revolution, it was referred to as "a barrel tapped at both ends."[22] The populations of both cities also provided independent markets for food.

Finally, perceptions of the land and its potential shaped land use from the first. The natural environment of New Jersey clearly impressed Europeans, as the earliest records document. European observations of the value to be found in New Jersey's environment were most accurate in those areas explorers and settlers could easily penetrate; thus, the area from Trenton southwest and the northeast were best known and most often described. The northern interior came to be known later, when the initial fascination with the New World had waned and environmental attributes had become too familiar to report.

Among the Dutch, Swedes, and Finns, the prime motivation for colonization was commercial—that is, to exploit the trade in furs with Native Americans.[23] Thus it comes as no surprise that many accounts describe wildlife extensively. Johannes De Laet, probably writing in 1624 and basing his work on official (many now lost) records of the Dutch West India Company, noted the abundance especially of deer and turkeys.[24] David De Vries, who had been involved in a failed colony on the Delaware River in 1630 and in settlements in northeastern New Jersey and on Staten Island between 1638 and 1644, mentioned in his 1655 account the prevalence of elk in the back country, as well as rabbits, foxes, wolves, wild cats, squirrels, beavers, minks, otters, skunks, bears, and other furbearers he could not name.[25]

A detailed description of the area's wildlife appeared in a report prepared between 1654 and 1656 on the shoreline and immediate interior from Delaware Bay to the falls at present Trenton by the Swede Peter Lindestrom, who had been trained in map making at Uppsala University.[26] The country harbored panthers, black bears, wolves, lynxes, skunks, wild cats, elks, fishers, raccoons, minks, beavers, otters, deer, foxes, muskrats (whose pelts, he noted, were splendid for coat lining), hares (rabbits), and squirrels. Rattlesnakes fascinated recently arrived Europeans, and many apocryphal stories circulated about them; Lindestrom, for his part, thought that a rattlesnake's jaws were powerful enough to bite off a person's leg. That all of Lindestrom's information on animal life had not been acquired firsthand may be surmised from his assertion that dragons existed in New Sweden, but such fanciful statements were not unusual in early European accounts of the region.[27]

Studies of the distribution of the pre-European fauna of New Jersey are limited in number,[28] but the many accounts of early Europeans amply document the wealth of furbearing animals. Some of the older Swedish residents told Peter Kalm that when southwestern New Jersey was first settled "there were excessive numbers of wolves . . . and their howling and yelping might be heard all night."[29] Elk, however, seem to have vanished early.[30] The mountain lion, or panther, certainly was present until the mid-eighteenth century, and wolves lingered in the north Highlands and in parts of the Ridge and Valley section into the nineteenth century. The commercially important beaver, though much diminished, was probably never completely eliminated. Some species now common appear to have either extended their range fairly recently (opossum) or to have been introduced in colonial times (red fox). Based on what is now known about the distribution of both animal fauna and Native American sites, it seems reasonable to suppose that, before extensive clearance had taken place, the least favorable habitat would have been the Outer Coastal Plain and north of the terminal moraine in the Highlands.[31] Human disturbance would have favored certain species in certain areas. Deer, for example, would have been favored by Indian clearance.[32] As permanent agricultural settlement took place and land was cleared, those areas least favorable for agriculture were those where most of the game could be found, the reverse of earlier circumstances.

Exploration and settlement accounts often mentioned the numerous birds and fish of the area as well. Observing that many inlets and rivers offered access to the area of the Outer Coast Plain, De Laet (and later writers) waxed eloquent on the number and excellent quality of the fish of stream and ocean. Henry Hudson's crew in 1609 spent some time in fishing near Sandy Hook, with good success.[33] Peter Lindestrom also noted the many streams flowing into the Delaware that sloops might navigate for good distances upstream. Many sites on the streams, he observed, were appropriate for various kinds of mills, and the streams themselves were full of fish. He mentioned especially shad, which he likened to salmon and which the Swedes and Finns valued for their fine taste. Bass and sturgeon also inhabited the fresh waters of the colony. On the major rivers the salt and fresh water fisheries overlapped. On the Hudson, Jasper Danckaerts and Peter Sluyter enjoyed fine striped bass in 1679. "They were fat and hard," they wrote, "with a little of the flavor of the salmon."[34] In coastal waters, clams and oysters also abounded, and whales in the waters off Cape May were viewed as a significant resource from as early as 1640. Peter Kalm devoted a great deal of space in his travel account to describing how oysters were prepared to be eaten and pickled for the very lucrative West Indian market.[35] Collectively, fish and shellfish may have been much more important in New Jersey's economy than were hunting and trapping for furs, as the many efforts of early legislators to regulate these resources suggest. Because most western Europeans came from a largely deforested landscape, they viewed the resources of the forest as a marvel. To Hudson's expedition of 1609, the view from Sandy Hook Bay was a "magnificent landscape . . . pleasant with Grasse and Flowers, and goodly Trees."[36] On shore, the expedition found "the finest oaks for height and thickness that one could ever see, together with poplars . . . and various other kinds of wood useful in shipbuilding." Swedes and Finns on the lower Delaware, who came from a forested region, were well aware of the uses to which the forest could be put. Early accounts note how high and thick the trees were and how suitable they seemed for cabinet work. Some of the evergreens had a much more pleasant smell than their Swedish counterparts, but Lindestrom pointed out that the gum tree smelled like raw fish, could not be split, and burned poorly.

Other accounts made note of additional promise the environment seemed to contain. In 1524, the Verrazano expedition found Lower New York Bay "hospitable and attractive" and noted that valuable minerals might lay in the hills.[37] Europeans also commented with wonder on the huge grapevines in the forest, which suggested successful viticulture. For the Swedish government, Lindestrom visited every stream in the area and reported his perceptions of the quality of soils and other factors of interest in 1653. He noted that the soils of the west bank were generally better than those on the New Jersey side, where hogs were being allowed to run free and were hunted as needed. Allowing livestock to range freely was also common in New Netherland at the time.[38]

Not all commentary on the settlement environment related directly to its potential use, however. Peter Kalm and other observers wrote at length about the pests that plagued early settlers, and, as no formal study of the insect life of colonial New Jersey is known to exist, these accounts are the best information available on the subject. With many others, Kalm singled out the mosquito as a special target of opprobrium:

> The gnats which are very troublesome at night here, are called mosquitoes. . . . In daytime or at night they come into the houses, and when the people have gone to bed they begin their disagreeable humming approach nearer and nearer to the bed, and at last suck up so much blood that they can hardly fly away. . . . After a rain, they gather frequently in such quantities about homes that their numbers are

legion. . . . On sultry evenings they accompany the cattle in great swarms from the woods to the houses or to town, and when they are driven before the houses. . . . [They] fly in wherever they can. In the greatest heat of summer they are so numerous in some places that the air seems to be full of them, especially near swamps and stagnant waters. . . When they stung me here at night, my face was so disfigured by little red spots and blisters that I was almost ashamed to show myself.[39]

Swedes living on the Maurice River in Cumberland County made fires in front of their houses to drive the mosquitoes away. Older Swedes thought that the numbers of mosquitoes had diminished in southwestern New Jersey (perhaps due to drainage projects) but that vast numbers could still be found on the coast.

Mosquitoes were not only unpleasant nocturnal companions but were also the vectors of disease—especially malaria, referred to generally as "ague." Kalm and others noted that ague was especially associated with poor drainage and the hot season.[40] The assumption at the time was that the evaporation of odoriferous, stagnant water produced vapor that, when inhaled, caused the disease. Indeed, the very term "malaria" means bad air. Kalm described the people afflicted with the disease as looking "as pale as death and . . . greatly weakened, but in general are not prevented from doing their work in the intervals." Attacks of fever were widely commented on, especially in the southern part of New Jersey, and although the precise consequences of the disease are not known it apparently forestalled labor in many places for days or weeks at a time. There is no evidence to support the notion that Europeans knew that draining land would prevent malarial fever, but certainly they cannot have thought draining would exacerbate the problem.

Kalm also commented on the depredation of "woodlice" (ticks)[41] and described the destruction of apple and peach trees by tent caterpillars, which settlers attempted to eradicate by burning their nests with a torch.[42] Other pests included a caterpillar that arrived in vast numbers every few years to lay waste to forest trees and "grass worms," which did great damage every few years in the meadows and corn fields. Relatively benign were the seventeen-year locusts and crickets and the introduced bedbugs, cockroaches, fleas, and moths that infested houses.[43]

Thus, the physical environment, land allocation system, cultural background, time and duration of settlement, population distribution, and location of New Jersey might be expected to have influenced land use through time. This book will explore each of these variables, in particular the influence of cultural background in varying patterns of land use in New Jersey. New Jersey was a cultural mosaic, with several very distinct culture areas. Did, for example, the slave labor available to the Dutch make a difference in the way they used land? Did the New England system of settlement, in nucleated groups within relatively large areas with periodic distributions of land, influence land use in the areas in which New Englanders predominated? Were there differences, as Robert G. LeBlanc has suggested, between the way "folk" and "elite" peoples used land?[44]

This study will also compare what actually transpired in New Jersey with a model developed early in the nineteenth century in northern Germany and later adapted by James Lemon in his useful study of southeastern Pennsylvania, *The Best Poor Man's Country* (map 9).[45] Although the systematic data that can be gathered from tax lists, store and farmers' account books, and other such sources vary consider-

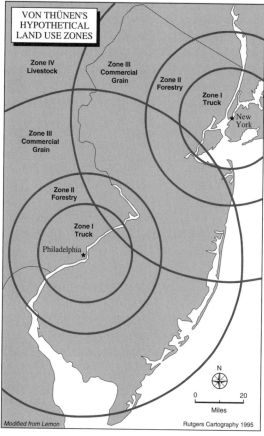

VON THÜNEN'S
HYPOTHETICAL
LAND USE ZONES

Zone IV
Livestock

Zone III
Commercial
Grain

Zone II
Forestry

Zone I
Truck

New
York

Zone III
Commercial
Grain

Zone II
Forestry

Zone I
Truck

Philadelphia

N

0   20

Miles

Modified from Lemon

Rutgers Cartography 1995

MAP 9

ably from place to place and through time, and although Lemon's time frame differs somewhat from the one examined here, some comparisons can be made between his findings for southeastern Pennsylvania and mine for New Jersey as a whole. In his study, Lemon adapted a model developed by Johann von Thünen in 1826 to describe land use in northern Germany.[46] The von Thünen model, widely used to explain land use in other places and times, assumes the existence of a totally isolated market center. It also assumes that the surrounding land surface is even, that the soil is of even quality, and that no transportation by water exists. He assumed too that people would act in an economically rational manner—that is, they would endeavor to maximize the profit to be made in using land. Under such conditions, von Thünen hypothesized, different kinds of land use would form a series of concentric rings around the market center. Those located near the market center would use their relatively expensive land more intensively than those located at a greater distance from the market, where land would generally be less expensive but the cost of transport to the market would be relatively high.

The first concentric ring around the market, according to von Thünen, would be given over to such products as fresh fruit, garden truck, and milk that could not be transported great distances by wagon. In effect, all of the land would be in use in the first ring: land values would simply be too high here to allow any land to lie fallow. Milk cattle, for example, would have to be stall fed because they would damage the small pastures; farmers would realize a greater profit by cutting and selling the clover on the market than by growing it to feed cattle. Hay would be grown for fodder because the cost of transporting such a bulky product from elsewhere would be very high. Crop production would be enhanced by the manure available from the town. Farmers in this first ring would produce some grain but largely for the straw byproduct, to be used on stall floors.

The second ring begins where the cost of drawing manure from the town and supplying it with produce by wagon becomes too high to allow a sufficient profit from the intensive land use of the first ring. Here, forestry becomes important. The market center of von Thünen's day required wood for fuel, lumber for building, and charcoal for cooking. So indeed did American cities before the widespread use of coal. Forests would not have been located further afield, von Thünen argued, because wood is bulky and expensive to transport, but land values in the first ring would be too high to encourage farmers to devote land to forest. Farmers in this second ring, however, could make greater profit from their lands by maintaining forests upon them than by using them to grow such products as grain, the return from which would not be sufficiently high to justify its production.

For southeastern Pennsylvania, Lemon combined several rings von Thünen had proposed because certain northern European conditions did not exist in colonial America. Farmers beyond the second ring would grow grain and would raise cattle to produce butter, which von Thünen judged to be uneconomic to produce near town. In this third zone, raising cattle for butter production made more sense than raising livestock to slaughter.

On the inexpensive, sparsely populated lands of the outermost ring, however, even growing grain would not be profitable because of the cost of bringing it to market; farmers would grow only enough grain to use themselves and supply the local market. Given the size of this zone, farmers sent very few animal products to the market. Here, beyond the area of commercial grain production, farmers would be more apt to raise livestock, largely in the summer on pasture grasses. In relation to its value, stock was a product less expensive to transport than grain because it could be driven to market; indeed, farmers in the third zone could easily obtain animals for slaughter from this outside ring. Von Thünen equivocated on whether stock would be fattened so far from the market and finally concluded that "the fattening process will be started in the outlying districts, but finished nearer the Town." Then, some fifty miles from the market, the zonal system ended; von Thünen theorized that here would be only a few hunters "living virtually like savages."

Von Thünen was the first to admit that his model was theoretical and, because it presumed level, equally fertile land, would not precisely mirror land use in every environment. Soils were not equal over large areas, and von Thünen acknowledged that he knew of no large town remote from transportation by water (including those reached by canal). Moreover, every sizeable country had many small market centers in addition to the major center.

For New Jersey, and indeed for Pennsylvania, other factors make von Thünen's model less relevant. Not only was New Jersey's agriculture drawn to two large regional markets, but both Philadelphia and New York were linked into an enormous Atlantic commercial system, including both the Old World and the Caribbean.[47] Further, the area had been recently settled, and patterns that had perhaps taken hundreds of years to develop in northern Germany might not have emerged in the colonies.[48] Von Thünen also allowed that government regulation such as tariffs might radically alter the zonal pattern of land use. Did external demand for New Jersey produce change due to unsettled conditions elsewhere—during the Napoleonic Wars, for example, or the War of 1812?

Moreover, neither Philadelphia nor New York, to which New Jersey was essentially hinterland, were "isolated" in any sense of the word. And New Jersey lacked the cultural homogeneity of northern Germany in the 1820s. An additional consideration is that New Jersey (and, in general, American) farmers were often criticized for poor land use practices; it is possible that they did not, in other words, always manage land in such a way as to maximize their profit. Von Thünen's model also did not take into account change over time; as cultural groups became acculturated, as new areas were settled to the west, as transportation improved, and as external markets changed, New Jersey farmers might be expected to have changed accordingly. And a final variable centers on the very different environmental circumstances of northern Germany and New Jersey. Because New Jersey summers were far warmer, crops such as corn that could not be grown in northern Europe became especially important in New Jersey. Did the production of corn affect other land uses?

This study relies on a wealth of data documenting land uses in early New Jersey. Systematic tax ratable data are available for much of New Jersey from 1772 to 1822, the ending date for this study. Early settlement narratives, advertisements of real estate sales, damage claims submitted by New Jersey farmers from the Revolutionary War, farmers' diaries and account books, and store daybooks and ledgers all contain extensive detail about the composition and activity of farms and of their laboring populations. Much of this data was collected so systematically that it could readily be transferred to maps which could then be compared to other distributions of phenomena, both physical and cultural.

These sources will be used to describe, first of all, how New Jersey's earliest settlers used the physical environment, as well as how legislators endeavored to curb exploitation of natural resources and practices that conflicted with commerce or agriculture. Regional and cultural differences in property ownership, agricultural labor forces, and types of farms will then be explored. The middle chapters will describe efforts to improve land through drainage, fertilization, and crop rotation, the cultivation of grain and non-grain crops, the dedication of land to orchards and vineyards, and the raising of livestock, fowl, and bees. The final two chapters will describe what township and county tax lists and farmers' account books reveal about land use in New Jersey and the seasonal round of activity on its farms and woodlands over the two centuries between settlement and the dawn of the industrial age.

Notes

1. Carl R. Woodward, *Ploughs and Politicks: Charles Read of New Jersey and His Notes on Agriculture* (New Brunswick, N.J., 1941), 229.

2. Hubert G. Schmidt, *Agriculture in New Jersey: A Three-Hundred-Year History* (New Brunswick, N.J., 1973); Carl R. Woodward, *Agriculture in New Jersey* (New York, 1930). Interestingly, both Schmidt and Woodward have produced very fine studies of smaller areas, Hunterdon County and Burlington County. See Schmidt, *Rural Hunterdon: An Agricultural History* (New Brunswick, N.J., 1945) and Woodward, *Ploughs and Politicks*.

3. This study does not deal with Amerindian land use in any direct way, as that subject has been covered adequately in Herbert C. Kraft, *The Lenape: Archaeology, History, and Ethnography* (Newark, N.J., 1986).

4. Adolph B. Benson, ed. and trans., *Peter Kalm's Travels in North America: The English Version of 1770* (New York, 1937), 1:89, 119–20, 174–75, 187–89, 317; Peter M. Lindestrom, *Geographia Americae* (Philadelphia, 1925).

5. For a discussion of New Jersey's physiography and geology, see Kemble Widmer, *The Geology and Geography of New Jersey* (Princeton, 1964) and Peter E. Wolfe, *The Geology and Landscapes of New*

Jersey (New York, 1977).

6. Beryl Robichaud and Murray F. Buell, *Vegetation of New Jersey: A Study in Landscape Diversity* (New Brunswick, N.J., 1973). Robichaud and Buell did not mention mountain laurel, though Kalm noted its presence in 1750. See Benson, *Peter Kalm's Travels,* 1:176–78.

7. Emily W. Russell, "Vegetational Change in Northern New Jersey Since 1500 A.D.: A Palynological, Vegetational and Historical Synthesis" (Ph.D. diss., Rutgers University, 1979), 126–33, 136–42, 187–94.

8. This was suggested to me by Lorraine Williams, Curator of Archaeology, New Jersey State Museum, Trenton.

9. Samuel Smith, *The History of the Colony of Nova-Caesaria or New Jersey* (Trenton, N.J., 1877), 511.

10. The American chestnut was all but eliminated by a blight introduced in 1904; sprouts of this tree, however, can be found today in both upland forest habitats.

11. A. Philip Muntz, "The Changing Geography of the New Jersey Woodlands, 1600–1900" (Ph.D. diss., University of Wisconsin, 1959), 41–42.

12. Calvin J. Heusser, "History of an Estuarine Bog at Secaucus, New Jersey," *Bulletin of the Torrey Botanical Club* 76 (1949): 385–406.

13. Russell, "Vegetational Change," 64.

14. Julian Ursyn Niemcewicz, *Under Their Vine and Fig Tree: Travels Through America in 1797–1799, 1805, With Some Further Account of Life in New Jersey,* ed. and trans. Mitchie Budka (Elizabeth, N.J., 1965), 229.

15. Benson, *Peter Kalm's Travels,* 1:23.

16. *Votes and Proceedings of the General Assembly of the State of New Jersey,* 1st sitting, 1784, 33. Also see note 19.

17. James T. Lemon, *The Best Poor Man's Country: A Geographical Study of Early Southeastern Pennsylvania* (Baltimore, 1972), 50–61.

18. Peter O. Wacker, "Swedish Settlement in New Jersey Before 1800," in *New Sweden in America,* ed. Carol Hoffecker (Newark, Del., forthcoming).

19. Unless otherwise noted, the general discussion of settlement and land division in New Jersey is derived from Peter O. Wacker, *Land and People: A Cultural Geography of Preindustrial New Jersey: Origins and Settlement Patterns* (New Brunswick, N.J., 1975), esp. chaps. 4 and 5.

20. Ibid., esp. chap. 3.

21. Maps of county and township boundaries are derived from John P. Snyder, *The Story of New Jersey's Civil Boundaries, 1606–1968* (Trenton, N.J., 1969).

22. This quote is generally attributed to Benjamin Franklin, but James Madison may have been its actual source. See John T. Cunningham, *New Jersey: America's Main Road* (Garden City, N.Y., 1976), 53.

23. Amandus Johnson, *The Swedish Settlements on the Delaware* (New York, 1911), 1:93–12.

24. J. Franklin Jameson, *Narratives of New Netherland, 1609-1664* (New York, 1909), 32–35.

25. Ibid., 183–85.

26. Lindestrom, *Geographia Americae,* 154–67, 177–78, 185–89.

27. Ibid., 185 n. 3.

28. David C. Parris, "New and Revised Records of Pleistocene Mammals of New Jersey," *The Mosasaur* 1 (1983): 1–21, esp. 4–5. I am indebted to Lorraine Williams for bringing this source to my attention. Also see J. McManus, "Checklist, Identification Keys, and Bibliography of New Jersey Land Mammals," *New Jersey Academy of Science Journal* 19 (1974): 52–58.

29. Benson, *Peter Kalm's Travels,* 1:150.

30. Stellan Dahlgren and Hans Norman, *The Rise and Fall of New Sweden: Governor John Risingh's Journal, 1654–1655, in Its Historical Context* (Stockholm, 1988), 215.

31. Although many sites have been found in the Outer Coastal Plain and northern Highlands due to more intensive field surveys in recent years, these regions appear to have experienced a much lower density of Amerindian occupation than did the rest of the state. For the best statewide general survey, see Dorothy Cross, *Archaeology of New Jersey* (Trenton, 1941), end map.

32. Leonard J. Wolgast, "Mammals of the New Jersey Pine Barrens," in *Pine Barrens: Ecosystem and Landscape,* ed. Richard T. T. Forman (New York, 1979), 454.

33. Jameson, *Narratives,* 18.

34. Jasper Danckaerts, *Journal of a Voyage to New York, and a Tour in Several of the American Colonies in 1679–80* (Brooklyn, N.Y., 1867), 165.

35. Benson, *Peter Kalm's Travels,* 1:125–26.

36. Robert Juet, *The Voyage of the Half Moon from 4 April to 7 November, 1609* (Newark, N.J., 1959), 29.

37. Quoted in Carl O. Sauer, *Sixteenth Century North America: The Land and the People as Seen by the Europeans* (Berkeley, Calif., 1971), 55.

38. Russell, "Vegetational Change," 123–24.

39. Benson, *Peter Kalm's Travels,* 1:76–77.

40. Ibid., 1:192–93.

41. Ibid., 1:280.

42. Ibid., 1:304–5.

43. Ibid., 1:213–18.

44. Robert G. LeBlanc, "The Differential Perception of Salt Marshes by the Folk and Elite in the Late Nineteenth Century" (Unpublished paper, 1978).

45. Lemon, *Best Poor Man's Country,* 193.

46. Johann Heinrich von Thünen, *Isolated State: An English Edition of Der Isolierte Staat,* trans. Carla M. Wartenberg, ed. Peter Hall (Oxford, Eng., and New York, 1966).

47. D. W. Meinig, *The Shaping of America: A Geographical Perspective on 500 Years of History,* vol. 1, *Atlantic America, 1492–1800* (New Haven, Conn., and London, 1986), 257–67.

48. Sheep are an interesting case in point. Von Thünen was unsure about the zone in which sheep would be raised because the superior Merino had just been introduced into Germany and the wool was bringing a very high price. Eventually, he suggested, sheep would be raised in the outside ring.

Third Month, March, 1819.

CHAPTER 1

EXPLOITING THE NATURAL ENVIRONMENT

In 1755–56, more than half a century after Cape May had been settled, longtime resident Jacob Spicer listed and estimated the value of what he termed Cape May's "exports," the goods and services leaving the area for sale elsewhere.[1] Spicer was in an excellent position to compile such estimates, because he owned a store and large amounts of land in the area. He was also recognized throughout the province of West New Jersey for his wide knowledge of economic conditions; his expertise led his colleagues in the legislature to appoint him to gather data for and formulate the new tax law of 1751.[2]

Cape May had been settled at the end of the seventeenth century at first by New Englanders, who came to exploit the whale fishery.[3] Although poor by New Jersey standards elsewhere, its sandy soils are among the best on the outer portion of the Atlantic coastal plain. Spicer's estimates show that despite the fact that the area had been actively farmed for decades, the local economy was still largely driven by products derived from exploitive uses of land:[4]

Cape May "Exports"

Cattle	£1,200
Pork Products	200
Hides and Tallow	120
Flax Seed, Neat's Tongues, Beeswax and Myrtle	80
Ship's Pilots (for the port of Philadelphia)	420
Mittens (knitted by local women from wool produced on Cape May)	500
Cedar Posts	300
White Cedar Lumber	500
Boards	200
Tar	60
Charcoal	30
Oysters	600
Deer Skins and Venison	120
Furs and Feathers	100
Total	£4,430

For some reason, Spicer's list did not include sheep, which he himself sold to butchers in Philadelphia and which other sources indicate were a significant "export" from Cape May at the time. Even allowing for this and other possible inaccuracies, Spicer's account makes clear that commercial crops were generally not leaving Cape May to be marketed elsewhere. The sole exception was flax seed, most likely a byproduct of the flax used locally. Spicer's diary documents that he grew wheat, but the yield was very low, and he probably regarded it as a subsistence crop. Cattle and hogs did bring in a large part of Cape May's (and Spicer's) income from the outside, but Spicer's diary again indicates that livestock except sheep received little care and were mostly pastured in the woods. Clearly, the bulk of the area's income derived from using what the environment already offered, not from settled field agriculture.

Exploiting the natural environment was the most important land use in the early years of settlement in New Jersey. Agricultural land uses, such as the supervised raising of livestock and the cultivation of crops, came later—in some cases much later. In some areas, agricultural activity remained less important than exploitive use of the physical environment. One such area was the Atlantic coast, where poor soils encouraged people to harvest the resources of the sea and the woodlands. And even in areas where agriculture was feasible and productive, exploitation of natural resources remained an important part of the economy.

By the 1750s, the income from hunting, trapping, and fishing was a small proportion of Cape May's total export income, but these activities remained important even as residents and lawmakers confronted the depletion of desirable species. Especially in newly settled areas and in parts of the Outer Coastal Plain, hunting, trapping, fishing, and lumbering probably made a big difference in the level of affluence settled farmers and farm laborers were able to attain.

The first European settlers in the region including New Jersey positioned themselves where the access to large numbers of furs was best—the Dutch at Fort Orange (Albany) on the Hudson and the Swedes at Fort Christina (Wilmington) in the Delaware Valley. Huge numbers of furs did leave the region. In 1626, 7,246 beaver pelts, 800 otter skins, and numerous mink, wildcat, and muskrat skins were shipped from New Netherland.[5] On the Delaware, between thirty and forty thousand beaver pelts were taken in 1662 alone.[6] Undoubtedly, some of these pelts came from New Jersey. By 1710 the beaver trade had collapsed. Yet scattered references to them indicate that enough remained to act as agents of landscape change.[7] In 1755 Spicer mentioned a beaver dam in southern New Jersey, and a survey in 1786 by Lemuel Cobb of land adjoining a small stream running into what later became Lake Hopatcong stated that the stream was "near to the beaver Dams."[8]

By the mid-eighteenth century, panther, deer, bear, wolves, wild cats, red and grey foxes, raccoons, and otters were also scarce in New Jersey; "old settled places have but few of those most voracious," Smith observed.[9] Yet, even as the beaver trade fell away, furs remained a significant part of the economy; into the nineteenth century inhabitants received credit in the account books of local merchants for furs. That it still paid to devote time to trapping or hunting is revealed in the prices furs commanded. In the early nineteenth century in northwestern New Jersey, for example, a muskrat skin was worth a day's work at hard agricultural labor.[10]

After the beaver, the most widely sought skin was that of the deer, which remained abundant in many places at midcentury. The early Swedish and Finnish inhabitants of New Jersey were great hunters of deer, on the Inner Coastal Plain in the seventeenth century and on the Outer Coastal Plain in the eighteenth.[11] In October 1764, Pastor Carl Wrangel described the catch of one Carl Steelman, who lived near Egg Harbor. "Around his house were high fences, on which were hung a considerable number of deer antlers; like trophies, they witnessed that here dwelt a mighty hunter," Wrangel wrote. "Here we . . . feasted on Swedish venison."[12]

By the mid-eighteenth century, however, many accounts attest a mounting concern about the disappearance of deer. Peter Kalm reported that the number of deer had much diminished from years before because of "increase of population, the destruction of the woods, and the number of people who kill and frighten the stags at present."[13] Yet he added that does could be easily tamed if captured very young and could be used to entice bucks during the rutting season. At least one farmer made it a practice to capture bucks in this way and sell them in Philadelphia for twenty-five to forty shillings (£0.25.0 to 0.40.0), a profitable enterprise. In 1765, Smith noted that deer were "plentier than one would expect" in all the counties of New Jersey despite the "great numbers . . . destroyed by traps and hunting."[14]

Smith described the enormous iron traps that endangered both man and beast and decried the practice of setting sharp stakes and loaded guns. In reality, legislators had banned iron traps larger than 3 1/2 pounds and the setting of loaded guns in 1760 in most of New Jersey, but traps were still permitted in Essex, Bergen, Morris, Somerset, and Sussex counties.[15] An "Act to Preserve Deer" of 1769 reveals clearly the extent of concern over the decline in deer population, as well as much about how the animals were taken in colonial New Jersey.[16] The act established a deer hunting season from September 1 to January 1 and prohibited hunting without permission on another's property and hunting with shot, which tended to ruin the skin and to waste a great many wounded deer.[17] An emerging elite interest in sport appears to have motivated the legislation's resriction of hunting on "waste and unimproved land" to those having enough personal wealth to qualify for the franchise (those holding one hundred or more acres as a freehold worth £50 or more) and to their sons over eighteen. "Great numbers of idle and disorderly persons make a Practice of hunting for Deer on the waste and unimproved lands in this Colony," the law declared, "whereby their Families are neglected and the Public is prejudiced by the loss of their Labour."

Only two years later, another law fined anyone except Native Americans who sold the skins or venison of green deer beyond the hunting season established in 1769.[18] By 1771, such larger game as bear, foxes, and wolves must have disappeared from all parts of New Jersey except the northern Highlands, because residents of Essex, Bergen, Morris, and Sussex counties were again permitted to set traps weighing more than five pounds to catch them. In Essex County, the last refuge for large game may have been parts of the Watchung Mountains or the Great Swamp, but in Morris Township by 1772 land clearance had probably progressed to the point that the only wooded refuge large enough to accommodate deer was the poorly drained Great Swamp, a legacy of the Pleistocene.

As early as 1749, thirty-six men, probably from the northern part of the colony, petitioned the Governor, Council, and General Assembly to ban the use of dogs to hunt deer in the snow. The petitioners offered the rationale that venison was poor during the winter and that the skins were damaged, but they were probably more concerned abut the depletion of the herd.[19] In 1769, hunters were no longer permitted to stand at night with a gun within two hundred yards of a road on unenclosed land in order to shoot deer driven by dogs, nor could they set guns to go off by a string or rope. In 1772, "for the better Preservation of Deer," Morris Township set a five-year moratorium on hunting. Anyone found to have killed, wounded, or otherwise destroyed a deer was to be fined the large sum of six pounds, and hunting with guns or dogs was banned entirely from the Great Swamp.[20] Furthermore, any dog found hunting in the Great Swamp could be killed with impunity. But hunters elsewhere continued the practice; in about 1820, hunters used dogs to drive deer into Lake Hopatcong, where they rowed to them, seized them by the hind legs, and then killed them. The severe winter of 1835–36 apparently exterminated deer in that region for some time.[21]

An 1735 account book kept at a general store in Bound Brook (whose hinterland then extended to northern Hunterdon County, just beginning to be settled) attests that deer and other animal skins retained economic importance well after initial settlement.[22] The store apparently kept a separate account book for the skin trade. In July of that year, John Breese was credited with the very respectable amount of £27.11.3 for thirty-nine deer skins. Christopher Banker had brought in two bear skins at £0.8.0 (eight shillings) a piece, one panther skin at five shillings, three minks valued together at eight shillings, twelve fox skins at three shillings each, and fifteen wildcat pelts at two shillings six pence each (£0.2.6). Compared to daily wages at about the same time (see table 13), a successful hunter and trapper apparently did quite well financially.

In Cape May, Spicer recorded the prices he paid for commodities at his general store in January 1756. For furs "catched between th 1st Dec'r. and the first of March" he paid £0.10.0 for otter; 0.3.0 for wolves; 0.2.8 for foxes and "cats" (wildcats); 0.2.4 for mink; 0.2.0 for raccoon; and 0.4.0 for muskrats. Fall deer skins brought 0.2.0 per pound and "summer red skins, two shillings six pence per pound."[23] Panther were no longer present, evidently, around Cape May, and they appear to have been scarce at Bound Brook.

Hunting panthers and wolves not only produced valuable skins but also eliminated the danger they presented to both livestock and man. A panther is recorded to have killed a man at Shrewsbury in 1768, and, judging from the bounties offered in both East and West New Jersey in the earliest years, wolves were far more numerous.[24] Even the twenty-shilling bounty for every wolf head offered in 1730 was apparently not enough to encourage hunters to take these predators: in 1751, the bounty was raised to sixty shillings.[25] At about that time Peter Kalm reported that wolves were "seldom seen" in southern New Jersey "but further up the country, where it is less inhabited, they are still very abundant." In 1769 a petition to the General Assembly from Sussex County complained "that Wolves are grown so plenty in that County, that they come in Companies, and destroy Colts, young Cattle and Sheep in Abundance."[26] Wolves remained a menace in the uncleared northern Highlands and Ridge and Valley section through the turn of the eighteenth century; in 1799 Newton Township offered an additional forty pounds "for Wolf Scalps," and in 1807 wolves killed a number of sheep at Hamburg. Great drives were organized in later years to hunt wolves in the mountains.[27]

Even smaller animals were hunted for their skins. In 1679 large numbers of raccoon pelts were accumulated at Bergen (now part of Jersey City) for export to

Europe.[28] Muskrats were trapped because their pelts were valued for coat lining and because they undermined mill races and banked marshes by burrowing into them.[29] Like muskrat, mink were hunted both for their pelts and to stop them from tunneling into dikes that kept low-lying meadows from flooding. Peter Kalm also noted the havoc they wreaked among some farmers who kept fowl. "When a brook is near the houses it is not easy to keep ducks and geese, for the mink, which lives near rivers, kills the young ones," he wrote. "It first kills as many as it can seize, and then it carries them off and feasts upon them."[30]

Mink skins brought £0.0.20 to 0.2.0 each and were either fashioned into muffs for local women or sent to England for distribution throughout Europe. Even rabbits and squirrels, whose skins were relatively worthless, were hunted for food and because they destroyed crops; Peter Kalm noted that squirrels especially were very fond of corn.[31] Even in the well-settled districts local residents lost no opportunity to profit from any animal or reptile they encountered. In what is now Irvington, for example, a rattlesnake skin fetched three shillings in 1760.[32]

Some birds were also hunted because of their depredations—crows ate freshly planted corn, and the Swedes called grackles "corn thieves"[33]—but most were hunted for food. By 1820, bird populations had diminished so greatly that legislation established a hunting season for moor-fowl, partridge, grouse, quail, woodcock, and rabbit.[34] Passenger pigeons, once plentiful but now extinct, were especially valued for food. Early records attest that pigeon trapping was an important economic and recreational activity. On March 5, 1781, in the northern Piedmont of Hunterdon County, James Parker recorded that one of his employees was "knitting [a] pigeon net" and had caught "about 10 Dozn" on March 23 of the year before.[35] On several days in January 1793 and once in February, Benjamin Scudder recorded "wild pigeons by thousands" between present Union and Springfield, then part of Essex County.[36]

In 1765, Samuel Smith called passenger pigeons "an article of consequence to the early inhabitants" and noted that, though they bred north of Burlington County, they were frequent visitors, flying "night and day, and thick enough to darken the air, and break trees where they settled." According to Smith, the pigeons had evidently subsisted on acorns in the open oak woods (probably on the Inner Coastal Plain in Burlington County), but the birds "have not been observed of late years so plenty as formerly."[37] Perhaps the incursions of increasing numbers of woods-ranging hogs, who also fed on the mast of the forest, had diminished the pigeons' food supply.

The amount and character of legislation about fish and mammal populations in streams, lakes, and sea conveys the measure of their importance to early New Jerseyans as well. For the most part, by the late eighteenth century, the fisheries were significant largely to a local market; the saltwater fishery was largely commercial, although the sparse coastal population did subsist in part on fish and shellfish.[38]

Although whaling was considered part of the general fishery and pursued at Cape May from perhaps as early as 1640, it was of little importance in the 1700s.[39] The inshore saltwater fishery devoted to supplying the Philadelphia market was instead preeminent. From the 1690s, the common land on Cape May was open to all who wished to engage in the fin or shell fishery. By November 1752, the disposition of what common land remained concerned residents of the area so deeply that about 150 persons formed an association to prevent Jacob Spicer, who had recently purchased ninety thousand acres of this land, from buying the remaining "parcel of broken and Sunken Marshes Sounds creeks barren Lands &c." and thus attempting to "Monopolize the Fishery Oystering &c which Nature Seems to have intended for a General Blessing for the poor and others who have bought the Lands & Settled contiguous thereunto." The association pledged to resist any attempt by Spicer to attach the oysters, fin fish, or shellfish they normally brought to the Philadelphia market and offered to buy the land from Spicer as tenants in common. A smaller group of Cape May residents were eventually able to purchase the formerly unappropriated lands, and in 1813 the legislature passed a private act "to incorporate the owners of certain fisheries in the Upper and Middle Townships, in the county of Cape May."[40]

Spicer was well aware of the economic value of fisheries in general and the Cape May oyster fishery specifically, as his diary of 1759 makes clear. "Elisha Crowell informed me he has been 3 times oystering this fall & not exceeding 3 tides, at a time and has got between 4 or 5 £ worth," he wrote. "That oysters in the season were always needed, indeed I have heard great inquiry for gatherers, & have understood the boat men are frequently nonplused," or unable to meet demand.[41] Spicer noted that Crowell intended to buy an "oyster sound" for himself and that others had the same idea in mind; the oyster fishery was thus not only lucrative but competitive as men of means aimed to buy up productive locations and, probably, bar those who had harvested oysters on them for many years.

Other contemporary records document increasing competition over increasingly scarce freshwater and saltwater resources. On May 22, 1765, freeholders in Little Egg Harbor township petitioned Governor William Franklin to bar people from other counties and states from their fishing grounds. "Our fathers and some of us, Settled This Poor Remote Part of the Province for the Sake of the Salt Meadows fishing fouling &c without which Priviledges we Cannot here Comfortably Subsist, The Land Otherwise Being So Poor as Not To Afford a Settlement," the petitioners claimed; outsiders, however, were "Catching Gathering and Carying of for Markit into the Neighboring Provinces Such Quantitys of fish Clams Oysters, That It hath allready Very Much Exhosted The Stock, and . . . will Effectually Distroy the same." They were especially incensed by a fisherman from neighboring Gloucester County, who went so far as to cut a local fisherman's net, and by threats of violence from those who wished to exclude the locals from either side of the Little Egg Harbor (now Mullica) River.[42] Two years later, Gloucester County fishermen "& a great many Egg harbour & Burlin [Burlington] Cape [May] people" petitioned the General Assembly to ban the practice of carrying fish to Philadelphia or New York by sea or land between June 20 and August 20, when the heat of summer caused many fish to spoil before they reached the market.[43]

These petitions were not successful, but legislators took special care to preserve the oyster fishery. Oysters were a very popular food among the New Jersey elite, who had them brought from the coast to their country seats far in the interior.[44] A 1719 law banned raking shellfish beds between April 10 and September 1; in 1775, the close of the season was moved to March 1, indicating serious depletion of oyster beds.[45] These laws also banned gathering oysters to burn for lime "whereby great Waste is made, and the Oyster Beds thereby in Danger of being entirely destroyed." The iron industry of the Outer Coastal Plain, however, continued to use oysters as a source of lime to act as a flux in its furnaces until 1817, when legislation banned such practices and the delivery of oysters to landings associated with the industry.

Other legislation attempted to regulate the oyster fishery in specific places and to stipulate how the shellfish might legally be propagated. In 1811, state legislators passed an act permitting only wading and picking oysters up by hand in the Navesink River; using rakes or tongs was prohibited there for ten years. In 1819 dredges were banned for gathering oysters.[46] The 1817 act encouraged efforts to propagate oysters and placed a fifty-dollar fine on anyone who attempted to destroy locks or gates erected for this enterprise.

> It shall and may be lawful for any person or persons owning marsh or meadow in this state, within the boundaries of which there shall be creeks, ditches or ponds, wherein oysters do or will grow, and where such creeks or ditches lead to no public landing, to lay or plant oysters therein, and for the preservation of which, to hang and affix gates or locks across [s]aid ditches or creeks, to prevent any person or persons from entering the same.[47]

In 1820 legislators extended the general act concerning oysters to prohibit nonresidents from gathering oysters, clams, or shells unless they were aboard a vessel owned in New Jersey. They also extended special privileges so that people owning flats or coves along tidewater between the Great Egg Harbor and Little Egg Harbor rivers in Gloucester County could set out stakes delimiting beds where clams and oysters were being propagated.[48]

Freshwater fishing was a very significant economic activity on the major rivers, as the amount of legislation about it again suggests. Shad were, without question, the most important fish on inland waters accessible to the sea.[49] Mill dams served to limit the access of these anadromous fish, which generally entered coastal waters by the second week in April. Before the Revolution, the shad caught in the Paulinskill River in the northwestern part of the Ridge and Valley section were larger than those generally brought to the Philadelphia market.[50]

Johann Schoepf described the shad fishery on the Raritan immediately after the Revolution.[51] Dams kept shad from ascending the Millstone, a tributary of the Raritan, but the fishery was so important that millers were obliged to leave a forty-yard passage over the dams during the shad run. Schoepf wrote, "Fishermen line the riverbanks, cast their seines with the flush tide, and at times catch during a running several hundred pounds' worth." With careful salting, Schoepf wrote, shad tasted like European herring and were "costly morsels" during the first part of the run. They were served fresh split, air dried, or smoked. Many were stored by salting, and a considerable number were exported to the West Indies as food for slaves.

Shad were so important to local economy that they sometimes served as currency. On May 15, 1780, James Parker accepted forty-three shad as part of one tenant's rent.[52] As many other store account books indicate, it made sense for a farmer or laborer to take time to gather shad during the season. On April 14, 1792, in Warren Township, Somerset County, Eli Dunham received for thirty shad a store credit of fifteen shillings, what he might have earned at the time for four full days of hard agricultural labor (see table 14).[53] In May and June of 1801 and 1802, storekeeper Benjamin Smith in Franklin Township, Somerset County, credited weaver Jacob Van Nostrand with one shilling a piece for shad; in those years, Van Nostrand received three shillings a day for ordinary labor and ten shillings during the height of the harvest. He himself paid only five pence a pound for veal, three shillings for a bushel of buckwheat, and nine shillings for a bushel or rye.[54]

Another anadromous species, of lesser economic significance but greater prestige than shad, was sturgeon, widespread on the Delaware River. Just below the falls at Trenton, a sturgeon fishery was attempted in 1763, quickly sold, and redeveloped in 1764; between April 1 and August 14 of that year, sixty kegs of sturgeon, each keg containing five gallons, had been pickled and placed on the ship *Myrtilla* in Philadelphia.[55] Again advertised for sale in 1765, the fishery contained a frame dwelling house, a cooper's shop with a stone cellar, a smokehouse, other out-buildings, an improved garden, and "two stone buildings under the bank, the one a boiling house, well contrived for ease and expedition in working; the other a cellar for curing sturgeon and herring, together with the kettles and every utensil sufficient and proper to carry on the business, all in order to go immediately to work." Further, there was "a great plenty of fish" and "a pond made for preserving the fish alive."[56]

A fishery known to exist near Trenton in 1767 may have been this same sturgeon fishery. Edward Broadfield, who had moved his operation there from Gloucester, claimed to have won a prize of fifty pounds sterling for the best fish cured in North America at his former location. Broadfield assured prospective consumers that he intended "the fish to go all through his own hands, not trusting to servants, so that he hopes to give a more general satisfaction than ever, as no struck or bruised fish will be kept by the subscriber." Broadfield's fish were sold only by Thomas Mullan at the Old Tun tavern in Water Street, Philadelphia.[57]

Other than shad and sturgeon, the freshwater fishery depended largely on trout (in northern New Jersey), pickerel, perch, sunfish, catfish, eels, suckers, and chubs. Although not of major economic significance, they did provide much-needed protein.[58] Kalm reported that frogs' legs were also a popular food in southwestern New Jersey.[59] On smaller streams, fish were taken with nets and three-pronged spears called gigs, but local people simply fishing for food used more basic methods, probably derived from the Amerindians. As late as 1774, people on the shores of the Delaware in Hunterdon County were "driving the same [fish] with brush swabs."[60] By contrast, Kalm noted, the more affluent constructed fish ponds to provide a ready source of more desired species. Generally placed below a running spring, these ponds were apparently widespread in central and southern New Jersey by mid-eighteenth century.[61] In 1747 Governor Belcher praised the "fish pond about 150 Rods from my door full of Bass - Pike - Eels and Perch" at his Burlington residence.[62]

To a certain extent, freshwater fishing was pursued as recreation, apparently among people of all classes. On April 22, 1782, Benjamin Scudder recorded four people drawing a seine "or fishing" below his mill dam on Rahway River on a Sunday. On April 24, 1789, James Parker found that so many of the northwestern Hunterdon County residents who had promised to help him resurvey a local estate "were gone down the River [Delaware or Musconetcong] boating and others fishing that we found it very difficult." They were probably fishing for shad and, like the Rahway River fisherman, probably used nets even though fishing tackle was available at that time. Scudder fished frequently below his mill dam from 1782 to 1791, especially in April when he often saw a "great run" of shad. On April 18, 1786, he went "to the fishing place and playd all Munday Night," and a year later he fished there for four days straight.[63] A 1769 advertisement for the sale of a property on Salem Creek also suggested its recreational potential: the land included "a good Seine Fishery for Rock and Perch, . . . and the Creek affords great Diversion for angling the whole Summer, within sight of the House."[64] The necessity to conserve fish stocks became evident by the mid-eighteenth century. In 1766, residents of Somerset and Middlesex counties successfully petitioned for a law to ban the summer practice of tying and fastening brush and other material together to drive fish into pounds or pots, which destroyed young fish on the Raritan and South rivers. Banned as well were seines or nets set across the entire stream into which fish were either driven and frightened. The law permitted hoop nets, which embraced a much smaller area.[65] Three years later, the law was amplified to ban any device that would "obstruct the Fish going up in the proper Seasons of the Year, and so preserve the fry and young Brood of Fish from being destroyed in the said Rivers," language that suggested the need to protect such anadromous fish as shad.[66]

Fisheries on the Delaware River received particular attention from the legislature. Such devices as fish pounds, weirs, and seines were claimed to impede navigation; boundaries between the fisheries on shore, islands, and sand bars were often disputed; and the modes of taking fish were increasingly circumscribed. A 1790 act appointed seven commissioners to whom people could apply to set fishing dams, pounds, and baskets in the river without obstructing navigation. The commissioners were to see that the deepest parts of the river were left open and a channel at least two hundred feet wide was left for the passage of boats and rafts of timber.[67] In 1808, legislators regulated the fishing season from place to place and the hours during which fish could legally be seined; such devices as the "weir, rack, basket, fishing dam, or pound" were declared illegal. No one was permitted in addition to use "any gilling seine or drift net, anchor any engine, or make use of any device whatsoever, except fishing with sweeping seine, hooks and lines, dart [the lure currently most used in the shad sport fishery], scoop nets, and eel baskets." Wing dams (jetties for diverting a stream's current) were also declared illegal, and vessels and rafts could not anchor in the river on the fishing grounds. The law was to go into effect when Pennsylvania passed similar legislation.[68]

Legislation regulating the shad fishery on South River was passed in 1804 and on the Hackensack in 1806. A decade later, it was clear that the shad fishery on that latter river remained endangered: legislation in 1816 regulated the placement of "nets and other devices, in the bay of Newark" on both the Hackensack and Passaic rivers.[69] Three years later, an act was passed regulating fishing on the Cohansey in south Jersey.[70] The construction of fish ponds, perhaps in part a prestige symbol, may also have have acknowledged the diminution of what had been a readily available resource.

Beyond fish, birds, and game, Europeans valued the land itself and its products within their utilitarian economy. The cranberries, blueberries, and huckleberries in

New Jersey bogs and upland woods were valued and gathered widely by local people.[71] Salt marshes produced cordgrass, widely gathered in southwestern New Jersey in the earliest years of settlement for roof thatching. Open areas in particular elicited comment from early European observers because they could be cultivated with greater ease and could serve as pasture for cattle and horses. In 1670 an English observer described the Raritan Valley as open and park-like and thus ideal grazing land.[72] Another report in 1683, also from East Jersey, cited the value not only of fresh meadow but also of the abundant salt meadows.[73] A century later, Johann Schoepf described the potential significance of the large salt marsh near Elizabethtown.

> The whole region is low, salt-marsh land exposed to the inflow of sea water. . . . In the dry season these salt-marshes go by the name of salt-meadows, but produce only a short hay, corse and stiff, for the most part rush, the usual meadow grasses not growing on such lands. Horses do not like this hay, and the milk of cows eating it rapidly sours. There is, however, one variety of salt-meadow grass, to whit *Juncus bulbosus L.* known as Blackgrass and the best forage for cattle. This is seldom sown, although the use of it would make the handling of such tracts very profitable.[74]

Pioneer European settlers used the grasses of both salt and freshwater marshes from an early period and undertook reclamation projects, especially in southern New Jersey, to control the flow of water and improve the productivity of these marshlands with an eye to optimizing pasture. Some species of marsh grasses were apparently almost eliminated by the fondness of the wide-ranging hogs of the early European settlers.[75]

Sand dune habitats located on the barrier islands were also especially valued for grazing stock, and in the earliest years of settlement (or where population remained sparse later), inhabitants valued unimproved land most highly for the subsistence of livestock running at large. Woodlands became the resort of hogs, cattle, and horses. Peter Lindestrom reported in the 1650s that Swedes used the New Jersey shore of the Delaware to raise hogs, which multiplied naturally and were hunted as needed. A century later Peter Kalm noted that his aged Swedish informant, Nils Gustafson, then ninety-one years old, referred to the practice as common during his youth in the earliest days of Swedish settlement in southwestern New Jersey.[76] Widespread burning, both by Native Americans and early settlers, also produced good grazing lands.[77] On the Outer Coastal Plain, initial succession in both the pine- and oak-dominated forests included plants useful to grazing animals, such as panic grass, horseweed, and ragweed. In the upland forests of south and north Jersey, the first stage of succession brought horseweed and ragweed as well as foxtail grass, goldenrod, and broom sedge. Even though these upland species were inferior to the perennial European species that have now supplanted them, they were good for grazing. However, the laurel prevalent in Jersey bogs was poisonous to domestic stock, especially to sheep; Peter Kalm noted that laurel was fatal to lambs and to older sheep in larger amounts. His mentor Linnaeus named the lovely but deadly mountain laurel *Kalmia latifolia* for him.[78]

Native Americans originally kept no domesticated animals except for the dog and thus did not fence their relatively small gardens. European livestock roaming at large often damaged their crops, and the legislative relief the Lenape sought presaged the raft of acts that attempted to constrain free-ranging livestock as European settlement grew denser and settled field agriculture became more prevalent.[79] Legislation in 1668 required every settlement to build a pound for stray animals but stipulated that livestock owners were not liable for damages if the farmers had failed to protect their crops and orchards by fencing them in.[80] The law also established the position of fence viewer and required that each town appoint two freeholders to the position.

In 1677, the Carteret administration required every township to make its own rules concerning hogs and their depredations.[81] The ownership of free-ranging animals was generally indicated by ear notches, each of which was recorded by the towns.[82] As early as 1684, this identification had already been abused. In East Jersey that year, lawmakers banned the cropping or cutting off of both ears "by which means ill disposed People may defect the marks of others, their Neighbours Cattle, and appropriate them unto themselves."[83] In the New England-settled northeast, the practice of ranging hogs in the woods was so common that legislation "to prevent disorderly taking up of Horses and Hogs out of the Wood" was enacted as early as 1675. Hogs rooting (or digging with their snouts) in the soil destroyed valuable meadowlands set aside to produce hay for livestock fodder.

Leaving the matter of free-ranging hogs in the hands of towns was apparently ineffective. In 1682 the General Assembly of East New Jersey permitted anyone to kill a hog found on one's enclosed land or in a town's meadows or streets. Hogs were to be fenced on one's own property because, the legislators observed, "we have found by daily experience, that Swine are Creatures that occasion Trouble and Difference amongst Neighbours, and rather prejudicial than beneficial to the Province, while they have Liberty to run at randum, in the Woods or Towns, they being so obstructive to the raising of Corn in the Province, and spoiling the Meadows."[84]

Yet the 1682 law was too restrictive. Less than a year later, it was deemed illegal to kill any hog except one trespassing on one's land, and if three-quarters of the inhabitants of a town or neighborhood agreed, hogs could be let out after October 10 (after harvest) and before January 1. In such event, even trespassing hogs could not be killed.[85]

Then, in 1686, East New Jersey lawmakers reversed themselves and returned the regulation of free-ranging hogs to communities, who were to appoint not more than seven inhabitants to formulate these rules. Clearly, the practice was vital to the general economy; the act indicated that banning free-ranging "tends much to the Impoverishment of the said Inhabitants, in regard they are denied liberty of keeping Swine, which was great Preservation to themselves and Families, and help likewise to defray their Debts contracted with Merchants and others."[86] Indeed, the legislation passed in East Jersey in 1692 dividing counties into townships was rationalized in part by the need to make "Orders amongst themselves respectively about Swine, Fences, &c."[87]

West Jersey was similarly engrossed in an effort to regulate free-ranging. In 1681, one act attempted to control the practice of hunting hogs in the woods by requiring prior consent for a hunt from two people living in the neighborhood and by declaring no hog wild until it had gone a year without being marked.[88] As in East

Jersey, West Jersey legislators ultimately empowered the towns to set rules about hogs in 1694, a duty to which Nottingham Township in Burlington County, just surveyed in 1688 and thus in the process of settlement, promptly attended.[89] To prevent "the frequent Nuisances dayly don by Hoggs, and for reducing their numerous Herds into lesser Companies &c.," the town voted unanimously that no one could keep more than six hogs and that all hogs had to have rings in their noses to prevent their tendency to root. The animals were also to be kept closely pounded.[90] Nottingham Township was in the midst of an affluent Quaker-settled area, and the landed gentry were clearly not as interested in running hogs in the woods as less affluent small farmers were. Yet even as late as 1770, provincial legislators were asked to pass an act preventing swine from running at large in nearby Haddonfield,[91] and one Hunterdon County farmer complained about the havoc unsupervised, unyoked hogs (those not fitted with a device to keep them from slipping through fences) continued to play with crops there in 1784:

> I have planted a peac of Corn too acars Un a haf un sod it with weat John Steves Son has a drov of hogs un never yoke one tha lay in my Corn un Weat day by day I give him notis time after time When I puld my Corn I had but part of a lod un Amost all Cobs. . . . When I hold in I stack my weat un then his Hogs lad in my Stack yeard un one stack with two hundred sheaves tor all to peses When I carred it in I had but fifty sheves left 1784 last Spring I planted five acarks un . . . haf John Steves Son his hogs un pigs layd . . . my Corn time after time when I geathered my [co]rn I had but 3 small lods left my petaters . . . s yet in the feald then his hogs at them . . . nd Ruted them a most all up.[92]

Hogs liked the tubers of freshwater marshes, and Peter Kalm noted that "great herds" of hogs fed on acorns in the oak woods near Philadelphia in October of 1748.[93] A 1778 advertisement for a five-thousand-acre tract in Newton Township, Sussex County (the Ridge and Valley section) explicitly recognized the relationship between hogs and oak-dominated forests. "The advantages of raising hogs thereon are . . . considerable," it stated, "on account of the great quantity of oak timber and acorns on it and many thousand acres of unimproved land, contiguous thereto afford, where they may be fattened at little or no expense to the owner."[94] As open oak woods fell under the plow and marshes were embanked and improved for meadows or pasture, free-ranging hogs declined in numbers in most places. But in Essex County and perhaps elsewhere, the practice of driving hogs and cattle into swamps in the fall continued for quite a time, and wild hogs continued to exist in swamps in southern New Jersey well into the 1820s. A "lean and speedy" wild hog weighing three hundred pounds was captured by a posse of eighteen men with a pack of dogs in Stoe Creek Township, Cumberland County, in 1821.[95]

Ranging hogs was clearly important to early New Jerseyans, but running cattle on undeveloped land was an even more significant economic activity. The Concessions and Agreements of Berkeley and Carteret in 1665 clearly gave permission for the settlers to graze their cattle on unappropriated land without payment of any fee, as long as they did not then pretend to have any rights to such land in the future.[96] By extension, settlers commonly ran their stock on land that had been sold by the proprietors to individuals. But, as with hogs, the abuses of this freewheeling system emerged quickly. In 1752 a petition from inhabitants of thinly populated Morris County was presented to the General Assembly "complaining of their Inconveniencies they suffer by having great Numbers of Cattle from the neighbouring Counties drove up into their County &c," and during the Revolution, inhabitants of much more densely settled Woodbridge and Piscataway filed a similar petition.[97]

Horses were also among the livestock permitted to graze freely in the woodlands, but in 1683 West Jersey legislators banned the roaming at large of "Stone Horses (small stallions)" less than fourteen hands (four feet, eight inches) high so as to insure the production of superior stock.[98] In 1684 the province of East New Jersey (and, somewhat later, West Jersey) established the position of chief ranger for each county to take up stray mares and geldings and to assure that drovers were not removing horses from the province that had not been properly acquired.[99] In 1705, Lord Cornbury, New Jersey's first royal governor, reported that "the woods are full of wild horses," but when he appointed a chief ranger to take up these horses, the proprietors claimed that the right to do so rested with them.[100]

The deposition of John Hayward to John Budd on May 1, 1732, documents the economic significance of running horses in the woods. Hayward claimed that the former Piscataway resident and blacksmith Benjamin Hillyard had told him of a scheme to steal horses and sell them to the back settlements in Maryland or to the Amerindians there. Hillyard allegedly told Hayward that horses "at this Season of the Year . . . were plenty in the Woods, being turned out to get Flesh against Ploughing time."[101] Although they needed greater protection against both predators and poisonous vegetation, sheep were also permitted to pasture in local woodlands. Kalm noted that, in early March each year, Swedish settlers let their sheep go "into the woods to seek their food, which was as yet very scanty."[102] But for much the same reasons as stallions were to be kept from free-ranging, the legislature in 1775 banned rams from running at large during rutting season, from August 20 to December 20.[103] The practice, the legislation's preamble stated, "tends not only to injure the Breed of Sheep, but also to the Introduction of Quarrels, Disputes and Lawsuits among Neighbours." Rams thus had to be confined to enclosures "secured by a Fence so close and high as not to admit Sheep to pass the same," and any ram found at large during rutting season could be impounded or castrated. Owners then were compelled to pay three shillings for either service, above compensating any other damage the ram might have caused. Two neighbors, one chosen by the animal's owner and the other by the person claiming damages, were to assess the damages. In 1788, this act was extended indefinitely.[104]

Land sale notices often included comments on land nearby that, without purchase, could be used to raise stock. One plot within four miles of New Brunswick was advertised in 1749 as being "very convenient to raise Stock, being in the Middle of a large Body of Land which in all Appearance, will not be improved in many years."[105] One 1767 notice for land in Upper Freehold Township, Monmouth County (on the margin of the Inner and Outer Coastal Plains) touted the area's relatively early spring season and used the common term "out-let" to denote such unimproved land. "Said Plantation lies very convenient to an Out-let, where Cattle may be turned out, and shift for themselves by the first of April, and some Seasons sooner."[106]

Map 10 depicts unimproved land that advertisements between 1726 and 1782

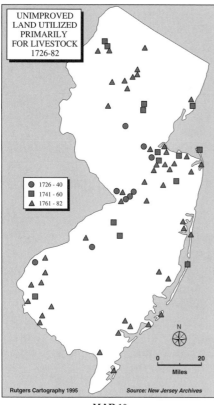

UNIMPROVED
LAND UTILIZED
PRIMARILY
FOR LIVESTOCK
1726-82

● 1726 - 40
■ 1741 - 60
▲ 1761 - 82

N

0   20
Miles

Rutgers Cartography 1995   Source: New Jersey Archives

MAP 10

indicated was used primarily for livestock.[107] In the earlier years such land was generally on the Inner Coastal Plain and Piedmont, but as settlement progressed these outlets tended to exist in the northern Ridge and Valley and Highlands sections and on the Outer Coastal Plain. In 1794, Theophile Cazenove recorded that farmers around present-day Washington, New Jersey, adjacent to the Highlands in the southern part of the Ridge and Valley, were buying up as much land as they could "not so much for cultivation [but for]. . . cattle and horses to pasture in the uncultivated woods."[108]

Before winter, farmers regularly drove cattle from the Inner to the Outer Coastal Plain, where the season was milder, for grazing on the salt marshes and uncultivated forests.[109] Longtime Swedish residents of southwestern New Jersey told Peter Kalm that they had built barns like those in Sweden when they first came to the area but that they later adopted the custom of English settlers, who had come from milder winters than the Swedes, of leaving their cattle out all winter. These Swedish settlers found, however, that the animals suffered greatly during cold winters, especially when a freeze following rain in the winter of 1741 killed many cattle.[110] Running cattle in the woods appears to have been a major support of the residents of the pines, who otherwise worked as lumbermen.[111] Even for Jacob Spicer, a wealthy resident of Cape May, free-ranging his cattle in Cape May and Cumberland County was a major activity.

Livestock also roamed free on the barrier islands because the surrounding water confined them there, away from crops. Pirates landing on Sandy Hook killed several hogs in the spring of 1698.[112] On June 20, 1755, Spicer recorded going to "the Beach" where he "saw 41 head of Cattle & 17 fine Calves in a Company," and in 1756 he saw "at Beach 13 old hogs 4 Young ones Since had 3 hogs from ye Beach."[113] Disputes over the use of islands for this purpose were resolved through legislation. In 1770 the General Assembly required landowners on Long Beach Island to meet yearly to determine, proportionate to the land each owned, how many stock each could run on the island.[114] One 1789 act regulating stock on Peck's Beach on Cape May acknowledged that overgrazing could be destructive in such environments. Each resident was permitted to graze ten head of horse or cattle—the more destructive hogs, sheep, and goats were entirely barred—for every one hundred acres owned. The grazing season was to be from September 1 to July 1, and the legislation set fines for grazing more than one's rightful share of stock.[115]

Some woodland and marshland in long-settled northeastern New Jersey (as well as in the northern sections of the Ridge and Valley and the Highlands) was used to run stock well into the nineteenth century, in part because of disputed title to the land.[116] In such a densely settled area, it was no doubt remarkable that some lands remained wooded, as the distinctive names assigned them—"Big-woods" in Bergen Township, "the wild Rough" in Harrington Township—suggest. Between 1801 and 1819, state legislators permitted owners of at least seventeen parcels of undeveloped lands to bar outsiders from using these lands after they were suitably fenced.[117] These lands were all in the Piedmont except for Franklin Township and Saddle River Township in Bergen County, which were in the Highlands.

Legislators and farmers alike attempted to calculate the merits and demerits of woodland grazing. In the 1750s, Charles Read estimated that twelve milch cattle, if given two quarts of rye slop morning and evening and grazed in "good wood range" for two months, would save mowing twelve acres of meadow, worth the large sum of £19.12.0.[118] But free-range grazing had a negative effect on the woodland flora. In a 1959 study of New Jersey woodlands between 1600 and 1900, A. Philip Muntz determined that litter and organic material were much reduced, soil compacted, and erosion accelerated. Grazing thus retarded the natural reproduction of desirable species and encouraged less valuable weed species.[119] At least some early New Jerseyans were aware of these negative effects. In 1748, Peter Kalm described how the elderly Ake Helm recalled the woodland pasture of southwestern New Jersey in the 1670s and 1680s.

> In his youth there was grass in the woods which grew very thick, and was everywhere two feet high, but that it was so much thinner at present that the cattle could hardly find food enough, and that therefore four cows now gave no more milk than one at that time. The causes for this change are easy to find. In the younger days of old Helm the country was little inhabited, and hardly a tenth part of the cattle kept which is there at present. A cow had therefore as much food at that time as ten now have. Further, most grasses here are annuals, and do not for several years in succession shoot up from the same root as our Swedish grasses. They must sow themselves every year because the last year's plant dies away every autumn. The great numbers of cattle hinder this sowing, as the grass is eaten before it can produce flowers and seed. We need not therefore wonder that the grass is so thin on fields, hills and pastures.[120]

In 1767, owners of parcels in the salt marshes "commonly called the Elizabeth-Town Great Meadows" complained to the General Assembly that horses, cattle, and "other creatures" turned out to pasture on the marsh were destroying valuable hay.[121] In late December 1796, English immigrant Gavin Scott, who had bought a small farm near Elizabethtown, described how he used this same marsh and the value its hay signified:

> I have three & half Acres of Salt meadow that often is covered when the tides is high this was mowed in Summer but not got at till Last week we have got 9 loads Home the wet bottoms is Left untill another frost sets in, a high-tide haveing melted the Ise that it will not carry waggons or Sleds. . . . I must give you some account of this meadow. Its siz appears to me as Large as all Balmburough Shire its Divided into shares with Stakes. . . . I Live about 2 miles from it my meadow is about 3 miles into it when the frost is hard then all farmers make it there bus-

ness to bring home this hay and all agree that if it was not for this meadow our Lands would produce very Little it makes a fine addition to the midding [cattle feed] when the hay time is over and vewed from an Emiance [*sic*] you see a dead plain all covered with stacks when it's an oppen winter a great part cannot be got of [due to the lack of snow or ice to support sleds]. . . . one advantage of both salt and frish [*sic*] meadows is they require no manure to make them produce.[122]

As late as 1899, the black grass of the salt marshes of the Outer Coastal Plain was still being used as fodder, but legislators had regulated grazing on these lands at least from the beginning of the nineteenth century.[123] In 1805, acts established the position of managers for salt marshes in Newark Township and Rahway and permitted farmers to build causeways to create better access to meadows.[124] A road was allowed to be extended in the salt meadows at Elizabethtown in 1813, and in 1817 legislation reinforced a 1799 ban on the trespass of cattle, horses, and sheep on the "Raritan Great Meadows" (Woodbridge and Piscataway).[125]

Some settlers attempted to improve woodland pastures to support cattle by burning them, though it is not known to what extent Native American example had influenced Europeans in this practice.[126] Niemcewicz, who traveled widely in New Jersey and lived, for a time, in Elizabethtown, described the practice and its results west of Little Egg Harbor in 1797.

> Again sand and pine forests, the more sad because it was all burnt over. This tremendous damage is caused by indigent inhabitants who, having no meadows in which to feed their cattle, burn the woods. The fire, running along the ground, turns the lower bushes to ashes; with this the earth is enriched and puts forth grass and other plants—in a word excellent pasturage for cattle. This advantage does not compensate for the harm done by the fires which rise from the lower growth to the tops and burn the taller and more useful trees . . . Our guide led us through swamp and burnt woods for 6 or 7 miles.[127]

Almost forty years earlier, Peter Kalm noted, burning was common at the end of March on the Inner Coastal Plain. He understood that burning was meant to remove the three or four inches of fallen leaves from the forest floor and thus to allow the grass to grow, but he charged that it killed much useful vegetation and consumed dead and hollow trees that could have been used for firewood and would thus have preserved some of the more valuable trees from that use. Also, he observed, burning destroyed the "upper mould," the rich organic material on the forest floor.[128]

One April 18, 1768, article in a New York newspaper revealed how common— and dangerous—burning the woods could be. The article noted that "the usual Practice of burning of Woods and Meadows in the Spring, has been more so than usual"; near Mount Holly, woods fires had destroyed three houses and a great deal of fencing.[129] Since 1683, colonial authorities had attempted to regulate the times for setting such fires.[130] On the Outer Coastal Plain, burning the woods was done not only to create "improved" pasture but to encourage native blueberry bushes, which put out shoots bearing unusually large berries after fires.[131] Peter Kalm also described how bayberries were used to produce candle wax; at about the same time, Spicer paid nine or ten pence per pound for "Myrtle wax."[132]

Gathering berries from poorly drained locations in southern New Jersey was a sufficiently significant economic activity to be regulated by legislative act as well. In 1770, four owners of "Cranberry Ponds" in Salem County asked the General Assembly to exempt their lands from planned drainage projects, and in 1789 the assembly set a season for cranberries located on common or unallocated land. Because "cranberries, if suffered to remain on the Vines until sufficiently ripened, would be a valuable Article of exportation," the law made it illegal to gather them between June 1 and October 10.[133] In 1755 Jacob Spicer paid four shillings per bushel of cranberries delivered to his Cape May store, and other accounts from stores in and near the Outer Coastal Plain similarly credited customers for these berries.[134]

By the 1790s in the more densely settled areas of New Jersey, inhabitants used the woodlands chiefly for lumber and firewood. The wealth of timber in New Jersey and the myriad uses to which it could be put had been noted often since settlement times. Although the more affluent could afford to build houses in brick or stone, where available, the overwhelming majority of New Jerseyans built houses of wood. In East Jersey, houses were built with sawn lumber, but in the west, borrowing on Finnish and Swedish tradition, log houses were common in the earliest years. White oak was an especially good building medium, and its prominence in the forests of the central region was of great utility to early settlers.[135]

Fuel or cordwood was another essential local need. New Jersey winters were longer and colder than most northwestern Europeans knew, and houses were notoriously drafty.[136] Early on, the nut trees, especially hickory, became known for providing the most heat for their bulk, and the presence of hickory and the various oaks in the central region was also a great boon to settlers.[137] A third major local use of wood was for fencing, of paramount concern because of the continuous peril to which wandering stock subjected crops. Most New Jerseyans used "worm" fencing, which contained large numbers of rails, but in areas settled by New Englanders and the Dutch, post-and-rail fencing was the rule. Chestnut, red cedar, and oak were most often used for fencing, the first two especially valued because they withstood rot longer than most other woods.[138] Both were relatively available in the central region, the red cedar (actually a juniper) being an early successor on cut-over land. Peter Kalm reported that the best wood for fence posts was red cedar, white oak, and black oak, while Charles Read declared that black ash made better fence rails than either cedar or chestnut.[139]

In his study of the changing geography of New Jersey woodlands, Muntz identified this central zone as one of three types of woodlands in the state.[140] This fertile corridor ran between New York and Philadelphia and the Kittatinny Valley— basically, the Inner Coastal Plain, the Piedmont, and the southwestern Ridge and Valley section. The southeastern zone included most of the Outer Coastal Plain, and the northwestern zone embraced the Highlands and the rest of the Ridge and Valley section.

Muntz distinguished between three major exploitations of woodlands, the first essentially local—cutting for building, heating, fencing, and other products such as shingles and barrel staves. The second type was commercial—lumbering, woodcutting, and the extracting of such other products as charcoal and tar to be carried and sold at a distance. Thirdly, woodlands supported extractive industries such as iron, whose demand for charcoal was insatiable. Muntz suggested that because the fertile central zone was settled earliest, it probably experienced greater total permanent clearance than the other two zones, while the soil-poor southeastern zone experienced the longest sustained lumbering effort.

Muntz could not precisely estimate the amount of cleared or forested land from place to place in New Jersey, but recently discovered tax records permit some approximate ratios from mid-eighteenth century on. Table 4 depicts the relative amounts of improved land from county to county from 1751 to 1784.[141] In little more than a generation, rapid development had increased the ratio of improved to total land area from one-half to more than four-fifths. The most "improved" region in New Jersey appears to have been the Piedmont (including all or most of Somerset, Essex, Middlesex, and Hunterdon counties). Of the total land area in Somerset County, only slightly more than 1 percent was unimproved by 1784. Counties lying totally (Cape May and Cumberland) or partially in the Outer Coastal Plain (Monmouth, Burlington, and, especially, Gloucester) lagged in development. After 1751, northwestern counties (Morris and, later, Sussex) boomed; subdivisions of land there surpassed those in counties in the Coastal Plain to the south, initially settled four or five generations earlier.

Examining improved land by township in 1784 reveals a more detailed picture of cleared and forested land, especially in the Inner and Outer Coastal Plains (map 11).[142] On the Inner Coastal Plain of Gloucester County, near Philadelphia, land was developed much as von Thünen's model suggested it should be. Several townships in this southwestern section showed relatively little improvement, which suggests the area was still forested; the Swedish settlers of this section were more oriented toward a wood economy than were others and, as Lindestrom's survey suggested, they perceived the soils of the Inner Coastal Plain to being too sandy to be productive.

But opposite New York, a different pattern of land use developed. Because Bergen and Essex counties lay closest to New York, they might have been expected

Table 4
Percent of All Land Taxed as Improved, by New Jersey County, 1751–84

County	1751	1769	1784
Middlesex	65.5	84.9	93.9
Monmouth	70.9	77.6	82.1
Essex	62.7	76.7	92.1
Somerset	87.3	87.9	98.4
Bergen	59.7	79.7	90.1
Burlington	64.1	71.6	77.8
Gloucester	39.3	49.1	53.9
Salem	61.5	75.6	76.6
Cape May	62.6	63.3	56.3
Cumberland	36.7	53.4	53.2
Hunterdon	70.9	88.6	94.3
Morris	24.7	71.7	83.7
Sussex		48.1	89.0
Total	**54.9**	**70.6**	**80.7**

to supply the city with wood. But the Dutch of Bergen County were profoundly agricultural in their orientation, and the New Englanders of Essex were settled on such small landholdings that a sustained production of wood was simply not possible. Yet the ease of waterborne traffic put southern Middlesex and northern Monmouth counties within a day's sail of New York, and, though relatively unimproved, placed farmers there in an excellent position to supply New York with cordwood. Had New Englanders settled the Inner Coastal Plain instead of Swedes, and had Swedes settled northeastern sections, land use might have been radically different. Another major contrast existed between the Piedmont, very much improved, and those townships lying to the north and west, not only settled later and much less accessible but also within the glaciated sections of the Highlands and Ridge and Valley.

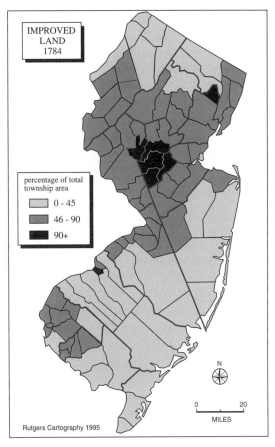

MAP 11

An 1787 letter to English friends, in which Thomas Capnerhurst described the wooded land west of his property in Flemington, Amwell Township, Hunterdon County, fleshes out this overall depiction. According to the map, more than three-quarters of Amwell Township, which lay in one of the most developed portions of the central region, was "improved" in 1784. Standing on a small hill, Capnerhurst discerned four times as much wooded land as cleared land in 1787 "and the boundaries of the horizon seemed to be one continuous wood, but we may suppose that the wood hid a great part of the cleared land."[143]

In the central region, where relatively good soils encouraged permanent clearance, only the marginal lands were used to produce wood and to provide rough grazing land for stock. In the earliest years of settlement, farmers here may have exported wood to the timber-poor Dutch, but apparently the lumber was not as good as the Netherlanders could import from the Baltic. Muntz has suggested that the poor quality of wood in the central region may have been due to the fact that open, park-like stands of trees were prevalent there. Individual trees would thus have been able to grow large, spreading branches at just a few feet above the ground, which would create so many knots that the wood would make inferior lumber.[144] No records apparently survive that document how the early Dutch or Swedes cleared New Jersey land, but elsewhere the Dutch are known to have cut down the trees, placed them in great heaps, and burned them to get rid of them.[145]

A large proportion of the Swedes were in fact ethnic Finns who had been transported to the New World because their slash-burn farming was deemed destructive in Sweden. In his reading of the earliest colonial documents, Muntz found no reference to the girdling of trees that characterized the later American frontier, but that girdling was practiced in New Jersey is beyond doubt. Early legislation refers to the practice. In 1717 an act acknowledged that "several Persons in Clearing of their Lands, through which the Publick-High Ways run, have only killed the Trees, and left them standing, which Trees, so killed, on every high Wind, are subject to fall across the Roads and are thereby dangerous."[146] A five-shilling fine was laid upon the feller for every tree killed laying within a chain (sixteen and a half feet) of a public road that had not been felled within a year. That the law dealt only with girdling along public roads and established a one-year grace period suggests that the practice was widespread and that legislators endeavored not to inconvenience farmers; in 1774, in fact, the grace period was extended to two years. The practice of girdling trees in these areas must have persisted: in 1817 a new law stipulated "that no tree shall be girdled or killed on the highways."[147]

Farmers usually located woodlots in steep, rocky places, in poorly drained areas, and on poor soils, sometimes at a considerable distance from their farmsteads. Writing to his brother in England in 1796, Gavin Scott marveled at how rapidly longtime settlers produced cordwood from the oaks, hickory, and chestnut, "stright as English firs," around Elizabethtown.

> You used to say Adam would make a good cutter of trees. if he was set along with the good fellers of wood here he would only be like a child strikeing a man. To give you an idea of what one man can cut in one day he can cut Eight cord in a day they begin at the edge of a wood they first fell the trees about a foot from the ground. . . . They cut of the branches and cut all the peaces from 4 inch diamitor to 18 inch Do into 8 foot Long then laying the 8 foot pces close packed at one another's side. . . . No small twiggs is Left on these peaces.[148]

Even farmers on excellent soils preserved woodlots. In 1765, on his 183-acre farm in present-day Franklin Township, Somerset County, John Van Liew kept rectangular wood lots at both ends, one of 8 1/2 acres and the other 58 acres.[149] In the winter of 1775–76, he sold cordwood from these lots to his neighbors—32 3/4 cords of oak and 12 1/2 cords of unspecified "wood" at £0.14.0 a cord, 2 cords of hickory at £1.0.0 per cord, and 1 cord of wood "in the barks" at £0.15.6 per cord. The "wood" was probably oak from which the bark had been removed for sale to a tanner. The local need for wood must certainly have encouraged some farmers to leave somewhat less productive land in wood, but no solid data are available in regard to amount and distribution of these lots. The importance of New Jersey lumber to the economy of Pennsylvania is evident in a statement Governor Lewis Morris presented to the Board of Trade in London in 1742. Without it, he declared, "Pennsylvania cannot build a ship, or even a tolerable House, nor ship of a Hogshead or a pine stave."[150]

New Jersey's central woodlands—most accessible, earliest settled, on the best soils, and most permanently deforested—also supplied the enormous demand for heating and cooking wood in New York City and Philadelphia, and there is little doubt that this trade employed more people and covered a larger area than did any other woodland exploitation. On September 16, 1702, the Swedish Lutheran Reverend Sandel recorded that fuel wood had just left Elizabethtown Point bound for New York. In 1760, Jonathan Hampton of Elizabethtown noted the "many fine Black-ash swamps for rails" on the 6000-acre Sussex County land he offered for sale.[151] In 1768, an advertisement for a farm in Middletown Township, northern Monmouth County, noted that the property was within a mile of a landing "very convenient to carry Wood to New-York" and bounded by a creek "where it is very convenient for carrying Logs or Cordwood."[152] As Muntz has indicated, carrying cordwood from northeastern New Jersey to New York was common through at least the time of the Revolution.[153]

Contemporary advertisements document the importance of the New York market in southern Middlesex and northern Monmouth counties. One property advertised for sale in 1758 on the southern shore of Raritan Bay was described as well wooded with oak and hickory and as having "a convenient Wharf lately built, sufficient to stow 500 Cord of Wood, from which Place a ten Cord Boat at any common Tide, may go loaded, and with a fair Wind may be at New-York Market in three Hours from said Wharf."[154] A decade later another tract in the same general area but somewhat more inland was advertised as being within a mile of a landing "from which a Boat may go all Winter, and not freeze up" and would thus be "very convenient to carry Wood to New-York." In 1768, "common sloops and wood-boats" were sailing up Berry's Creek in the Hackensack Meadowlands to be loaded, presumably with timber for the New York market.[155] It would make sense, although no evidence proves it, that deforestation occurred first on lands lying immediately on the bays and later on a path up navigable local waterways. It would also make sense to suppose that poor and rocky land, of which much lay in the Hudson Highlands in New York, also supplied wood to the city by way of the Hudson River. Unimproved land remained on the Inner Coastal Plain very close to Philadelphia as late as 1780. A 1758 advertisement for a farm within seven miles of Philadelphia promoted its three hundred acres of "Wood and Timber Land" and the existence of a landing on Newtown Creek "to transport Wood or Timber to Philadelphia." In 1771, a property on Alloway's Creek in Salem County was promoted for being only "two miles from a noted landing" (Quinton's Bridge) from which an "abundance of staves and cord wood are transported to Philadelphia."[156] And on November 19, 1764, Jacob Spicer wrote to Philadelphia merchants to report his activities on their behalf:

> The Teams have been already imployed better than a Month, and by them I forwarded Orders to the person Intrusted to look out for flatmen intending to engage em in readiness for Carrying over the Wood just before the River Closed, when a Better price might have been expected, but through a Mistake of my Instruction the Overseer Sat them to work some time past, Since which they have Carried and Vended, the most of what has been hitherto Carted as I am informed at 24/6 to 25/ per Cord which can't now be remedied, . . . Before my Departure [for Bergen] I should be Glad to know whether you need any wood for winters firing that I may give orders accordingly, having at present both green & dry hickory & dry Oak on hand.[157]

Spicer wrote a week later to thank the merchants "for your thoughtfulness & care in getting over my wood, while Surface of Delaware form'd a Bridge"—that is, while it was frozen over.

Flatboats, which often appeared on the tax lists of southwestern New Jersey townships bordering on the Delaware and were often operated by Swedish settlers, were generally used to carry wood to Philadelphia.[158] Wealthy landowner George Reading marketed a tract in the Swedish area of settlement on the basis of the economics of transporting wood. The tract, on Repaupo Creek, had much white oak, red oak, and hickory that "with a trifling expence might be cleared out so as to raft logs, and carry wood and staves from along side of the tract, which would prevent some expence in carting." Reading further labeled the tract "the best timber land in these parts that is so near the landing" and suggested that "as timber grows scarce this land would suit ship builders, coopers, brewers, &c &c." Countering Swedish perceptions, Reading termed the soil "remarkable good, so that after the timber is off, the land will be valuable, and would make a good plantation."[159]

That southwestern New Jersey wood continued to be harvested for the Philadelphia market in the nineteenth century is clear. In 1812, Joshua Brick and Thomas Lee of Port Elizabeth on the Maurice River in Cumberland County contracted to supply Joseph Jones of Philadelphia "One thousand Cords of good Sound and Merchantable Oak wood."[160] Two years later, a private act of the legislature permitted inhabitants of Pittsgrove Township in Salem County to open and clear navigation on Muddy Run to carry "timber, plank, boards, wood and other articles to market by water."[161] In 1840, as Muntz determined from census data of cordwood production, the Outer Coastal Plain continued to harvest a vast amount of cordwood, some of it for the steamboats and locomotives of the day.[162]

Throughout the period, the tendency to preserve woodlots to maximize income from them made timber expensive in the area. Peter Kalm noted the dense Pennsylvania forest near Philadelphia was largely owned by "people of quality and fortune . . . [who] leave the trees for times to come, expecting the wood will become very expensive."[163] The high cost of overland transport clearly encouraged wood production close to the city, and advertisements suggest that landowners well understood the importance of preserving timber and the cost of transporting it. One 1762 advertisement for a woodland tract across the Raritan River from Bound Brook announced that after a bridge across the river was finished, "the Timber and Wood thereon will become exceedingly beneficial to the Town, as the Carting from the Land to Town is but a very small Distance."[164] In 1768, a white cedar swamp in the Hackensack Meadowlands was advertised as being accessible by water to New York. "The timber and wood of every kind in the cedar swamp, is now in great perfection," the notice stated, "as the present owner has preserved it, and has prevented any of the wood being cut for near upon 30 years."[165]

Making barrels and shingles also consumed great quantities of New Jersey wood. In the 1780s, as he cleared "new" land at Shipley, his farm on the Piedmont in Hunterdon County, James Parker was careful to save good "hoop poles," oak or hickory saplings or coppice that was split to provide barrel, keg, and firkin hoops. Because such goods as flour, preserved meat, butter, and apple brandy were transported in wooden casks, hoop and staves were a staple well into the latter nineteenth century. Staves, almost invariably made of white oak, were gathered and exported from the central region, and references to finished casks and cooperage abound in store account books.[166] One 1778 offering of a parcel of land in New Brunswick advertised "timber of the largest and best kinds, from which great quantities of staves may be made, and readily sold to the millers in the vicinity, of which there are several from two to six miles distant, who are all purchasers of wheat and other country produce."[167] On February 1, 1762, New York merchant John Watts ordered staves from James Neilson in New Brunswick:

> I desird you a few days ago to send me up what White Oak hhd: [hogshead] Staves you had, not exceeding three thousand & to let me know what Number I might probably depend upon, in a fortnight or three weeks time. As I am affraid I shall be press'd for this kind of Lumber I must beg if you cannot supply me yourself, so as to be here in all this Month with about twenty thousand, you would engage them where they are to be had and can be delivered within the time upon my giving Orders as they shall be wanted which I apprehend will be pretty fast after about a week has passed.[168]

On May 18, Watts sent seven thousand of "the best" white oak hogshead staves and fifteen thousand shingles (probably from the Outer Coastal Plain) on the sloop *Little Molly,* bound for Martinique.[169] Thus, white oak from the rapidly developing Raritan Valley was transported to the Caribbean as an integral part of the sugar trade. Other New Jersey merchants also participated in the West Indian trade: surviving account books from present-day Atlantic County list thousands of feet of lumber being sawn in the region, some for house frames prefabricated for the Caribbean trade in the 1790s.[170] Julian Niemcewicz also reported on the vast amount of lumber being taken out of the region at the same time.[171]

Another likely product of the clearance of the central region and elsewhere, especially where old oak timber was present, was potash. Little evidence exists that directly refers to potash production, although the papers of the Hendrickson family, who lived on Monmouth County's fertile Inner Coastal Plain, contain a long handwritten treatise (probably written between 1750 and the Revolution) on "the method of makeing Potashes as practised in Hungary, Poland, and Germany." In 1765, based on "Experiments made in the Neighboring Colonies," Governor William Franklin advocated that the legislature encourage the production of potash, which suggests the product was not commercially produced in New Jersey at that time.[172] One of the recently arrived Capnerhursts, on Hunterdon County's fertile Piedmont, commented in 1788 that "Betty scarce likes the thought of going so far back, but says she will help her mother and Jo burn the logs and the brush and take care of the ashes . . . burnt that they may be sold to the potash manufactory."[173] Store accounts often credited individual customers for "ashes" especially near the iron works in northern New Jersey around the turn of the nineteenth century. It is likely that their ultimate destination was a potash manufactory.

Oaks and especially hemlock from central and northwestern New Jersey forests were also harvested for tan bark, a major product of the wooded land remaining on the poor soils drained by South River in southern Middlesex County well into the nineteenth century.[174] Settlers also gathered chestnuts and other nuts (as well as berries) from forested lands, and at least one observer in 1788 commented upon the "Excelant sugar . . . from the sugger maple and I am told they make great quantities of it."[175]

Another use for cordwood occurred during the Revolution, when salt, normally imported from the Caribbean, could not be easily obtained. Along the coast, several salt works burned wood—evidently a great deal, according to contemporary descriptions of the process—to hasten evaporation. So many private salt works operated in New Jersey that in 1778 the legislature rescinded its plans for a public enterprise.[176] On the Outer Coastal Plain, trees were also burned for tar and charcoal. Pastor Reincke, preaching at Maurice River in 1745, found "many Germans, who burn tar, were present from Cohansey." Tarkiln Creek, a small stream flowing into Delaware Bay in Maurice River Township, Cumberland County, commemorates the activity.[177] Spicer bought "pitch" at both Egg Harbor and Maurice River in 1755.[178] Charcoal increased in importance after ironworks were established at Batsto and Atsion. Because trees of all sizes could be used to produce charcoal (itself used to melt metallic iron from the bog ores in this region), clear-cutting was prevalent and probably affected the forest much more seriously than did lumber or cordwood production. Charcoal production also encouraged more destructive fires: an estimated minimum of twenty thousand acres of woodland were needed to support each furnace on a sustained yield basis, and one thousand acres were cut each year.[179] The iron industry greatly expanded in the pines during the nineteenth century and had an enormous impact on the woodlands there, an effect exacerbated by the rise of glassworks in the same region. Some charcoal was also sent out of the region: in 1755, it was among Spicer's "exports" from Cape May. And in areas so remote as to make transportation of such a bulky commodity to Philadelphia or New York unfeasible, a substantial iron industry existed early on and was intact for much of the initial settlement of the region. Especially in the glaciated Highlands, the iron industry lasted well into the nineteenth century and denuded large areas of woodland in order to make charcoal; the industry itself recognized such devastation as a threat even before 1800.

Abundant evidence documents that building, heating, fencing, and other needs required such huge amounts of wood that the very existence of woodland in the northeastern sections of the state was endangered by midcentury. By 1760, the Great Swamp was promoted as the last great regional source of wood, "chiefly a Timber Swamp" with "plenty of Oak fit for Staves, Ship-planks, Building and Fencing; also great plenty of fine Chest-nut, Black-Ash, and Hickery."[180] Woodlands may also have remained in some places because they were part of an overall land hunger among those who could afford to buy it; investment in undeveloped land was after all perceived as abundantly rewarding in the long term. Cazenove described this appetite in northern New Jersey in 1794.[181] Landholders who did not need money simply left the larger part of their land alone, a practice that was encouraged by the relatively high cost of labor. Niemcewicz described the attitude among such affluent landowners on the Outer Coastal Plain:

> The owner holds his land at a high price. It is rare to find an American who is not fully convinced that the land must, with time, rise in value, that in a short while it will become ten times more valuable than now. These dreams may be barren, and then perhaps, with the upset and persecutions in Europe, they may come true. But

these hopes contribute, as I have said, not a little to the postponement of the cultivation and settlement of many parts of America.[182]

In the 1760s, Watts complained how "scarce and dear" lumber had become, and in 1768 New York merchants applied to the city to set standards for white oak hogshead staves because "Stave-Getters from New Jersey and other Parts" had moved on to the white oak of the Hudson Valley.[183] In a letter to Governor Livingston in 1785, Baron von Steuben noted the paucity of wooded land at the northeastern New Jersey house and property the legislature had given him. The nearest lot "on which there is a stick of Wood" was three quarters of a mile distant, he wrote; though unowned, it had not been included with the property he received, and the "great part of the Wood is cut off & the destruction daily increases."[184] By the 1790s even interior Hunterdon County farmers were concerned about setting aside wood lots.[185]

The shortage of wood also promoted thievery, and absentee owners were always fair game. On December 21, 1787, James Parker wrote to John Stevens about a local man who had formerly taken wood from undivided land they jointly held in Hunterdon County. The man, whom Parker had engaged to assure that stealing did not continue, complained that the owners' agent had illegally taken wood from the tract to make rails for several area farms. Parker wrote Stevens, "I believe it that not a Smith's or nailers fire in German Town [New Germantown, now Oldwick] but what is kindled with the coals made of our timber."[186] Years earlier, in 1773, James Parker had complained that some twenty men from "Sandwich Township" had taken timber from their lands and made staves of it, and were prepared to raft them down the Delaware as soon as the river rose. Parker probably meant Sandyston Township, located in the extreme northwest where the Kittatinny Ridge approaches very near the Delaware and good agricultural land was limited; as only forty-eight taxables were listed for Sandyston in 1774, a comparatively large percentage of men were engaged in this illegal activity, which undoubtedly greatly supplemented or surpassed their income from purely agricultural activities.[187]

Parker seems to have been plagued with thievery from his wood lots. Again in 1773, he wrote Stevens, "The great demand for pine Joyce [joists] for frames for N York Nova Scotia & the West Indies sets every body to work in the unlocated Lands that can use an ax and all the Landings in the Country from Shrewsbury to South River are full of wood and timber pillaged off the common lands of the proprietors."[188] Even individual proprietors themselves were involved in such shenanigans: one 1794 law banned them "from cutting timber on the unlocated Lands of this State."[189] Even in the second decade of the nineteenth century, laws attempted to regulate timber thievery, which must have been important in local economies where agriculture and other activities failed to provide sustaining income.[190]

The depletion of New Jersey forests naturally had profound ecological effects, especially as certain valued trees were overharvested. On the Outer and Inner Coastal Plains and the Hackensack Meadows, the Atlantic white cedar was probably the single most important tree.[191] These tall, straight trees grow in dense stands in swamps. White cedar wood, though soft and weak, is straight-grained, nonresinous, extremely durable, and slow to burn, properties that made it valuable for shingles, cooperage, boat building, and fencing.[192] As early as 1693, West Jersey

Proprietors set relatively large two-shilling fines on anyone who unlawfully "ffelled [*sic*] Several Cedar Trees in ye Swamps."[193]

Peter Kalm, who appeared fascinated by the species, noted that all the houses in Philadelphia were covered with white cedar shingles, many sent from Egg Harbor; other places on the coast sent shingles to New York for reshipment elsewhere. The shingles John Watts shipped to Martinique were probably white cedar, and Kalm noted that some New Jersey coastal residents carried on a direct trade in white cedar shingles with the West Indies, so much that Kalm feared "the inhabitants here are not only lessening the number of these trees, but are even extirpating them entirely . . . by these means many swamps are already quite destitute of cedars."[194]

Kalm might have overstated the case in 1750 except for the cedar swamps of the Inner Coastal Plain. On the Outer Coastal Plain in 1755, a New York newspaper reported that "a very great Fire happen'd in the Cedar Swamps, on the 20th of May last, and burned with such Violence, that in a few Days time it render'd desolate Lands to the Extent of near thirty Miles, the Trees and ready cut Shingles being intirely burnt to Cinders"; the fire reduced "most of the Inhabitants . . . to meer Penury and Want."[195] On August 15 of the same year, an anonymous writer apparently employed as a lookout in northern Monmouth County recorded seeing "on the Vast Atlantic Ocean Twenty-Seven Vessels. And Seven of them that was inwards bound I perceived to be Cedar Men."[196]

Despite Kalm's suspicions, white cedar had clearly not been extirpated by 1750. Jacob Spicer recorded in his diary on September 24, 1756, that "half the cedar swamps at Little Egg Harbour were burnt over and two third diminished, that good swamp within two miles of a landing was worth 5 or 6 £ per acre but fallen of late." Spicer also cited the prices South Jersey merchants were offering for shingles at the time. At New York, a thousand shingles could be traded for £3 in goods or £2.15.0 in cash; in New Brunswick, merchants offered £3 to £3.15.0 in cash. At nearby Oyster Bay on Long Island, thirty thousand three-foot shingles sold each year at about £3 or £3.10.0. Spicer also noted that bakers valued the slow-burning tops of cedar trees. "John Schuyler sells cedar tops to the bakers cut into cord wood for 18s per cord & has sent for a great deal in New York." And in a March 1764 letter, Spicer expressed doubt about whether he could supply the Philadelphia merchant Abel James with white cedar shingles because of problems not with the wood supply but with transportation:

> The hands I Imployed for the Winter Season & yet remain in the Swamp have been kept to getting three feet Shingles which I esteem more profitable than Rails, except I could have been assured of a price adequate in which case I Intended to have got some extraordinary in quantity for . . . out of the Tops of Shingle Trees, but receiving no advice relative thereto declined it, having before on hand a quantity of merchantable, out of which I should be much pleased to furnish you with 1000 but receiving the advice directly before my Departure had not time to make Order thereabout, and Indeed I very much question whether I can get them freighted till sometime in the Summer, as not long Since I was in quest of a Vessel to carry shingles, & with great Difficulty obtained one, being the only one I could procure.[197]

Cedar swamp continued to be advertised and cut over into the 1770s.[198] Muntz has argued that the best and most accessible stands of white cedar had been cut over by the end of the eighteenth century, although a second growth of trees may have been responsible for reviving the industry in the early nineteenth century. He theorized that the clear-cutting of white cedar from early colonial times onward eventually caused such hardwoods as red maple to become the dominant tree species in swamps of the Outer Coastal Plain.[199]

Other than white cedar, the primary trees of commercial interest were the oaks and pines, though most of this wood was probably not of good quality. Still, exceptions must have prevailed in some places. Muntz has cited the existence of a large shipbuilding industry that relied on a local supply of lumber, probably atop Pleistocene deposits such as the Cape May formation and on clay soils bordering rivers.[200] In remoter northwestern sections that had access to the Delaware River, farmers were harvesting black walnut and white pine to send as timber, boards, planks, and staves to Philadelphia and Trenton mills.

By the 1790s, a lumber shortage may have emerged on the better soils bordering rivers flowing into the Delaware, as indeed it had in many other parts of the state. Still, in the glaciated sections far from the Delaware, the high cost of overland transport confined wood to local uses; little of it left the region.[201] Much of the rougher land away from the iron industry remained in high forest at the end of the eighteenth century; the presence of wolves well beyond 1800 in Sussex County suggests that extensive areas of forest remained. Following the valley of the Wanaque River in 1781, the Marquis de Chastellux remarked that the area was "entirely wild"; north of the iron center of Ringwood was "the wildest and most desert country" he had passed through in America so far. Chastellux discovered one family carving a farm out of the forest, which happened with more frequency as the better soils became occupied. Stone wall fences in the Highlands and on some of the ridges in the Ridge and Valley section bear witness to these marginal enterprises.[202]

Even south of the terminal moraine, some Highland areas remained relatively undeveloped at the end of the eighteenth century. Theophile Cazenove reported in 1794 that except for German (Long) Valley and the valley of the Musconetcong, the land between Black River (Chester) and the Musconetcong Valley contained "very few farms and almost everything is woods and uncultivated land." Local farms had two-thirds of their acreage in the valley and one-third on the slope of the mountain, presumably in wood lots.[203] One 1797 map of New Jersey shows numerous roads and villages south of the Wisconsin terminal moraine and only a few roads and ironworks to the north.[204]

As timber grew scarcer, disputes between landowners over boundary lines arose more frequently. Jonas Phillips, who probably lived in Sussex County, wrote Robert Morris in 1784 about just such confusion:

> Sir I understand you was up at your plais Last Sunday & ordered ye Rails to be Brought of which I Say is on my Land I Desire you wont move one Rail till we Chouse Each a man & prize ye damig for it Cant Be asertained after ye Rails is gon I will atend ye Bizness if I am well any Day you will a pint Except Sunday.[205]

Robert Morris well knew the value of wooded land and the relative values of individual tree species. In 1792, he involved himself in a lengthy dispute with Joseph Insley, a tenant on his uncle's farm a few miles from New Brunswick, whom he had several times warned, at least once by letter, not to cut timber on the property. According to his lease, Insley apparently had the right to cut rails on the property, but the chestnut rails he cut in 1792 were, he claimed, "Short of the Number I was to get According to bargain." He wrote Morris that if he could cut no more white oak for fence rails, "I Shall Expect Allowance as the Bark is Some Compensation for my Labour." Morris responded in no uncertain terms four days later.

> If you will persist in cutting the white oak timber against Mr. Morris's will intentions & my explicit protestation you must do it at your peril and I will neither license nor countenance your conduct but will order suits against you if any waste you have committed or shall commit is unauthorized by the terms of your Lease. I cannot but think that you or your people at the time of falling a tree could [not] distinguish between one fit for rails & crooked trees too winding to split, if it had been your or their wish to distinguish & I do not know of any right or authority you have to carry any wood or timber off the farm for fuel or any other purpose and I neither can nor will license or countenance your doing so.

Morris added, after signing the letter, "as to there being no full grown Chestnut or black oak timber on the place fit for rails I fancy a jury of the neighbourhood will be able to decide."[206]

When soil quality and the cost of water transport to market are taken into account, use of woodlands by the end of the eighteenth century in New Jersey does appear to mirror von Thünen's model. Part-time work and gathering in the woods benefited small farmers everywhere, especially in the earliest years of settlement and especially in the Outer Coastal Plain, where indeed woodlands exploitation was the full-time enterprise and agriculture part-time. In many poor-soil areas, farmers actively sold cordwood to New York and Philadelphia markets. Large landowners on good soils recognized the value of their wood resources and sold them off prudently, which also in a sense subsidized agriculture by paying for the high cost of clearance.[207]

Notes

1. William Ellis, "Diary of Jacob Spicer, 1755–6," *Proc. N.J.H.S.* 63 (1945): 37-50, 82–117, 175–88; "Extract from a Diary of Mr. Jacob Spicer of Cape May County," *Proc. N.J.H.S.*, 1st ser., 3 (1848): 103–4, 192–98; and Jacob Spicer Diary, Jacob Spicer Papers, NjHi.

2. "Extract from a Diary," 196–97.

3. Lewis T. Stevens, *A History of Cape May County, New Jersey* (Cape May City, N.J., 1897), 23.

4. Peter O. Wacker, "The New Jersey Tax Ratable List of 1751," *NJH* 107 (1989): 23–24.

5. Edmund B. O'Callaghan, ed., *Documents Relative to the Colonial History of the State of New York* (Albany, N.Y., 1853), 1:37–38.

6. John B. Linn and William Egle, eds., *Pennsylvania Archives* (Harrisburg, Pa., 1896), 7:727.

7. By 1765, when Samuel Smith published his history of New Jersey, few beaver remained in the colony. Smith, *History of the Colony*, 502. See also Russell, "Vegetational Change," 126.

8. Ellis, "Diary of Jacob Spicer," 39; Alexander Papers, New York Historical Society.

9. Smith, *History of the Colony*, 502.

10. "Account Book of Jesse Knowles," Knowles Family Papers, NjHi. In 1813 in Knowleton Township, Sussex County, a muskrat skin brought a man three shillings, as much as he could earn in a day of hard labor threshing oats.

11. Terry G. Jordan and Matti Kaups, *The American Backwoods Frontier: An Ethnic and Ecological Interpretation* (Baltimore, 1989), 79.

12. Carl M. Anderson, trans. and ed., "Pastor Wrangel's Trip to the Shore," *NJH* 87 (1969): 13.

13. Benson, *Peter Kalm's Travels*, 1:311.

14. Smith, *History of the Colony*, 502.

15. *N.J. Laws* 4:52–53.

16. Ibid., 582–85.

17. In 1818, the season for deer hunting was again set at September 1 to January 1; in 1820, hunters were allowed to begin hunting on August 1. *N.J.S.L.*, 1820:66–67. Unless otherwise indicated, a first sitting and a public law is assumed.

   For qualifications to vote, see *N.J. Laws*, 2:53.

18. *N.J. Laws* 5:69–72.

19. "Petition of Sundry Persons to the Governor Against Killing Deer With Dogs, 1749," Governor's Manuscripts, New Jersey State Archives, Trenton.

20. *N.J. Laws* 5:162–63.

21. E. D. Halsey, ed., *History of Morris County, New Jersey* (New York, 1882), 231.

22. "Janeway Account Book," Vol. 1, Special Collections, NjR.

23. Ellis, "Diary of Jacob Spicer," 176.

24. *Docs. Rel. N.J.*, 1st ser., 26:51; Aaron Leaming and Jacob Spicer, *The Grants, Concessions, and Original Constitutions of the Province of New Jersey* (Somerville, N.J., 1881), 102, 261, 315, 356, 448, 557.

25. *N.J. Laws* 1:407-8, 2:177. The bounty for wolf whelps rose from five to ten shillings.

26. *Votes and Proceedings of the General Assembly of the Province of New Jersey* (Woodbridge, N.J., 1769), 8.

27. "Monies necessary to be raised by the Township of Newton for the year 1799," Anderson Papers, NjHi; Alanson H. Haines, *Hardyston Memorial: A History of the Township and the North Presbyterian Church, Hardyston, Sussex County, New Jersey* (Newton, N.J., 1888), 13–14.

28. Danckaerts, *Journal of a Voyage*, 156.

29. William M. Johnson, comp., *Memoirs and Reminiscences Together with Sketches of the Early History of Sussex County, New Jersey, by Casper Schaeffer* (Hackensack, N.J., 1907), 80.

30. Benson, *Peter Kalm's Travels*, 1:242.

31. Ibid., 1:164–68, 233–34.

32. Joseph Camp Daybook, Camp Family Papers, NjHi.

33. *N.J. Laws* 244, 248–51.

34. *N.J.S.L.*, 1820:66.

35. James Parker Diary, James Parker Papers, NjHi; Charles W. Parker, "Shipley: The Country Seat of a Jersey Loyalist," *Proc. N.J.H.S.*, n.s. 16 (1931): 117–38. See also Jonathan Holmes Diary, Holmes Family Papers, NjHi.

36. Virginia S. Burnett, transcr., and Elmer T. Hutchinson, ed., "Marginal Jottings from the Almanacs of the Scudder Family," *Proc. N.J.H.S.* 63 (1945): 222–23 (notes for 4 and 7–15 January and 26 February 1793).

37. Smith, *History of the Colony*, 511.

38. John Rutherfurd, "Notes on the State of New Jersey," *Proc. N.J.H.S.* 1 (1867): 87.

39. Stevens, *History of Cape May*, 29–30. Newspapers gave special mention to the few whales killed, especially at Cape May and Great Egg Harbor. See, for example, *Docs. Rel. N. J.*, 1st ser., 11:46, 203, 592.

40. "Spicer-Leaming Indentures," Jacob Spicer Papers, Historical Society of Pennsylvania, Philadelphia; *N.J.S.L.*, 1813, S.S., Priv.& Temp.: 77–81.

41. Spicer Diary, 20, NjHi.

42. "Petition of the Inhabitants of Little Egg Harbour Township, May 22, 1765," Governors' Manuscripts, NJSA.

43. "Petition of the Freeholders of Great Egg Harbour to The General Assembly, January 20, 1767," Stewart Collection, Savitz Library, Glassboro State College, Glassboro, N.J.

44. On June 10, 1778, James Parker, for example, sent a wagon from his country seat in Hunterdon County to New Brunswick in order to fetch clams or oysters. Parker Diary, NjHi.

45. Additional legislation regulating oysters was passed in 1769 and 1774. See *N.J. Laws* 2:262, 4:585–87, 5:240–41, 313–14.

46. *N.J.S.L.,* 1811, S.S.: 307–308; 1819: 24.

47. *N.J.S.L.,* 1817: 3–5. In 1820 a private act of the legislature encouraged the planting of oysters in the Manasquan River. See *N.J.S.L.,* 1821, Priv. & Temp.: 153–154.

48. Ibid., 1820:165.

49. Rutherfurd, "Notes on the State," 86.

50. Johnson, *Memoirs and Reminiscences,* 35.

51. Johann David Schoepf, *Travels in the Confederation, 1783–1784,* ed. and trans. Alfred J. Morrison (Philadelphia, 1911), 1:28–30.

52. Parker Diary, NjHi.

53. Edward F. Randolph Account Book, Special Collections, NjR.

54. Benjamin Smith Farm Ledger, 1797–1828, Special Collections, NjR.

55. Woodward, *Ploughs and Politicks,* 84–85; *Docs. Rel. N.J.,* 1st ser. 24:505.

56. *Docs. Rel. N.J.,* 25:459.

57. Ibid. That Broadfield's fishery may have been the one Read first established is indicated by the description of "a pond near a quarter of a mile long, and, at low water, contains 5 or 6 feet in depth, and a constant supply every tide from the river, which is their own element, not spring water, so that it is in his power to put up fish most part of the winter."

58. See, for example, Johnson, *Memoirs and Reminiscences,* 35; Smith, *History of the Colony,* 510; Samuel Dennis to John Stevens, January 18, 1713, Steven Family Papers, NjHi; Warren Fretz, "Old Methods of Taking Fish," *Papers of the Bucks County Historical Society* 5 (1926): 361–72 and Thaddeus S. Kenderine, "Hunting, Traping [*sic*], and Fishing in Bucks County," Ibid., 736–40. Bucks County, Pennsylvania, lies across the Delaware River immediately west of central New Jersey.

59. Benson, *Peter Kalm's Travels,* 1:298.

60. *Docs. Rel. N.J.,* 1st ser., 29:443.

61. Benson, *Peter Kalm's Travels,* 1:161–62.

62. *Docs. Rel. N.J.,* 1st ser., 8:93.

63. Burnett and Hutchinson, "Marginal Jottings," 154–73; Parker Diary, NjHi; *Docs. Rel. N.J.,* 2d ser., 2:239. See also the description of the fishing expedition of Bailey Brus, April 10, 1810, in Doty and Southard General Store Day Book, Basking Ridge, New Jersey, Special Collections, NjR.

64. *Docs. Rel. N.J,* 2d ser., 26:357.

65. *N.J. Laws* 4:405–406.

66. Ibid., 4:509.

67. *N.J.S.L.* 1790:702–3. In 1765 several residents of the "Minisinks" [Delaware Valley north of the Water Gap] petitioned the legislature to be allowed to continue placing pounds, weirs, and the like in the river. *N.J.S.L.* 1765:343–45. The 1790 act amended a 1784 law concerning navigation and the fishery on the river.

68. Ibid., 1808:104–11. In 1814 the New Jersey act was supplemented by shifting the responsibility of prosecuting offenders and receiving fines to the Overseers of the Poor. Ibid., 1814, S.S.:71–72. In 1819, the state passed legislation bounding individual fishing operations on the Delaware; see ibid., 1819:18–19.

69. Ibid., 1804, S.S.:286–87; 1806:744–45; 1807:58–59; Ibid., 1816, Priv. & Temp., S.S.:113–14.

70. Ibid., 1819, Priv. & Temp., S.S.: 1.

71. A. Capnerhurst to her sister in England, May 31, 1788. Capner-Exton-Hill Papers, Hunterdon County Historical Society, Flemington, N.J.

72. Daniel Denton, *A Brief Description of New York* (New York, 1937).

73. G. Lockhart, *A Further Account of East New Jersey* . . . (Edinburgh, 1683).

74. Schoepf, *Travels;* Blackgrass is now known as *J. gerardi.*

75. Benson, *Peter Kalm's Travels,* 1:260–61.

76. Lindestrom, *Geographia,* 159; Benson, *Peter Kalm's Travels,* 1:266.

77. Richard T. T. Forman, "The Pine Barrens of New Jersey: An Ecological Mosaic," and Peter O. Wacker, "Human Exploitation of the New Jersey Pine Barrens Before 1900," in Forman, *Pine Barrens: Ecosystem and Landscape,* 574–75, 18–20. See also Jack McCormick, "The Vegetation of the New Jersey Pine Barrens," in ibid., 229–42.

78. Benson, *Peter Kalm's Travels,* 1:177–78.

79. In 1668, one of the first acts of the Carteret administration was to negotiate with the Lenape concerning the damages brought about by livestock.

80. Leaming and Spicer, *Grants,* 82.

81. Ibid., 127.

82. Many of these records are extant. See, for example, Frank G. Speck, *Earmarks of Livestock of the Settlers of Woodbridge, New Jersey, 1716–1799* (Philadelphia, 1938).

83. Leaming and Spicer, *Grants,* 278.

84. Ibid., 252–53.

85. Ibid., 260.

86. Ibid., 288–89.

87. Ibid., 320.

88. Ibid., 433.

89. Ibid., 538. In West Jersey, a 1683 law made those keeping hogs that injure a neighbor's marsh or meadow liable for the resulting damages. In 1689 the Council of West Jersey Proprietors forbade anyone who was not a Proprietor from hunting wild hogs on the proprietary lands that had as yet been undivided.

90. "A Copy of the Minute Book of Nottingham Township," *Proc. N.J.H.S.* 58 (1940): 24–25.

91. *Docs. Rel. N.J.,* 1st ser., 18:197.

92. Complaint to Jacob Race, 1784, Race-Emley Collection, Hunterdon County Historical Society.

93. Benson, *Peter Kalm's Travels,* 1:151, 87.

94. *Docs. Rel. N.J.,* 1st ser., 28:423–24.

95. R. Wayne Parker, "Taxes and Money in New Jersey," *Proc. N.J.H.S.* 7 (1883): 147; Frank H. Stewart, *Salem More than a Century Ago* (Salem, N.J., 1935), 15.

96. *Docs. Rel. N.J.,* 1st ser., 1:37.

97. "The Votes and Proceedings of the General Assembly of the Province of New Jersey," 3d session, Library of Congress, *Records of the States of the United States of America: A Microfilm Compilation* (Washington, 1949), 389; *Docs. Rel. N.J.,* 1st ser., 3:297–98.

98. Leaming and Spicer, *Grants,* 475.

99. Ibid., 262–63, 531.

100. *Docs. Rel. N.J.,* 1st ser., 3:79–80. That free-ranging horses were important economically may be gathered from the fact that the reason given for one of the two members of the General Assembly from Bergen County being absent from the meeting of that body in May of 1716 was that he was "said to be gone into the Woods to catch horses." *Docs. Rel. N.J.,* 1st ser., 14:23.

101. *Docs. Rel. N.J.,* 1st ser., 11:280–81.

102. Benson, *Peter Kalm's Travels,* 1:178.

103. *N. J. Laws* 5:340–41.

104. *Acts of the Twelfth General Assembly of the State of New Jersey* (Trenton, N.J., 1788), 465.

105. *Docs. Rel. N.J.,* 1st ser., 12:471.

106. Ibid., 25:324.

107. The dates reflect the years during which such advertisements commonly appeared.

108. Rayner W. Kelsey, ed. and trans., *Cazenove Journal, 1794, A Record of the Journey of Theophile Cazenove through New Jersey and Pennsylvania* (Haverford, Pa., 1922), 15.

109. Anderson, "Pastor Wrangel's Trip," 11–12.

110. Benson, *Peter Kalm's Travels,* 1:234.

111. Anderson, "Pastor Wrangel's Trip," 11–24.

112. *Docs. Rel. N.J.*, 1st ser., 2:214.

113. Ellis, "Diary of Jacob Spicer," 184; Spicer Diary, 107.

114. *N.J. Laws* 4:41–43.

115. *N.J.S.L.* 1789:521–22. Legislation concerning Manasquan Beach in 1804 raised the proportion of horses and cattle to twenty per hundred acres owned but shortened the grazing season to from September 15 to December 1st. Hogs, sheep, and goats were barred there as well. *N.J.S.L.* 1804:484–85.

116. *N.J. Laws* 4:257–62. In northeastern New Jersey, despite the relatively higher population density, some open areas remained "commons" for many years because both the Dutch authorities and Carteret had allowed freeholders in the townships to distribute undivided land periodically. Carteret had prescribed the method of land division in a charter that reconfirmed Peter Stuyvesant's patent, but because the office that was designed to manage the process no longer existed, much - undivided land remained more than one hundred years after initial settlement. One area with a great deal of such land lay largely in the Hackensack Meadowlands. Residents of Bergen Township petitioned for the commons to be divided, and an act was passed in 1763 setting up a commission of outsiders to oversee the process, but conflicts arose over a regrant by Stuyvesant that confused title to the land.

117. These enclosed lands were among those the legislature acted upon: 1801—woodland in northeastern Bergen County just south of New York state line; 1804—meadow near Overpeck Creek; 1808—"Bergen woods" in Bergen Township; 1811—"Big-woods" in Westfield Township, and woodland on the Palisades near Fort Lee; 1813—Moonachie Swamp, "the Rysen," and the unenclosed woodland south of Hackensack; 1814—woodland in Big Swamp, Saddle River Township; woodland in New Barbadoes Township; woodland called "the Wild Rough" in Harrington Township; woodland called "the Glouf" in Franklin Township, Bergen County; 1816—another woodland in Saddle River Township; 1817—Managhia Swamp and other adjacent woodland, New Barbadoes Township; 1818—Campgaw Mountain, Franklin Township, Bergen County; and 1819—Closter Mountain, Harrington Township, and swampland called "the Great Piece" in Caldwell Township. See *N.J.S.L.* 1800:52–55; 1803:306–8; 1808:39–42; 1810:440–42; 1812:71–77; 1813:192–95, 200–25, 243–47; 1814:136–39; 1815:15–17; 1816:40–41; 1818:67–69; 1819:109–11.

118. Woodward, *Ploughs and Politicks*, 342.

119. Muntz, "Changing Geography of the New Jersey Woodlands," 63–64.

120. Benson, *Peter Kalm's Travels*.

121. *Votes and Proceedings of the General Assembly of the Province of New Jersey, 1770, Second Sitting* (Woodbridge, N.J., 1770), 5.

122. Gavin Scott to his brother, December 31, 1796, Scott Family Papers, NjHi.

123. John Gifford, "The Forestal Conditions and Silvicultural Prospects of the Coastal Plain of New Jersey," *Annual Report of the State Geologist for the Year 1899* (Trenton, 1900), 248–49.

124. *N.J.S.L.* 1805:506–10.

125. Ibid., 1813: S.S., Priv. & Temp., 94–95; 1817: S.S., Priv. & Temp., 29–31; 1799:569–72.

126. Smith, *History of the Colony*, 511.

127. Niemecwicz, *Under Their Vine*, 217–18.

128. Benson, *Peter Kalm's Travels*, 279–80.

129. *Docs. Rel. N.J.*, 1st ser., 26:143.

130. Leaming and Spicer, *Grants*, 476.

131. Gifford, "Forestal Conditions," 268–69.

132. Benson, *Peter Kalm's Travels*, 1:101, 189; "Diary" [copy of extracts], 4, Jacob Spicer Papers, NjHi.

133. *Votes and Proceedings of the General Assembly*, 8; *N.J.S.L.* 789:516.

134. "Diary," 3, Spicer Papers.

135. The United States Department of Agriculture rates woods according to properties considered valuable for construction purposes on a scale from A to C, A being most desirable. White oak rates an A in most of the important criteria for building. Its only rival appears to be locust, which, on the basis

of early records of vegetation, was not present in large amounts in New Jersey. See James H. Whitaker, *Agricultural Buildings and Structures* (Reston, Va., 1979), 34. I wish to thank Karen Lang for bringing this source to my attention.

136. Benson, *Peter Kalm's Travels,* 1:235–36.

137. Muntz, "Changing Geography of New Jersey Woodlands," 53.

138. Benson, *Peter Kalm's Travels,* 1:238.

139. Ibid.; Woodward, *Ploughs and Politicks,* 320.

140. Muntz, "Changing Geography of New Jersey Woodlands," 68–72.

141. In New Jersey in this period, all land that had been surveyed off from the collective proprietary domain and had been improved in any way was taxed, and such "improved" land could remain extensively forested. Nevertheless, Table 4 still suggests the extent and changes in the cleared landscape. See Chap. 6 for graphs of the changes in the amounts of taxed improved and unimproved land for selected counties between 1751 and 1822.

142. The 1751 tax list may be found in the Jacob Spicer Papers, NjHi. See my "New Jersey Tax Ratable List," 33. The 1769 tax ratable list was published in *Votes and Proceedings of the General Assembly,* 1769:50. Data for 1784 are found in abstract form in "County Tax Ratables, 1772–1822," Division of Archives and Records Management, New Jersey State Library.

143. T. Capnerhurst to John, Samuel, and Rowland Coltman, November 17, 1787, Capner-Exton-Hill Papers, Hunterdon County Historical Society.

144. Muntz, "Changing Geography of New Jersey Woodlands," 59–60.

145. Ibid., 62.

146. *N.J. Laws* 2:201.

147. *N.J.S.L.* 1818:43.

148. Gavin Scott to his brother, 1796, Scott Family Papers, NjHi.

149. "Abstract of Deed and Map of Lands of John Van Liew [ca. 1765]," Van Liew Family Papers, State Archives, New Jersey State Library. William Wright brought this source to my attention.

150. William A. Whitehead, ed., "The Papers of Lewis Morris," *Collections of the New Jersey Historical Society* 4 (1852): 156.

151. "Archivum Americanum," Upsal Documents Relating to the Swedish Churches on the Delaware Transcribed and Translated from Documents Held in the Consistory of Upsal in Sweden for C. J. Stille under the Supervision of Col. Elfving and Dr. Wuselgrin, 1891, Historical Society of Pennsylvania, 1:120; *Docs. Rel. N.J.,* 1st ser., 26:142.

152. *Docs. Rel. N.J.,* 1st ser., 26:142.

153. Muntz, "Changing Geography of New Jersey Woodlands," 104.

154. *Docs. Rel. N.J.,* 1st ser., 20:303.

155. Ibid., 26:142, 245.

156. Ibid., 20:185, 27:375–76.

157. Jacob Spicer to Messrs. James and Dunker, November 19, 1764, Jacob Spicer Papers, NjHi.

158. See, for example, the tax ratable list for Upper Penn's Neck Township, 1774. "County Tax Ratables, 1773–1822," Department of Education, Division of State Library, Archives and History Microfilm and Records Unit, Trenton. Swedes, in numbers of "wood boats" and "flats" and in capacity, were involved in ownership in much greater amounts (one-third and more than one-half, respectively) than their proportion of the total number of taxpayers (one-quarter) warranted.

159. *Docs. Rel. N.J.,* 1st ser., 26:372–73.

160. "Cord Wood Agreement," Thomas Lee Papers, Special Collections, NjR.

161. *N.J.S.L.* 1814: S.S. Priv. & Temp., 143–44.

162. Muntz, "Changing Geography of New Jersey Woodlands," 101–2, 256.

163. Benson, *Peter Kalm's Travels,* 1:50–51.

164. *Docs. Rel. N.J.,* 1st ser., 24:62.

165. Ibid., 26:245.

166. Parker Diary, NjHi; *Docs. Rel. N.J.,* 1st ser., 26:4.

167. *Docs. Rel. N.J.,* 2d ser., 2:203.

168. Dorothy C. Barck, ed., *Letter Book of John Watts, Merchant and Councillor of New York* (New

York, 1928).

169. Ibid., 54.

170. Somers Account Books, Savitz Library, Glassboro State College.

171. Niemcewicz, *Under Their Vine*, 219.

172. *Docs. Rel. N.J.*, 1st ser., 17:386.

173. Mary Capnerhurst Exton to her mother, Mary Capnerhurst, May 18, 1788, Capnerhurst-Exton-Hill Family Papers, Hunterdon County Historical Society.

174. Muntz, "Changing Geography of New Jersey Woodlands," 118.

175. A. Capnerhurst to her sister, May 31, 1788, Capner-Exton-Hill Papers, Hunterdon y Historical Society.

176. Muntz, "Changing Geography of New Jersey Woodlands,"161; *Votes and Proceedings of the General Assembly*, 1778, 35.

177. "Reincke's Journal of a Visit among the Swedes of New Jersey, 1745," *Pennsylvania Magazine of History and Biography* 33 (1910): 101; Thomas F. Gordon, *A Gazetteer of the State of New Jersey* (Trenton, N.J.), 169.

178. "Diary," 4, Spicer Papers.

179. Charles S. Boyer, *Early Forges and Furnaces in New Jersey* (Philadelphia, 1931), 1.

180. *Docs. Rel. N.J.*, 1st ser., 20:414.

181. Kelsey, *Cazenove Journal.*

182. Niemcewicz, *Under Their Vine*, 222.

183. Barck, *Letter Book of John Watts*, 17, 30, 115.

184. Frederick Wilhelm August von Steuben to Governor Livingston, November 13, 1785, Manuscripts Collection, State Archives, New Jersey State Library. Von Steuben's property at River Edge is now a state historic site.

185. "Articles of Agreement between John Emley and John Allen," January 1, 1794, Race-Emley Papers, Hunterdon County Historical Society.

186. James Parker to John Stevens, December 21, 1787, Stevens Family Papers, NjHi.

187. New Jersey Tax Ratables, Sandyston Township, Sussex County, September 1774; James Parker Papers.

188. Stevens Family Papers, NjHi.

189. *N.J.S.L.* 1794, T.S.: 888.

190. For example, see *N.J.S.L.* 1816, S.S.: 6–7.

191. Benson, *Peter Kalm's Travels*, 1:296; Muntz, "Changing Geography of New Jersey Woodlands," 153.

192. Benson, *Peter Kalm's Travels*, 1:299–301.

193. Council of the Proprietors of the Western Division of New Jersey, "Minutes, 1688–1951," 1:57.

194. Benson, *Peter Kalm's Travels*, 1:300.

195. *Docs. Rel. N.J.*, 1st ser., 19:503.

196. Beekman Family Papers, Special Collections, NjR. I am indebted to David Fowler for bringing this source to my attention.

197. Spicer Diary, James Spicer Papers, NjHi; Spicer to Abel James, March 31, 1764, Spicer Papers, NjHi.

198. *Docs. Rel. N.J.*, 1st ser., 27:25–26, 77.

199. Muntz, "Changing Geography of New Jersey Woodlands," 23.

200. Ibid., 157–59.

201. Muntz, "Changing Geography of New Jersey Woodlands," 183.

202. Howard C. Rice, Jr., trans., *Marquis de Chastellux Travels in North America in the Years 1780, 1781 and 1782* (Chapel Hill, N. C., 1963), 1:189.

203. Kelsey, *Cazenove Journal*, 14.

204. D. F. Sotzman, "New Jersey" (Hamburg: Carl Ernst Bohn, 1797), cited in Muntz, "Changing Geography of New Jersey Woodlands," 181.

205. Jonas Phillips to Robert Morris, June 22, 1784, Boggs Papers, NjHi.

206. Robert Morris to Joseph Insley, May 8, 1792, Robert Morris Papers, Special Collections, NjR.

207. In 1769, John Scott of Hanover Township, Morris County, proposed to a tenant interested in renting his farm for seven years that he could clear the land for grain "and the wood on said Land will pay for the clearing." See *Docs. Rel. N.J.*, 1st ser., 26:401.

Fourth Month, April, 1819.

CHAPTER 2

LANDHOLDING, LABOR, AND FARM TYPES

In August 1786 John Rutherfurd, a member of the wealthy proprietary class and later a United States Senator from New Jersey, set down an outline of the history and economy of the province and state in a piece that he called "Notes on the State of New Jersey."[1] Rutherfurd was concerned about the "great Emigrations from this State, which not only lose the Hands that might be turned to many useful Improvements and Employments, but some of them privately dispose of their Effects, run off and defraud their Creditors, while others sell considerable Property, and carry the amount to other States to the southwestward, or to the western wide Wilderness, which is settling too fast, and a century too soon."

Rutherfurd believed that lower agricultural yields due to poor husbandry, great tax increases, and shrinking farm sizes had hastened this exodus from the state. Farm land was quite valuable—"near considerable Towns," he observed, "it is from £20 to £50 pr. acre, as the Land is generally better and may have the help of manure"—but he and other land owners could not secure adequate rents from tenants. "Generally farms are leased at 3 or 4 pr. cent of their value, while the legal Interest is 7 pr. cent," Rutherfurd noted. ". . . If Landlords therefore in this State could sell their Lands, and otherwise invest the Value in Security [presumably at 7 percent] it would be much to their Advantage."

Rutherfurd did not provide any information on variations in farm size or land costs within New Jersey. These factors, however, differed greatly from place to place, as did the nature of tenure—whether one was a freeholder, a squatter, or a tenant. And all of these factors affected land use, relative affluence, and the nature of the cultural landscape.

Land hunger was a powerful force for the entire population, stimulated at least in part to assure that one's children would be freeholders. In 1740, Governor Lewis Morris attributed the lack of money in circulation in New Jersey to the tendency of farmers to hoard cash income from grain and other sales "in Order to make purchase of Land for their children."[2] But evidence suggests that decent farmland was increasingly hard to come by for most residents of middling incomes. And even for those who could afford to buy farms, land purchases were sometimes hindered by the complex and ambiguous process of land allocation.

The history of land distribution in New Jersey is the history of the involvement of the Dutch West India Company, proprietors Berkeley and Carteret, the Councils of Proprietors of East and West New Jersey, and subsequent private dealings. In both East and West New Jersey, the Councils of Proprietors periodically assigned the "rights" to a given number of acres to individual proprietors depending on how many proprietary shares they held. A proprietor could take his allocation and have it surveyed for his own use or for sale, either in whole or in part, or he could sell his right in whole or in part. Surveyed land, whether parceled out to a proprietor or to someone who had purchased it from him, was to be registered with the respective proprietors' council.

Table 5, compiled by Dennis Ryan,[3] is a useful view of the land patents officially recorded by the East Jersey proprietors in their earliest years. Patents in the Dutch-settled area were relatively modest, averaging seventy-five acres. In Bergen County, the Dutch grants in existence in 1664, few in number and rarely containing more than fifty acres, were reconfirmed, but later Dutch settlers purchased large tracts in the Raritan Valley and northern Monmouth County from individual proprietors. The less affluent among the Dutch group moved from New York to become tenants on the Ramapo Tract, a very large holding in northern Bergen County begun by speculators.

In the early New England settlements south of Raritan Bay, individual tracts were quite a bit larger. In what became northern Monmouth County, they averaged more than two hundred acres; in addition, very large tracts were distributed to council members and others who were neither Dutch nor from New England. New Englanders had been encouraged to migrate to New Jersey by the Duke of York's governor in New York before he had been informed that the colony had been granted to Berkeley and Carteret. A great deal of grief was to come from this unfortunate coincidence, especially in Elizabethtown, whose settlers were earliest on the scene and claimed a vast area to the west. In the first years of settlement, these New Englanders generally came in groups; they acquired land jointly and periodically distributed it among themselves, to descendants, and to settlers who later received

Table 5
East New Jersey Land Patents, 1665–82
(Chart does not include, among town patents, those given to Council members, citizens of New York, or the out-plantations of Bergen)

Town	1667	1668	1669	1670	1671	1672	1673	1674
Bergen	2*	33	4	6	3	1		
	154**	54	50	86	93	44		
Newark								
Elizabethtown								
Woodbridge			6	39	2	2	3	
			232	159	146	243	128	
Piscataway								
Middletown								
Shrewsbury								
Council Members	1	1	10	13	2		1	
		2602	7792	3361	845	144	2	

Source: East Jersey Deeds, Liber 1, 2, 4.

* = # patents   ** = average # acres per

a right to a portion of lands yet undistributed. Newark was a New England settlement, as were Woodbridge and Piscataway when they were divided from part of the Elizabethtown claim. These large tracts all subsequently became townships.

However, unlike their counterparts in East Jersey townships to the north, the New Englanders who settled the Middletown and Shrewsbury tracts cooperated with the proprietors from an early point and thus received relatively large individual landholdings. Also, because the proprietors reserved a seventh part of their grants to the New England towns for themselves, quite large parcels within these townships were owned by those deriving title from the proprietors and not from the New England towns.

Most New Englanders settled north of the Raritan not only had smaller parcels, but often an individual's holdings were not contiguous. Those who had settled New England's first towns had been assigned village house lots and other lands that they held collectively. In New England and in New Jersey places settled by New Englanders, the first inhabitants usually received a salt or fresh meadow lot as part of the general division. In 1697, Eliphalet Johnson, a prosperous resident of Newark, owned 390 acres "English Measure" that was divided into twenty separate parcels.[4] After a standard 10 percent "allowance" for "Highways" and errors in surveying, Johnson's parcels included a house lot and a piece of "upland in the Great Neck" (the Ironbound District), each ten by six chains in area, thirty-six acres "Lying on the Hill," twelve acres "in the Neck by the two Mile Brook" over which one John Brown had legal right to carry hay from his adjacent meadow, sixteen acres "Lying at ..ulsoms Milstone," and fifty acres at the foot of the first Watchung Ridge. He had four acres of "the fresh Meadow," probably on the Passaic River, two acres at "Beefe point," and tracts in the Watchung Mountains, on both sides of the "third river," "on the stone house plain" (possibly South Orange), on the Rahway River, and in the Great Swamp. Finally, another fifty-two acres of Johnson's land

Table 5 (cont.)
East New Jersey Land Patents, 1665–82
(Chart does not include, among town patents, those given to Council members, citizens of New York, or the out-plantations of Bergen)

1675	1676	1677	1678	1679	1680	1681	1682	Total
1		5	6				1	62*
40		34	128				120	75**
16	8		1	31				56
109	97		85	103				103
	24	4	19	9				56
	176	157	179	130				168
2	1	2	3					60
106	94	100	140					162
			37			2	1	40
			130			201	178	138
	13	29	2	1	1	2		48
	338	235	232	209	24	308		261
		1		3	6	42	14	66
		904		195	185	192	293	224
			1			3	6	28
			191			628	2189	2479

lay in six tracts—meadow land, tracts next to Two Mile Brook, Morris's Creek, and Maple Island Creek, two acres on the bay, and twelve acres of "Boggs in Tomkens Cove."

In West Jersey, except among New Englanders in southern Cape May County and on the Cohansey River in what became Cumberland County, there was much less incidence of group settlement. Although groups of Quakers did settle from Burlington County south, most moved to their own large farms soon after they arrived. Many of the Quaker settlers, entrepreneurs who had been tradesmen in England, were themselves proprietors or held portions of a proprietary share. Of sixty-four taxable persons listed on one 1687 tax list for southern Gloucester County, thirty-four with non-Swedish surnames—presumed for the most part to have been Quakers—had mean land holdings of 474 acres.[5] The mean holding for the thirty landowners with Swedish surnames was only 224 acres. Several very large landholdings among the non-Swedes—including one 2,400-acre tract, one of 2,200 acres, one of 1,350 acres, and two of 1,000 acres each—skewed these figures. In the first year of settlement in Nottingham Township, just south of present-day Trenton in Burlington County, twenty-four property owners, all with English surnames, held parcels ranging from 30 to 1,350 acres; the mean size was 459 acres.[6]

Advertisements of real estate for sale provide some idea of the process of private subdivision of the proprietary lands.[7] Of the 142 properties advertised for sale from 1720 to 1738, 58 percent were unimproved, and the mean size was 1,403 acres (table 6). Almost all of these parcels were in the hands of absentee owners. Improved properties, 58 percent of which were held by absentee owners, averaged 405 acres. In effect, then, tenants occupied more than half the improved properties in the sample. As the pace of settlement quickened in the decade before the Revolution, from 1766 to 1775, the sale of real estate escalated; only 17 percent of

Table 6
New Jersey Ownership and Sizes of Agricultural Land Advertised for Sale,
by County or Region, 1720–38

| County | N | | Unimproved | | | | Improved | | |
		Percentage	Mean Area (Acres)	Resident Owner (%)	Absentee Owner (%)	Percentage	Mean Area (Acres)	Resident Owner (%)	Absentee Owner (%)
Bergen	2	—	—	—	—	100	450	50	50
Essex	9	56	474	—	100	44	114	25	75
Hunterdon	40	97	2,219	—	100	3	200*	—	100
Somerset	13	8	500*	—	100	92	460	8	92
Middlesex	28	46	866	8	92	54	358	53	47
Monmouth	5	—	—	—	—	100	443	60	40
Burlington	14	7	1,666*	—	100	93	344	69	31
Gloucester	15	67	462	30	70	33	782	40	60
Salem	14	79	531	—	100	21	412	—	100
Cape May	—	—	—	—	—	—	—	—	—
Outer Coastal Plain	2	100	1,133	—	100	—	—	—	—
Aggregate	142	58	1,403	5	95	42	405	42	58

*Only one property listed.

the land advertised remained unimproved, but absentee ownership prevailed (table 7). The mean size of unimproved parcels had fallen to 472 acres, a third of their size in the 1720–38 period. In these later years, mean acreage of improved parcels had fallen to 234 acres, and absentee owners—largely New Yorkers, Philadelphians, or residents of the two provincial capitals, Perth Amboy and Burlington—held two-thirds of these tracts.

Complicating the West Jersey situation was the formation in 1692 of the West Jersey Society, a joint stock company based in London. One of its holdings was the "Great Tract," more than 92,513 acres in Hunterdon County. Later acquired by a consortium of wealthy East Jersey proprietors, this tract and others were managed for absentee owners who had subdivided them and rented out parcels to tenants. Before midcentury, almost all of this relatively inaccessible and late-settled area in northwest Hunterdon and, later, in Morris and Sussex counties, was unimproved. Absentee owners held large tracts averaging 2,219 acres. This area grew rapidly before the Revolution, and holdings there accounted for more than a third of the properties listed for sale (see table 7). Less than a fifth of these, all owned by absentees, were described as unimproved. Here, the size of unimproved tracts had fallen from 2,219 acres to 517 acres. More than four-fifths of the properties listed were occupied farms. Eighty-seven percent of these farms, which averaged 262 acres (a little larger than the mean), were owned by non-residents. Thus tenancy was significant in the region.

Real estate advertisements present a biased view of land ownership; they are skewed toward larger properties and were more prevalent in some areas than in others. New Englanders and the Dutch, for example, tended not to advertise in the newspapers of the day. Nevertheless, these notices document in some measure the ongoing process of land division and the fact that a large percentage of improved tracts were occupied by tenants and not by freeholders.

Surviving records of some of New Jersey's major landlords make plain that tenants did not have the same attitude toward the land that owners did. Many, if not most, tenants cared little for land they occupied, a fact that landlords attempted to mitigate (often with little success) by monitoring their tenants' agricultural activities.[8] Complicating this effort was the fact that both titles and property boundaries were uncertain in many areas, and substantial agrarian unrest beset northern New Jersey in particular, especially from the mid 1740s to the early 1750s.[9] Both circumstances must have greatly affected the attitudes of many farmers, especially as they contemplated their future on the land they tilled.

In New Jersey, tenants were landholders, but not landowners. After 1751, tax lists almost always list the occupant of the property; owners were listed instead of occupants only if they lived in the township where the property was located. Taxes were recorded this way because it was easier for collectors to gather tax monies from occupants; land owners were often living many miles away. Also, because squatting was widespread, at least in earlier years, local collectors realized it made more sense to collect taxes from those who used the land, without regard to who owned it. Thus assessors estimated acreages and collected from those who claimed to have the right to occupy the land.[10] Assessors also recognized that owners frequently represented tracts to include fewer acres than they actually did. James Parker admitted in his diary that he deliberately falsified lease agreements to reduce

Table 7

New Jersey Ownership and Sizes of Agricultural Land Advertised for Sale,
By County or Region, 1766–75 (20 Percent Sample)

County or Region	N	Unimproved				Improved			
		Percentage	Mean Size (Acres)	Resident Owner (%)	Absentee Owner (%)	Percentage	Mean Size (Acres)	Resident Owner (%)	Absentee Owner (%)
Bergen	4	—	—	—	—	100	132	25	75
Essex	8	—	—	—	—	100	191	75	25
Hunterdon	16	6	100*	—	100	94	260	33	64
Morris	14	7	144*	—	100	93	345	31	69
Sussex	38	26	596	—	100	74	223	—	100
Hunterdon Morris Sussex (Old Hunterdon)	68	18	517	—	100	82	262	13	87
Somerset	9	11	Several Hundred*	100	—	89	171	50	50
Middlesex	19	11	478	—	100	89	196	38	62
Monmouth	14	14	600*	50	50	86	321	33	67
Burlington	15	20	623	33	66	80	187	58	42
Gloucester	23	17	117	—	100	83	179	47	53
Salem	11	9	500*	—	100	91	318	50	50
Cumberland	2	—	—	—	—	100	528*	—	100
Salem Cumberland (Old Salem)	13	8	500*	—	100	92	337	32	58
Cape May	2	—	—	—	—	100	100*	—	100
Outer Coastal Plain	12	58	489	14	86	42	151	20	80
Aggregate	187	17	472	16	84	83	234	34	66

*Only one property listed

taxes.[11] Such falsification was probably more prevalent in recently settled areas or where large tracts had recently been subdivided—in other words, places of which local assessors lacked intimate knowledge. And for their part, New England-settled towns often failed to register their periodic distributions of land with the proprietors so as to avoid paying annual fees, or quit rents, to them.

County tax lists of about 1780 indicate great contrasts in the size of landholdings in New Jersey at that time (table 8).[12] In New England-settled Essex County, the mean holding was 72.5 acres, or less than half the mean for the entire state. In Quaker-settled Burlington County, the mean was 224 acres, or almost 50 percent higher than the state mean. In general, tracts in West Jersey counties were larger than those in East Jersey; if Morris County, settled mostly from adjacent Essex, is combined with East Jersey counties, mean landholding in East Jersey would be 128.7 acres, while in West Jersey it would be 174.6 acres.

Table 8
Mean Landholdings by New Jersey County, ca. 1780

County	Mean Acreage
Bergen	122.9
Essex	72.5
Morris	112.5
Somerset	159.9
Middlesex	138.8
Monmouth	165.8
Sussex	134.7
Hunterdon	152.5
Burlington	224.0
Gloucester	209.7
Salem	167.1
Cumberland	153.5
Cape May	229.8
State	**149.9**

The distribution of mean landholdings by township (map 12) permits more detailed comparisons between the sizes of landholdings, physiographic divisions, and cultural groups. The Outer Coastal Plain had generally large acreages, but many of its large tracts were unallocated and therefore did not appear on tax lists until 1779, when unimproved land was first taxed. The term "farm" may actually be inappropriate for tracts on the Outer Coastal Plain, because cleared acreage for crops was small; land use was oriented far more toward lumbering and running cattle in the woods.

Also, the large West Jersey farms of the fertile Inner Coastal Plain, settled by Quakers, spilled over into Quaker-settled portions of Monmouth County in East Jersey. Similarly, the small farms in the New England sphere of settlement in Essex County spilled over into adjacent Morris County. New England-settled Wood-bridge and Piscataway farm sizes were considerably below the mean for the state. The same held true in several small townships in Cumberland County settled largely by New Englanders. Dutch-settled portions of the Raritan Valley and northern Monmouth County contained larger farms than the state mean, while farms in the Dutch-settled northeast were generally smaller, probably because they were initially smaller and because lands had already been subdivided due to the region's early settlement.

Mapping landholdings from twenty-five to forty-nine acres (map 13) highlights the contrasts between areas settled by New Englanders, the Dutch, and Quakers. In many areas of northeastern New Jersey, more than 10 percent of the farms contained fewer than fifty acres. A map of farms from fifty to ninety-nine acres (map 14) again isolates the area of New England settlement, though the small farm sizes in Franklin Township, Bergen County, are less easy to explain. A map of farms containing more than two hundred acres (map 15) clearly depicts the great differences between areas settled by New Englanders and English Quakers, as well as the general contrast between the north and east and west and south in 1780.

Generally, New Jersey's farms were larger than farms in parts of England at the time; in 1796 in Gloucestershire, for example, a twenty- to thirty-acre farm was considered very small, and it was thought impossible to make a decent living on

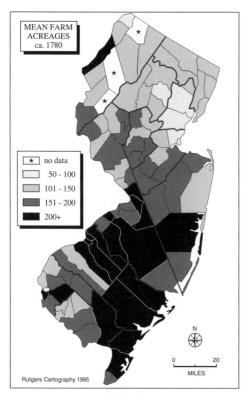

MAP 12

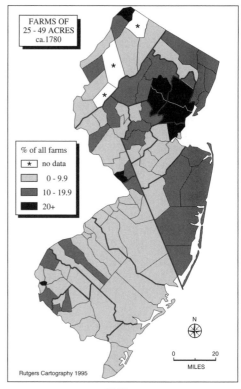

MAP 13

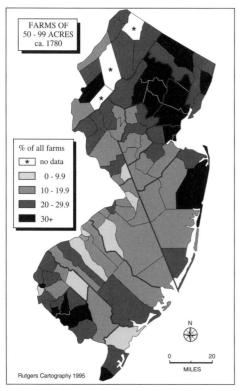

MAP 14

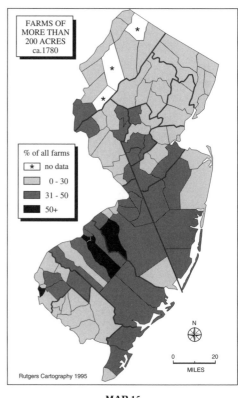

MAP 15

96/Land Use in Early New Jersey

fewer than one hundred acres.[13] New England farms were smaller on average (and grew smaller over time),[14] while Lemon found the average southeastern Pensylvania farm to be 125 acres. In Pennsylvania, farms near Philadelphia were smaller than 125 acres on average, while New Jersey farms near this city were much larger. Lemon argued that "even on the fertile Lancaster Plain, farms of only 60 to 75 acres apparently would have been inadequate to sustain families,"[15] a fact that suggests how precarious farms in the New England-settled section of New Jersey might have been.

Much evidence suggests that landless men who had no real property inheritance and little money found it difficult to obtain a freehold, particularly after the Revolution. In 1786, Rutherfurd had estimated land values at twenty to fifty pounds per acre for better lands near larger towns; eight years later, on his trip across northern New Jersey, Theophile Cazenove noted that good land accessible to the New York market commanded about ten pounds per acre, while good land farther from this major market and less improved went for about three to four pounds per acre (table 9).[16] Buyers were customarily asked to put up a third of the purchase price as downpayment and had only a few years to pay off the mortgage. At that time, Cazenove estimated, an agricultural worker could command wages of thirty to forty pounds a year. Thus, even a relatively small farm on "medium land" near Hanover in Morris County would have required a downpayment of 160 pounds, or four years of top farm wages if every penny of those wages were saved. At this time, too, a pair of oxen for plowing cost twenty to thirty pounds, a horse twenty-five pounds, and a milch cow seven pounds; farm implements were another necessary investment. Cash-poor farmers could raise the livestock of others on "shares," but for many tenancy was the only escape from hiring oneself out as ordinary farm labor.

Rutherfurd's sense in 1786 that farm rents were low was true if compared to European standards, and in his view they could be blamed on four facts of life in early New Jersey. First, land was not as productive as it looked and was plagued with "great Droughts, violent and long Rains, and great Heats and Colds" that were not so prevalent in Europe. Second, the cost of labor was very high, from one-third to two-thirds of a dollar a day, or from sixty to eighty dollars a year. Third, many farmers were simply "very unskillful and bad husbandmen" who could not derive enough income from their holdings to pay higher rents. Fourth, landlords found it difficult to sell their lands. Rutherfurd maintained that "an industrious thriving man" in New Jersey could always buy a farm for himself, but there must have been few such men in New Jersey at the time. Thus those who did not wish to become tenants tended to leave the state; "annual Swarms" of the descendants of Scots-Irish, German, and New England settlers from the "back Counties," Rutherfurd declared, were emigrating in 1786.[17]

Those who stayed to work New Jersey farms, if not landholders themselves, were the sons of landholders, landless white laborers who worked by the day or on contract, free blacks, slaves, and indentured servants. Landless whites were, without question, the largest in total numbers; at about the time of the Revolution, according to Lender, they constituted 37 percent of the white population.[18] Tax lists of about 1780 permit these landless persons to be mapped (map 16). With few exceptions (that is, free blacks), landless people were white males, generally termed in tax

Table 9
Land Values and Descriptions Recorded by Theophile Cazenove
in Northern New Jersey, 1794

Location	General Description	Price per Acre	Farm Description (Price)
Springfield to Chatham	Ground very bad, sand and broken stones, "miserable huts," few inhabitants.	£3	200–250 acres, mostly raising cattle, wood almost gone. Pair of oxen £20–30. Horse £25. (£2,000–2,500).
Chatham	Valley more level, ground better, many pastures.	£10	120–150 acres, wheat, corn, buckwheat. More and more cattle raised. Milk cow £7. (£750).
Hanover	Ground better for cultivation, less suited for pasture.	£7–8 (good land) £4–5 (medium)	150 acres, 40 acres in wood for farm, 80 tillable, 20 meadow. Corn, little wheat. (£750).
Morristown vicinity	High hills, stones, medium soil (glaciated Highlands).	£5	
Morristown	One-hundred-foot frontage in village.	£100	
Musconetong Valley	Land pretty good as far as Easton.	£3–4	200 acres, 2/3 in valley, 1/3 on mountain. Corn, buckwheat, Easton market. (£600–800).

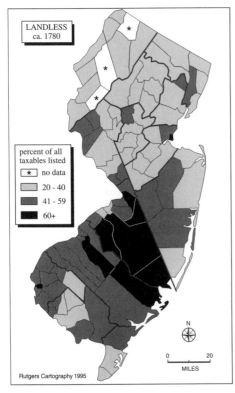

LANDLESS ca. 1780

percent of all taxables listed
★ no data
20 - 40
41 - 59
60+

N

0   20
MILES

Rutgers Cartography 1995

MAP 16

lists "single man," "single man with horse," and "householder." A single man was a male over sixteen who held no land and worked for hire. If he worked for his father he was not taxed. If a single man owned a horse, he was taxed at a slightly higher rate. House-holders, a term implying responsibility for others living under the same roof, were almost all married men, though some wid-ows and widowers were also listed. Though they held no real property within the town-ship, some few may have rented where they lived and leased land elsewhere to others.[19]

Widely spread throughout New Jersey after the Revolution, the landless white labor force was most heavily concentrated in southern New Jersey. On the Outer Coastal Plain, most were undoubtedly lumbermen; others must have been ironworkers. On the fertile Inner Coastal Plain, they were largely agricultural workers. In northern New Jersey landless whites were fewest in parts of the Dutch-settled area, in the more recently settled northwest, and in parts of the New England-settled area, where holdings, though small, were widely dispersed throughout the male population.

Also a large part of the agricultural labor force, particularly in earlier years, slaves from 1726 on were most prevalent in the areas of Dutch settlement and least in the areas of English Quaker settlement.[20] In 1790, 20 percent of Bergen County inhabitants were black at a time when blacks were less than 8 percent of New Jersey population as a whole. The availability of slave labor correlates well with improved land by township (see table 10 and map 11). Small farmers in the New England-settled section could not afford slaves, nor could the impecunious tenants of the northwest. But in the Dutch-settled areas, slaves took the place of landless white laborers, who apparently could not compete; presumably, many (including the sons of relatively small farmers) were compelled to leave the area.

Of the slaves offered for sale in newspaper advertisements between 1704 and 1782, almost three-quarters were listed as farmers. Blacks and whites appear to have worked alongside each other on a regular basis; James Parker noted that his slaves and white hired hands worked at the same tasks in the same fields each day at his large farm in Hunterdon County.[21] Advertisements indicate that some slaves were in charge of substantial properties; others regularly ran errands for their owners and handled cash transactions on their behalf, often at some distance from where they lived.[22]

Free black laborers and indentured servants filled out the labor force for agri-

Table 10
Patterns of Landholding and Potential Agricultural Labor Supply
Selected Groups of Townships, ca. 1780

Location[1]	Number of Taxables	Percentage[2] Holding 25 Acres or More	Percentage[2] Holding 100 Acres or More	Labor Supply[3]	Labor Supply as a Percentage of Holdings 100 Acres or More	Slaves[4] as a Percentage of the Labor Supply
Bergen County plus Acquackanonk Township, Essex County (Dutch–settled Piedmont)	1,381	58.87	36.28	772	154.09	41.06
Essex County, without Acquackanonk Township, plus adjacent Middlesex County. (New England–settled Piedmont	2,850	51.75	16.46	1,022	217.91	16.46
Somerset County (Dutch–settled Piedmont)	1,329	54.18	39.58	799	151.90	38.92
Burlington County (Quaker–settled Inner Coastal Plain)	1,127	39.57	30.88	668	191.95	6.14
Salem County (Quaker-settled Inner Coastal Plain)	1,309	50.11	35.52	644	138.49	10.40
Total	7,996			3,905		
Mean		51.40	28.88		169.12	22.99

1. Townships located on poor soils or possessing largely urban functions have been excluded.
2. Percentage of total of taxables.
3. Whites holding no real property, plus slaves and a very few free blacks.
4. A few free blacks have been included for Salem County.

cultural work. Though the size of both groups is difficult to determine precisely, neither was probably a very large part of this work force. The presence of free blacks varied widely through the state: by 1800, more than 90 percent of Gloucester County's small black population of 707 was free, but less than seven percent of Bergen's substantial black community of 3,027 enjoyed that status (table 11).[23] The practice of indentured servitude survived into the nineteenth century, and toward the end of the century previous Europeans tended to believe that farmers who had populated American places farther afield than the first settlements were indentured servants. According to Cazenove, "Most of them have, either themselves or their fathers, come to America from Germany, Scotland, and especially Ireland, poor, from among the poorest country-people, and spent their first years in servitude (as is the custom for that class) from 2 to 6 years, and then become mechanics or farmers."[24] But available official data does not support this supposition, at least for New Jersey. In 1751 and 1769, tax lists combined servants and slaves in one category, and by comparing the 1751 figures with the number of male slaves listed in the New Jersey county census of 1745, a rough estimate of the number of servants in the state at midcentury may be developed (table 12).[25] Some allowance must be made for the fact that censuses listed black males of all ages, while tax lists showed only black males older than sixteen.

The census of 1745 listed 2,588 black males, while 1751 tax lists show 2,293 servants and slaves. Probably few of the black males in the 1745 census were under sixteen, because there were more men than women at the time (the sex ratio was 128 black men to 100 black women) and thus relatively few marriage partners for black males. If that is so, there must have been relatively few white servants in New Jersey in 1751, though during this period white migration into the state was rapid.[26] In a few counties such as Somerset, Salem, Hunterdon, and Gloucester, there were

Table 11
Total Numbers of African Americans,
Percentage African American, and Percentage of
All African Americans Free by County, New Jersey, 1790 and 1800

| | 1790 | | | 1800 | | |
County	Total Numbers	Percentage of Total Population	Percentage Free	Total Numbers	Percentage of Total Population	Percentage Free
Middlesex	1,458	9.11	9.41	1,827	10.24	14.40
Essex	1,331	7.48	12.02	1,719	7.72	11.52
Monmouth	1,949	11.52	18.11	2,101	10.57	22.28
Somerset	1,957	15.91	7.51	2,038	15.90	8.59
Bergen	2,493	19.78	7.70	3,027	18.97	6.67
Burlington	825	4.55	72.48	958	4.45	80.38
Hunterdon	1,492	7.36	18.90	1,790	8.18	29.89
Gloucester	533	3.98	81.23	707	4.39	91.37
Salem	546	5.23	68.49	692	6.09	87.72
Cape May	155	6.02	9.03	178	5.81	44.94
Morris	684	4.21	7.01	875	4.93	11.43
Cumberland	258	3.12	53.48	346	3.63	78.32
Sussex	404	2.58	12.89	616	2.73	16.56
State	**14,185**	**7.70**	**19.45**	**16,824**	**7.94**	**26.17**

Table 12
Servants and Slaves, Single Men and Householders, 1751 and 1769

County	1751		1769		
	S. & S.	S.M.	S. & S.	S.M.	H.H.
Middlesex	221	81	303	179	594
Monmouth	262	194	281	203	581
Essex	158	121	258	86	513
Somerset	378	94	440	192	276
Bergen	306	8	422	34	164
Burlington	227	229	230	336	896
Gloucester	161	211	173	292	538
Salem	141	113	147	302	286
Cumberland	32	107	49	59	245
Cape May	26	47	29	45	40
Hunterdon	299	274	360	193	615
Morris	82	91	129	105	300
Total	2,293	1,570	2,903	2,187	5,270

fewer male slaves in 1745 than there were servants and slaves in 1751. Thus these counties must have had the largest numbers of servants, but still their overall numbers were few.

When data from the 1769 tax list is compared to the incomplete census of 1772, the imbalance between black men and women had grown more extreme, and so a smaller proportion still must have been under the age of sixteen.[27] Of 173 servants and slaves listed for Gloucester County in 1769, some were probably servants; only 178 black males were listed there in 1772, some of whom were probably younger than sixteen. Salem County contained 169 black males in 1772 and 147 servants and slaves in 1768, which again suggests the presence of at least a few bound servants. The combined servant-slave category was dropped in subsequent tax laws, perhaps because of the relatively small number of servants; thereafter, the category included only black slaves. Finally, apprentices who were bound over for a term of years to learn a trade may also have been agricultural laborers, but again their numbers appear to have been relatively small.

On the better soils where the Dutch, New Englanders, and Quakers had settled, the number of laborers potentially available for agricultural work correlates roughly with the average size of farms (see table 10).[28] The data are divided into two sets—those farms of fewer than one hundred acres and those containing more, based on the assumption that the holder of one hundred largely improved acres on good soils probably could have used some extra seasonal help. One hundred acres was below the mean farm size in New Jersey at the time, but such a farm would have been larger than the seventy-five-acre tract Lemon determined necessary for subsistence in southeastern Pennsylvania.

In the part of Essex County settled by New Englanders, the ratio of landless whites to holdings over one hundred acres was very high, in part because farms on the whole were so small. In the southwest, the percentage of landless men was higher, but so was the number of large holdings. Thus that region's potential labor force was smaller than in New England-settled Essex, where small farmers and their sons were generally available for casual day labor. Potential labor supply was also of course greatly affected by the great differences in population densities from place to place (see map 4).[29] In 1790, there were seventy-four people per square mile in Essex County but only twenty-two in Burlington County. Of course, much of Burlington lay in the Outer Coastal Plain, but nevertheless the densities in Essex were much greater than on the better (Inner Coastal Plain) soils of Burlington (see map 4). This meant that agriculture could be pursued with greater intensity in Essex County. Thus agricultural land was used much more intensively in Essex County, whose forest clearance had begun more than two generations earlier. Moreover, potential labor in Essex was probably drawn to its early industries, many of which were directly tied to agriculture; Moreau de St. Mery described one Newark shoe factory that employed three hundred people in 1794.[30] Skilled industrial work paid better or provided off-season employment not available in a more purely agricultural economy.

Because systematic information on the relatively poor majority is hard to come by, it is difficult to generalize about the habits and activities of this labor force. Account books and diaries make occasional mention of landowners' dealings with tenants and hired labor. In June 1756, Jacob Spicer of Cape May agreed to let one tenant keep a cow, a horse, and eight to ten hogs (provided they were kept from rooting in the grain fields) and to live in a house on the property, in return for which the tenant was to look after Spicer's cows and calves and supply him and his people with milk and butter when they visited. He agreed to provide new fence rails if the tenant kept the fence in good repair. The tenant was allowed to store his grain in the barn, to have fruit for his table, and to use dead wood for heating and cooking, but Spicer was to receive all of the hay produced on the place and one-half of the grain crop. Spicer's cousin, another man then in "Carolina," and he and his men were to have a room in the house whenever they wanted to occupy one.[31]

Whether this intricate agreement worked out as planned is unknown, but many landowners seemed to have difficulty with tenants. On July 7, 1737, Jonathan Holmes at Middletown Point, now Matawan in northern Monmouth County, complained about the local agricultural laborers in his diary. "I was at home a doing Some harvest work; and walking a mongst the harvest folks to see that they did make good work which was a hard matter to make them do."[32] In 1763, James Parker wrote Robert Emley about a mare Emley had sent from Parker's farm in Hunterdon County to Perth Amboy. "I wish you had agreed with the man that brought down the Mare what to allow him for it unless a Positive agreement is Made they allways Expect to be more than paid for their time & trouble and are for leaving it to my generosity which is a method of asking a Price that I don't very well like."[33]

Absentee owners clearly felt that hired or slave help had to be managed closely in order to get a good day's work. James Parker noted that both blacks and whites tended to take it a bit easy when he was unable to supervise them directly. In an April 1730 letter to his son John about his Monmouth County estate at Tinton, Lewis Morris complained about the small crop his previous overseers had produced and stated that he suspected "Embezzlement of Cattle, Sheep, &c.," though he could not determine whether his overseers, slaves, or both were responsible. He advised his son to watch with care the amount of corn slaves planted, for they would "follow their owne way if not carefully looked to," and he suggested sowing more wheat than his neighbors used because birds would carry away some and slaves would steal more.[34] The independence of some slaves clearly unnerved potential owners. In 1781, David Frazer of Lebanon Township in northern Hunterdon County declined to purchase a slave from John Stevens because he had heard "that he is not only Sausy, and Idle, but that he has taken even your Sleigh, and Horses, without your leave or knowledge, and used them where and when he pleased, . . . I could expect no better usage from him, which would by no means suit me as I would be obliged to put all my Farming, Horses &c under his care, and am so Sickly myself that I cannot anser almost any of my business as I ought to do."[35]

Theophile Cazenove believed that the lack of supervision newly freed blacks enjoyed had harmed their characters and made them poor farmers. "You do not see one out of a hundred . . . that can make a comfortable living, own a cow, a horse," he wrote in 1794; "they remain in their cabins where they live miserably, barely raise some corn, but do not rise to anything, are worse off than when they were slaves, although the race is open to them the same as to white people." But clearly, the race did not take place on a level course, as Cazenove's own wage data makes clear. On farms around Newark at harvest time, a white worker could demand five shillings per day in 1794; in present-day Chester, Morris County, harvest workers could earn six shillings a day. But around Morristown, free black males were paid only three shillings a day during the summer, and black women could command only four shillings per week. And in Eastern Precinct (Franklin Township), Somerset County, white laborers earned more in the winter of 1775–76 than a slave hired from his owner (table 13).

By Old World standards, American labor was generally considered to be well paid. "Working people of all kinds in this country are all paid well and all people are upon a level," the itinerant millwright Thomas Capner wrote to his English sister in 1795 from Hunterdon County. "These people seem to doubt my veracity when I tell them a labourer at sometimes in England works a whole week for a bushel of wheat." Capner valued wheat in Hunterdon County at from ten to fourteen shillings per bushel and laborers at eighteen to twenty-seven shillings for a six-day week.[36] Thus, laborers in Hunterdon County were paid almost double the going rate in England at that time.

Still, the wages paid agricultural workers varied greatly by season, region, race, and through time. In the New England-settled area of East New Jersey, workers in densely settled Newark Township engaged in various commercial and industrial activities as well as in agriculture, while Warren Township (Somerset County) was far more rural (table 14).[37] In 1753 and 1754, cutting wood in the winter brought only three shillings per day in Newark, but cradling wheat during the peak of the harvest (July 26) brought a daily wage of five shillings. The four-shilling rate on July 12 for cradling wheat suggests that the higher wage two weeks later reflected a sense of urgency in getting the crop in, perhaps after a spell of inclement weather. Similarly, the six-shilling rate (August 30) for cradling buckwheat, a crop of relatively low value, must reflect extraordinary circumstances.

Generally, in the 1750s a day of agricultural labor brought from £0.3.0 to 0.3.6 in Newark, and in the next decade, perhaps due to the effects of the Seven Years' War, the average daily wage rose to 0.4.0. Rates during the harvests continued to

Table 13
Wages of Labor, in Shillings and Pence,
Selected New Jersey Locations, 1748–1816

Date	Location	Type		Rate
1748—Sept.	Near Phila.	Various		2/6–3/0 day
1755—Oct. 30	Lower Twp.	Various	30/0 mo.	2/0 day
1764—Mar. 12	Bedminster Twp.	Various	40/0 mo.	1/8 day
1770—Growing Season	Bedminster	Various	30/0 mo.	1/3 day
1774—May	Bedminster Twp.	Various	37/2 mo.	1/6 day
1775—Dec.	Franklin Twp.	Slave	25/0 mo.	1/.5 day
1776—Feb.	Franklin Twp.	White	40/0 mo.	1/8 day
1778—Apr.	Alexandria Twp.	Various		2/6 day
		Cleaning Lime Kiln		3/9 day
1779—Summer	Middletown Twp.	Various		4/6 day
1780—Summer	Middletown Twp.	Various		4/3 day
1781—Summer	Middletown Twp.	Various		4/3 day
1782—Summer	Middletown Twp.	Various		5/0 day
1788—Summer	Egg Harbor Twp.	Tending Corn		4/6 day
1788—Summer	Egg Harbor Twp.	Carpentry		5/0 day
1789—Summer	Egg Harbor Twp.	Various		2/6 day
1789—July	Egg Harbor Twp.	Reaping		3/0 day
1789—Summer	Egg Harbor Twp.	Sprouting and Grubbing		3/5 day
1791–1794—Winter	Chesterfield Twp.	Various		2/0 day
1794—Harvest	North Jersey	Various	£30–40 yr.	5/0 day
—Spring				3/0–4/0 day
		18–25 yr. slave		£100
1794—Harvest	Chester	Various		6/0 day
—Growing Season				4/0 day
—October				3/0 day
—Summer		Free Black	60/0 mo.	3/0 day
1794—Winter	Morristown	Various		4/0 day
		Carpentry		6/0–7/0 day
		Masonry		8/0 day
1795—Year	Hunterdon Co.	Various		3/0–4/6 day
		Carpentry		5/0–7/6 day
		Masonry		6/5–7/6 day
		Millwrighting		6/5–10/0 day
1796—Winter	Elizabethtown	Fence Mending		6/0 day
1796—May	Elizabethtown	Various		7/0 day
1796—Harvest	Elizabethtown	Harvesting		9/5 day
1802—July 14	Franklin Twp.	Harvesting		10/0 day
1802—July 26	Franklin Twp.	Work at Flax		3/0 day
1802—Oct. 7	Franklin Twp.	Work at Buckwheat		3/0 day
1806—Summer	Newark Twp.	Hoeing Broom Corn		8/0 day
1807—Dec. 19	Knowlton Twp.	Dressing Flax		3/0 day
1808—Sept. 5	Knowlton Twp.	Threshing Rye		4/0 day
1810—July 14	Knowlton Twp.	Mowing, Making Hay		5/0 day
1811—Oct. 14	Knowlton Twp.	Husking Corn		3/0 day
1812—July	Knowlton Twp.	Various		4/6 day
1813—June 4	Knowlton Twp.	Threshing Oats		3/0 day
1814—July 25	Knowlton Twp.	Pulling Flax		7/6 day
1814—Aug. 17	Knowlton Twp.	Loading Dung, Threshing Flax		5/7 day
1816—July 3	Knowlton Twp.	Raking Clover		5/6 day

Table 14
Wages of Labor, in Shillings and Pence,
Newark Township and Warren Township, 1753–1803

Date	Location	Type	Rate
1753—May 10	Newark Twp.	Covering Corn	3/6 day
1753—June	Newark Typ.	Hoeing Corn	3/6 day
1753—July 12	Newark Twp.	Cradling Wheat	4/0 day
1753—July 13	Newark Twp.	Taking Up Wheat	3/0 day
1753—July 26	Newark Twp.	Cradling Wheat	5/0 day
1753—Aug. 30	Newark Twp.	Cradling Buckwheat	6/0 day
1753—Oct. 6	Newark Twp.	Threshing Buckwheat	3/6 day
1753—Dec.	Newark Twp.	Cutting Wood	3/6 day
1754—Jan.	Newark Twp.	Cutting Wood	3/0 day
1754—Mar. 16	Newark Twp.	Pruning	4/0 day
1754—Oct.	Newark Twp.	Gathering Corn	3/6 day
1754—Nov.	Newark Twp.	Moving Fence	3/6 day
1755—May	Newark Twp.	Hoeing Corn	3/6 day
1755—Sept. 20	Newark Twp.	Gathering Corn	3/0 day
1760—Sept. 20	Newark Twp.	Making Hay	4/0 day
1761—June 8	Newark Twp.	"Work"	4/0 day
1762—Jan. 3	Newark Twp.	Work on Road	4/0 day
1762—Oct. 12	Newark Twp.	Threshing	4/0 day
1762—Dec. 18	Newark Twp.	Sawing Staves	4/0 day
1763—Feb. 24	Newark Twp.	Fanning Wheat	5/6 day
1763—Mar. 1	Newark Twp.	Cutting Logs	4/0 day
1763—Mar. 31	Newark Twp.	"Work"	3/9 day
1763—April 1	Newark Twp.	Carting Dung	5/0 day
1763—June	Newark Twp.	Hoeing Corn	4/6 day
1763—Aug.	Newark Twp.	Cutting Oats	6/6 day
1763—Aug. 31	Newark Twp.	Mowing in Salt Meadow	5/6 day
1763—Sept.	Newark Twp.	Work in Meadow	4/9 day
1763—Nov. 26	Newark Twp.	Sawmill Op.	5/6 day
1763—Dec.	Newark Twp.	Taking Up Flax	4/0 day
1764—Feb. 6	Newark Twp.	Cutting Timber	4/0 day
1764—June	Newark Twp.	Breaking Stones	7/0 day
1765—Apr.	Newark Twp.	Breaking Stones	6/6 day
1765—May 16	Newark Twp.	Covering Corn	4/0 day
1765—Sept. 11	Newark Twp.	Cider Mill Op.	5/9 day
1766—Aug.	Newark Twp.	Household (Female)	4/6 day
1766—Dec. 11	Newark Twp.	Butchering	5/0 day
1770—Jan. 29	Newark Twp.	Cutting Timber	4/6 day
1771—Oct. 2	Newark Twp.	Cider Mill Op.	5/0 day
1772—June 22	Newark Twp.	Breaking Stones	6/0 day
1774—June 4	Newark Twp.	Hoeing Corn	4/4 day
1774—July	Newark Twp.	Harvesting	6/0 day
1775—Feb. 16	Newark Twp.	Cutting Wood	3/5 day
1775—June 22	Newark Twp.	Haying	5/0 day
1776—May 29	Newark Twp.	Shearing Sheep	4/0 day
1790—July	Warren Twp.	Ditching	5/0 day
1790—July 27	Warren Twp.	Harvesting	7/5 day
1790—Aug. 15	Warren Twp.	Mowing	4/6 day
1790—Oct. 15	Warren Twp.	Digging Potatoes	3/6 day
1790—Oct. 16	Warren Twp.	Threshing	3/6 day
1790—Nov. 11	Warren Twp.	Husking Corn	3/6 day
1791—Sept. 18	Warren Twp.	At Corn	3/0 day

Table 14 (cont.)
Wages of Labor, in Shillings and Pence,
Newark Township and Warren Township, 1753–1803

Date	Location	Type	Rate
1791—Oct. 19	Warren Twp.	Threshing	3/0 day
1972—Aug. 31	Warren Twp.	Masonry	7/0 day
1792—Sept. 30	Warren Twp.	Harrowing	3/6 day
1793—July 5	Warren Twp.	Mowing & Cradling	5/0 day
1793—July	Warren Twp.	Harvesting	6/0 day
1793—Nov. 18	Warren Twp.	Killing Hogs & Hauling Stalks	3/3 day
1793—Nov. 25	Warren Twp.	Taking Up Flax	3/0 day
1794—Dec.	Newark Twp.	Sawmill Op.	80/0 month (about 3/4 day)
1795—Oct. 18	Warren Twp.	Masonry	8/0 day
1799—June 15	Warren Twp.	Carpentry	6/0 day
1800—Mar. 8	Warren Twp.	"Work"	40/0 month (about 1/8 day)
1801—Mar. 13	Warren Twp.	Carpentry	8/0 day
1801—June 22	Warren Twp.	Planting	4/6 day
1803—Nov. 14	Warren Twp.	Work at Corn	4/0 day

be higher, and more difficult or onerous tasks also brought greater rewards. A worker carting dung in April 1763 earned 0.5.0 a day; another breaking stones (probably quarrying brownstone) in June 1764 earned a daily wage of 0.7.0. Taking on non-agricultural work in the off-season certainly brought greater returns: on November 26, 1763, operating a sawmill brought 0.5.6 a day, compared to 0.4.0 for gathering the flax crop in December. Such distinctions in wage rates also characterized the 1770s in Newark Township.

The record for Warren Township dates from the 1790s, and even at that later date ordinary daily agricultural wages were lower than in Newark Township in the 1750s and 1760s. Typical daily wages in Warren Township appear to have ranged from 0.3.0 to 0.3.6. Harvesting brought up to 0.7.6 a day; at that time, the standard daily wage for a mason was 0.7.0. In Newark Township during the winter of 1794–95, long-term employment at a sawmill brought only about 0.3.4 a day, but for the great majority of workers, unemployed or employed only irregularly during the agricultural off season, such a daily wage would probably have looked very good.

More scattered data on wages in New Jersey between 1748 and 1816, a useful benchmark for measuring contemporary prices for land, produce, and other items, indicate that these trends prevailed generally through the state (see table 13).[38] As in Newark and Warren townships, the cost of agricultural labor varied with the season; workers received the highest wages during the July harvest of such winter grains as wheat and rye and the early fall harvest of summer grains such as corn. In 1788, William Canniday paid £3.3.0 to Richard and Constant Somers for "14 days tending corn at Long Point," probably near Great Egg Harbor.[39] Lengthy periods of hire, including during the off-season, brought proportionately lower compensation on a daily basis partly because men who were employed for long terms probably lived on the employer's farm and were supplied with their daily sustenance.

The type of labor also affected price. More skilled labor was more highly paid, and heavier or more unattractive tasks also appear to have been compensated somewhat better. In 1789, one man at Somers Point on Great Egg Harbor in the Outer Coastal Plain was paid 0.2.6 for sundry agricultural work, 0.3.0 during harvest, and 0.3.5 for "grubbing."[40] In 1778, James Parker paid the "lime burner" John Whiting £4.17.6 for laying limestone in his kiln and firing it; over the course of that year, he agreed to pay Whiting twenty-six dollars (probably at 0.7.6 to the dollar, or £9.15.0). For fourteen days of other work around the farm Whiting received 0.2.6 per day and for emptying the kiln 0.3.9 per day.[41]

Wage rates were probably also affected by periodic labor scarcity, induced on some occasions by the absence of men with military commitments. This scarcity must have been especially pronounced in southwestern New Jersey, which so greatly relied on hired white farm workers. Samuel Allinson of Burlington wrote to his uncle in England about this problem on June 26, 1761, as the winter grain harvest approached. "The prosecutn of the present [French and Indian] war has Stript the Country very much of Its Laborers," he wrote, "which Lays some Farmers under great Difficulties & subjects them to loss at this annl Season wch is now very near."[42]

There also appears to have been a rural-urban differential in wage rates, as the data from Newark and Warren townships suggests. Wages in Newark Township in 1806 were higher than in Knowlton Township, Sussex County, from 1807 on. Similarly, wages in "urban" Elizabethtown in 1794–96 were higher than they were in the interior of northern New Jersey, but rapidly increasing grain prices at that time may have stimulated atypically high rates. Clearly, there was greater competition for labor in densely settled places. An unskilled, landless man in the more rural areas could work at lumbering or could hunt and fish in the earlier years of settlement, but with the deforestation of better soils, agricultural employment was often the only work available.

The numerous letters written back to England in the 1790s by the Scott Family, who had settled at Elizabethtown, offer a closer view of wages in densely settled Essex County. Gavin Scott paid 0.6.0 a day for off-season labor, such as mending fences, and 0.9.6 (or $1.25) for work during the harvest. These rates were high, but they were evidently not sufficient. "A man here that works for Days wages does well in summer," Thomas Mather, Scott's relative, wrote to his brother in England to discourage him from emigrating in July 1798, "but the winter eats up all as there is so Little to do every farmer does the Little of work there is to do himself."[43]

Agricultural laborers often sought long-term commitments from local farmers to ensure regular employment. For many relatively impecunious farmers with several sons, hiring one or more of them out was a welcome source of additional support. On March 12, 1764, just as the agricultural season was beginning, Guisbert Sutphen of Bedminster Township, Somerset County, hired the son of a neighbor.

William Wortman Hired to me his Son William Wortman being a grade for between ous some time afore but Intered at this Date for a Year if we both Likes onen other after the first siks months Expired and Et Dont Sute me ane Longer then I am to Give hem forty shillen per month but Ef I Chuse to Ciep him a hole Yeare I am to Give him Eighteen pound in mony and to find hem In Shouse for his whare Conieneweng hies Yeare and to Give hem up that Note of Eleven shillen that Thomas Jouns has[44]

Sutphen let Wortman go six months later with a pair of trousers, a shirt, two pairs of shoes, and the redemption of a note he owed in the amount of 0.11.6. Wortman went home with £9.9.9 on October 12, 1764.

Five years later, Sutphen hired "Hue Sotten" for six months. In April, during his first week, Sotten lost half a day "to Cote firewode to your self," which suggests that he may have been a local man who was cutting wood for his family: that Sotten was married is clear from Sutphen's note that he had paid 0.8.0 "for a pare of Shuse for your wife." Sutphen housed Sotten—the man "moved In the House" on April 10— but Sotten received no pay soon afterward for a "black day" (a term used throughout New Jersey to indicate a day lost to an employer and for which a laborer received no pay) Sotton used "to plant your Corn." That Sotten was planting corn certainly suggests that he was local. Sotten also lost time for plowing his corn and for attending "at John phenix stone frolick."

That some hired hands must have been true unfortunates is apparent from the account book of Frederick Van Lieuw, who lived in what is now Franklin Township, Somerset County.[45] Van Lieuw hired one "Eastor Horn" periodically from 1769 to 1771. When he hired Horn January 1769, he apparently paid him with clothing for him and his wife. On June 28, 1770, Horn was "taken Sick with the fits"; Van Lieuw calculated that "this Sickness and Sickness in the spring and Lost Days in all Makes one Munt." Again on July 30, Horn was "taken Sick with another Spel of fits Lasted a half a mont," an illness so serious that Van Lieuw paid a physician fifteen shillings to attend Horn the next month and another fourteen shillings "for the Second Spel of Sickness" later. On February 24, 1771, Horn left Van Lieuw's employ, and he was paid a mere ten shillings, the money remaining after all of his expenses were deducted from his wages.

Van Lieuw had a more favorable experience with a weaver named John Fonck, to whom he rented a house for one year in 1768. Fonck was "to have prevelidge of the house and a Spot of Ground for a Gardain twoo Couws and one horse in the pastor and wood for one fire." Fonck and his wife paid part of their account with Van Lieuw with the products of their labor, and they also bought some of his produce—turnips, hay, tallow, beef, buckwheat, wool, and flax. They paid, partly with a hog and a cowhide, an extra 0.9.3 to pasture a cow for three months and three weeks. There is no evidence that Fonck did farm work for Van Lieuw, but he clearly had his own small farm on the land. Wages too were often paid in kind. In June 1778, James Parker paid his lime burner partly with cash and partly with a draft for wheat to be retrieved from another man with whom Parker had dealings. He paid the lime burning crew with three bottles of whiskey, and in November that year he paid one of his seasonal laborers in buckwheat. The next year, Parker, who had agreed to pay the lime burner thirty shillings for each kiln burned, compensated him with ten pounds of wool and four bushels of wheat.[46]

Cazenove suggested that small farmers hired themselves out to larger landholders. According to Cazenove, the owner of one 1,650-acre tract on the poor, glaciated soils of northeastern Morris County could not find workmen and so hired local farmers to "go shares in hay-making" so that he could get his lands cut. These small farmers must have preferred working for hay for their own stock, rather than for cash.

But, as Thomas Mather noted, many small farmers got around the high cost and relative unreliability of labor by doing the work themselves, as one man near Rocky Hill, north of Princeton, told Johannes Schoepf in 1783. "I am a weaver, a shoemaker, farrier, wheelwright, farmer, gardner, and when it can't be helped, a soldier. I bake my bread, brew my beer, kill my pigs; I grind my axe and knives; I built those stalls and that shed there; I am barber, leech, and doctor." Schoepf declared that the man "could do anything, as indeed the countryman in America generally can, himself supplying his own wants in great part or wholly."[47]

Small farmers also relied on "frolics" to get things done at relatively little cost. Frolics, popular in the New England-settled area and in the northwest, pooled neighbors to accomplish such labor-intensive tasks as getting wood for buildings, raising houses and barns, plowing, and, among women, seasonal sewing.[48] In 1788, Ann Capnerhurst near Flemington in Hunterdon County wrote her sister that "frolics appear to me to have been very necessary in a new settled country"; even the search for the body of a young man who had drowned was so organized. "In the morning, as all extraordinary things here are done by frolic, so was the search for the corps," Capnerhurst wrote.[49]

A farmer and his wife generally provided food and drink at the end of each day during a frolic for the farm laborers who attended. Some, including Hue Sotton, worked at frolics while technically employed elsewhere and thus were docked for "black days." Between May 10 and December 14, 1813, Jesse Knowles in Knowlton, Sussex County, recorded that his employee Jacob Lance lost time for "Regiment training," "raising Saml Dilts mill," "Masonic meeting," "mowing clover for Lanning," "John Dilts flax frolick," "Lannings mowing frolick," "Jacob Raub's mowing frolick," "Peter Freas's (at dung)," "John Dilt's dung frolick," "Stouts husling match," "Samuel Dilts dam," and "drawing loggs."[50] Lance's peregrinations not only suggest that he was relatively gregarious and footloose but that his arrangement with Knowles was quite flexible. Lance was thus probably not a married man (householder).

Just as the size of landholdings, the form of tenure, and the availability and compensation of labor varied greatly from place to place and through time, so too did the types of farms. Rutherfurd described the typical farm in 1786 to have been from fifty to four hundred acres. Its arable land was laid out in four fields rotated every four years: in the first year, summer crops such as corn, oats, flax, and buckwheat were planted; in the second year, the field lay fallow; in the third year it was put to wheat and rye, and in the fourth year to grass.[51] Agreements between landlords and tenants universally stipulated that tenants on newly settled farms were to clear and fence several different fields, which suggests that while not everyone rotated crops in this way, the ideal was to divide one's farm into several fields, separated by fences.[52] Rutherfurd described each farm as having an orchard, a piece of natural meadow, and a parcel amounting to about one-quarter of the tract that was wooded to supply fencing, firewood, and other necessities. That Rutherfurd was describing an ideal farm is clear from data that show the amount of wooded land to have varied tremendously from place to place and that such features as orchards were also valued differently.

The gentleman's farm or seat probably best typifies what a New Jersey farm was supposed to be. Before the Revolution, such estates were most apt to be situated within a reasonable distance of Burlington and Perth Amboy because the men who possessed enough wealth to create them were often also involved in politics and needed to be near the provincial capital.[53] Moreover, because both capitals were convenient by water routes to New York and Philadelphia, farms near them were in a favorable market position. Because gentlemen farmers were the primary agricultural innovators, they also valued a location on good soils, and they sought as well a pleasant location and a view, or prospect. Thus, gentlemen's seats tended to be found in the Delaware Valley, mostly between Burlington and Trenton, the Raritan Valley between Perth Amboy and a little upstream of New Brunswick, around Elizabethtown, and in the Passaic Valley a little upstream of Newark. Others were near Princeton and in fertile Hunterdon County in central New Jersey.

Gentlemen's seats in these areas no doubt helped earn the colony the label "the garden of North America," assigned it by Andrew Burnaby in 1759.[54] As he traveled up the Raritan Valley from New Brunswick, Burnaby noted that "the country I passed through is exceedingly rich and beautiful and the banks of the river are covered with gentlemen's houses. At one of these I had an opportunity of seeing some good portraits of Vandyck, and several other small Dutch paintings."[55] Another estate on the Raritan was that of Edward Antill, who had inherited a great deal from his father, a New York merchant.[56] Antill devoted himself to agricultural experimentation and to disseminating this knowledge among his neighbors and acquaintances. When his estate came up for sale in 1772, two years after his death, it consisted of 336 acres, of which 63 were improved meadow ground lying between the house and the river.[57] Woodland took up 70 acres, not quite the one-quarter of the total that Rutherfurd advocated. But 70 acres was a goodly amount for the lower Raritan Valley at that time, given the fact that the College of New Jersey had declined to locate in New Brunswick a few years before because of the paucity of woodland.

The remaining 203 acres of Antill's estate were cleared for cultivation. Ten of these cleared acres were devoted to an orchard containing many exotic fruit trees. Antill had also planted an extensive vineyard on the slope leading down to the river, for which he had won a prize from the London-based Society for Promoting Arts and Agriculture. Other sources document that Antill raised potatoes, hogs, and cattle.

The advertisement pointed out that Antill's estate was only about thirty miles from New York and within half a mile of "several Gentlemens Seats." From the house, "an excellent well-built Brick House" fifty-six by forty-two feet with a large central hall, "a most pleasing Prospect presents itself to View." Other structures on the property included a new barn, a coach house, a fowl house, and other "convenient Buildings" including a brew house adjoining the site that was to be sold or leased separately.

Gentlemen's seats were often assembled from several smaller properties. Governor William Franklin's estate of six hundred acres on the Rancocas between Burlington and Mount Holly was originally two large farms and one small one.[58] Franklin placed the property on the market in 1774 when he moved to Perth Amboy, where the proprietors had erected a house for him. The advertisement noted that "two good farmhouses and two small tenements," the latter presumably for landless white laborers and their families, were on the property; one of the farmhouses "stands on a fine healthy spot . . . has been lately enlarged, new roofed, and put into thorough repair."

Even though there was no impressive dwelling on the tract, the property was described as making "an elegant COUNTRY SEAT for a Gentleman who chooses retirement." It had a "fine situation for a mansion-house, with a Park containing about 175 acres, in which there are between 30 and 40 deer." Also, there were "several pleasant shady walks, particularly in a young grove of pines, where many more might be made at small expence." Though the number of fields into which the estate was divided was not specified, the notice stated that nearly twenty thousand cedar rails were "in good fence" and divided the tract "into proper fields." There was a large range for young cattle, several fields of upland meadow, about thirty acres of meadow that had been double banked, an orchard, a garden, and a fish pond. There was also a dairy, stables, a barn, stalls, and sheds for cattle.

The brief descriptions of farms often advertised in the newspapers of the day make it clear that many in New Jersey had numerous enclosed fields and that in most places arable land predominated over the use of land for pasture and meadow, which were on the better-watered parts of the property. The areas on a farm devoted to grass were primarily of two types, pasture for grazing animals, to keep them healthy or to fatten them for slaughter, and meadow or mowing land that produced hay for stock that had not been slaughtered and would be kept in stalls through the winter. Pastures were also established to serve the animals of those who owned no land or were traveling through. The Swedish Pastor Sandel recorded catching a boat for New York from Elizabethtown on September 16, 1703, and leaving his party's horses "with a man who was to graze them in his pasture ground. There are people who always have such pasture grounds in readiness for strangers and who charge not more than 2 shillings a week for each horse."[59] In 1773, Dr. John Cardy owed Grant Gibbon of Salem £1.5.0 for pasturing his horse at Cape May for ten weeks.[60] In the New England-settled section, meadows were widely separated because of the region's method of land allocation, and many small farmers who could not afford their own wagons paid to have hay hauled to their barns.[61] Most Englishmen kept their hay in "cocks" until it could be stored in a barn, while the Dutch used a moveable-roofed structure called a hay barrack.[62]

Gardens, orchards, and activities demanding everyday surveillance were typically located near the house, which itself was built on a rise to permit good drainage and a view of as much of the land as possible. Gardens for kitchen use and for ornament were established very early on. One 1672 account describes how two men vandalized the garden of Richard Michell in Elizabethtown; they "plucked up the pallasades of the garden, and before I came, the hoggs, within an hours tyme had rooted up and Spoiled all that was in the garden, which was full of necessary garden herbs."[63] In 1698, Gabriel Thomas described the much more opulent garden of John Tateham, a wealthy resident of Burlington, as containing a "variety of Fruits, Herbs, and Flowers; as Roses, Tulips, July-Flowers, Sun-Flowers (that open and shut as the Sun Rises and Sets, thence taking their Name), Carnations, and many more; besides abundance of Medicinal Roots Herbs, Plants, and Flowers, found wild in the Fields."[64] In his 1759 travel narrative, Andrew Burnaby made note of the unusual garden—apparently at least partly glassed in—kept by Colonel Peter Schuyler, who resided north of Newark. It featured, Burnaby wrote, "a very large collection of citrons, oranges, limes, lemons, balsams of Peru, aloes, pomegranates, and other tropical plants."[65]

Kitchen gardens mentioned in advertisements were often described as being "paled"—that is, surrounded by a paling fence. Such gardens were widely distributed through the state, except, perhaps, in the Dutch-settled northeast (map 17). In 1776, one 166-acre farm in Amwell Township was advertised to include "an excellent kitchen garden handsomely fenced with new pales last spring."[66] In 1786, John Rutherfurd noted how New Jersey women were commonly responsible for this part of the farm. "All of them make good Gardens of a variety of good Vegetables," he wrote, "which is half the support of their Families."[67]

Alice Manning's study of nineteenth-century farmsteads on the Inner Coastal Plain—properties that often had eighteenth-century origins—suggests the norm for an earlier period.[68] Farmhouses were most often at the top of a rise for the view, drainage, and water supply, were generally oriented toward the south, southeast, or southwest to take advantage of solar heating, and were usually located from one hundred to more than eight hundred feet from through roads. Today, many surviving eighteenth-century dwellings front immediately on older roads or are within a very short distance of them. Manning also found that most eighteenth-century barns were located behind or beside the farmhouse, and a little more than half the Inner Coastal Plain farmsteads were organized around an open courtyard. Apparently also of eighteenth-century origin, this plan was popular in the nineteenth century as well. According to Manning, the literature in the later nineteenth century specified that the barn was to be near the house and near a water source so that farmers wasted no time driving the cattle to a remote location. Other outbuildings were to be placed near the barn but separated from it to reduce the possibility of damage from fire. The layout of the entire farm was to emphasize easy and direct access and reduce long hauls. The Passaic farm was organized in much this way.

The farms Manning surveyed were prosperous, and thus neither they, most real property sale notices, and descriptions of country estates provide a direct glimpse of the properties of marginal farmers. Cazenove described farmers living in "miserable huts" near Springfield in 1794; other observers described the "rock farms" in the glaciated Highlands begun by those who

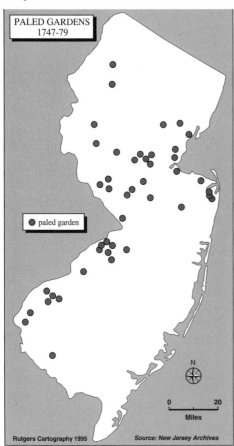

MAP 17

could not afford to go elsewhere.[69] Still, descriptions such as those of Manning or Rutherfurd would probably have applied in a very general way to many farms in New Jersey.

Notes

1. Rutherfurd, "Notes on the State."

2. Lewis Morris quoted in *Docs. Rel. N.J.*, 6:1030.

3. Dennis Ryan, "Six Towns: Continuity and Change in Revolutionary New Jersey" (Ph.D. diss., New York University, 1974), 459.

4. "Tracts of Land Belonging to Eliphalet Johnson in Newark by Patent, January 18, 1697," Lindsley Family Papers, Free Public Library of Morristown and Morris Township, Morristown, N.J.

5. "Tax List of the Lower Division of Gloucester County, 1687," *The Genealogical Magazine of New Jersey* 53 (1938): 10–12.

6. "A Copy of the Minute Book of Nottingham Township," *Proc. N.J.H.S.* 58 (1940): 22–38.

7. The advertisements were reprinted in *Docs. Rel. N.J.* The time periods chosen for the tables demarcate the time during which county boundaries remained the same. As many more advertisements appeared as the density of population increased, only every fifth advertisement was used for the second table. In each, a 20 percent sample is analyzed.

8. This is abundantly clear from the records and correspondence of major landowners and their agents. See, for example, the Race-Emley Papers, Hunterdon County Historical Society.

9. Gary S. Horowitz, "New Jersey Land Riots, 1745–1755" (Ph.D. diss., The Ohio State University, 1966); on unclear property boundaries, see Wacker, *Land and People*, 233 ff.

10. Peter O. Wacker, "The New Jersey Tax Ratable List of 1751," *NJH* 107 (1989): 29–30.

11. On May 23, 1789, Parker wrote that "the lease mentions only 200 acres but that is to lighten the Tax it contains more" and "his lease mentions his place to contain 109$^1/_4$ acres but it contains 209$^1/_4$ This was done to lighten taxes." James Parker Papers, NjHi.

12. "County Tax Ratables, 1772–1822," Division of Archives and Records Management, New Jersey State Library.

13. J.V. Becket, "The Debate Over Farm Sizes in Eighteenth and Nineteenth Century England," *Agricultural History* 57 (1983): 313.

14. Charles S. Grant, *Democracy in the Connecticut Frontier Town of Kent* (New York, 1961), 32–33; Kenneth A. Lockridge, "Land, Population, and the Evolution of New England Society, 1630–1790" *Past and Present* 39 (1968): 67.

15. Lemon, *Best Poor Man's Country*, 89–91.

16. Rutherfurd, "Notes on the State," 84; Kelsey, *Cazenove Journal*, 2.

17. Rutherfurd, "Notes on the State," 84.

18. Mark Lender, "The Enlisted Line: The Continental Soldiers of New Jersey" (Ph.D. diss., Rutgers University, 1975), 7.

19. Woodward, *Ploughs and Politicks*, 229.

20. Peter O. Wacker, "The Changing Geography of the Afro-American Population of New Jersey, 1726-1860," in *Pattern and Process: Research in Historical Geography*, ed. Ralph E. Ehrenberg (Washington, D.C., 1975), 42–43.

21. James Parker Diary, NjHi.

22. Peter O. Wacker, "The Changing Geography of the Black Population of New Jersey: A Preliminary View," *Proceedings of the Association of American Geographers* 3 (1971): 176.

23. Wacker, *Land and People*, 194.

24. Kelsey, *Cazenove Journal*, 17. Historian Hubert Schmidt also believed that there were large numbers of such servants in Hunterdon County. See *Rural Hunterdon*, 68. Not until 1790 did censuses distinguish free from enslaved blacks.

25. Wacker, *Land and People*, 415.

26. Ibid., 137.

27. Ibid., 415.

28. "Potential" labor is used because it is impossible to determine if the available people actually

worked at agricultural tasks.

29. Wacker, *Land and People,* 138.

30. Kenneth Roberts and Anna M. Roberts, ed. and trans., *Moreau de St. Mery's American Journal* (Garden City, N.Y., 1947), 113.

31. Jacob Spicer Diary, NjHi.

32. Jonathan Holmes Diary, Holmes Papers, NjHi.

33. James Parker to Robert Emley, May 7, 1763, Race-Emley Papers, Hunterdon County Historical Society.

34. Lewis Morris to John Morris, April 22, 1730, Morris Papers, NjR. I wish to thank Robert Burnett for this source.

35. David Frazer to John Stevens, March 14, 1781, Stevens Family Papers, NjHi.

36. Thomas Capner to Mary Capnerhurst Exton, January 1, 1795, Capner-Exton-Hill Papers, Hunterdon County Historical Society.

37. Camp Family Record Book, Camp Family Papers, NjHi; Edward F. Randolph Ledger, NjR.

38. The following sources were used to generate typical wage data: Camp Family Record Book, David Camp Day Book A, and Joseph Wheeler Camp Record Book, NjHi; Thomas Capner to Mary Capnerhurst Exton, January 1, 1795, Capner-Exton-Hill Papers, Hunterdon County Historical Society; Kelsey, *Cazenove Journal,* 3, 8, 12; Ellis, "Diary of Jacob Spicer," 115; Samuel Harrison Account Book, NjHi; Accounts of Daniel Hendrickson, Hendrickson Family Papers, NjR; Benson, *Peter Kalm's Travels,* 1:67; Jesses Knowles Account Book, NjHi; Edward F. Randolph Ledger, NjR; Gavin Scott to Mather Scott, June 9, 1796, Scott Family Papers, NjHi; Benjamin Smith Farm Ledger, NjR; Richard and Constant Somers Ledger and Somers Account Book, Glassboro State College; Spicer Diary, 115, NjHi; Guisbert Sutphen Account Books, NjHi; and Account Books of Johannes Van Liew, Van Liew Papers, New Jersey State Library. I wish to thank William Wright for bringing this last source to my attention.

39. Richard and Constant Somers Ledger A, Job Point Store, Stewart Collection, Savitz Library, Glassboro State College.

40. Somers Account Book, Savitz Library, Glassboro State College.

41. Parker Diary, James Parker Papers, NjHi.

42. As quoted in Woodward, *Ploughs and Politicks,* 144.

43. Thomas Mather to his brother, July 1798, Scott Family Papers, NjHi.

44. Guisbert Sutphen Account Books, NjHi.

45. Van Lieuw Family Papers, New Jersey State Library.

46. Parker Diary, NjHi.

47. Schoepf, *Travels,* 1:30.

48. See, for example, Burnett and Hutchinson, "Marginal Jottings," 156, 170, 172, 173; and Schmidt, *Rural Hunterdon,* 80. 81, 248, 258, 277.

49. Ann Capnerhurst to Mary Exton, August 31, 1787, and May 18, 1788, Capner-Exton-Hill Papers, Hunterdon County Historical Society.

50. Jesse Knowles Account Book, NjHi.

51. Rutherfurd, "Notes on the State," 81.

52. See, for example, the Stevens Family Papers, NjHi.

53. Thomas L. Purvis, *Proprietors, Patronage and Paper Money: Legislative Politics in New Jersey, 1703–1776* (New Brunswick, N.J., 1986), 237.

54. Andrew Burnaby, *Travels through the Middle Settlements in North America in the Years 1759 and 1760* (Ithaca, N.Y., 1963), 73.

55. Burnaby, *Travels,* 104.

56. William Nelson, *Edward Antill, A New York Merchant of the Seventeenth Century, and His Descendants* (Paterson, N.J., 1899), 311n.

57. *Docs. Rel. N.J.,* 28:311.

58. *Docs. Rel. N.J.,* 29:226–27.

59. "Archivum Americanum," Upsal Documents Relating to the Swedish Churches on the Delaware transcribed and translated from documents held in the Consistory of Upsal in Sweden for C.J. Stille under the supervision of Col. Elfving and Dr. Wuselgrin, 1891, 1:120, Historical Society of Pennsylvania.

60. Grant Gibbon Store Ledger, Salem, New Jersey, 1764–1778, Loose Paper, Sinclair Collection, Alexander Library, NjR.

61. See, for example, Camp Family Record Book, August 7 and October 18, 1755, NjHi.

62. Hans Kurath, *A Word Geography of the Eastern United States* (Ann Arbor, 1949), 54; Peter O. Wacker, "Folk Architecture as an Indicator of Culture Areas and Cultural Diffusion: Dutch Barns and Barracks in New Jersey," *Pioneer America* 5 (July 1974): 38.

63. *Docs. Rel. N.J.*, 1st ser., 1:85.

64. Gabriel Thomas, *An Account of Pennsylvania and West New Jersey* (Cleveland, Ohio, 1903), 346.

65. Burnaby, *Travels*, 107.

66. *Docs. Rel. N.J.*, 2d ser., 1:13.

67. Rutherfurd, "Notes on the State," 85.

68. Alice E. Manning, "19th Century Farmsteads on the Inner Coastal Plain of New Jersey," Office of New Jersey Heritage, Department of Environmental Protection, Trenton, New Jersey. I am indebted to Olga Chesler for bringing this source to my attention.

69. Kelsey, *Cazenove Journal*, 2; Muntz, "Changing Geography of New Jersey Woodlands," 81.

CHAPTER 3

DRAINAGE, IRRIGATION, AND SOIL ENHANCEMENT

"This state has all the varieties of soil from the worst to the best kind," Jedediah Morse wrote of New Jersey in his *American Geography* of 1789.[1] Though Morse was surely unaware of the reason for this variation at the time, remote geological events had indeed wrought great differences in the parent materials of New Jersey soils, and early settlers were clearly drawn to those accessible areas whose soils they believed would provide the highest yields.

New Jersey's best soils are on the Inner Coastal Plain, the eastern part of the Piedmont, and in the limestone-floored valley of the Musconetcong south of the Wisconsin terminal moraine (map 18).[2] The poorest soils covered much of the Outer Coastal Plain, the Highlands north of the terminal moraine, the bed of glacial Lake Passaic (Great Swamp), a portion of the Piedmont on the Hunterdon Plateau, the Palisades, and the Kittatinny Ridge.

Soils were fair to good in a contiguous belt running from the southwest through the western Piedmont and fair to poor on the margins of the Outer Coastal Plain, on marine terraces formed during the Pleistocene Era such as Cape May.

A systematic evaluation of New Jersey lands for tax purposes in the records of the General Assembly for January 1752 appears to reflect legislators' perceptions of the inherent fertility of the soil, as well as, probably, the effect that development and location near the markets of Phila-

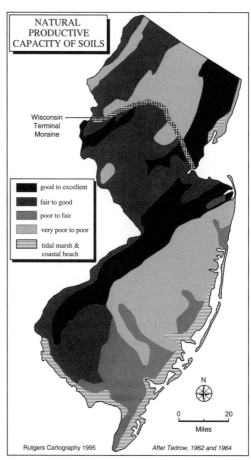

NATURAL PRODUCTIVE CAPACITY OF SOILS

Wisconsin Terminal Moraine

good to excellent
fair to good
poor to fair
very poor to poor
tidal marsh & coastal beach

N

0   20
Miles

Rutgers Cartography 1995   After Tedrow, 1962 and 1964

MAP 18

delphia and New York had on land values (table 15).[3] Assembly members ranked the Piedmont and Inner Coastal Plain counties highest in the value of their soils; long-settled Cape May, on the better soils of the Outer Coastal Plain, was assessed at only half that value. Bergen and Gloucester counties, which lie close to New York and Philadelphia, were not ranked as highly as other Piedmont and Inner Coastal Plain counties, so perceived soil fertility must have accounted for the difference; the lower values for Hunterdon and Morris counties may have been a function both of their recent settlement and their locational disadvantage. The soils of Cumberland County, also just beginning to be settled, were perceived to be poor.

The only other contemporary references to soil fertility in New Jersey were real estate advertisements (which were apt to overstate the case) and the relatively superficial remarks of travelers and official reports. The isochronic map of settlement in the state (see map 2) strongly suggests that settlers understood inherent differences in soil fertility and located their farms in the most accessible areas where the soils were thought to be best for agriculture; these areas, including those on the Piedmont and the Inner Coastal Plain, filled up rapidly. Then, in the less accessible northwest, the Musconetcong Valley was settled, and as late as 1765 the Outer Coastal Plain was settled for most part only on its better soils; there, maritime activities and lumbering were of paramount importance, and lumbering in most cases did not lead to extensive permanent settlement. Large parts of the Palisades, the Great Swamp, the northern Highlands, and the Kittatinny Ridge remained essentially unoccupied in 1765. The maps of improved land and population density in 1784 tell essentially the same story (see maps 11 and 4).

The sandy loams of the Inner Coastal Plain elicited much comment from the time of the earliest Swedish settlements forward. In their part of the Old World, sandy soils had resulted from glacial outwash and were very poor.[4] Peter Kalm noted, however, that this perception mistook the quality of the soil in this region. In 1748, when he crossed the Delaware from Philadelphia to the New Jersey side, he noted that "the land here is very different from that in Pennsylvania, for here the

Table 15
Valuations on One Hundred Acres of Improved Land,
in Pounds Sterling, by New Jersey County, 1752

County	Highest Value	Lowest Value
Monmouth	45	9
Essex	45	9
Somerset	45	9
Burlington	45	9
Salem	45	9
Middlesex	40	8
Bergen	40	8
Gloucester	40	8
Hunterdon	40	8
Cumberland	30	6
Cape May	20	5
Morris	20	5

ground is almost entirely sand, while in the other province it is mixed with a good deal of clay, and this makes the soil very rich." Kalm went on to say that "one might be led to think that a soil like this in New Jersey could produce nothing, because it is so dry and poor. Yet the corn which is planted on it grows extremely well, and we saw many fields covered with it."[5] Corn, rather than wheat, came to be the major crop here.

Kalm also commented on the characteristic reddish color of the "sometimes rich and sometimes poor" soil of the Piedmont. He thought the material was limestone, but the soils here actually derived from the red Brunswick shale that underlies much of the area. Further on, near New Brunswick, "the ground in general was level, and did not seem everywhere of the richest quality."[6] Kalm's Swedish informants in southern New Jersey, some of them resident for three generations, told him that natural vegetation was a good indicator of soil fertility. In southern New Jersey, for example, the hazel was taken to indicate good soil.[7] Because birch grew on some of his Burlington County lands, Charles Read took the soil to be of a "Cold Nature" (that is, heavy soil that heated slowly in the spring) and so planted several grasses he judged suitable for such areas to see which ones did best.[8] Contemporary advertisements stressed that once the good stands of such trees as white oak had been cut off, the underlying soil would be excellent for tillage.

In many places, the process of clearance was probably quite casual: settlers on occasion girdled trees and let them stand for more than a year after having planted the area. Where enough labor was available, however, workers would "grub" out roots with a mattock and remove stumps as soon as possible.[9]

The potential benefits of efforts to improve New Jersey's soils for cultivation and grazing were widely perceived. A short time after the Revolution, John Allinson described at length his plans and vision for the so-called "Drowned Lands," the poorly drained valley of the Wallkill River in northwestern New Jersey, to the noted French traveler and commentator Michel-Guillaume St. Jean de Crèvecoeur.[10] Crèvecoeur and his companion were amazed at the rapid development of the area and curious about how it would appear "in a matter of a few years." Allinson responded at length.

> The time when everything you see becomes transformed into grain and useful grass is still far off. The cultivation of this vast plain is a conquest reserved for our posterity: here as in Egypt, we will be obliged to cut drainage canals, although this prairie land is not very apt to be flooded over; we will have to build dikes and causeways, to divide the properties by a great number of ditches, put lasting boundaries to determine the limits and subdivisions, and to establish the line of demarkation [the boundary with New York] across New Jersey. The boundaries will be trees; then on all sides one will see willows, cypress, poplars, sycamores. What embellishment! What richness! What great utility the coolness of their shade will be during the summer heat! The monotony you see today will be replaced by variety; the green sombreness of this bleak horizon will no longer blend with the brilliant blue of a beautiful day; our population will be increased.

Allinson then speculated about what it would be like "for a man born, as I was, in this country during its early infancy, to see it again when these great spaces, today useless and uncultivated, will be covered with fine crops; . . . What a luxury of vegetation this fat and fertile land will exploit! . . . What a great number of horses and cattle will be bred to fatten off this land, today so abundant in useless weeds and wild growth."

Allinson was especially mindful of the benefits to be realized from draining wetlands; in other areas plagued by dryness, New Jersey farmers irrigated fields, and to compensate for poor soils many, though perhaps only the more prosperous, fertilized with mud, clay, manure, and lime. Soon after they had made a successful start raising stock and growing crops, farmers turned to these soil improvement projects, many of which were aided by private legislative acts.

Drainage was especially crucial to the production of hay, which was often in short supply; at midcentury Kalm noted that winter travelers through Maryland, Pennsylvania, and New Jersey had trouble finding food for their horses because hay was scarce.[11] Hay production could be very much enhanced by diking salt and freshwater marshes, draining them, and growing hay on them, which could be mowed several times a year (fig. 1).[12] Drainage was more important in the saltwater marshes because only some of the vegetation (especially the grasslike black grass on the landward margins of the marsh) could be used for fodder. Banked meadows were a popular way of dealing with the hay shortage early on in southwestern New Jersey. In many places where the physical conditions were right and where they were well maintained, these meadows were an important part of the agricultural economy and constitute an enduring change on the landscape to the present day.

In both Pennsylvania[13] and New Jersey in the eighteenth century, banked meadows had a very distinct distribution, centering on the lower Delaware (map 19). Salt and freshwater marshes could have been diked in other parts of New Jersey, and so their concentration here is significant. The presence of meadows producing hay for stock was such an important feature that they were very often mentioned in advertisements between 1724 and 1750 (map 20). The New England-settled northeast and the southwestern portion of New Jersey used such meadows quite differently. In the northeast before the late eighteenth century, very little improvement took place; New Englanders in such places as Woodbridge and Piscataway constructed ditches to drain their marshes, fenced them, and built bridges over the

Fig. 1. A New Jersey banked meadow, from Robert J. Sim, *Pages from the Past of Rural New Jersey* (1949). Courtesy New Jersey Agricultural Society.

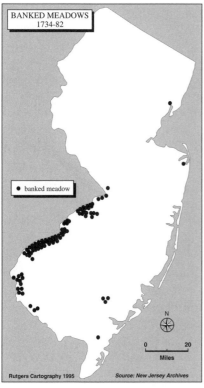

MAP 19

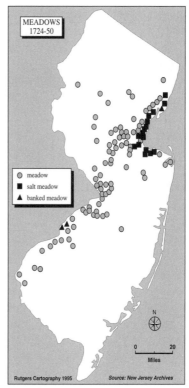

MAP 20

ditches, but with one known exception they did rarely diked these meadows. The atypical "One Hundred and six Acres of fresh Meadow, all bank'd in" at New Barbadoes Neck in Bergen County in 1744 may well have been a legacy of Dutch settlement in the area.[14]

In a study of perceptions and uses of salt marshes in tidewater communities in the northeastern United States in the nineteenth century, Robert G. LeBlanc proposed that improvements such as diking were characteristic of an agricultural "elite," farmers who belonged to agricultural societies, read the agricultural literature of the day, and had the capital to invest in reclamation schemes.[15] By contrast, the agricultural "folk" were tradition-bound and often scoffed at any departure from time-honored methods. If LeBlanc is correct, the wealthy Quakers of the Inner Coastal Plain behaved as an elite; as Rutherfurd noted in 1786, Quakers, "frugal and industrious People . . . have banked off many valuable meadows."[16]

There is no question that the Dutch introduced the technique of diking (or banking) to the lower Delaware Valley,[17] but they neither applied the practice very widely nor seem to have used it elsewhere (with one noted exception) in New Jersey. No evidence indicates that the Swedes and Finns who settled in southwestern New Jersey utilized the technique. Indeed, they were for the most part relatively poor people who lacked the resources and perhaps the inclination for such projects. The English Quakers, on the other hand, saw early the potential of the marshes and quickly attempted to secure ownership of such parcels on the Pennsylvania side of the river.[18] In New Jersey, Jasper Danckaerts noted on November 18, 1679, Quakers who had only settled in the area the year before occupied a banked meadow on Matinnaconk Island (between present-day Bordentown and Burlington) that had "formerly belonged to the Dutch governor . . . [who] dyked and cultivated a large piece of meadow or marsh, from which he gathered more grain than from any land which had been made from woodland into tillable land."[19]

The interest in reclaiming marsh land spawned many private legislative acts. One 1685 act established the position of burgess in Salem. Elected by a majority of the freeholders in the town, the burgess was to call inhabitants together to make local rules of governance and in this instance appears to have been appointed specifically because certain residents had borne the expense of public improvements. "A Ditch and Bank for a Road, a Landing Place and other Considerations" had been built "for which there hath been several Sums of Money expended by some particular Persons for the Performance thereof, whereby others receive the same Benefit that have expended none, which if allowed on, will become prejudicial to all therein concerned."[20] In 1693 a similar act passed to appoint five men, two to be chosen by the town and three by the Council of Proprietors, to survey and list all "the Swamp and wet Land" in Burlington. These men were then to divide the swamp land proportionally among those holding an interest in the town, provided that "they do engage to bear a proportionable Share of the Charge for the draining of the said Swamp and wet Land by their Subscriptions, to a Paper or Instrument drawn up to that effect."[21] In 1711 the first private act passed after the merger of East and West New Jersey concerned "the Owners of the Meadows and Marshes adjoining to and on both Sides of the Creek that surrounds the Island of Burlington, to stop out the Tide from overflowing them."[22]

The mechanics of setting up an organization to undertake reclamation in the Burlington legislation was a forerunner of the many later bills that applied to other localities. From this time on, especially immediately before the Revolution, local interests petitioned legislators to allow the formation of associations to organize drainage projects. One 1772 act applied to "Sundry of the Owners and Possessors of Meadows and Tide-Marsh lying on English's Creek" in Mansfield Township, Burlington County "to erect and maintain a Bank, Dam and other Waterworks across the said Creek in order to prevent the Tide from overflowing the Same, and to keep the former Water-course of Said Creek open and clear, and to make the Said Dam when erected a publick Landing."[23]

Not all property owners wished to be included in these projects, probably because of their expense and because of concern that navigation might be impeded and thus make it harder to deliver agricultural products to market.[24] When the legislature finally passed an act dealing with all the tidal swamps and marshes in the state in 1788, it established a procedure to accomplish such projects in the event that not everyone in a township would support it. Should "the whole" not agree to improve "any Body or Tract of Marsh or Swamp exposed to the Overflow of the Tide, and capable of being laid dry and put in a proper State for Improvement by one general Bank or Dam," two-thirds of the landowners were to advertise their intent to proceed with the project and, three weeks later, apply formally to do so to the county's Court of Common Pleas. The court was to appoint as commissioners three disinterested men who were "well acquainted with banking and improving Tide Meadows" to visit the site of a proposed project, listen to all parties concerned in it, and then, if they deemed it proper, "lay out the Bank, Dam, Sluices,

Floodgates or other Works necessary." They were to produce an exact survey of the placement of such improvements, establish, name, and set a meeting time and date for a company to manage the project, and return a certificate of the proceedings to the clerk of the court, who entered the proceedings in the county's road book.[25] Today, these entries document well the diffusion of this method of reclamation in New Jersey.

The act noted that differences of opinion about diking projects might arise, as they had in Mansfield Township in 1772, over the question whether they would hinder navigation. The commissioners were forbidden to stop up any navigable water "the Use of which Navigation may, in the Opinion of the Majority of the Men appointed as aforesaid, be of more than Half the Value to the Inhabitants of the Neighborhood that the Improvement of the Meadow would be to the Owners thereof." Nor were they to impede in any way the trade in cordwood, especially important in the southwest where most of the banking was taking place. "Stopping out any Creek or River capable of Navigation for Shallops or Flats that can carry eight Cords of Wood" was specifically banned. Alloway's Creek in Salem County had a bank to stop tidal flow above Hancock's Bridge as early as 1697. By "neglect" the bank was destroyed and never repaired, probably because it hampered the passage of wood and lumber down the creek.[26]

The 1788 act also called for levying a special tax to cover the expense of erecting and maintaining drainage works, to be assessed according to the value of individual holdings in the reclaimed area. The managers of a newly established association were to inspect the condition of the works at least once every three months and were authorized to order "Mud, Sand, or other Earth" to be dug for repairs and "to lay or erect any Works without the Banks, to prevent the Wash from damaging the Banks or Works." Further, breaching the bank or opening a sluice to let in the tide—which encouraged the deposit of soil-enriching sediment—was not permitted between April 1 and December 1. No cattle or swine were to be grazed on the bank without the permission of the managers; that livestock were normally grazed in such areas is evident in the fact that line ditches nine feet wide at the surface, four and a half feet wide at the bottom, and three feet deep that lay on a muddy bottom were declared lawful fences.

Northeastern New Jersey began to show similar interest in improving tidal meadows after the Revolution. One 1788 legislative act enabled the owners of meadows lying in "the Elizabeth-Town Great Meadows, adjoining and contiguous to a Ditch, commonly called the Great Ditch, to clear out open and enlarge the same, and to make and maintain Sluices and Dams to keep out the Tide, and drain the said Meadow." In 1789, the area to be drained was extended.[27] Elizabethtown had been settled a century earlier, and its New England settlers were clearly slow to accept this Dutch and later Quaker practice; New Barbadoes Township appears to have been one of the few places in northeastern New Jersey with banked marshes aside from Elizabethtown before the Revolution.

In 1794, John Stevens received permission to erect a bank across a salt marsh at Hoboken, probably the same "Piece of Salt Marsh" he leased to Charles Loss in 1809.[28] A drawing shows it to have been only 1.62 acres in extent and to have been enclosed by dams on two sides and by the turnpike from Hoboken to Hackensack on the third side (fig. 2).[29] A sluice had been built where Hoboken Creek met the

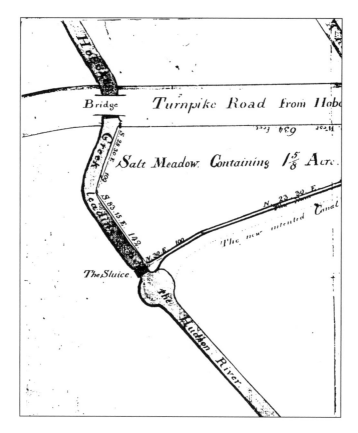

Fig. 2. Diagram of a sluice, property of John Stevens, Hackensack Meadowlands, 1794. Courtesy New Jersey Historical Society.

Hudson. The strategic location of this small tract—next to the turnpike in a heavily traveled area where hay must have commanded a premium price—probably justified its reclamation. Stevens noted that it was more profitable to sell the hay it produced locally than to bring in cattle to feed on it.

However, banking tidal marshes did not really catch on in the northeast until after the War of 1812. In 1816, legislative acts authorized banking tidal land between the Hackensack and the Passaic and constructing "a sluice and dam across Munaghia Creek"; two years later, reclamation of the salt marsh at Kingsland's Creek in New Barbadoes was authorized as was "the banking and improving of certain meadows, marsh and swamp" in Shrewsbury and Middletown townships in northern Monmouth County.[30]

In the same year, the legislature incorporated the New-Jersey Salt Marsh Company, whose principals included Cadwallader D. Colden and several other eminent and wealthy men. The group cited the "great public utility and great benefit to the interest and encouragement of agriculture and internal improvement" that might result from "embanking, draining, ditching and cultivating, certain large tracts of salt meadow or marsh, in the county of Bergen."[31] In 1820, the North River Meadow Company was formed for similar purposes in Shrewsbury.[32] Even into the second half of the nineteenth century, state geologist George Cook believed that much additional salt marsh could be profitably reclaimed. "Our

marsh lands are as susceptible of improvement, and as productive when in cultivation, as those of England or Holland," he wrote in his annual report for 1869, "and
they are so near the great markets of our country that their improvement is a matter of necessity."[33] But by the 1890s, state geologist John Gifford took a contrary
view. Even though he admitted that the salt marshes of the Outer Coastal Plain
were unusually productive, he declared that diking these lands was not worthwhile;
with only a little effort, they would still produce sustained yields of salt hay and
black grass, the latter especially still being used for fodder.

> Owing to the fact that these marshes already yield a good income, that is, a fair
> rate of interest on the amount invested, and probably more than cultivated fields
> would pay, by producing year after year a good grade of hay without any labor
> except the reaping, and a little ditching now and then, it would be a precarious
> investment to bank and drain them as has been done to similar land in Holland.[34]

In 1869, when Cook reported on the construction of banks in New Jersey, many
of the traditional methods of building were evidently still in use.[35] First, a trench
four feet wide and two "spits" (a spit was probably eighteen inches) deep was dug
to remove the sod and grass roots and provide a firm foundation. Next workers dug
a ditch twelve feet wide and three spits deep outside the trench on the water side
to supply earth for the bank. The pieces thrown out of the ditch were cut up and
fit tightly into the bank just as one would lay up a stone wall. When well packed,
the bank formed a very strong and durable wall if it was kept moist, a requirement
flood tides generally satisfied; if a bank was permitted to become too dry, it would
crumble.

Workers dug these ditches with a "skiver," a narrow, spade-like tool about four
feet long usually of ash, maple, or sassafras.[36] The skiver had a blade fifteen inches
long and about five inches wide, slightly concave in front and tipped by two or three
inches of steel kept very sharp. Workers used it to pare off an eighteen-inch strip of
wet mud from the wall of the trench and, with a turn of the wrist, to break each
strip loose and throw it some fifteen feet or so. Where brackish meadows encouraged tougher roots, the "heart shovel," whose entire blade was sharp steel, was
used.

Some inhabitants of southwestern New Jersey worked permanently on drainage
projects; some members of Swedish congregations were described as "ditchers"
rather than farmers.[37] In Salem, where the daily wage at the time was probably
about £0.2.0, a ditcher probably expected to dig at least eleven cubic yards in a
day; in an October 20, 1766, entry in his store ledger, Grant Gibbon recorded paying John Grace £5.4.0 for digging "52 rods Ditch, 6 by 3"—0.2.0 per rod, or 0.1.0
for every five and one half cubic yards excavated.[38]

According to Cook, banks in Salem rose four feet above the meadow, were eight
feet wide at the bottom, and were three feet wide on top. They commonly sloped
one half to one on the inside and nearly one to one on the outside. Exposed banks
were built higher and deeper. At Finn's Point on the Delaware in Lower Penn's
Neck Township, where the shore was very exposed for two or three miles along the
river, the bank was ten feet high, twelve feet wide on the top (wide enough for a
wagon road), and thirty feet at the bottom. The outside of this bank was faced with

stone in the nineteenth century. In Cumberland County, banks ranged from three to seven feet high and were built directly on the surface of the meadow.

Typically, banks were built a little distance from the edge of the water, leaving a strip of marsh a rod wide or more (called the guard or shore) to protect the bank and supply the mud used to repair it. At intervals, ditches were cut to drain the meadows: in Cook's day they were two feet deep and seven feet wide, or, if used as a boundary, nine feet wide. Where the water was very salty, a newly banked meadow would require two or three years to freshen before it would grow anything other than salt grass.

These banked meadows required constant observation and maintenance. Fiddler crabs and muskrats burrowed into and through the banks, which made them susceptible to being breached in high water. Accordingly, during periods of low water, farmers would dig out muskrat burrows by hand. Unusually high tides and storms were also a problem, and on occasion the banks and sometimes entire meadows would settle. Banks that crossed a meadow and were built on organic matter such as peat were most prone to settling; Cook declared that some banks had settled as much as ten feet in ten years. Whole meadows overflowed at high water when the tide marshes were open and unbanked; saturated, they remained near the level of the high tide. After they were banked and drained, they dried out, and as their organic base slowly decayed the entire surface sank. Tillage speeded this process. After some years the meadow surface fell to the level of low water; water could no longer drain by gravity and cultivation had to cease. But such meadows could be reclaimed if the banks were breached at several points so that water could flow onto them again, thus depositing sediments that quickly restored meadows to their proper levels in many places. According to Cook, Salem Creek and the Maurice River carried down a great deal of mud while the Cohansey did not; in ten years a mud deposit two feet deep built up in one of the meadows left open near Salem.

In many places it was a matter of course to open the sluices during the winter season and allow sediments to deposit, both to mitigate the problem of settling and to enhance fertility. Different muds were deposited in different locales: Cook believed that blue and gray muds resulted from soil erosion itself brought on by deforestation. In his day and earlier, during the eighteenth century, the meadows were used to grow not only grass but various other crops. The banked meadows of Salem and Cumberland counties were excellent grazing land, and meadows on the Maurice River in Cook's day produced "enormous crops" of timothy, grains, and roots.

No statistics are known to document the profits or losses farmers realized from banking projects. That they were expensive to maintain is evident from the great amount of enabling legislation that specified mechanisms to collect taxes for their support. In 1765 residents of Newport Creek, between Greenwich Township and Stow Creek Township in Cumberland County, petitioned the legislature to regulate drainage there because the twenty-year-old bank and sluices on the creek "for want of . . . being kept up in an effectual Manner, is become almost useless."[39] Property owners in Gloucester County asked the same legislative session to compel all who had benefited from the banking of Little Mantua Creek to share in the expenses; three years later, Grant Gibbon paid a hefty bank tax of £1.16.0 for this purpose.[40] In 1773, when Whitten Cripps and others in Salem County asked the legislature's permission to bank meadows in Penn's Neck, Samuel Nicholson protested that the application had not been advertised as provided by law. Cripps charged in turn that "his Meadows had lain under water at times for near twelve months past occasioned by the Said Nichelson or his tenants neglecting to keep up their adjoining Banks."[41]

More common and widespread than the practice of banking marshes inundated by tidal waters was the ditching of poorly drained areas. In many parts of southwestern New Jersey, farmers were routinely digging ditches before groups were formed to bank the tidal lands. Tidal areas were also ditched in northern New Jersey, and the glaciated section began to be drained after initial occupation had taken place because of the great glacial derangement of stream flow there.

Like banking, ditching aimed to enhance the hay production to feed cattle in winter and pasture them in summer. In a 1727 advertisement for Joshua Grainger's large property in Penn's Neck, on the Delaware in northwestern Salem County, three hundred acres of one meadow "joyning to one of the lower Creeks" was described as "good hard Marsh Meadow Ground, that the Hay may be fetched at any Time, and bears very good Hay." It was probably salt marsh. On the upper side of the plantation was a parcel, probably largely a freshwater marsh, "of about 200 Acres of good Meadow, 90 Acres of which is drained and cut into 7 or 8 Acres Fields by Ditches." Grainger claimed that the plantation could support three or four hundred head of cattle "with Winter and Summer Food sufficient, besides a very good Outlet; and by the 9th or 10th of March there is most commonly Grass for Cretors, in the Meadows aforesaid, being they lye so warm" (that is, there was an early beginning to the growing season).[42] Soon after they had addressed their more pressing problems, farmers commonly began a regular program of ditching their lands. In northern New Jersey, leasing agreements often required tenants to drain swamp and produce meadow. The "Articles of Agreement" between tenant David Phillips and John Stevens dated November 21, 1772, clearly spells out Phillips's obligation on Stevens's farm, probably in northern Hunterdon County or in Sussex County.

> The said Phillips hereby Obliges himself to Clear fit for the Sythe all the Swamp ground Contained in his Lease above and below the road that goes from Stepn. Hagertys to his House in which he is to cut up and burn all the brush & loggs and Saplins reserveing Such poles as may do for fenceing The swamp to be Cleard on Each side above the road to the upland as far as the Alders growes & below the Road to the upland on one Side & to Sd Hagertys line on the other side.[43]

Phillips was to be excused £35.0.0 of his annual rent in proportion to the amount of the swamp he cleared that year, and he was allowed "the geting of 1500 Rails towards fenceing the Same."

Swamps were considered to be a valuable asset because of their ability to support grass for stock. A 1772 sale notice for a 210-acre parcel in "the Great Meadows" noted that 70 of its 160 acres of meadow astride the Pequest River were "ditched and improved."[44] In 1775, William Kelly of London advertised a large tract of land in Newton Township, Sussex County, an area of northern New Jersey just beginning to be occupied. Its "considerable quantity" of good swamp was unimproved, but Kelly noted its potential to be "easily cleared and brought into grass; so that upon the whole there are few (if any) lands in that part of the country better calculated for raising stock."[45]

In about 1749, a letter to Jared Eliot from Charles Read of Burlington County describing his drainage efforts at "Sharon," his 289.5-acre farm northeast of Mt. Holly (fig. 3), shows how important draining meadows could be in enhancing agricultural yields.[46] Read was reasonably wealthy and a very prominent political figure, and he criticized his neighbors for not being as innovative as he was. He thus described the process of draining an individual farm in great detail, presumably so others who could afford to do so could follow a similar procedure.

> I began with a Meadow, on which there had never been much Timber, but it was always overflowed; the Soil of it is very Fine and black about three foot then it comes to a fatt Bluish Clay; of this deep Meadow I have about Eighty Acres, forty of which had been Ditched and mowed the Grass which comes in first after Ditching is Spear grass and white clover, but the weeds are to be mowed four or five years before they will be Subdued, as the Vegetation is very Luxuriant. This meadow had been ditched & planted with Indian Corn of which it produced about Sixty Bushells pr acre. I first Scoured up my Ditches & drains & took off all the Weeds, then I plowed it and Sowed it with Oats in the last of May, In July I Mowed them down, together with the Weeds, which grew plentifully among them, and they made good fodder. I immediately Plowed it again, & kept harrowing 'till there was an appearance of Rain and on the twenty-third of August I sowed near thirty Acres with red Clover and Herd grass.

Pleased with his results, Read noted that the meadow "is well matted and looks like a Green Corn field." He then drained a pond.

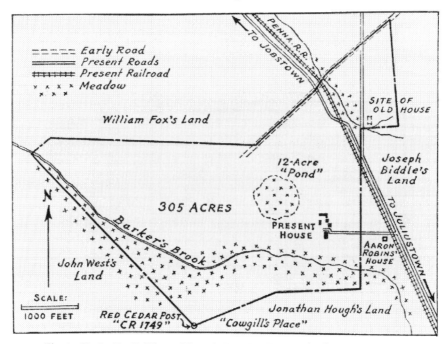

Fig. 3. Charles Read's "Sharon," boundaries as in 1750, drawing in Carl R. Woodward, *Ploughs and Politicks* (1941). Courtesy Rutgers University Press.

My next undertaking was a Round Pond of Twelve Acres; Ditching round it with a large Drain through the Middle and other smaller Drains laid it perfectly dry, this, after first taken up all the Rubbish, I plowed up and Harrowed it many times over till it was smooth, its Soil is blackish but in about a foot or ten Inches you come to a Sand of the same colour with the upland.

On these soils that Read judged to be "cold," he planted rye, Salem grass, timothy, rye grass, blue bent, and red clover. The rye did well, he wrote, and though the timothy and Salem grass looked good he feared it would decline in dry weather "from the Sands laying So near the Surface."

Read sold "Sharon" in 1750 and bought a 492-acre tract between the north and south forks of the Rancocas River near Mount Holly in 1761. The soils on this farm, which he called "Breezy Ridge," were largely light and sandy, and so Read engaged a ditcher to ditch and bank his marshland (fig. 4).

In northern New Jersey, as John Stevens knew, even small areas of wetland could have great economic value if drained. On June 10, 1766, Stevens's nephew, Fenwick Lyell, described the meadows in the glaciated Highlands at Hardyston Township, Sussex County, then in a very early phase of settlement. Only very small areas of arable soils existed there, so Lyell must have been impressed by the productivity of meadowland.

I have this day been with Mr. Ogden to View a Bogg Meadow of his, plow'd with the Same plow I told you of (when here) and planted, the Corn is Exceeding Thrifty, and have been to View another Meadow of Harlows, which is planted the Second year, and I dare to Say you never see any thing of the kind to Exceed it, I have been at Pollenskill [Paulinskill River in the Ridge and Valley Section] lately

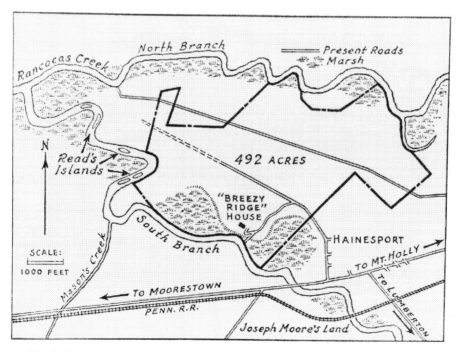

Fig. 4. Charles Read's "Breezy Ridge," boundaries as in 1761, drawing in Carl R. Woodward, *Ploughs and Politicks* (1941). Courtesy Rutgers University Press.

and The Indian Corn Flax and hemp of my Uncle Richard looks Very Well, That I am Quite Satisfied that the Meadow will answer, I have planted a few Hills of Indian and a little of Every Other Seed for Experimt.[47]

Other evidence attests the significance of such poorly drained locations as bog meadows in this general area. On March 8, 1779, John Stevens sold Thomas Gustin of Sussex County 179 acres (probably in the Kittatinny Valley) in several very irregular parcels, including two "Bog Meadows" (fig. 5).[48] The area was in a very early state of settlement, and no mention was made of any effort to ditch these meadows. Still, some ditching would probably have been done to lower the water table a bit in order to grow crops or to improve grass and hay production.

Other than these accounts, little evidence of individual drainage efforts appears in the public record, but references to the work of communities and groups are

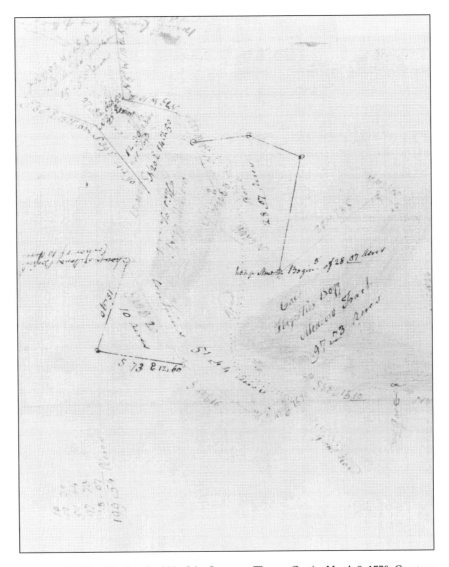

Fig. 5. Parcel with "Bog Meadows" sold by John Stevens to Thomas Gustin, March 8, 1779. Courtesy New Jersey Historical Society.

abundant. From the 1760s such groups seem to have been especially busy with drainage projects, which indicates that the basic job of clearance had been completed. "Divers Inhabitants" of Newark petitioned the legislature in 1767 to be allowed to cut ditches and put in sluices to drain the meadow between Wheeler's Point, Maple Island and Tompkin's Point on the Passaic.[49] Four years later, residents of the upper Passaic were authorized to clear and deepen existing ditches and to dig new ones to drain more effectually the "Meadows and Swamps . . . lying on Pinch Ditch, Black Brook, and part of Whiponong [Whippany] River in the County of Morris."[50] An eighteenth-century map exists of a drained portion of the Whippany meadows, part of the large system of swamps lineally descended from glacial Lake Passaic (fig. 6).[51] Here, workers built an outlet ditch running parallel to the river and emptying downstream from the area drained. Line ditches emptied into the outlet ditch. The meadow was divided into lots, most of them long lots of three to five acres lying back from the river in three tiers; one holding was more

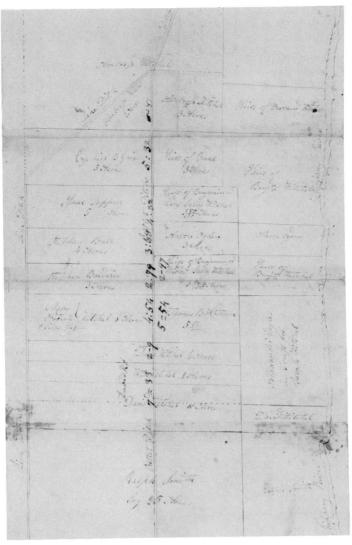

Figure 6. The drained portion of the Whippany Meadows, early 1700s. Courtesy the Joint Free Public Library of Morristown and Morris Township.

than twenty-five acres. The rectilinear form of the lots undoubtedly eased the process of subdivision due to inheritance, evident on the map. These ditches, like the banked meadows of the southwest, formed property boundaries in addition to draining land.

Drainage on the Passaic proper—a matter, apparently, of great controversy for years—was authorized in 1772 seven years after a petition to cut a new channel for the river had been tabled over complaints of some residents "that they have received great Damage occasioned by a Mill-Dam built across said River belonging to Samuel Woodruff, Esq." By 1772 Woodruff had died, and owners of "the Meadows Swamps and low lands on the Rivers Pasaick and Dead River" petitioned to be allowed "to clear the same and remove every obstruction to the free Passage of the Waters" from the late Woodruff's former saw mill. Obstructions in the river, legislators noted, had caused the water to overflow some public roads for part of the year as well as "many Thousand of Acres of valuable Meadows and Land" thus "rendered in a great Measure useless to the Owners thereof."[52] In proportion to the value of the lands they owned that benefited from the undertaking, lowland onwers were to pay for the clearance and maintenance of the river.

This Passaic legislation encouraged other drainage projects, including one on the Assunpink in 1774 and another on the "Drowned Lands" bordering the northward-flowing Wallkill River in the Kittatinny Valley, which straddled the boundary between New York and New Jersey.[53] The boundary with New York had not been agreed upon until 1772, which may have kept the legislature from acting earlier.[54] In addition, this area had only recently been settled, and much of the land was still held in common by the East Jersey proprietors, who were probably less interested in the agricultural benefits of drainage than in the fact that the association between wetlands and unhealthfulness made the land harder to sell or lease. The bill noted that the fact that the land overflowed for part of the year "rendered [it] of little Benefit to the Proprietors . . . the Water being long stagnated thereon, the adjacent country is rendered very unhealthy."

Drainage projects were so vital that they were even authorized during the Revolutionary War, when manpower was at a premium and New Jersey was the site of many major military engagements (see map 25). In 1779, farmers living at Fresh Pond in the South Ward of New Brunswick asked the legislature to compel those whose property bordered a two-mile ditch leading to the Lawrence Brook to contribute to its upkeep. The ditch kept filling in, the farmers claimed, and rendered "useless" at least eight hundred acres of "marsh swamp and Lowe Lands Capable of being made good Meadow."[55]

Legislative relief was also sought because ditches often had to be constructed through the properties of others, which naturally gave rise to disputes.[56] After the Revolution, one act made the two surveyors of the highways and two freeholders chosen by the township responsible for viewing sites to be drained, determining the best course for the ditch, and collecting taxes from those benefiting from the drainage to apportion to those "damaged" by it. Apportioning construction and maintenance costs was complicated in the glaciated northwest, where a great deal of land required drainage, by the fact that it was surrounded by the unimproved and undivided land of the proprietors. To recover costs in such circumstances, all drainage projects had to be advertised three weeks in advance. If proprietors failed to respond, officials were permitted to proceed against them by selling off some of their lands.

This act was evidently unsatisfactory, for in 1792 it was repealed and supplanted by another that called for ditches to be laid, when possible, along the property lines of the interested parties. Sections of these ditches were assigned to individuals, who bore the responsibility for clearing them out every year between September 1 and May 1; the mud thus excavated was to be cast equally on both sides of the property line.[57]

In the early years of the nineteenth century, numerous private legislative acts authorized draining the "Drowned Lands" on the Wallkill (1806), improving a local stream feeding into the Wallkill in Wantage Township (1818), ditching and draining the Bog and Fly Meadow in Pequannock Township, Morris County (1811), and draining "Maidenhead Great Meadows" in present-day Lawrence Township (1812).[58] The Maidenhead meadows were divided into widely held five- or ten-acre lots used, as elsewhere, to support livestock; they had become very much diminished by 1814, when almost all of them were located far from Stoney Brook.[59]

Farmers confronted with dry lands rather than wetlands irrigated meadows from an early date. In 1748, Peter Kalm described the practice in eastern Pennsylvania, where the hot summers often dried out the grasses.[60] Local farmers routed water from springs in the general vicinity of a meadow to the highest portion of the land and then dug narrow channels running down to the lower parts. In low places wooden gutters would be laid to channel the water to flow farther. To raise the water level at its source, Kalm noted, high dikes were built near the springs, and water was diverted sometimes more than a mile through channels dug along hillsides and wooden pipes implanted where necessary. Such meadows were mowed three times in a summer. "One that has not seen it himself, cannot believe how great a quantity of grass there is in such meadows, especially near the little channels," Kalm wrote; "while others, which have not been thus manage[d], look wretched." The practice of irrigating meadows appears to have been widespread in eastern Pennsylvania and may have been a survival of European, especially German, practice; one authority speculated that its decline in the nineteenth century was due to the introduction of superior perennial grasses on the uplands and the amount of labor required to keep the ditches clear.[61]

The practice of irrigating meadows diffused into northwestern New Jersey from Pennsylvania. In 1760, a farm on the South Branch of the Raritan included seventy acres of meadow, "25 thereof watered with springs."[62] On July 16, 1778, James Parker recorded sending Peter Thackery "into Potts Meadow to lead the water properly" and went there himself on March 19, 1781 "to prepare it for watering."[63] He had his men level "the ground the hogs had rooted last year," plant it in timothy, and build fencing around the meadow. On April 24, Parker recorded that "Barnabus Maddon, the man that promised to come and ditch for me came here this day and not proper weather to go into the meadow I employed him on the garden." In 1791, Parker credited his tenant Jesse Warnick of Alexandria Township in northern Hunterdon County with £30.0.0—half his yearly rent for the farm—for "clearing a piece of meadow and making the dam &c.," which, according to this lease the next year, impounded a creek "that Waters the meadow."

In addition to drainage and irrigation, farmers, perhaps especially gentlemen farmers, directly attempted to enhance the soil. Charles Read and Lord Stirling recorded their ideas about soils and sought to correct what they perceived to be their deficiencies.[64] Read lived in Burlington County, probably in the forefront of agricultural experimentation in New Jersey. His notes about the activities of his neighbors and acquaintances suggest that knowledgeable people were greatly altering the natural state of the soils, at least in the general area of Burlington County. Decades later, farmers there formed the Burlington Society for the Promotion of Agriculture and Domestic Manufactures in 1790.

In 1756, Read described the experiments of John De Normandie, who grew a fine crop of wheat yielding twenty-five bushels to the acre after plowing one thousand loads of mud into a sandy soil that had earlier not been very productive. De Normandie apparently extended the practice to other land. This often-mentioned "blue mud," which Carl Woodward has suggested was the same green-sand marl that became a well-known calcareous fertilizer in the nineteenth century, altered the structure and moisture retention of the soil. Woodward has also noted that De Normandie's son was the first president of the local agricultural society and advocated the use of plaster of paris as a manure, the cultivation of more root crops and clover to feed hogs and cattle, more systematic crop rotation, more frequent plowing, and the systematic destruction of weeds. Read frequently mentioned the fact that farmers were spreading mud from low-lying areas on sandy soils, so such fertilization projects must have been fairly widespread. Yet they required substantial capital and labor. Farmers needed at least a wagon to draw substantial amounts of sand or any other material to the fields, and tax lists reveal that few farmers possessed these vehicles. Most farmers probably could afford to do only as much as they could do with carts or sleds.

Read described another experiment on the Rancocas River, where Joshua Fenimore had added forty loads of "Hassocks" (tufts of grass or sedge, probably from a poorly drained area) per acre on poor sandy soil in 1754. He cut these hassocks in pieces, let them rot, and then plowed them in. Two years later he grew a fine crop of thirty bushels per acre of corn. Read noted that the hassocks should be rotted in a pile where they would deteriorate nicely in two years; if they were spread out at once, "they roll about a field several years."

Read also advocated burning clay (probably a calcareous marl) and using it as a "Cheap Dressg" on all sorts of land. One English experiment, he noted, added sand to marshy ground and had much improved it; the same was being done in New Jersey. Read reported that the meadow above the saw mill in Mount Holly "is now so improved by Sand that it bears excellent White Clover as I have ever seen." Read pointed out too that dung was in wide use. The best was dung from swine, who yielded four to eight loads (but over how much time Read did not say); one load of swine dung was as good as two loads of the dung of any other livestock "but too hott to use alone." Horse dung, even dry, had fertility. Cow dung was less effective but "None better mixed," Reed noted. Sheep dung "Loses its Virtue the soonest of any if Exposed - best for Cold [clay] Land," but it could be very much enhanced if the sheep were folded (penned up) and fresh earth brought into the pen every week.

As Rutherfurd had suggested, the value of land was greater "near considerable Towns" partly because of "the help of manure," probably horse manure from the towns' stables and perhaps cow manure from those who kept a cow but lacked space for a kitchen garden.[65] There must have been keen competition for manure in these locations. Gavin Scott noted twelve years later, in 1798, that its scarcity doomed him to make "but small progress in improveing" his 68-acre farm near Elizabethtown.[66]

Read noted that lime had been used for fertilizer in England and may have been available in the form of ship ballast from Jamaica, but his brief mention suggests that it was not in wide use in southern New Jersey, where the calcareous properties of the local marl made it less necessary in any event. According to Lemon, lime had come into agricultural use in southeastern Pennsylvania by about 1750, at which point its ability to improve sour soils was well known.[67] Writing about Pennsylvania and west New Jersey in 1698, Gabriel Thomas observed that there was "very good Lime-Stone in great plenty, and cheap, of great use in Buildings, and also in Manufacturing Land (if there were any occasion) but Nature has made that of itself sufficiently Fruitfull."[68]

In northern New Jersey, the agricultural use of lime predated the Revolution. In 1760 a sale notice for a farm on the South Branch of the Raritan, most likely in present Long Valley, noted the "good Lime-Rock and Kiln on the Premises, by which Manure may be made for the Land, if wanted."[69] Lime was a necessary addition for good crops of clover, and this farm had seventy acres of meadow "under clover and timothy grass." Lime would indeed have been wanted if the farm were to produce cattle. In 1773, a property in the limestone-rich valley of the Musconetcong was advertised to include "good conveniences for burning lime to manure the land."[70]

From 1778 through at least 1794, James Parker produced and used large amounts of lime on his farm three miles from Clinton, a town that produced lime in great quantities in the early nineteenth century.[71] On June 12, 1778, on Robert Allen's recommendation that he was "a person to burn lime," Parker hired John Whiting and another man, and the next day the two began, with the aid of two of Parker's farm workers, to lay limestone in the kiln and fire it. On August 7, Whiting came again, but workers had not yet taken the last lime produced out of the kiln; Whiting helped with the oat harvest instead.

By August 17, Parker had his laborers draw the lime out of the kiln, pile it into heaps eighteen yards apart, and cover all except one 160-bushel heap with earth. Parker's men drew 686 bushels out of the kiln, sold 50 bushels in small amounts to neighbors, and carried 636 bushels "out on the land." A week later, his workers began to spread the lime evenly from the four bushel heaps by throwing it with shovels, but Parker thought that the heaps were too far apart to achieve an even application this way; he made a note to have the men make two bushel piles nine yards apart next time. The lime was laid on ground that had been plowed once; it was then distributed more thoroughly by harrowing twice and plowing once more.

On August 27th, Parker's men emptied the kiln of 518 bushels of lime which they carried out to the fallow land. The next day they slacked the lime by placing water on each heap. High winds over the next six days made it hard to spread, but by the morning of September 5 the job was finished, and by September 22 his men had finished sowing the limed land with either wheat or rye.

Early the following March, the men began to haul limestone with three teams.

John Whiting arrived on March 7 to burn the lime, but heavy snows forced him instead to work inside swingling flax. By March 15 Whiting was at work clearing the kiln for thirty-eight loads of limestone the teams had brought in, and Parker set his men to cutting wood to fire the kiln on March 19. Two men remained in constant attendance at the kiln for three days, when it burned out. On March 31 Parker's men began to draw lime out of the kiln; in early April they hauled more limestone, cut more wood, hauled lime to the fields, and continued to burn limestone. Parker continued to engage Whiting to burn lime, and in 1794 he was was receiving thousands of bushels of the fertilizer.[72]

Parker's kiln was very likely a "set kiln" built into the side of a hill (fig. 7).[73] One of apparently two types of early lime kilns, the set kiln had an egg-shaped interior which was filled through the top with alternating layers of limestone and wood. The top was covered with sods before the fire was started, and the kiln burned continuously until all the wood was consumed.[74]

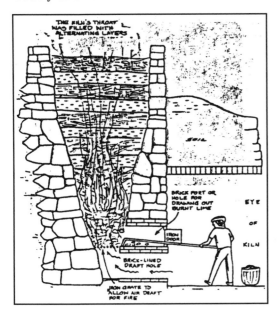

Fig. 7. A set kiln, drawing in Robert J. Sim, *Some Vanishing Phases of Rural Life in New Jersey* (1941). Courtesy New Jersey Department of Agriculture.

Use of lime on the fields during the sowing of wheat seems to have been fairly widespread among the more affluent farmers in northwestern New Jersey, who could obtain it easily by burning local limestone. Rutherfurd refers to "some" being used to advantage at forty bushels to the acre (the amount Parker used) in 1786.[75] By 1798 the Scotts were contemplating using lime on their small acreage near Elizabethtown. They evidently would have preferred to use manure but it was scarce at the time.[76] The Scotts were fairly far from the nearest sources of lime in valleys in the Highlands, so the prices they had to pay must have been relatively high. But, as with other New Jersey farmers of some means, their perceived need to "improve" their soil must also have been great.

Notes

1. Jedediah Morse, *The American Geography* (Elizabethtown, N.J., 1789), 286.

2. John C. F. Tedrow has given a thorough description of New Jersey soils, although he said very little about productivity; see his *Soils of New Jersey* (Malabar, Fla., 1986). This map, which I published first in *Land and People* (10, 12–15) is based on Tedrow's earlier work and very greatly generalizes regional differences based on a sliding scale of the descriptions of the productive capacities of soil series under modern tillage methods.

3. *Votes and Proceedings of the General Assembly of the Province of New Jersey* (Philadelphia, 1751), 28.

4. Norman J. G. Pounds, *An Historical Geography of Europe, 450 B.C.–A.D. 1330* (Cambridge, Eng., 1973), 3.

5. Benson, *Peter Kalm's Travels,* 1:89.

6. Ibid., 1:120.

7. Ibid., 1:101, 189.

8. Woodward, *Ploughs and Politicks*, 70–79.

9. Woodward, *Agriculture in New Jersey*, 28. See also James Parker Diary, 3–4, NjHi.

10. Percy G. Adams, ed., *Crèvecoeur's Eighteenth-Century Travels in Pennsylvania and New York* (Lexington, Ky., 1961), 140–41.

11. Benson, *Peter Kalm's Travels*, 1:181.

12. See Robert J. Sim, *Some Vanishing Phases of Rural Life in New Jersey* (Trenton, N.J., 1941).

13. Lemon, *Best Poor Man's Country*, 175, 196, 213.

14. *Docs. Rel. N.J.*, 1st ser., 17:365.

15. Le Blanc, "Differential Perception of Salt Marshes," 138–43.

16. Rutherfurd, "Notes on the State," 87–88.

17. Clinton A. Weslager and A. R. Dunlap, *Dutch Explorers, Traders, and Settlers in the Delaware Valley, 1609–1664* (Philadelphia, 1961), 204–5.

18. Israel Acrelius, *A History of New Sweden*, trans. William M. Reynolds (Philadelphia, 1874), 126.

19. Bartlett B. James and J. Franklin Jameson, eds., *Journal of Jasper Danckaerts 1679–1680* (New York, 1913), 97.

20. Leaming and Spicer, *Grants*, 515–16.

21. Ibid., 523–27.

22. *N.J. Laws*, 1:100.

23. Ibid., 5:107.

24. *Votes and Proceedings of the General Assembly*, 1765, 9.

25. *N.J.S.L.* 1788:507–13.

26. Robert G. Johnson, *An Historical Account of the First Settlement of Salem in West Jersey by John Fenwick, Esq., Chief Proprietor of the Same* (Philadelphia, 1839), 78.

27. *Acts of the General Assembly of the State of New Jersey*, 1788, 504; 1789, 558–61.

28. Anonymous, June 7, 1794, Stevens Family Papers, NjHi.

29. John Stevens to Charles Loss, "Lease for a Piece of Salt Marsh [1809]," Stevens Papers, NjHi.

30. *N.J.S.L.* 1816:180–184, 93; 1819, Priv. & Temp.:94–97; 1818:15, 20–22.

31. Ibid., 1819:97–99.

32. North River Meadow Company Records, NjHi.

33. George H. Cook, *Annual Report of the State Geologist 1869*, 36.

34. Gifford, "Forestal Conditions," 249.

35. Cook, *Annual Report. . .1869*, 24.

36. Sim, *Vanishing Phases*, 94–97.

37. "Archivum Americanum," 1:465–92.

38. Grant Gibbon Store Ledger, Salem, N.J., 1764–1778, NjR.

39. *Votes and Proceedings of the General Assembly of the Province of New Jersey*, 1765, 7.

40. Ibid., 9; Grant Gibbon Store Ledger, NjR.

41. *Docs. Rel. N.J.*, 1st ser., 18:365–66.

42. Ibid., 11:116–17.

43. Stevens Family Papers, NjHi.

44. *Docs. Rel. N.J.*, 1st ser., 29:215.

45. Ibid., 27:424.

46. Woodward, *Ploughs and Politicks*, 70–79, contains an excellent discussion of Read's drainage efforts in southwestern New Jersey around the middle of the eighteenth century. Woodward discovered that this letter to Eliot, long attributed to Benjamin Franklin, was actually written by Read.

47. Stevens Family Papers, NjHi.

48. "Map of Hagertys & the Other Meadow and Three Other Surveys Joining," March 8, 1779, Stevens Family Papers.

49. *Votes and Proceedings of the General Assembly of the State of New Jersey*, 16.

50. *N.J. Laws*, 5:99.

51. Untitled, undated map of Whippany Meadows, Kitchell Family Papers, Joint Free Public Library of Morristown and Morris Township, Morristown, N.J.

52. *N.J. Laws*, 5:145–47.

53. Ibid., 5:265–67, 288–93.

54. Wacker, *Land and People,* 372.

55. "Petition of the Inhabitants of New Brunswick to Governor William Livingston," November 3, 1779, Governors' Manuscripts, Division of Archives and History, New Jersey State Library.

56. *N.J.S.L.* 1783:65–67.

57. Ibid., 1792:796–99. Such legislation made it possible for people such as Jacob Lantz of Sussex County to drain his "bog meadow" through his neighbor's property in 1810 with a ditch six feet wide and as deep as necessary; see Sussex County Road Return Book, July 24, 1810, Division of Archives and History, New Jersey State Library. In some places neighbors came up with an agreement on their own: in Westfield in 1785, one group agreed that a ditch there only needed to be three feet wide and eighteen inches deep. See "Agreement on Drainage, Westfield, 1785," Ross Family Papers, NjHi.

58. *N.J.S.L.* 1806:747–750; 1808:196–200; 1818:41–43; 1811:472–475; 1812:98–100.

59. "Historic Land Map, Lawrence (Maidenhead) Township, Circa 1776," (Lawrenceville, N.J., 1978); see also *N.J.S.L.* 1814:130 for an act authorizing the clearing of Stoney Brook.

60. Benson, *Peter Kalm's Travels,* 1:162–63.

61. Robert C. Bucher, "Meadow Irrigation in Pennsylvania," *Pennsylvania Folklife* 11 (1960): 24–32.

62. *Docs. Rel. N.J.,* 1st ser., 20:426.

63. James Parker Diary, NjHi.

64. Woodward, *Ploughs and Politicks,* 235–51.

65. Rutherfurd, "Notes on the State," 84.

66. Gavin Scott to his brother, January 15, 1798, Scott Family Papers, NjHi.

67. Lemon, *Best Poor Man's Country,* 174.

68. Thomas, *An Account,* 30.

69. *Docs. Rel. N.J.,* 1st ser., 20:426.

70. Ibid., 29:22.

71. James P. Snell, comp., *History of Somerset and Hunterdon Counties, New Jersey* (Philadelphia, 1881), 549; James Parker Diary, NjHi.

72. "Miscellaneous" Folder, Parker Papers, NjHi.

73. Sim, *Vanishing Phases,* 9.

74. Alanson H. Haines, *Hardyston Memorial: A History of the Township and the North Presbyterian Church, Hardyston, Sussex County, New Jersey* (Newton, N.J., 1888), 93.

75. Rutherfurd, "Notes on the State," 86.

76. Scott Family Papers, NjHi.

Sixth Month, June, 1819.

CHAPTER 4

THE CULTIVATION OF CROPS

In 1748, the aged Swedish residents of southwestern New Jersey who spoke to Peter Kalm told him that they had never suffered a crop failure in their New World home and that the people had always had plenty to eat.

> Sometimes the price of grain rose higher in one year than in another, on account of a great drought or bad weather, but still there was always sufficient for the consumption of the inhabitants. Nor is it likely that any great famine can happen in this country, unless it please God to afflict it with extraordinary punishments. The weather is well known from more than sixty years experience. Here are no nights cold enough to hurt the seeds. The rainy periods are of short duration and the drought is seldom or never severe[1]

Even if a stretch of bad weather hurt crops from time to time, Kalm noted, the length of the growing season and the diversity of crops farmers planted would virtually ensure success.

> The chief thing is the variety of grain. The people sow the different kinds, at different times and seasons, and though one crop turns out bad, yet another succeeds. The summer is so long that of some species of grain they may get two crops. There is hardly a month from May to October or November, inclusive, in which the people do not reap some kind of cereal, or gather some sort of fruit.

Kalm allowed that this history of success made farmers ill prepared for possible failure, "for here, as in many other places, they lay up no stores, and are contented to live from hand to mouth, as the saying goes." In 1788, in a letter to her daughter in England, Mary Capnerhurst suggested that many farmers in fertile, wheat-producing Amwell Township, Hunterdon County, viewed the eventual depletion of agricultural lands as an inevitable process:

> In England there is more farming than farms; here there is more farms than people. Those that have wore out their old farms are very desirous to sell and go back [move to the frontier]. I was once talking with a farmer about spoiling the land. Said the English landlords would be much displeased if their lands was used so. Landlords, he answered, we like to be our own land lords. I replyed if they was they spoiled their land. He did not seem to think that could be avoided, and one reason he gave was that It should ware out and could find no remedy against it.[2]

From the first, European settlers in New Jersey were clearly impressed by the relatively benign environmental conditions that prevailed in the area, a factor that may have encouraged farmers not only to plant a diverse array of crops but also to approach agricultural lands with the casual attitude Kalm and Capnerhurst described. There is no doubt that New Jersey's climate was generally favorable to agriculture. Though precipitation varied from place to place, it generally averaged more than forty-four inches per year, almost double what many parts of northwestern Europe received, and it was (and is) well distributed throughout the year, with a slight summer maximum. But New Jersey summers were much hotter than those of northwestern Europe, a fact that elicited much comment from settlers: Gavin Scott of Elizabethtown Township wrote in mid-July 1798 that "the other week we had three days the warmest I ever felt we were making hay I changed my shirt four times in one day."[3]

With the vegetative need for water and evaporation at their highest points, summer dry spells were a problem for New Jersey farmers, especially those on sandy soils. A serious drought plagued Cape May in August 1755 and must have especially hurt crops such as corn.[4] Cold, long winters were also a problem from time to time; Samuel Allinson of Burlington County noted that the winter of 1760–61 was uncommonly cold and snowy, circumstances he thought would lead to "very Fruitful Crops of Corn."[5] But the following spring was so dry as to strike many as unprecedented. In August 1762, the New York merchant John Watts recorded that "all necessarys for Life both for Man and Beast are astonishingly dear & scarce, owing in great Measure to the most severe Drouth that ever was known in this part of the world."[6] The inflation of wheat prices documented in local account books probably reflects the effects of this drought (table 16). Poor winter weather (perhaps lack of snow cover), a late spring, and the dryness induced an early harvest, which had driven prices up; so had quartering and supplying troops for the French and Indian War.[7]

New Jersey and the middle Atlantic region have long been known for changeable

Table 16
Wheat, Representative Prices Per Bushel
Credited to Local Accounts, in Shillings and Pence, 1675–1822

Year and Date	Location	Price
1675—Year	East Jersey (Summer Wheat)	4/6
1675—Year	East Jersey (Winter Wheat)	5/0
1735—July 29	Bound Brook	4/3–4/6
1753—June 28	Newark Township	5/6
1753—Sept. 24	Newark Township (seed wheat)	6/6
1757—Aug. 1	Newark Township	5/0
1762—Dec. 27	Newark Township	8/8
1763—Sept. 13	Newark Township (seed wheat)	8/6
1765—Mar. 12	Hardwick Township	5/0
1769—Jan. 11	Newark Township	7/0
1769—Aug. 26	Amwell Township	5/0
1770—Feb. 17	Hardwick Township (seed wheat)	5/0
1776—June 12	Newark Township	7/0
1787—?	New Jersey	7/6
1789—Feb. 12	Alexandria Township	10/0
1795—Jan. 4	Amwell Township	10/0–14/0
1796—Aug. 19	Warren Township (seed wheat)	8/0
1822—Jan. 2	Knowlton Township	8/11

daily weather and temperature extremes; at New Brunswick midwinter temperatures of 70 degrees Fahrenheit have been recorded, while temperatures during
some summers have dipped below 40 degrees. The winters of 1697–98, 1740–41,
and 1779–80 appear to have been especially severe, and the summer of 1816 was
infamous for its low temperatures throughout the Northeast.[8]

Still, the historical record of average temperatures indicates southern New Jersey
was relatively mild, as Kalm had perceived (maps 21 and 22).[9] Although winters in
the northwest are cold, air of continental origin reaching southern New Jersey is
moderated by passing over Delaware Bay and produces winters that are, on average, above freezing. Moreover, the length of both the frost-free season and the
growing season was extremely favorable to agriculture, though again great variation
exists between the south and the extreme northwest (maps 23 and 24). The frost-
free season at Cape May, for example, is fully two months longer than it is in the
Minisink Valley in the northwest. Most of the Piedmont has almost six frost-free
months. The growing season begins when temperatures average at least 43 degrees
Fahrenheit, by March 15 on the southern Inner Coastal Plain and about two or
three weeks later in the Highlands and Ridge and Valley sections. Thus in the south,
as advertisements so often mentioned, cattle could be turned out onto pastures earlier, stock could be wintered on the coastal marshes and islands, and wheat harvests
were earlier. Two summer crops a year were thus certainly possible, as Kalm suggested, in southern sections.

New Jersey tax laws did not tax crops, so the systematic valuations Lemon had
for southeastern Pennsylvania are lacking in New Jersey.[10] However, important
crops such as wheat, corn, and rye, as well as orchards and meadowland, were mentioned fairly regularly in farm sale advertisements, particularly in the corridor
between Philadelphia and New York (Inner Coastal Plain and southern Piedmont).[11] Another source of data are farmers' damage claims. After the Revolution,
the legislature authorized non-Loyalist farmers to file for damages to their lands as
a result of the actions of either British or American forces.[12] These claims list systematically what aggrieved farmers lost and its value; they were also attested by two
neighbors of good character who had personally witnessed the property loss or
destruction. Because a great part of the Revolutionary War was fought on New
Jersey soil, a great deal of damage occurred in the province, not only from such
major engagements as the battles of Princeton and Trenton but, perhaps more
extensively, from foraging expeditions and troop bivouacs (map 25). Not all the
damage claims have survived to the present day, but several thousand are available
from the contemporary counties of Bergen, Essex, Middlesex, Somerset,
Burlington and Hunterdon. Those for Bergen, Essex and Middlesex—the New
England- and Dutch-settled areas that tended not to advertise farm sales—are not
only complete but specify locations. The record for Somerset County is complete,
but locations are not as specific; Hunterdon and Burlington entries are only scattered and do not list locations (map 26).[13]

Advertisements, damage claims, farmers' journals, store account books, and
travelers' observations permit some judgement about the distribution of grain crops
in New Jersey, and there is little question of the mid–eighteenth-century preemi-
nence of wheat (map 27). Along with other middle colonies, New Jersey had earned
renown as a great producer of wheat, and these grain yields were tied into a vast

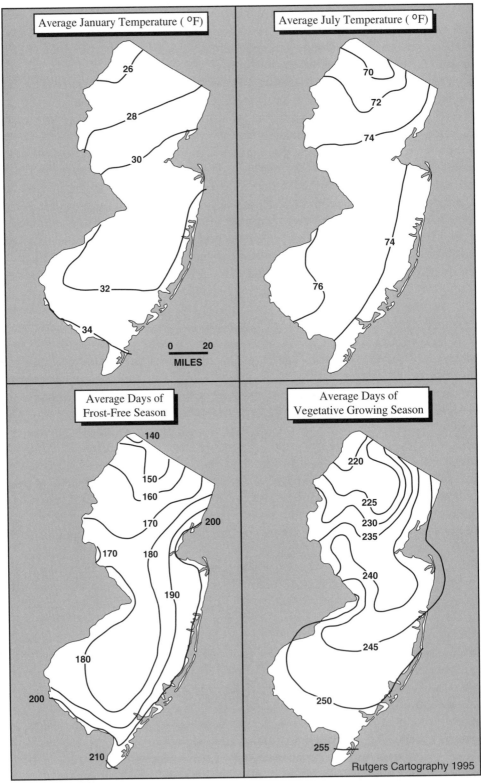

MAP 21

Average January Temperature (°F)

26

28

30

32

34

0   20
MILES

MAP 22

Average July Temperature (°F)

70

72

74

74

76

Average Days of Frost-Free Season

140

150

160

170

170   180

200

190

180

200

210

MAP 23

Average Days of Vegetative Growing Season

220

225

230

235

240

245

250

255

Rutgers Cartography 1995

MAP 24

transatlantic trade. In 1764, John Watts recorded his concern about the rapid escalation of wheat prices on both the New York and English markets due to "a call from the Streights" and suggested that a shortfall had occurred in the eastern Mediterranean wheat harvest: "even Sicily itself was encluded," he wrote, "perhaps one of the greatest Granarys in the World." Watts noted that New York port received wheat from Maryland and Virginia and exported at least half of the harvest in Connecticut and New Jersey.[14]

That wheat was the preferred grain crop in New Jersey is clear too in the fact that rye and wheat—planted and harvested in the same way and at about the same time, and productive of similar yields on better soils—commanded uniformly different prices; wheat always brought farmers much more per bushel. Wheat was certainly considered New Jersey's staple crop, but it was not dominant everywhere, and in some places it was rarely grown. Wheat assumed more importance among farmers on the lower Cohansey, around Greenwich, for example, than it did in most of the rest of southern New Jersey. And its overall prevalence seems to have diminished after the Revolution, as other grain crops became more common.

Map 27 distinguishes between "actual" wheat—that which advertisements state was then growing and would be sold with the property—and "reputed" wheat, which embraces such statements as that the land was good for wheat or that the area generally produced a great deal of this grain. The war damage claims used for the map described only wheat in a field, not wheat in storage, as the latter

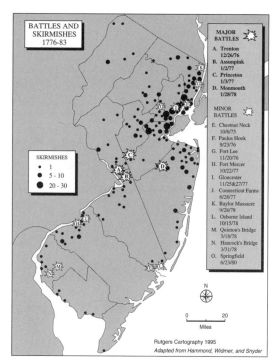

MAP 25

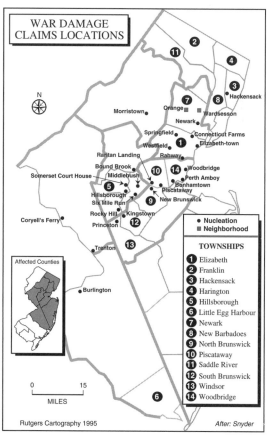

MAP 26

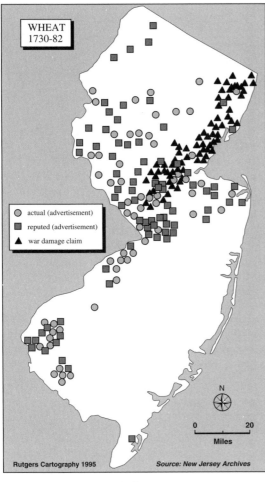

MAP 27

could have been brought in from else-where; thus the map is probably a conservative representation.

The data suggest that little wheat was grown in the extreme northwest, on the Outer Coastal Plain, or on the Inner Coastal Plain of Gloucester and southern Burlington counties. Settlement in the northwest was so recent that few advertisements were issued from this section, which may well account for the paucity of wheat in that area. Other documents attest its importance there. A letter from the Reverend Uzal Ogden in recently founded New-Town, Sussex County, noted that farmers there "sent their Iron, Wheat, Flaxseed, Cattle, Hams, Butter &c." chiefly to Philadelphia and New York markets. Ogden noted, "The country is mountainous, the soil in common pretty good and produces excellent wheat."[15] But in the north-east around Springfield, where the sandy soils from glacial outwash were fine for summer grains, "wheat dies in the winter from dampness and frost," Theophile Cazenove noted in 1794.[16] And very little wheat was grown on the Outer Coastal Plain because of its infertile soils, though the better Pleistocene terraces could support a decent crop. Jacob Spicer recorded finishing his wheat harvest at Cape May on July 15, 1762; Sarah Thomas mentioned that Judge Ebenezer Tucker of Tuckerton had very highly cultivated land with "very fine wheat" on June 24, 1809.[17]

Wheat was also relatively absent on the southern part of the Inner Coastal Plain. Following the early Swedish perception, residents judged the soils there to be poor. For example, in 1765 Samuel Smith wrote approvingly of the fertility of the soils of the Inner Coastal Plain in Monmouth County, which same soils he called only fair in Burlington.[18] Wheat certainly was grown there, but it appears that corn and rye were far more important. Moreover, for many years settlers demonstrated a greater tendency to keep the area near Philadelphia permanently in woodland, most likely a heritage of early Swedish settlement or a calculation of the potential to sell wood to the urban market, a reflection of the utility of von Thünen's land use theory in this instance.[19]

At the time of initial settlement, farmers in New Jersey apparently grew both summer and winter wheat, as the 1675 General Assembly valuation of grains indicates. Compiled for tax payments in lieu of cash, the list valued winter wheat at five shillings per bushel and summer wheat at six pence less.[20] By the mid-eighteenth century winter wheat, sown in the fall and harvested in the summer, was more common than summer wheat. Because wheat was a commonplace well known to Englishmen, few accounts describe its cultivation. But in his attempt to explain the light harvest of 1783, Johann Schoepf described the best conditions for the growth of both types:

> This summer the wheat harvest in Jersey turned out very moderately. There had been too little rain in the fall, and the winter was too mild and open. The farmer is well pleased, therefore, if his winter wheat, towards the end of December or in January, is covered with snow and thus protected against rain and frost, by which (when snow falls) the tender, exposed sprouts are killed or are pushed out of the freezing ground. Here as in the other middle provinces almost no spring wheat is sown, but that is not the case more to the south and more to the north, as for example in Carolina and in Massachusetts. Winter grain does not thrive in the southern provinces, because of the warmth of the autumn, the mildness of the winter, and the lack of snow, which very seldom falls; the young sprouts therefore grow faster, and a frosty winter night often kills off entirely the soft, exposed seed. What with extreme cold and early winters, spring wheat also does better in colder provinces.[21]

In the mid-eighteenth century, Peter Kalm noted that wheat fields in Delaware were prepared in the "English manner," with numerous furrows four to six feet apart (rather than ditches) for draining water.[22] In southern New Jersey, Kalm stated, the same method was in use, though heavy rains were known to wash out the wheat and rye seed. These grain fields were laid out in flat, rectilinear sections not elevated in the middle (as they would perhaps have been in Sweden) or divided into lots about twenty feet wide and separated from each other by furrows. Kalm's comments also suggest that southwestern New Jersey farmers used a system of shifting cultivation to produce grains (presumably including wheat), a survival of an Old-World Finnish practice:

> When a grain field has been obliged to bear the same kind of product for three years in succession it does not after that produce anything at all if it be not well manured, or allowed to lie fallow for a few years. Manure is very difficult to obtain and therefore people rather leave the field uncultivated. In that interval it is covered with all sort of plants and trees, and the countryman in the meanwhile cultivates a piece of ground which has till then been fallow, or he chooses a part of the ground which has never been plowed before and he can in both cases be pretty sure of a plentiful crop.[23]

Toward the end of the century, major landholders such as John Rutherfurd were advocating more sensible rotational schemes. The typical lease included the stipulation that tenants would not "plow any Part of the Premises more than once in [three or four] years for Winter Grain [rye and wheat]."[24]

There really is no way of telling precisely how much wheat was grown. By modern standards, certainly, the total land on any farm devoted to wheat was relatively small. As late as December 1781, a farm near Princeton was advertised for sale with "about 16 acres of green wheat in the ground."[25] On February 16, 1789, Robert

Johnston recorded yields that suggest he had planted about twenty-four acres in wheat on the generally excellent soils near Salem—"in the field Next Egle point 370 Bushels of Wheat Not Quite 15 Bushels to the Acre."[26]

Naturally, holders of large parcels of land grew more wheat, and they were most able to afford the labor to sow, tend, and harvest it. Lewis Morris, the absentee owner of Tinton Manor in Monmouth County, estimated that the wheat harvest in 1729 amounted to twelve to thirteen hundred bushels.[27] His son, who was to be responsible for the plantation in 1730, proposed to sow eighty acres with wheat that year. If he had cropped this much the year before, the yield would have been fifteen bushels to the acre. Morris suggested that his son be generous in the amount sowed per acre:

> The generallity of that country incline to thin Sowing, and boast the Successe of it: but I never saw any of the best of their wheat, comparable to my own, when I was there, & for that reason Still adhere to my own way of Sowing, a bushell & halfe & halfe a peck on an Acre: but this must not be A guess'd, but a measured Acre. . . . It should be plow'd in, not harrowed in: & considering the careless Husbandry that has been used there, by wch meanes the ground is foule, I think it Should be sow'd in Six Furrow ridges, that it may be . . . clean'd from rye, cockle, and drips, the certain concomitants of ill Husbandry: & considering how farr tis from home, how Subject to breachy cattle, & how much used too many people are there, to throw down fences to turn cattle in, no care in well fencing and watching of it can be too much.

Kalm had reported that on the better soils in southwestern New Jersey (clay mixed with sand and organic material) a bushel of rye or wheat would return twenty; barley on such soil, well prepared, should return thirty bushels.[28] So Morris's fifteen bushels per acre must have been a moderate yield (table 17). One farm advertised as "excellent for wheat" in Mendham Township, Morris County, in 1772 was claimed to yield twenty-four to twenty-seven bushels per acre weighing sixty-three to sixty-five pounds.[29] But on Cape May at about the same time, new land initially cleared of forest was promised to yield eight to ten bushels of wheat and twenty to thirty bushels of Indian corn.[30] When Spicer tallied up his entire wheat harvest on Cape May on July 15, 1762 (amid very severe drought), he counted 1,256 sheaves of "table wheat" and 287 of "seed" wheat (the best of the crop). At twenty sheaves to the bushel, he had only seventy-seven bushels "in the whole," indicating a poor yield and a small area under cultivation.[31]

In the northwest's worked-out soils, yields may have even been lower. An undated Revolutionary-era memorandum, probably describing a northern Hunterdon County location, indicates the yield of "Old ground wheat about two acres 200 sheaves," or "about 9 busl."[32] At the beginning of the Revolution, Francis Rush Clark, Inspector and Superintendent of His Majesty's Provision Train of Wagons and Horses, judged New Jersey's ability to grow wheat not very promising.

> The Soil of Jersey [probably the Piedmont] is in Genl. thick: Clay Grounds are very good for Grass when Manured, but without great Tillage, not favourable for Wheat, which is very apt to be destroyed in the Winter, in such grounds by Rains, or hurt by the droughts of summer—Loomy Lands are reckoned the best, they are

Table 17
Wheat, Yields per Acre in Bushels, 1749–1800

Year and Date	Location(s), Conditions	Yield
1749—March	Gloucester County—clay loam, well prepared	20 bu
1755—July 15	Lower Township, Cape May	4 bu +
1756—Year	Burlington County—mud (greensand marl?)	
	added to sandy soil	25 bu
1772—Year	Mendham Township—soil "excellent for wheat"	24—27 bu
1774—Year	Cape May—"new land"	8—10 bu
1777—Year	Northern New Jersey—loams best—"old Farms"	10—12 bu
	"well tilled and manured"	20—24 bu +
Revolutionary War	Probably northern Hunterdon County—	
	"Old Ground"	4.5 bu
1783—Year	Central New Jersey—	
	poor land	10—12 bu
	better land	15—18 bu
1787—September	"New Jersey"—	
	wet clay	5 bu
	seed drilled	10 bu
	well manured 20 bu	
1787—Year	Northern New Jersey—	
	normal	6 bu
	better soils	8 bu
1789—July	Salem Vicinity	15 bu
1794—Year	Hanover, Morris County—medium to good land	15—16 bu
	Musconetcong Valley	10 bu
1800—October	Elizabethtown Vicinity—an excellent farmer	
	(English)	40 bu

warm in winter, and stand the drought in Summer better than any Clay."[33]

"In the Old Farms," Clark stated, yields were ten to twelve bushels per acre, but where the soil was "well till'd and Manured will bring Double & more." In the chief wheat-growing area, Hunterdon County as well as Somerset County, farmers realized yields of about thirty bushels to the acre before the Revolution, but evidence suggests such high production rates were uncommon elsewhere.[34] Wheat was still a considerable item of trade in central New Jersey at the end of the war, Schoepf observed, and yields ranged from ten to twelve bushels per acre on poorer land and fifteen to eighteen on the better soils, with one bushel sown to the acre.[35]

After the Revolution, however, wheat yields were much diminished, a fact farmers attributed to played-out soils. In 1787 John Rutherfurd complained that lands (presumably in northern New Jersey, where his own properties lay) "are very much Exhausted" and that "winter crops" (wheat and rye) averaged only six bushels per acre and only in some places more than eight bushels "except when manured."[36] Lemon reported similar circumstances in southeastern Pennsylvania. After midcentury farmers could produce only five to twelve bushels per acre on old land, while twenty to forty bushels were reported on newer land.[37]

Evidently even more significant than soil depletion in the decline of wheat immediately after the Revolution was the arrival of an insect pest, the so-called "Hessian fly." Native to Eurasia, the fly allegedly arrived in eastern North America in the straw bedding of Hessian troops. "Our wheat . . . will be eaten up with an insect called an Hessian fly," one of the Capnerhursts wrote from Flemington in Hunterdon County in May 1788; "its first appearance was near the place where the

Hessians landed and yearly advances into the country. It is devouring the wheat all round they tell me."[38] On July 12, 1787, New England botanist Rev. Manasseh Cutler recorded the "immense injury to wheat" the fly had done on one Princeton farm. In 1794 near Morristown, Theophile Cazenove noted, "The Hessian Fly has been in these districts a great deal."[39]

In the spring, the female Hessian fly lay eggs on young wheat, barley, or rye plants. Larvae hatched several days later and fed on the sap of the plant. Once they reached maturity, the flies lived about three days but laid eggs in that time; the next generation passed the winter as pupae on the wheat and developed into adults in the spring.[40] But the fly apparently did not extirpate wheat in central New Jersey, or, if it had, the crop had recovered by the time Cutler wrote about the fields south of New Brunswick on July 11, 1787. "The crops of wheat, rye, barley, oats and flax, which I observed in the course of this day's travel were very fine." Later in the year, probably in October, he visited his uncle, a farmer near Morristown, and declared his crop of wheat "unusually large."[41]

Cutler pointed out that Colonel George Morgan of Princeton, famed as an agricultural innovator, had conducted "experiments" (perhaps including deep plowing) with controlling the Hessian fly that had enabled farmers to "get rid of an insect that had wholly cut off the crops of grain for several years successively." A letter from Gavin Scott near Elizabethtown to his brother in England in October 1800 also suggests that the fly was no longer a problem for Jersey farmers. One nearby English emigré farmer, he wrote, was "running as fast before the farmers in this new country as ever he did in the old," his eighteen acres of wheat having produced forty bushels to the acre that year. He expected to be able to sell this seed wheat for the very high price of $2.50 per bushel.[42]

The wheat crop was also hurt by what was probably a black stem rust that lived on barberry bushes. In 1745, farmers singled out the barberry as the culprit in a blight affecting grain in northern Monmouth County.[43] Schoepf noted that "the mildew" had attacked wheat between the first and tenth of July, just before harvest, in 1783, and cited New Englanders' belief that the barberry was injurious to the grain. "But," he added, "the New Englanders are known for other strange beliefs and practices as well, and it was among them that witch trials, at the beginning of the century, were so grimly prosecuted."[44] The black stem rust affected other grains as well, but no evidence is known to document its impact on the production of wheat or any other grain by region or over time.

Before the Revolution, most farmers probably used their own seed wheat or purchased enough to plant from others nearby. On September 10, 1754, for example, Mary Wheeler paid ten shillings for a bushel and a half of "Seed wheat" in what is now Irvington, a suburb of Newark.[45] At the same time, some of the more affluent and experimental farmers were probably already trying seed from elsewhere. Philip Kearny's account book records that on October 21, 1773, Stephen Skinner was in debt to him for "four [bushels] Algrs Barbary Wheat."[46] Kearny's business in Perth Amboy imported wine from Madeira and Lisbon extensively, whence probably came this wheat.

Seed wheat of course brought a higher price than table wheat and returned to farmers a significant premium over the other grains as well. The Assembly's 1675 valuation for winter wheat, five shillings per bushel, placed it above both rye and barley, valued at four shillings per bushel, and Indian corn, valued at three shillings.[47] Tenants on the Ramapo Tract in 1713 were reportedly paying the equivalent of $1.02 to $1.20 for a bushel of wheat, $0.72 to $0.90 for rye, $0.99 to $1.08 for corn, and $0.72 for buckwheat depending upon the season; grain values were lowest at the time of harvest and gradually rose higher as stocks were depleted.[4]

The ledger book of Onesimus Whitehead of Mendham Township, Morris County, documents grain prices from 1782 to 1800 and presents evidence of both seasonal and annual variations in value, as well as of consumption patterns. Whitehead was an ordinary farmer holding between seventy and eighty-five acres, two horses, up to eight cattle, and, at least in 1781, two hogs. Not a merchant in any sense, Whitehead yet recorded a series of transactions he carried on with Rebeckah Whitehead, probably his unmarried sister who lived either with Onesimus or nearby.[49] Figure 8 summarizes the prices debited to Rebeckah for the various grains between January of 1782 and December of 1800.

These figures are probably reliable, as the transactions involved the same two people living in the same area for almost two decades. For Rebeckah Whitehead, wheat was by far the most costly of grains, followed by rye, corn, and buckwheat. But, judging by her transactions with Onesimus, she used more corn than any other grain and used wheat least of all of them. She kept hogs (Onesimus slaughtered them for her), so perhaps she bought some of the corn to feed them. Rebeckah generally bought her corn at the beginning of the winter, when the harvest was in and the prices were lower, which also suggests that she used it for feed. The buckwheat she bought may have been for her own use or to feed her poultry.

Grain prices over this eighteen-year period apparently fluctuated according to

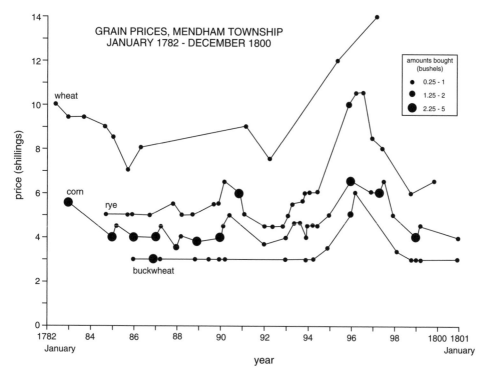

FIGURE 8

external market factors and weather conditions. Demand for all grains except buckwheat (low in value and generally not counted as a commercial crop) was high in 1790, and prices began to climb again in 1792. By the fall of 1794, even the price of buckwheat increased, which indicates that bad weather elsewhere or political events (possibly in France) had made all grain scarce locally, most of it having been exported.

Tables 16, 18–20, and 22 are attempts to compile the prices of the various food-stuffs over the same years to pinpoint why grain prices might have varied. They show that grains were valued most highly in the more accessible locations, where the cost of transport to a potential market would have been considerably less. Among the European winter grains, the prevalence of rye in New Jersey was second only to wheat. But because it was not valued as highly as wheat, advertisements mentioned it much less often. Its distribution appears to have been very much like that of wheat, except that it was far more likely to be grown in the Outer Coastal Plain than was wheat (map 28). On May 23, 1758, Jacob Spicer reported that one of the Swedish settlers of the Maurice River area "has two fields that has been tilled, every other year for this 30 years by information, and that one now in rye, the rye looks good and the other in corn is likely to produce a good crop by appearance." Pastor Wrangel reported seeing good stands of rye on his visit among Swedish-born residents of the Outer Coastal Plain in 1764. The journal of Julian Niemcewicz also states that rye rather than wheat was commonly grown on the better soils in this region. On June 8, 1797, five to six miles beyond the "sand and pine forests" near Egg Harbor, Niemcewicz came upon "oak trees and better land [undoubtedly the Cape May Formation] covered with a rather good-looking stand of rye."[50] Swedish and Dutch immigrants and their descendants used rye widely for food, a practice that other groups may have adopted when wheat harvests declined after the Revolution. Kalm observed that rye was planted and tilled in the same way that wheat was in Gloucester County, and on good soil yields were about the same.[51]

Corn, called maize or Indian corn in the earliest years, was valued as food for both people and livestock. The Dutch picked up the trait of eating cornmeal mush from the Indians early on.[52] There is a great deal more contemporaneous description of corn than of wheat or rye, undoubtedly because this American domesticate was unfamiliar to Europeans. Corn was one of the "summer" grains, sowed in the spring and harvested by early fall; it did well in the long summers of the Middle Colonies but could not mature in the shorter, cooler summers of northwestern Europe. For his part, Kalm was fascinated

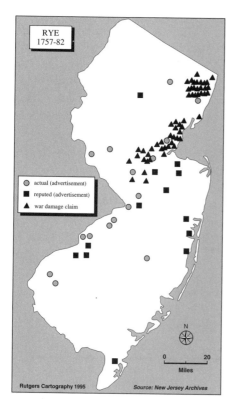

RYE
1757-82

○ actual (advertisement)
■ reputed (advertisement)
▲ war damage claim

N

0   20
Miles

Rutgers Cartography 1995   Source: New Jersey Archives

MAP 28

with corn and wrote two studies on the grain for Swedish readers. In southwestern New Jersey, he wrote, "The Swedes and all the other inhabitants of the country plant great quantities of corn, both for themselves and for their cattle. It is asserted that it is the best food for hogs, because it makes them very fat and gives their flesh an agreeable flavor, preferable to all other meat."[53] Kalm also noted that in Pennsylvania corn stalks were cut at harvest time below the ear, dried, and put up in narrow stacks to serve as cattle food during the winter. Charles Read advocated topping the corn after the silk dried and the kernels had grown hard. The tops were to lay twenty-four hours, then be bound in sheaves, allowed to dry further, and then stored away in a barn or barrack. He felt they made especially fine fodder for sheep. Corn tops were also widely used in the New England-settled section.[54] Another way to use corn for livestock was to feed it to hogs while it was "soft & milky Stalk & all. They chew & suck ye Stalk. They eat Cobb as well as Corn."[55] In one sale notice for a Princeton area farm in 1772, the corn contained in the "choice waggon-house with a good hay-loft and two cribs under the same roof" holding "near 1000 bushels of corn" was most likely feed.[56]

But by the middle of the eighteenth century in at least some places, corn apparently dominated in the human consumption of grains, at least according to an Englishman resident for more than six years in northern Monmouth County.

Table 18
Rye, Representative Prices per Bushel Credited to Local Accounts,
In Shillings and Pence, 1675–1822

Year and Date	Location	Price
1675—Year	East Jersey	4/0
1755—Year	Lower Township	2/9
1767—Sept. 17	Newark Township	5/0
1769—Aug. 26	Amwell Township	4/0
1772—March	Hardwick Township	4/3
1783—Dec. 22	Amwell Township	3/9
1784—March	Amwell Township	5/0
1784—April	Amwell Township	5/0
1789—Feb. 12	Alexandria Township	5/0
1790—Dec. 27	Warren Township	5/6
1791—May 18	Warren Township	4/6
1791—Oct. 30	Warren Township (seed rye)	5/6
1793—Mar. 27	Warren Township	5/3
1795—Jan. 4	Hunterdon County	7/6–8/0
1800—June 19	Franklin Township	9/0
1800—July 7	Warren Township	7/0
1800—July 29	Franklin Township	8/0
1800—Aug. 13	Franklin Township	7/0
1802—May 15	Franklin Township	5/6
1802—July 19	Franklin Township	5/6
1802—Aug. 2	Franklin Township	5/6
1802—Sept. 15	Franklin Township	5/6
1803—Apr. 21	Franklin Township	5/0
1806—February	Kingwood Township	5/0
1808—Sept. 13	Knowlton Township (seed rye)	6/0
1811—Aug. 21	Knowlton Township	5/0
1822—Feb. 12	Knowlton Township	4/6

This country's provisions are not of the best, but such as will relish very well with those that are not too nice a palate. The people live chiefly upon salt meat and roots, of the same as grow in England, besides pompions and squashes, of which they eat plentifully and with their victuals. But their most reigning dish is maize ground, and boiled into a diet they call suppaun. With this the board is crowned three times a day.[57]

Corn was not valued as highly as wheat, varying from about 50 to about 70 percent of wheat's price per bushel (table 19). And, like rye, it was not mentioned as often as wheat in real estate advertisements (map 29). Some limited amount, much less than wheat, was exported. John Watts wrote Col. William Amherst from New York on August 17, 1765, that "not one Bushell can I get of the Growth of this Colony New Jersey or the Eastward, where the best is produced, so scanty was the last Crop that the Country people send to Town for the Growth of Virginia for their own consumption." Watts indicated that if he could not get corn in Philadelphia, Amherst would have to wait until winter when the next crop would be available for shipping. He reckoned the price at twenty pence per bushel, the freight about the same, with a cask containing three bushels costing twelve pence. These prices,

Table 19
Corn, Representative Prices per Bushel Credited to Local Accounts,
In Shillings and Pence, 1675–1815

Year and Date	Location	Price
1675—Year	East Jersey	3/0
1755—Year	Lower Township	2/0
1765—Mar. 7	Newark Township	3/6
1766—Apr. 8	Newark Township	3/6
1766—Dec. 5	Newark Township	3/6
1769—May 5	Newark Township	4/0
1769—August	Amwell Township	3/6
1776—May	Newark Township	3/6
1788—Mar. 5	Millstone	3/6
1790—Feb. 27	N. Morris County	5/5
1790—Dec. 27	Warren Township	3/6
1791—July 7	Warren Township	3/4
1793—Mar. 30	Warren Township	5/0
1794—Mar. 3	Warren Township	5/0
1794—Mar. 21	Warren Township	4/6
1794—June 14	Warren Township	4/9
1794—June 21	Warren Township	5/0
1794—Sept. 27	Warren Township	5/0
1795—Jan. 4	Hunterdon County	7/6
1796—February	Hardwick Township	4/0
1796—Aug. 19	Warren Township	8/0
1796—Sept. 23	Warren Township	8/0
1796—Oct. 29	Warren Township	6/0
1798—June 4	Franklin Township	4/8
1799—May 29	Franklin Township	4/6
1800—Apr. 8	Warren Township	6/4
1800—May 26	Warren Township	7/0
1800—July 7	Warren Township	7/0
1803—Oct. 13	Franklin Township	5/4
1815—Feb. 27	Knowlton Township	5/0

which include the expense of the cask, indicate that it must have been corn for human consumption.[58] Few records document shipments of this grain, though, and those that do indicate that exports were small: Stephen Skinner was credited by Philip Kearny with delivery of 728 bushels of corn to be shipped to Madeira on June 11, 1773.[59]

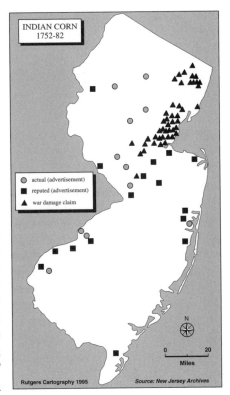

MAP 29

Peter Kalm described the corn in southwestern New Jersey reaching as high as eight feet and growing, in Amerindian fashion, in hills five and a half feet apart in all directions. Like rye but unlike wheat, corn grew well on the Outer Coastal Plain, where yields were two to three times greater than wheat yields. "Well dunged" upland at Little Egg Harbor advertised in 1767 was claimed to bear "as large a Crop of Corn as almost any land in the Jerseys"; one property at Toms River Bridge was advertised in August 1779 to include a field of twenty acres planted in Indian corn.[60] Jacob Spicer recorded his experience with corn on his farm at Cape May about the first of January 1756.

> Note. Planted 1¾ acres of indian corn in the orchard near my dwelling, and it was esteemed good especially next the house, and it yielded by measure but 19 bushels per acre good and bad together. I am at a loss to reconcile what I have heard with respect to the great yield of corn. I am sure 20 bushels per acre may be esteemed very good corn.[61]

However, the heavy clays of the Piedmont, according to Francis Rush Clark in 1777, were not favorable for the cultivation of wheat or corn. "Clays are not kind for Indian Corn, all Looms & even sand are," he wrote. "In Sandy Ground, I have known Indn Corn yield 40 Bushl. p. Acre, the common yield of Indian Corn with tolerable care is twenty and thirty Bushl. p Acre."[62]

In sandy soils, Clark advocated using a shovel full of aged dung per hill of corn, but on clay soil it should be covered with "Coarse litter, or Salt Hay, which keeps the soil loose" during dry spells in the summer. Other contemporaneous accounts of the cultivation of corn indicate that Clark described the common practice of the day.

In southern New Jersey rye was occasionally sown between the hills of corn in the fall before the corn had fully matured. Charles Read advocated a great deal of cultivation of corn both with a harrow and by hand with a hoe. Account books from Essex County contemporaneous with Read also mention hoeing during the growing season.[63] Thus, corn was seen to demand a great deal of labor, a fact that farmers surely kept in mind in deciding whether to grow it or one of the winter grains.

James Parker's detailed account of the cultivation of corn at Shipley, his estate in Hunterdon County, makes clear how labor intensive it was. On May 16, 1778, five of his workers were "dressing" corn, a practice he deemed well worth a farmer's while. Much as Francis Rush Clark had advocated, Parker dressed the crop to enhance the ability of the soil to receive and store moisture and to remove any vegetation competing with the corn. Parker acknowledged that his method went "against the Common practice" and that not all farmers were apt to follow it, but its evident success must have prompted him to detail it at length.

my corn was ridged which I by no means think the best way. The Hills were dunged with lime compost not sufficiently seperated [slacked] it was a dry time when it was planted and about a week after it came up there was a flood of Rain that rather hardened the Ground than otherways the first work after the planting was to plow out the Vacancies between the rows which was done when the ground was rather too wet the next process was to go with a heavy Harrow up and down between every two Rows across the plowing the Next to plow the same way with the Harrow which was begun this day In doing this the dirt is thrown up by the plow so as to bury many of the Hills of Corn which must unavoidably be the case this makes it necessary to have a man follow the plow to clear the Corn which one man can hardly do but more ought to be done at this time two plows should be employed and giving them about ten rows the start they will employ four men if they do their work properly to follow them for not only the dirt should be thrown off the Hill of Corn but it should be well set up and all the old dirt for about half an Inch deep skimmed off with the Hoe & fresh fine earth (of which the plowing makes a plenty) drawn up with the Hoe in its stead or if you should loosen the Earth from nine to twelve inches each side of the Corn as deep at least as you judge the Root to be and all the Course dry dirt thrown of & a little moist fine Earth drawn up in its place & so proceed from Hill to Hill till finished taking particular Care to cut up clean all the grass weeds & bushes of every kind whatever that is left untouched by the plow particularly round & in the Hill this is great Labour but it is well worth while for the Corn at this time which is about four or rather five weeks from the time of planting is very tender and wants all the Help of Art as well as Nature to give it a start which is particularly necessary in this State of Infancy as I may say for on its striking Root and the ground (at this time particularly) being well pulverized round the Hill as well as in the Hill your crop greatly depends and this contributes more than anything else to this end I know amongst farmers in general it is thought to be too early to do anything but Harrow wch I judge proceeds from a prevailing opinion that the Corn is too young and apt to be hurt or destroyed by the many Rubs & bruises it gets in this tender state but this really is not the Case it being much better able to stand this bruising now than when it is older as it gives way easily to the Harrow & plow & only bends to it when at a later time it would not so well bear the Treatment as if is Stouter an much more brittle[64]

Scratching up the soil between the rows, Parker declared, "prepares the ground for the Reception of all small rains and dews as well as possible can be and gives the Corn a much better chance in a dry time than it possibly can have any other way." But dry spells were not the only problem confronting Parker's corn crop. "No working today except Joseph Snider & his boys who went into the Corn which in many places was badly come up the black worm eat much & other bad appearances," he wrote on June 4, 1781. Luckily, in a region blessed with a long growing season, Parker simply replanted his corn.

Robert Kenedy, who probably also farmed in Hunterdon County, described his method of cultivating corn in a 1797 letter to John Stevens, a document that shows his process to have been much like Parker's.[65] Kenedy's furrows were about five feet apart in "rich" and "mellow" soil. The seed was soaked in dung water for twenty-four hours, rolled in plaster of Paris, and then planted about six inches apart. Harrowing and plowing were done much as Parker had described. Farm hands were kept busy using rakes to destroy all vegetation but the corn. More plaster was applied when the corn was a foot high, but only in damp weather. Kenedy claimed that William Johnson had followed these methods on four acres and had harvested a carefully measured 92.25 bushels per acre.

Mentions of buckwheat appear often in local personal and store accounts but rarely in the official record, because it was not a commercial crop and was not, for the most part, transported to distant markets. It was not even included in the 1675 listing of crops accepted for the payment of taxes. And because of its low value (table 20), contemporary advertisements did not often mention buckwheat. However, other records suggest that it was grown throughout New Jersey, except perhaps on the Outer Coastal Plain. Its noncommercial nature generally shielded it from the price fluctuations commercial grains experienced; that its price skyrocketed in the 1790s in Mendham Township was surely an anomaly. Buckwheat could grow in a relatively short season; a crop could be sown and harvested between the harvest of winter grains in the summer and their planting in the fall. And it could

Table 20
Buckwheat, Representative Prices per Bushel Credited to Local Accounts,
In Shillings and Pence, 1765–1815

Year and Date	Location	Price
1765—July 9	Newark Township	3/0
1767—July 17	Newark Township	2/9
1771—January	Newark Township	3/0
1776—Oct. 28	N. Morris County	3/0
1783—Dec. 22	Amwell Township	3/0
1790—July 16	Warren Township	4/0
1790—Dec. 27	Warren Township	2/6
1791—Oct. 15	Warren Township	2/0
1795—Jan. 4	Hunterdon County	4/6
1795—Oct. 14	Warren Township	5/4
1796—February	Hardwick Township	3/0
1800—Oct. 20	Warren Township	4/0
1801—Feb. 23	Warren Township	4/0
1802—Oct. 29	Franklin Township	3/0
1802—Nov. 18	Franklin Township	3/0
1802—Dec. 3	Franklin Township	3/0
1806—February	Kingwood Township	4/3
1807—Dec. 7	Knowlton Township	2/6
1813—Dec. 13	Knowlton Township	5/0
1814—Jan. 15	Knowlton Township	5/0
1815—Nov. 10	Knowlton Township	5/0
1817—Oct. 18	Knowlton Township	3/9

be quickly substituted for a failed crop of another winter grain or summer grain. Kalm was probably referring to buckwheat when he noted that two crops of grain could be produced in southern New Jersey in a year.

Irrespective of its market value, buckwheat was highly esteemed as food. Peter Kalm described buckwheat cakes baked in a frying pan or on a stone, buttered, then eaten when still warm with tea or coffee in the morning. He thought they were very good and noted that they were a common dish in Philadelphia (which implies that some commercial production of the grain took place) and in the other English colonies. Buckwheat was also widely used for feeding poultry and hogs. Chickens fed this grain, Kalm stated, "lay more eggs than they do from other food." And fields of buckwheat formed excellent pasture for bees, which were also to be found very widely.[66]

Charles Read called buckwheat "French-wheat" and advocated sowing half a bushel per acre except on sandy soils; one of his neighbors had cultivated eight acres with a return of sixty bushels per acre, which Read judged a very good result.[67] Kalm indicated that buckwheat was sown by the middle of July in southwestern New Jersey. If sown later, the frost would ruin it; if earlier, "it flowers all summer long, though the flowers drop and no seed is generated." During wet years, the best for buckwheat, harvests varied between twenty and forty bushels from a bushel sown.[68] Buckwheat was often used as an initial crop on newly cleared land over which a knotty log had been drawn. The grain was then broadcast and harrowed in with heavy brush.[69]

Poorer people probably grew and ate more buckwheat than did others. James Parker's account of "Grain in the hands of Jesse Warrick my thirds of the farm he lives on in Alexandria," a township in Hunterdon County, documents that Warrick, his tenant, produced more buckwheat than any other grain between 1789 and 1791 (table 21).[70] In 1791, the summer grains appear not to have yielded as well as the year before, more evidence in favor of the inclement weather in these years. Wheat may not have appeared in the latter two years on this account because Parker could readily market this grain.

Oats were also probably widely cultivated. The early Scottish settlers in East Jersey ate them,[71] but elsewhere oats were produced primarily for horses. Like buckwheat, oats were rarely mentioned in advertisements or local account books. Nor were they listed in the 1675 Assembly list (table 22).

By the mid-eighteenth century, cultivation of barley was rare. Barley had been used mostly to make beer in the seventeenth century, and as the taste of later inhabitants shifted toward other alcoholic beverages, its cultivation may have declined accordingly.[72]

Table 21
Grains Left with Jesse Warrick as a One-Third Share
Due James Parker, 1789–91

	1789	1789	1791
Buckwheat	—	100 bu	45 bu
Corn	—	38 bu	30 bu
Oats	—	—	28 bu
Rye	37 bu 28 lbs	28 bu	40 bu
Wheat	18 bu 18 lbs		

Table 22
Oats, Representative Prices per Bushel Credited to Local Accounts,
In Shillings and Pence, 1765–1808

Year and Date	Location	Price
1765—Mar. 12	Hardwick Township	2/6
1784—April	Amwell Township	2/6
1788—Mar. 5	Millstone (seed for relative)	2/6
1795—Jan. 4	Hunterdon County	2/9
1801—Apr. 14	Franklin Township	2/6
1808—Apr. 25	Knowlton Township	3/0

Mention of other small grains appears in the record from time to time, indicating that some experimentation was probably taking place. On April 29, 1756, Charles Read sowed millet in his garden; on August 24, he harvested sixty-seven bushels per acre. He thought it could best be utilized green for the cattle.[73] In 1806 and 1807, Joseph Wheeler Camp, a teacher in Newark, recorded debts to neighbors for "the use of Land for Broom Corn" and for a half-day's hoeing of broom corn.[74] In 1804, Calvin Green of Hanover, Morris County, recorded earning more than one hundred dollars for making brooms from his crop of broom corn; in 1805, he earned more than two hundred dollars from the sale of seven hundred brooms from nine acres. Green continued to raise the crop on reduced acreage and to manufacture brooms through at least 1812.[75] Growing broom corn made sense as urban populations and markets expanded in the New England-settled section of the state.

Non-Grain Crops, Orchards, and Vineyards

New Jersey farmers grew a wide array of non-grain crops throughout this period, as numerous records attest. In an advertisement in one of the Philadelphia newspapers in 1772, Richard Collings, a self-described "Gardiner" in Newton Township, Gloucester County (now Camden), just across the Delaware from Philadelphia, offered a "great variety" of seeds, all available by March 12, and, in addition to "8 or 9 different sorts of early pease and beans, of his own raising, excellent in their kind," between forty and fifty distinct kinds of produce:

> Savoy, turnip cabbage, sugar loaf ditto, colliflower, colliflower brocoli, purple ditto, cale, radish, early Dutch turnip, red ditto, sellery, sallet ditto, celeriac, white-cross lettice, brown Dutch ditto, asparagus, scarlet running beans, white Turkey prickly cucumbers, long orange carrot; onions, of different kinds; white mustard seed, cresses, union peas; melons of different sorts; early chanton pease; marrow fat ditto, Spanish moralto ditto, dwarf sugar ditto, early masagon ditto, long-kid ditto, toker pease, Windsor ditto, white blossom ditto, white dwarf ditto, yellow ditto, speckled ditto, horseshoe ditto.[76]

A few years before Collings advertised his seed and produce, Charles Read, who lived a little north of Collings's farm, made extensive notes about the crops he planted. In addition to many of the same kinds of produce Collings grew, Read also cultivated "poke" (pokeweed, used for dyeing; its edible shoots resemble asparagus), kidney beans, watermelons, squashes, pumpkins, "4 o'Clocks & french mallow" (possibly used as herbs), "Convolvolus" (a member of the potato family), potatoes, spinach, parsnips, hops, and "Calavance peas" (cowpeas).[77] Peter Kalm reported in 1749 that farmers around Salem were growing saffron and had also been experimenting with cotton, having obtained the seed either in raw cotton they had purchased or directly from the Carolinas.[78]

Of course, such diversity may only have characterized the enterprise of more affluent and more market-oriented farmers, who also carried out important experiments with various fruits, particularly grapes. But most farmers in New Jersey probably planted potatoes and peas, and both flax fields and apple orchards were ubiquitous. Like grains, the prevalence of crops showed great variation by region: apples and flax were more apt to be found in north Jersey, peaches and cowpeas in the south, and hemp and vineyards in central sections.

Of all non-grain crops, potatoes were clearly the most important for New Jersey farmers. Because potatoes were low in commercial value and bulky to transport, they were not often mentioned in the records of merchants and farmers. Small farmers probably planted potatoes for their own consumption: on July 21, 1818, according to the accounts of Jesse Knowles of Knowlton Township, Sussex County, his worker Henry Thomas "Lost one day hoeing his potatoes," and Peter Kalm reported that sweet potatoes were in wide use more than a half-century earlier.[79] Larger farmers also grew them: James Parker planted forty bushels of potatoes on three and a half acres of his Hunterdon County estate in May 1778 and placed dung "from before the barn door" on his potato furrows in 1781.[80] And in a letter to the Royal Society of Art and Letters in London in 1769, Edward Antill of Piscataway in the Raritan Valley explained how potatoes might be cultivated when labor costs made hiring seasonal help less feasible:

> as the Wages of Labourers are very high with us, I beg leave to mention the method which Necessity obliges us to pursue, in Order to raise them in the cheapest manner. We plough a peice of Ground up time enough to rot before we Plant, containing one two or more Acres, according to the Number of Hogs we have to fatten, and of those we intend to keep over, which are called Store Hogs; we strike strait furrows through through [sic] the Ground from Side to Side, but not deep, some three, some four Foot asunder, in which we plant the Potatoes, a foot asunder, some with early ripe, some with later ripe, and cover them over with the mould that came out of the Furrow; The large Potatoe cut into four or sic Peices according to its bigness, We find to grow better and to yeild more and larger Potatoes, than the small Seed Potatoes do: and we find a warm Sandy Soil, that is in good Heart, but by no means rich, to be best for the purpose where choice is to be had When the Blade appears about four Inches above Ground, we Plough a furrow on each side to every Row, and heap up the Earth to the Potatoes, so that the blade does but just appear, and this we do a Second Time when the Blade is grown four Inches high, but some do it but once and say it is best that the Sun warms the Ground the better, that the Potatoes grow the larger and are the dryer and that they are the easier taken up: when the Potatoes are ripe and fit for use, we run a Plough under some of the Rows, and the Potatoes are turned up to Sight and thus we take up as many as we think proper for present use: they generally yeild from two to three hundred Bushels to the Acre.[81]

In his notes, Charles Read reported that a farmer in New Hanover Township, Burlington County, had planted two hundred hills of potatoes on about a seventh of an acre in 1767. Read calculated the return at fourteen pounds per hill and the value at least one pence a pound, so his crop, if all of it were to be sold, would fetch £80 per acre.[82] But by the 1760s, most farmers apparently grew potatoes, like corn, as a major source of food for hogs. Antill explained how harvested potatoes were boiled in a large kettle or cauldron, cooled and then fed to hogs, which "fatten very fast upon this food, and it makes very Sweet, firm good Pork, without the help of any Grain." Antill claimed the value of potatoes as hog feed was discovered in the Raritan Valley, but Charles Read, far to the southwest, knew of it fully a decade earlier. In 1767, he cited the instance of one farmer who had bought two pigs weighing about fifteen pounds each at harvest time (perhaps mid-July) and had fed them his unsold surplus of raw potatoes until Christmas. When the pigs were slaughtered, they each weighed 150 pounds, and they made, Read observed, very good pork. Read noted, however, that the pork would have been better if the potatoes had first been boiled.[83]

Edward Antill described a "yet Secret and new discovery" the year before his death concerning the substitution of potatoes for milk in feeding calves. After the cow had given birth and had licked her calf, Antill took the calf away so that the mother could not see or hear it. The cow was then milked. In the morning and evening, Antill fed the warm milk to the calf for two days and then mixed the milk into a thin "pap" with as much water and boiled potatoes to feed the calf on the third and fourth days. On the fifth day the milk was entirely withdrawn, and the pap was thickened as the calf required it, Antill wrote, "until they are turned to Grass." After ten days Antill put sweet grass in slit sticks before the calves who in a little time, he wrote, would "eat it heartily." After a month the calves were put into "a piece of Sweet turf near the place where they are kept," along with a yearling that would teach them to graze. The use of the pap continued until the calves "Eat Grass enough to keep them hearty."

Antill also began to feed potatoes to his stall-fed oxen. Formerly they had eaten "the best of Hay and Indian Corn" ground into meal. Now one-third to one-half of that mixture was mashed boiled potatoes, Antill wrote, "and they fatten very fast and extremely well on this Food." Antill's sheep were fattened in the same way. He also fed cows potatoes, though, if they did not like them, Antill both mixed bran into the potatoes and put it on top of the mixture until the cows took to it. "Their Milk," Antill wrote, "more than doubles the Expence of Hay and Potatoes."[84]

Unlike potatoes, which had little commercial value, peas had been included on the 1675 list of crops acceptable for tax payment in East Jersey in lieu of specie. They were valued at three shillings per bushel, less than winter wheat but the same as Indian corn.[85] In 1713 peas were valued at only a little less than wheat in northeastern New Jersey but more than corn, rye, or buckwheat.[86] But for some reason, peas are cited less frequently in advertisements and other sources later in the eighteenth century, which suggests their prevalence had declined. Though Collings and Read planted them, Peter Kalm noted that the cultivation of peas had much declined by midcentury in southwestern New Jersey. Old Swedish settlers told him that "a little despicable insect" deposited its eggs into the growing peas and that its larvae destroyed the peas in storage.[87] However, "Calavance peas," or cowpeas, were apparently common in this part of New Jersey at the time, judging from the number of references Read made to them; it is now a common crop only much farther south. Good for humans and all kinds of cattle, cowpeas may have been a specialty of farmers in the region south and southwest of Mount Holly, and they were an item of commerce at Cape May at about the same time.[88] One grower advocated sowing two bushels on ten acres of "the poorest of ground & coarsest of Sand"; another advocated growing them with manure but on loose soil in rows two and a half to three feet apart. Plowing the rows to keep the "crabb grass" down, this latter farmer produced more than twenty-three bushels of cowpeas to the acre. When they were ripe, cowpeas were cut with a hook and taken to a threshing floor, constructed of rails about two feet above the ground. Through that floor the peas would drop on a cloth.

Other vegetables were also sown for both humans and livestock. Swedish settlers had eaten turnips since the earliest times, Kalm observed, and the local Indians had also developed a fondness for them. Jacob Spicer of Cape May also planted them to eat; his 1761 crop was, he noted, "pretty good being very sweet but not large."[89] Using a drill instead of broadcasting the seed, Read planted turnips in late July or early August in a sandy, moist soil. They grew best in cool weather, and ashes sown lightly over the crop in the evening would destroy insect pests. And in Elizabethtown in 1755, Charles Read saw two oxen "very fatt & very full" that had been raised on turnips.[90]

Cabbages had a more limited use as feed. They were fine for "fatting" cattle but not for dairy cows; cows fed cabbage would produce ill-tasting butter. Read's calculations showed it would cost a farmer £17 to raise cabbage for twenty cows for more than two months. One acre would produce 14,520 cabbages, and a cow would eat twelve cabbages a day. A field hand with one horse could be hired to tend the cabbages at £7 for the period; another £7 would be spent planting the crop and £3 for pulling the plants.[91]

Asparagus and pumpkins, by contrast, were probably raised widely for human food. Then as now, asparagus grows wild in South Jersey soils; Peter Kalm reported it "growing near the fences in a loose soil on uncultivated sandy fields."[92] Farmers often alternated "pompions" with corn as Native Americans had.[93] Parker planted pumpkins on three June days in 1778 in hills in a field whose furrows were ten feet apart; the "Dutch" rule, by contrast, was to space furrows twelve feet from each other. Parker fertilized these pumpkin hills with a mixture of hog's dung and ashes; three years later, he "planted Pumpkins in the usual place," covered the seed lightly with dirt, and lay rotten dung [probably cattle] and hog dung on the hills.[94]

Of nonedible field crops, flax and hemp were most prevalent in the state, flax particularly in northern New Jersey. Both the seeds and fibers were valuable; longer flax fibers were woven into linen, while the shorter, less desirable fibers made a coarser cloth called tow. Yet because a great deal of hard and tedious labor was required to prepare the fiber for use, farmers generally did not raise large quantities. Very few farm sale advertisements specifically mentioned flax, which makes its distribution difficult to determine, but those that did invariably described properties in the Raritan Valley (map 30). By 1751, the region apparently was known for the production of flaxseed (also called linseed). In a letter that year to John Stevens in Perth Amboy, Henry Gamble of Londonderry, Ireland, declared "that amboy is a place that flaxseed is to be gote on reasonable terms, and could we cultivate a correspondence, I Doubt note but wou'd be to our mutual advantage." Gamble told

Stevens that he was associated with merchants in Philadelphia who owned a vessel that could take on two hundred hogsheads of flaxseed; he would pay Stevens in linen or "bills on London." In February 1753, Stevens recorded delivering sixteen hogsheads of flaxseed to a vessel, probably lying at Perth Amboy.[95]

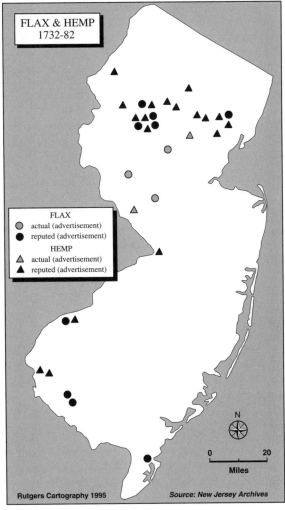

FLAX & HEMP
1732-82

FLAX
○ actual (advertisement)
● reputed (advertisement)
HEMP
△ actual (advertisement)
▲ reputed (advertisement)

Rutgers Cartography 1995   Source: New Jersey Archives

MAP 30

As the correspondence between Stevens and Gamble documents, flax was exported to Ireland in these years. Kalm reported that large quantities of linseed were sent to New York from New Brunswick in 1746 and observed that the port of New York sent a great deal of flaxseed to Ireland, presumably, he thought, because the flax in Ireland was harvested before the seed was ripe.[96] Indeed, Scots and Scots-Irish settlers may have made flaxseed a significant product of the region. It made a significant portion of the produce local farmers proffered for credit at various general stores, and legislation to pay farmers a bounty for growing it (as well as hemp) was enacted in 1765.[97] This bounty, proposed by Governor William Franklin, remained in force until October 1772; another act during the Revolution offered bounties on flax, hemp, and wool to help mitigate the fabric shortage.[98]

In Hunterdon County in the late eighteenth and early nineteenth centuries, flax was traditionally sown on Good Friday in fields divided into sections ("lands") seven paces wide.[99] Charles Read advocated sowing it in "Heavy Strong land," by which he probably meant to indicate clay loam. About the first of August, when the bolls began to turn a pale brown, the harvest began. Workers then set about the exceedingly hard work of pulling the plants up by the roots—most individuals pulled less than an acre a day—and binding them into sheaves three or four inches in diameter. Eight to twelve of these sheaves were set up in shocks to cure the stalks and ripen the seeds.

After the flax had cured for a few days, it was hauled into the barn, threshed to remove the seeds, and then retted, or rotted: the sheaves were placed on short grass and turned over periodically to allow the outer bark to separate. Then the flax was bound into bundles and stored until winter, when it would be tied to green poles to dry in a flax kiln. Workers then used a tool called a flax brake to break the fibers apart. Next was swingling—using a wooden knife to beat out the rotten particles between while holding the flax over an upright board. The fibers were then dressed and could be marketed or spun and woven into fabric at home.

Charles Read recorded that one farmer on very good land harvested two hundred pounds of "Swingle Flax abt 150 lb hatchelld & 10 bushells of seed - Ordinary flax will hatchell away ¹/₂." This was a good crop, he suggested. Another farmer, most likely residing near Trenton, had gotten two crops of flax in a year but no seed in the second crop.[100] James Parker practiced intertillage and sowed flax on May 1, 1781, "in the orchard by old house."[101]

Hemp was mentioned more often in advertisements than flax was, but it was always described as a crop that was known to do well, not as one actually growing in the fields (map 30). The distribution of the places reputedly good for hemp correlates very closely with areas immediately north of the Wisconsin terminal moraine where swamp land had been drained; hemp grew better in moist soils. Franklin's 1675 bounty proposal may actually have been instigated by a petition requesting such an incentive from inhabitants of Hunterdon County that year. In their view, hemp had the potential to be a new staple profitable enough, the legislation observed, to "enable them to pay the vast Sums for which they continually became indebted to Great Britain" since a recent change in British law had foreclosed "West India Markets" to them.[102] Hemp was grown in Amwell Township in that county in 1769 and remained an important crop in northern Morris County, at least until 1789.[103]

By midcentury hemp was being shipped out of the Raritan Valley. On November 8, 1747, the anonymous ledger of a merchant shipper in New Brunswick listed a credit to Robert Camell of Princeton of £2.4.4 for "76 lb of hampe at 7d." On the same day Camell had purchased 118 gallons of rum, which suggests that he was himself a merchant who had received hemp in trade from his customers. The same ledger credited Andrew Reed of "Trinton" with £59.9.6 for 2,379 pounds of "hampe" in January 1747 and £167.15.0 for 6,710 pounds of hemp valued at £0.0.6 a pound on April 8, 1748. Reed must also have collected these large amounts of hemp from many different farmers. It was worth far more than the flour he sold the same New Brunswick merchant.[104] Evidence documents that tobacco, too, was grown from early settlement times, probably for a farmer's own consumption; it was rarely mentioned in advertisements and thus was probably not thought of as a commercial crop. One farmer in Greenwich Township, Gloucester County, planted tobacco on June 23, 1770, either simply late or so that its harvest would not conflict with that of another crop.[105] In 1822, Henry Thomas of Knowlton Township, Sussex County, lost one and a half days' pay in June for working "at his tobacco patch fencing & planting & etc."[106]

Orchards were an essential component of New Jersey farms and ubiquitous in all areas of settlement by midcentury (map 31). A 1770 description of Edward Antill's orchard in Piscataway Township near New Brunswick attests the great variety of fruit trees in this region; Antill had ten acres planted with "a large Collection of the best Fruit Trees, (all grafted or inoculated by Mr. William Prince, of Long Island) such as Apricots, Nectarines, Peaches, Plumbs, Pears, Medlars, hard and soft-shell Almonds, early Apples and English Cherries."[107] In 1780 James Parker counted 77 pear, 42 plum, 13 cherry, and 825 apple trees on his property and noted which had the reputation for bearing unusually delicious fruit and which produced fruit that stored well. Parker also experimented with grafting—he obtained scions for grafting his apple trees largely from friends in New Brunswick, Trenton, Elizabethtown, and Amwell Township[10]— but in Burlington County Read noted his disappointment with grafted trees. A grafted tree, he declared, did not live as long as "a natural tree" and produced less satisfactory cider. "Tis found by Experience that Grafted fruit when the trees grow old, have a black rott wch makes ye Cider bitter - Let your trees bear before yo graft that yo may know yr fruit & graff Winter fruit on Winter fruit stocks otherwise you will be deceived."[109]

Parker indicated that apple trees were without question of the greatest economic significance. They were especially prized because apples were used to produce cider, by midcentury the dominant locally produced beverage. Older Swedish-born

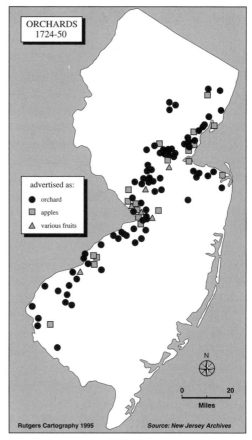

MAP 31

residents of southern New Jersey told Kalm that apple trees were comparatively rare in the days of their youth but were now common: "The Swedes brewed beer and that was their common drink. But at present there are very few who brew beer, for they commonly make cider."[110] It seemed to Kalm that Elizabethtown was especially to be noted for its orchards, and on his October 30, 1749, trip to Staten Island, he noted that its orchards and cider presses resembled those in Trenton, New Brunswick, Woodbridge, and Elizabethtown, through which he had passed en route.

> Near every farmhouse was an orchard of apple trees: the fruit had for the greatest part been gathered already. Here, and on the whole journey before, I observed a cider press at every farmhouse, made in different ways, by which the people had already pressed the juice out of the apples, or were just busy with that work. Some people made use of a wheel made of thick oak planks, which turned upon a wooden axis by means of a horse drawing it, much in the same manner as in crushing woad [a European dye plant], except that here the wheel runs upon planks.[111]

In New England, where European grains did poorly in the initial years of settlement, hard cider had replaced beer as the preferred beverage by the end of the seventeenth century; Connecticut in particular became well known for cider, and it may be that the famed Newark cider of later years had its origins among Connecticut people who settled this town.[112] Less than twenty years after its initial settlement, Newark was producing quantities of cider "exceeding any that we have from New England, Rhode Island or Long Island," according to East Jersey Governor Philip Carteret; he placed the community's cider production at one thousand barrels in 1682.[113] Newark and New Jersey ciders generally had an excellent reputation: in 1789, in the first edition of his well-known and widely used geography of the United States, Jedediah Morse called New Jersey cider "the best in the world" though, being a theologian, he thought it unfortunate that cider was a distilled beverage.[114] Five years later, Moreau de St. Mery stayed over in Newark on his way to New York and ranked the local cider. "Newark cider is generally reputed to be the best in the United States, and although that of Philadelphia is held to be close behind it, the superiority is justly awarded to the former," he wrote. "However, my colleague Michaux [André Michaux, the famous botanist], finds it inferior to that of St. Lo, of Coutances and of Bayeux," all made in the French province of Normandy, still famous for its apple brandy.[115]

Commercial mills around Newark processed large volumes of cider. Millers charged farmers who brought their apples to these cider mills by the number of barrels produced—one shilling per barrel was the going rate in the late 1750s. A farmer was charged less if he used another's mill to do the work himself. On December 15, 1757, Ephraim Camp recorded his dealings of both sorts with Joseph Day. "When we Reconed, their was Due to me over & above the one pound, fifteen Shillings & three pence, Eight barrels of Cyder for which I was to have Sixteen Gallons of Spirits. they was put into a barrel & when I brought them from the Still their was but Seven Gallons & a half and a pint for I measured it by the Quart."[116] Camp also made beer—for which he charged £0.1.6—but he mentioned doing so rarely, which again suggests that cider had by then become more common. The Camp family was still in the cider business in the first decades of the nineteenth century, dealing with thousands of gallons per year.[117]

The success of apple production is what must have allowed the very small farms of Essex County to remain in some measure viable into the early nineteenth century. As Lemon has suggested about small southeastern Pennsylvania farms, these New Jersey farms probably could not have supported a family had such a specialty been unavailable to them.[118] One 1770s advertisement suggests the intensity of orchard development in the area; one 22.25-acre "lot" on the Passaic River in Newark was stated to include a cider mill and "an orchard remarkable for making the best cyder, 200 barrels having been made in a plentiful season."[119]

The success of the Essex County farmers encouraged farmers elsewhere to plant apple trees. In 1794, Theophile Cazenove described the orchards on the "not very good" soils in the hollows between the hillier parts of the Highlands, south of the Wisconsin terminal moraine in adjacent Morris County. Based on figures local farmers gave him, Cazenove calculated that an acre of such land planted with sixty-five to seventy trees twenty feet apart would produce 250 bushels of apples in good years. (His estimates suggest that at least six and a half acres of the 22.25-acre farm in Newark was devoted to orchard.) Eight bushels of apples made thirty-two gallons (a barrel) of cider which, when distilled, made four gallons of spirits, which sold for £0.6.0, or $.75. These Morris County farms could thus produce 125 gallons of spirits per acre and realize a gross profit of £37.10.0, or $93.75. Wheat, the crop highest in value, produced a poor profit by comparison. In Morris County at the time, land sold for £3–4 per acre; even on better soils, then, wheat yields were only about fifteen bushels an acre. At a 1796 price of £0.8.0, this crop of wheat would only produce a gross return of £6 per acre, or about $16.00. The "great produce" of apples, Cazenove pointed out, "encourages every farmer to enlarge his orchard," as did the exports of spirits "to New York, and from there to the south; and the excise, instead of stopping the distilleries, has attracted attention to the advantages of this manner of making the best of this poor ground."[120] In 1799, Gavin Scott had reached the same conclusion about how to use the land on his family's small farm most profitably and had been expanding his orchard continuously. "I intend to plant 100 Apple & Peach trees this spring," he wrote; "we find them to be a profitable as any way we can put the Land fine Brandy is made from the Peach when New made it will sell at a Dollar the Gallon if keept one year 1$\frac{1}{2}$ Dllar if two years at two Dollars."[121]

Apple trees were also grown for their dried fruit, a delicacy among the wealthy planters of the Caribbean before the end of the eighteenth century. Crèvecoeur remarked after the Revolution, "Many people have carried the former manufacture of drying apples to a great degree of perfection in the province of New Jersey." Especially built ovens were used to dry the apples. One agriculturalist remarked that "shiploads" of apples were being sent to the Caribbean immediately before the Revolution.[122]

Apple production remained important in Essex County and elsewhere in northern New Jersey well into the nineteenth century. In 1804 in Amwell Township, Hunterdon County, five and a half bushels of apples made one gallon of "cyder spirits." The Williamsons brought 595 bushels of apples to the local mill and still in 1804, 225.5 in 1805, and 374.5 in 1806; their orchard must have brought the family a very respectable income in those years. They used hired hands extensively to plant new trees and prune the existing orchard.[123] On October 30, 1804, James Throckmorton presented an accounting of the 338 apple trees he had provided to Abraham Williamson—there were twenty-nine different types, most of them "Newtown Pippin" and many others "Newark Pippin" and "Newark King Apple."[124] By the 1820s, temperance activity among Methodists and Presbyterians in Essex County appears to have inspired a decline in the consumption of hard cider and thus apple production there, but the ledgers of cider mills amply document that apples remained a significant farm product through 1830 in poor-soil areas such as Denville in the glaciated Highlands.[125]

Apples were chiefly important in northern New Jersey, where peaches, susceptible to the region's late spring frosts, were far less prevalent. But in southern New Jersey, as the accounts of Charles Read and others attest, peaches were the orchard crop of choice. As was also true of apples, the dried fruit of peach trees had value: on December 4, 1787, Samuel Mickle of Woodbury in Gloucester County credited Richard Wood, Jr., of Cumberland County with fifteen shillings for two bushels of "dried Peaches."[126] Read was relatively uninvolved with arboriculture, yet he went into some detail in his diary about the cultivation of peaches. He believed that different soils produced fruit of different tastes. In addition, he advised that trees planted in sandy soil be branched low or staked to keep the wind from blowing them over and that the area around their trunks receive a treatment of walnut hulls mixed with earth to ward off a worm (borer) that attacked trees at the root. Read also grew plums, and he noted that horseradish planted around these trees would protect them from "the Bugg"; he also grew mulberries, for he suggested propagating them by rubbing the fruit in sand as soon as it dropped and sowing it in a bed.[127] Account books show, too, that New Jersey farmers grew and received general store credit for quince.

Compared with orchards, vineyards were never widespread in New Jersey, but they were well known abroad because two agricultural innovators in the central part of the state made serious attempts to establish them and to produce wine. Between 1762 and 1767, the Royal Society of Arts and Letters in London offered prizes for the successful establishment of vineyards north and south of the Delaware River. At their meeting in London on October 27, 1767, they discussed the application of Edward Antill, who had planted eight hundred vines "near New Brunswick."[128] In their certification of Antill's operation, New Brunswick mayor William Ouke and city recorder James Neilson testified that they had visited the vineyard across the Raritan, in Piscataway Township "within sight or our Town," on August 28, 1765. There, eight hundred vines "of different sorts," chiefly Madeira, Burgundy, and Frontiniae, were planted six feet apart in rows five feet wide "on the side of a Hill fronting the South" in "a dry warm Soil sufficiently rich" and kept free of weeds.[129] The certificate added that Antill had an "Eye to the publick," meaning that he intended to use the results of his experiment to encourage others to explore viticulture.

"I have been thought by some Gentlemen as well as by Farmers, very whimsical in Attempting a Vineyard; it is looked upon as an absurd undertaking as a force upon Nature, as though I meant to extort from her what is not in her power to yield," he wrote to the Society on May 9, 1766. "As if America alone was to be dinyed those cheering comforts which Nature with a bountiful hand Stretches forth to the rest of the World."[130] But Antill felt his critics overlooked the potential of vineyards in North America. "These Men forget that there are Vines, natives of America, which for Magnitude & luxuriency of growth give place to none, I believe, in the known world; if their fruit be not so luscious as those of Europe, it is because they are wild, Shaded & uncultivated; however this plainly shewes what Nature can & will do under proper Management & due cultivation."

With his "Eye to the publick," Antill had planted his vines along the River Road in Piscataway Township. In his own correspondence with the society, he pointed out that slopes were best for vineyards because the soil drained quickly; on flatter surfaces in the area, the soil's high clay content caused water to puddle on the surface after downpours, which were much more intense in the summer in New Jersey than in England.

Of the society's five awards for the introduction of viticulture in North America during these years, two were made to New Jersey agriculturalists Antill and Thomas Burgie, the self-described "principal Gardner" to the Earl of Stirling, who had planted 2,100 vines on Stirling's estate in northern Somerset County.[131] Antill conveyed his thanks for the ƒ200 premium in a letter to the society on February 28, 1769, in which he also assured the group that he had done everything in his power—including writing pieces for the newspapers—to further viticulture and the making of wine in America. He also urged the society to be patient with Americans.[132]

The Society will consider that all their encouragements, can only tend to set these Things on Foot in America, and, cannot in the Nature of things, expect them immediately to be brought to perfection; that must be a Work of Time; for an Apprentice cannot be supposed to turn off his Work with the same expedition and perfection, as an able and experienced Workman; Arts and Sciences are not the Work of a Day, the People of America are raw and unexperienced, and quite unacquainted with the several undertakings proposed by the Society. . . . The Bounties so generously offered by them are a powerful Spur to the making the several attempts, and when the People by experience find that they coincide with their own Interest, they will continue and carry them on with Vigour.

Antill later reported to the society that he was writing a treatise on viticulture at the request of men in Pennsylvania and New York who had read his pieces in the newspapers.[133]

Viticulture apparently caught the fancy of other New Jersey agriculturalists. James Parker's diary entry for April 22, 1780, notes that he "set out slips of Grape I brought from Brunswick out of Saml Kembles Garden that he got from Capt OBrien they are esteemed the finest grape in America."[134] Kemble had commercial dealings with Antill, so it seems likely that Parker's interest in vineyards was stimulated by Antill's work. In 1773, a sale notice for an Elizabethtown property, declared suitable for a gentleman's "country seat," advertised "a large garden stored with grapes of the best quality."[135] Even Cazenove, who complained in 1794 of the "lack of gardens and improvements" in the northwestern Highlands and Ridge and Valley sections, admitted that the region's "delapidated" vineyards were "large and productive."[136]

As at the Elizabethtown property, most farmers probably grew grapes in gardens, not in vineyards, and many gardens apparently yielded produce in quantity for the urban markets of Philadelphia and New York. In 1748, Peter Kalm noted that Swedish farmers in Gloucester County used canoes to bring their produce to the Philadelphia markets twice a week and described the city's market in detail.

There are every week two market days, *viz.* Wednesday and Saturday. On those days the country people in Pennsylvania and New Jersey bring to town a quantity of food and other products of the country, and this is a great advantage to the town . . . You are sure to find on market days every produce of the season which the country affords. But on other days they are sought for in vain. Provisions are always to be got fresh here, and for that reason most of the inhabitants never buy more at a time than what will be sufficient till the next market day. In summer there is a market almost every day, for the victuals do not keep well in the great heat. There are two places in town where these markets are kept, but that near the court-house is the principal one. It begins about four or five o'clock in the morning and ends about nine in the forenoon.[137]

By the 1760s, real property advertisements began to refer to the production of garden truck for the Philadelphia market. In 1761, a property opposite Philadelphia containing almost an acre planted "with the largest Battersea Asparagus" was advertised for rent.[138] Clearly an acre of asparagus was far more than a family could consume, so it seems likely that much of the produce went to Philadelphia for sale.

One Greenwich Township, Gloucester County, property sixteen miles from Philadelphia on the road from Salem was offered with a direct appeal to its commercial advantages: here, one could "raise Produce for supplying the Philadelphia Market weekly."[139] To the northeast, fronting the Delaware in Chester Township, Burlington County, another farm was advertised in 1769 as only nine miles from Philadelphia and "exceeding fertile for raising market truck." New Jersey farmers may also have sent produce to a market in the town of Burlington itself, as advertisements sometimes mentioned the proximity of this city.[140]

Richard Collings of Newtown Township sold garden truck and seed at the Philadelphia market regularly at, his 1772 advertisement noted, "the Covered Stall, at the upper end of the Jersey-market." The ledgers of general stores in southwestern New Jersey places having ready access to Philadelphia also suggest that local farmers brought in small amounts of such produce as cabbages and onions for sale at this market. And one anonymous letter in a Philadelphia paper in 1770 indicated that even farmers in East Jersey depended on Philadelphia:

> I am *a Native of East New Jersey,* an aged Man, who have enjoyed much good Living in my Time, for which I acknowledge myself indebted to the Philadelphia Market, for enabling me to produce not as a Purchaser, but as a Seller . . . Being a *Farmer,* I generally carried my *Truck* there and disposed of it for Cash.[141]

More typically, farmers in northeastern sections probably brought garden truck to New York, where the markets, Peter Kalm observed, were set up somewhat differently. "The country people come to market in New York twice a week, much in the same manner as they do in Philadelphia, with this difference, that the markets here are kept in several places, and one has to go from one to another sometimes to get what one needs," Kalm wrote.[142] Read noted in 1757 that one farm about a mile and a half from New York produced "garden truck" on fields fertilized with stable manure from the city.[143]

By the 1770s inexpensive waterborne transport carried produce from farms on the Hackensack River to the New York market on a daily basis.[144] In 1787, Manasseh Cutler noted that Bergen (now Jersey City), lying immediately across the Hudson from Manhattan, "is said to be remarkable for its wealth. The people are mostly farmers. . . . It is well situated for supplying the markets in New York, which the Dutch people know how to improve to the best advantage."[145] Northern Monmouth County farmers may also have sent produce to New York across the easily traversed Raritan Bay. Wood was shipped from there to New York regularly, and scattered references hint that truck crops also were. The area was noted in 1770 for the "great commerce carried on from thence to New-York," and from the early 1750s farmers there produced large quantities of onions for export to the Caribbean. Such evidence suggests that New Jersey farmers used land much as the von Thünen model proposed they would, at least as far as garden truck is concerned.

Notes

1. Benson, Peter Kalm's Travels, 1:286.

2. Mary Capnerhurst to Mary Capnerhurst Exton, May 18, 1788, Capner-Exton-Hill Papers, Hunterdon County Historical Society.

3. Gavin Scott to Thomas Scott, July 16, 1798, Scott Family Papers, NjHi.

4. See Ellis, "Diary of Jacob Spicer," 114, and *Minutes of the General Assembly of the Province of New Jersey*, August 20, 1755, 32.

5. Allinson cited in Woodward, *Ploughs and Politicks*, 144.

6. "Letter Book of John Watts, Merchant and Councillor of New York," *Collections of the New-York Historical Society* 61 (1928): 79–80.

7. Woodward, *Ploughs and Politicks*, 143–44.

8. David M. Ludlum, *The New Jersey Weather Book* (New Brunswick, N.J., 1983), 146–47; Ralph H. Brown, *Historical Geography of the United States* (New York, 1948), 95.

9. Maps 21 to 23 are from United States Department of Agriculture, *Climate and Man* (Washington, 1941), 1006, 1008. Map 24 is from Erwin R. Biel, "New Jersey's Climate," *The Economy of New Jersey*, ed. Salomon J. Flink (New Brunswick, N.J., 1958), 75.

10. Lemon, *Best Poor Man's Country*, 208-11.146. *Docs. Rel. N.J.*, 1st ser., 27:133; see also Hendrickson Family Papers, Alexander Library, NjR.

11. References to New Jersey in newspapers appearing through the Revolutionary War are reprinted in *Docs. Rel. N.J.*, 1st ser. and 2d ser. For a discussion of the interpretation of maps derived from the advertisements of real property, see Peter O. Wacker, "Historical Geographers, Newspaper Advertisements and Bicentennial Celebration," *The Professional Geographer* 26 (1974): 12–18.

12. "Damages by the British in New Jersey, 1776–1781," 5 vols., and "Damages by the Americans in New Jersey, 1776–1782," 1 vol., Division of State Library, Bureau of Archives and History, New Jersey State Library.

13. Map 25 is adapted from a map by John D. Alden, "Battles and Skirmishes of the American Revolution in New Jersey," Trenton, 1974. Boundaries and place locations in Map 4.x are based on John P. Snyder, *The Story of New Jersey's Civil Boundaries: 1606–1968* (Trenton, 1969).

14. "Letter Book of John Watts," 259, 355.

15. "Copy of a Letter from the Rev. Uzal Ogden, Missionary to Sussex County, New Jersey, to the Secretary of the Society for the Propagation of the Gospel," *Proc. N.J.H.S.* 4 (1852): 152.

16. Kelsey, *Cazenove Journal*, 3.

17. Jacob Spicer Diary, NjHi; Sarah Thomas, "Journal, June–August, 1809," Alexander Library, NjR.

18. Smith, *History of the Colony*, 491, 496.

19. Benson, *Peter Kalm's Travels*, 1:50–51.

20. Leaming and Spicer, *Grants*, 102.

21. Schoepf, *Travels*, 1:44.

22. Benson, *Peter Kalm's Travels*, 1:88.

23. Ibid., 1:85. For shifting nature of cultivation also see p. 55. Kalm noted that rye, wheat, and buckwheat were harvested with the sickle but that oats were mowed with a scythe. He also stated that "the field lies fallow for a year, and during that time the cattle may graze on it." Perhaps both practices were followed at the same time in southwestern New Jersey.

24. Leases of this sort can be found in the James Parker Papers or the Stevens Family Papers, NjHi.

25. *Docs. Rel. N.J.*, 2d ser., 5:341.

26. Robert Johnston Account Book, Salem, N.J., Alexander Library, NjR.

27. Morris claimed that all but four hundred bushels had disappeared through "Embezzlement." See Lewis Morris to John Morris, April 22, 1730, Morris Papers, Alexander Library, NjR. Thanks to Robert Burnett for calling this source to my attention.

28. Benson, *Peter Kalm's Travels.*

29. *Docs. Rel. N.J.,* 1st ser., 28:365.

30. Ibid., 29:484.

31. Spicer Diary, July 15, 1762, NjHi.

32. "Purchased of John Dunlap by John Tomson," James Parker Papers, Alexander Library, Rutgers University.

33. Francis Rush Clark to John Strutt, March 29, 1777, Francis Rush Clark Papers, Sol Feinstone Mss, David Library of the American Revolution, Washington Crossing, Pa. I wish to thank David Fowler for bringing this source to my attention.

34. Woodward's thirty-bushel estimate was probably too optimistic for most of New Jersey. See *Ploughs and Politicks,* 275.

35. Schoepf, *Travels,* 45.

36. John Rutherfurd, "Notes on the State," 81.

37. Lemon, *Best Poor Man's Country,* 134.

38. A. Capnerhurst to Mr. Cottman, May 31, 1788, Capner-Exton-Hill Papers, Hunterdon County Historical Society.

39. Joseph F. Tuttle, ed., "New Jersey, Pennsylvania and Ohio in 1787-8, Passages from the Journals of Rev. Manasseh Cutler, LLD," *Proc. N.J.H.S.* 3 (1872–1874): 91–92; Kelsey, *Cazenove Journal,* 10.

40. *The New Encyclopedia Brittanica: Micropaedia,* s. v. "Hessian fly."

41. Tuttle, "Journals of Rev. Manasseh Cutler," 95.

42. Ibid., 91–92; Gavin Scott to his brother, October 23, 1800, Scott Family Papers, NjHi.

43. Fred Shelley, ed., "A Letter from New Jersey," *Proc. N.J.H.S.* 74 (1956): 301.

44. Schoepf, *Travels,* 45.

45. Camp Family Record Book, Camp Family Papers, NjHi.

46. Philip Kearny Merchant Accounts, 1772–1779, Alexander Library, NjR.

47. Leaming and Spicer, *Grants,* 102.

48. E. S. Rankin, "The Ramapo Tract," *Proc. N.J.H.S.* 50 (1932): 389–90.

49. Whitehead's holdings were listed in Mendham Township Tax Ratable Lists for 1787, 1788, and 1802. Department of Education, Archives and History Microfilm and Records Unit, New Jersey State Library. I am indebted to Ethel Black for pointing out that Onesimus had a sister named Rebecca and also married a woman named Rebecca. See Barbara Hoskins et al., *Washington Valley: An Informal History* (Ann Arbor, Mich., 1960), 139, 146. For the account, see the Whitehead Papers, Joint Public Library of Morristown and Morris Township, Morristown, N.J.

50. Spicer Diary, NjHi; Anderson, "Pastor Wrangel's Trip," 11; Niemcewicz, *Under Their Vine,* 219.

51. Percy W. Bidwell and John I. Falconer, *History of Agriculture in the Northern United States* (Washington, D.C., 1925), 14; Benson, *Peter Kalm's Travels,* 1:274.

52. Kurath, *Word Geography,* 17, 24.

53. Benson, *Peter Kalm's Travels,* 1:89.

54. Ibid., 84; Woodward, *Ploughs and Politicks,* 279–80; "Damages by the British in New Jersey, 1776–1781," Essex County, New Jersey State Library.

55. Woodward, *Ploughs and Politicks,* 280.

56. *Docs. Rel. N.J.,* 1st ser., 28:99–100.

57. Shelley, "Letter from New Jersey," 301.

58. "Letter Book of John Watts," 377–78.

59. Kearny Merchant Books, 1772–1779, NjR.

60. *Docs. Rel. N.J.,* 1st ser., 25:447. 1767; Ibid., 2d ser., 3:590.

61. Spicer Diary, January 1, 1756, NjHi.

62. Clark to Strutt, March 29, 1777, Clark Papers, David Library.

63. Benson, *Peter Kalm's Travels,* 1:89; Woodward, *Ploughs and Politicks,* 278–80; see also the Camp Family Record Books, NjHi.

64. Parker Diary, NjHi.

65. Robert Kenedy to John Stevens, Esq., April 8, 1797, Stevens Family Papers, NjHi.

66. Benson, *Peter Kalm's Travels*, 1:184; John W. Lequear, *Traditions of Hunterdon* (Flemington, N.J., 1957), 86.

67. Woodward, *Ploughs and Politicks*, 283.

68. Benson, *Peter Kalm's Travels*, 1:183–84.

69. Ralph Ege, *Pioneers of Old Hopewell, with Sketches of Her Revolutionary Heroes* (Hopewell, N.J., 1908), 191.

70. Parker Diary, NjHi.

71. "A Letter from Gawen Lawrie to a Friend of his at London," March 26, 1684, reprinted in William A. Whitehead, *East Jersey under the Proprietary Governments*, vol. 1 of *Collections of the New Jersey Historical Society* (Newark, 1846), 287.

72. Bidwell and Falconer, *History of Agriculture*, 14.

73. Woodward, *Ploughs and Politicks*, 283.

74. Joseph Wheeler Camp Record Book, NjHi.

75. "Calvin Green's 'Diary': The Life of Calvin Green," *Proc. N.J.H.S.* 69 (1951): 124–27. Robert Burnett was kind enough to bring this source to my attention.

76. *Docs. Rel. N.J.*, 1st ser., 28:105–6.

77. Woodward, *Ploughs and Politicks*, 293–308.

78. Benson, *Peter Kalm's Travels*, 1:294.

79. Jesse Knowles Account Book, NjHi; Benson, *Peter Kalm's Travels*, 1:95–96.

80. Parker Diary, May 28 and 29, 1778, June 9, 1781, NjHi.

81. E. Antill to Dr. [Peter] Templeman, Royal Society of Arts and Letters, February 28, 1769, New Jersey Tercentenary Commission, New Jersey Records (selected) in the Public Record Office and other British Repositories, 17th–18th Century Obtained Through Dr. Richard P. McCormick, 1960, Sinclair Collection, Alexander Library, NjR.

82. Woodward, *Ploughs and Politicks*, 296.

83. Ibid., 296.

84. Edward Antill to Dr. Peter Templeman, Royal Society of Arts and Letters, February 28, 1769, New Jersey Tercentenary Commission, Sinclair Collection, NjR.

85. Leaming and Spicer, *Grants*, 102.

86. Rankin, "Ramapo Tract," 389–90.

87. Benson, *Peter Kalm's Travels*, 1:91–92.

88. Woodward, *Ploughs and Politicks*, 305–8; "Diary," Spicer Papers.

89. Spicer Diary, September 4, 1761, NjHi; Benson, *Peter Kalm's Travels*, 1:267–68.

90. Woodward, *Ploughs and Politicks*, 299–301.

91. Woodward, *Ploughs and Politicks*, 303–4.

92. Benson, *Peter Kalm's Travels*, 1:89; Woodward, *Ploughs and Politicks*, 89–90, 304–5.

93. Woodward, *Ploughs and Politicks*, 280.

94. Parker Diary, NjHi.

95. Stevens Family Papers, NjHi.

96. Benson, *Peter Kalm's Travels*, 1:122, 135–36.

97. Ned C. Landsman, *Scotland and Its First American Colony, 1683–1765* (Princeton, 1985), 212–13, 216–17.

98. *Docs. Rel. N.J.*, 1st ser., 17:386; *Acts of the General Assembly of New Jersey* (Trenton, 1778), 42.

99. For information on flax, see Hubert G. Schmidt, *Flax Culture in Hunterdon County, New Jersey* (Flemington, N.J., 1939), 6–8.

100. Woodward, 290, *Ploughs and Politicks*, 314–15.

101. Parker Diary, NjHi.

102. *Votes and Proceedings of the General Assembly of the Province of New Jersey, 1765*, 26.

103. "Inventory of John Williamson, August 26, 1769," Williamson Papers, Alexander Library, NjR; Stephen Brant Account Book, NjHi.

104. New Brunswick (N.J.) Merchant Shipper's Ledger, 1730s–1750s, Rutgers University Library.

105. Restore Lippincott Diary, Gloucester County Historical Society.

106. Jesse Knowles Account Book, NjHi.

107. *Docs. Rel. N.J.*, 1st ser., 28:311.

108. Parker Diary, NjHi.

109. Woodward, *Ploughs and Politicks*, 314–15.

110. Benson, *Peter Kalm's Travels*, 1:268.

111. Ibid., 40–41, 48, 51–52, 86, 97, 123–4, 143–44. The quotation appears on 124.

112. Harry B. Weiss, *The History of Applejack or Apple Brandy in New Jersey from Colonial Times to the Present* (Trenton, N.J., 1954), 10-11.

113. William H. Shaw, comp., *History of Essex and Hudson Counties, New Jersey* (Philadelphia, 1884), 1:560.

114. Morse, *American Geography*, 287.

115. Roberts and Roberts, *Moreau de St. Mery*, 114.

116. Ephraim Camp Record Book, NjHi.

117. "Apple Book, 1810–1822," and "Apple Book, 1800–1810, Caleb Camp," Camp Family Papers, NjHi.

118. Lemon, *Best Poor Man's Country*, 90–91.

119. *Docs. Rel. N.J.*, 1st ser., 28:210–11.

120. Kelsey, *Cazenove Journal*, 11–12.

121. Gavin Scott to his brother, April 1799 and April 1, 1798, Scott Family Papers, NjHi.

122. St. John De Crèvecoeur, *Sketches of Eighteenth Century America* (New Haven, Conn., 1925), 104. By the time Crèvecoeur wrote this, of course, New Jersey was a state, not a province. The statement about Caribbean shipments appeared in *American Husbandry*, cited in Woodward, *Ploughs and Politicks*.

123. "Memorandum Book," Williamson Papers, NjR.

124. "J Throckmortons bill of young apple trees & rect," Oct 30, 1804, Williamson Papers, NjR.

125. Weiss, *History of Applejack*, 94, 132; "Denville Apple Ledgers. 1822–1827," Cobb Collection, Joint Free Public Library of Morristown and Morris Township, Morristown, N.J.

126. Samuel Mickle Daybook and Journal, Stewart Collection, Savitz Library, Glassboro State College.

127. Woodward, *Ploughs and Politicks*, 262, 312.

128. Royal Society of Arts, "Minutes of Committee of Colonies and Trade," October 17, 1767, New Jersey Tercentary Commission, Sinclair Collection, NjR.

129. Ibid., "Guard Book 10," #19.

130. Ibid., "Guard Book 12," #38–39; Edward Antill to Dr. Templeman, May 9, 1766.

131. Ibid., "Colonies and Trade," 18. Two of the remaining three society awards went to South Carolina growers and the third to a Virginian.

132. Ibid., "Guard Book A," #69.

133. Ibid., Edward Antill to Dr. Peter Templeman, March 20, 1769. Antill died, at the age of 69, in 1770. See *Docs. Rel. N.J.*, 1st ser., 28:311.

134. Parker Diary, NjHi.

135. *Docs. Rel. N.J.*, 1st ser., 28:446.

136. Kelsey, *Cazenove Journal*, 16.

137. Benson, *Peter Kalm's Travels*, 1:30, 85.

138. *Docs. Rel. N.J.*, 1st ser., 28:288.

139. Ibid., 29:226.

140. Ibid., 26:388–89, 28:288. Another farm in Chester Township, advertised in 1772, located on

Rancocas Creek, twelve miles from Philadelphia, was declared to be "very convenient for raising market truck" and just five miles from Burlington.

141. Ibid., 27:26–27.

142. Benson, *Peter Kalm's Travels,* 1:136.

143. Woodward, *Ploughs and Politicks,* 286.

144. *Docs. Rel. N.J.,* 1st ser., 28:456; 29:104–5.

145. Tuttle, "Journals of Rev. Manasseh Cutler," 88–89.

CHAPTER 5

GRASSES, LIVESTOCK, FOWL, AND BEES

We wish you could procure from London two or three pounds of Burnet grass seed to send by the Grange [a vessel] this Spring. . . . You will be inclined to think we have no grass but you are mistaken for we have blew grass, spear grass, swale grass, summer grass, Indian grass, red and white clover, timothy grass and English grass, I dont know the name of. I have before this wrote for Rye grass, Bent seed, Saint Foine, some good seeds out of a hay barn floor.

In 1787, Ann Capnerhurst, who had moved to the area around Flemington after the Revolution, wrote to her sister in England for grass seed even as she sought to assure her that grass was plentiful in New Jersey.[1] For farmers like the Capnerhursts, the amount and quality of forage grasses were of enormous importance to the health and growth of livestock, much of it raised for urban markets in Philadelphia and New York.

Before the Revolution, in his history of the province, Samuel Smith had observed that pork was the staple of his home county, Burlington, and an important product of Middlesex, Sussex, Gloucester, and Salem counties as well (table 23). Indeed, as Gavin Scott of Elizabethtown told his brother in England, "swine flesh is the favourit meet here."[2] Pork was also a chief product in Hunterdon County, but, as Smith noted, the cultivation of wheat was by far the county's most important agricultural activity. Smith found cattle to be a "staple" of no single county but important in most of them; in Cumberland County on the Outer Coastal Plain, he observed, both cattle and sheep were raised for graziers, who fatted cattle—perhaps on the rich meadows of Salem County—before slaughtering them or taking them to market.[3]

Throughout the eighteenth century, knowledgeable farmers imported and sowed new forage crops with an eye toward creating larger animals, tastier meat, and grasses that, when cut, cured, and dried into hay, would keep better over a winter. Peter Kalm observed that "foresighted farmers have procured seeds of perennial grasses from England and other European states, and sowed them in their meadows, where they seem to thrive exceedingly well."[4] Miscellaneous notes and receipts from the early 1790s in the papers of the Stevens family indicate an interest in various species of grasses and clovers, including lucerne (alfalfa), a legume.[5]

By the middle of the eighteenth century, Charles Read clearly knew about many pasture and forage crops, though he may not have grown all that he mentioned in his journal.[6] Read surely grew red clover, timothy, fowl meadow grass, trefoil, and ryegrass and perhaps also white clover, herd grass, alfalfa, and sainfoin. One November, he sowed timothy in a field that had been used earlier that year for flax and then for buckwheat; after a northeaster, he wrote, "weeds came up & ye Timothy was poor." His experiments with red clover, introduced to England from Flanders a century earlier, were more successful. He rotated it with other crops— with corn in "pretty good orchard ground," with flax on "a good piece of upland," and by itself in "a rich Meadow." Because of the long growing season in southern New Jersey, he was able to mow the clover several times a year. Read got three and a half wagon loads per acre in the first mowing from the rich meadow, but the seed planted on the orchard and the upland did not yield well; the orchard red clover did not come up until the following year. Read noted that while red clover did poorly in poor soil, rich soil would yield two bushels per acre and some 120 pounds in seed, enough to sow twelve acres.[7]

Read recorded the experiments of other farmers in his region with different grasses. In 1753, he wrote, a resident of Trenton "fatted Eight Cattle well" on less than two acres of "not very rich" soil in 1753. He cut red clover for the cattle and fed them three times a day "in Racks" from April to November; the amount of milk his milch cows produced increased by one-third. An acquaintance who probably resided in Salem County wrote Read that he had fatted two oxen twice as rapidly on white clover as he had been able to do by keeping them on "Excellent pasture & well Watered." An acre would support the oxen for 107 days if they were fed freshly mown white clover three times a day, and stall feeding the animals saved pasture land. An ox, he wrote Read, "destroys more wth feet, Dung and Urine than He eats, yt Urine in a hott day destroy even ye roots of ye grass where it falls." Read also recorded the advice of friends who told him to "burn yr Hay that is to give it the brown cast not ye white Mould feeds best & makes the Cattle Drink much."[8]

Hay was a bulky, low-value product that did not travel well, so few records permit a reasonable estimate of its distribution and yields in these years (map 32). The account books of average farmers often made note of mowing and making hay, but they rarely described planting it or the results of any experiments they might have undertaken with various species of grass to increase yields and thus support more livestock. However, the record of losses New Jersey farmers suffered during the Revolution did include estimates for hay either consumed or destroyed, especially in northern New Jersey; from these and other evidence about livestock, it is clear that the production of hay for fodder was ubiquitous, except perhaps on the poorer soils of the Outer Coastal Plain (table 24). Even there, grasses were

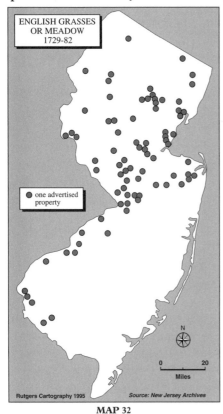

ENGLISH GRASSES OR MEADOW 1729-82

● one advertised property

N

0   20
Miles

Rutgers Cartography 1995   Source: New Jersey Archives

MAP 32

Table 23
Smith's Description of the Agricultural Economies
of New Jersey Counties, 1765

County	Soil Situation	Agricultural Products	Market
Bergen	Opposite and adjacent to New York, lands generally good for grass, wheat, or any grain.	Not mentioned	New York
Essex	Good land, small farms more improved than other counties.	Wheat, beef, sheep "and generally what is common from good land"	New York and exported in bottoms of their own
Morris	Late settled, but populous.	Grain and cattle, timber	New York
Middlesex	Land high and dry in good air, Scots proprietors worked hard to improve, land is in part very rich.	Beef, sheep, some pork, most sorts of grain, staves, firewood, and lumber	Perth Amboy as good a port as any on the continent but with little success. Export and New York market
Somerset	Rich land, much improved by Dutch.	Wheat the staple	Flour to New York
Monmouth	The lands in Shrewsbury, Middletown, and part of Freehold (townships— Northern Inner Coastal Plain) are most remarkably good.	Grain, beef, butter, cheese, and other produce	New York
Burlington	Arable land indifferent, but profitable, due to good meadows. The climate not as favorable as in some other places.	Pork the staple. Beef, mutton, and cheese also important. Little hemp or flax here or in the other counties	Situation for trade is good but eclipsed by Philadelphia, West Indies market. Products carried to Philadelphia
Hunterdon	Late settled but is the most populous and opulent county in the province. Land generally good for tillage.	Wheat the staple	Flour to both Philadelphia and New York markets
Sussex	Newest county, not much improved but few inhabitants. Excellent low interval land in Minisink Valley.	Some wheat, pork and cattle, lumber	New York and Philadelphia markets
Gloucester	Uplands poor, meadows are good and improve fast. Situation vis à vis Philadelphia market gives great opportunity.	Beef, pork, mutton, butter, cheese	Philadelphia
Salem	Land and meadows rich and productive. Old settlements. Improvements considerable.	Beef, sheep, pork, butter, cheese, and grain	Exportation
Cumberland	Land mostly poor. Good meadows and marshes. Newly settled so little improved.	Cattle and sheep for graziers	Not mentioned
Cape May	Land poor.	Cattle and horses in salt marshes. Fish and oysters "afford . . . an easy maintenance"	Not mentioned

grown on the better soils: in 1777, one property lying on a Pleistocene terrace within view of Little Egg Harbor was advertised to include "a fresh meadow which promises to be as fruitful for Timothy grass, red and white clover, as any in the province, the latter coming in, in great plenty."[9]

On their damage claims, farmers referred to losses of "fresh hay," "hay or grass," "English hay," "salt hay," and corn tops, all but the last two possibly describing the same thing. As Kalm noted, native grasses were annuals, and overgrazing eliminated them before they could mature and produce seed. Farmers thus tended to cultivate imported grasses; "English grass" appears to have been applied to several different perennial Old World species including blue grass, timothy, and red clover.[10] The grasses near Morristown Mrs. Martha Bland described in May 1777, the ideal month to view meadowlands, were probably European perennials. "The farmes between the mountains are the most rural sweet spots in nature, their medows of a fine luxurient grass which looks like a bed of velvet interspersed with yellow blue and white flowers."[11]

Damage claims suggest that salt hay must have been extremely important in Middlesex County, a fact the recently arrived Scott family noted from their home near Elizabethtown. Essex County farmers lost comparatively little hay, perhaps because their small farms could devote relatively little land to meadow. The damage claims also indicate that Somerset County farmers depended extensively on corn tops for fodder, while farmers in Bergen County, also settled by the Dutch, appear to have used little for this purpose.

New Jersey farmers raised cattle for sale at urban markets (much of it undoubtedly in barrelled form), for milk, cheese, and butter to consume themselves and to sell, and for milk to feed swine. Making butter and cheese was traditionally considered women's work, as Gavin Scott noted in a letter to his brother in England in 1799. Scott complained that the mother and daughter who did his housework were "as good as any around us yet there is no altering the practice of the country when we have milk and make cheese then they make no butter this may do, but when they make Butter they will not make cheese as they do not think Scimed milk fitt for

Table 24
Revolutionary War Damage Claims Pertaining to Fodder

| | | Percentage of Total Claims | | | | |
County	Total Claims	Fresh Hay	Salt Hay	Hay or Grass	English Hay	Corn Tops
Bergen with Acquackanonk Twp. (Dutch)	436	0.9	0.7	19.3	3.2	1.1
Burlington (English)	230	0.4	1.7	32.6	1.7	3.5
Essex without Acquackanonk Twp. (New England)	234	1.7	2.9	6.8	9.4	0
Middlesex (Heterogeneous)	321	10.3	28.9	18.7	15.3	3.4
Somerset (Dutch)	114	2.6	6.1	6.1	2.6	36.8

anything but swine."[12]

Early tax lists enumerated cattle, but they did not indicate whether the animals were oxen, beef cattle, or milch cows.[13] The county tax list summaries of 1751 and 1769 combined cattle and horses in a single category. Cattle do appear on the tax lists of the Revolutionary War period, but because they provided food for the armies, their distribution was very much impacted by the war. Still, a map of the distribution of cattle in about 1780 (map 33) does show relatively large numbers of cattle in relation to total population in some southern Jersey townships, especially in Salem County, where the fatting of cattle on its rich banked meadows for the easily reached Philadelphia market is strongly suggested. Dairying was evidently a major enterprise among some farmers there as well. Some of the townships in the Outer Coastal Plain also held relatively large numbers of cattle per taxable unit, testimony, no doubt, to the long-standing practice of running them in the sparsely populated, undeveloped woodlands.

Mapping cattle per one hundred acres of land (both improved and unimproved) per township in 1784 reflects perhaps a more normal distribution than what prevailed in the war years (map 34). Those townships in the northeast settled by New Englanders and easily accessible to the New York market apparently specialized to some extent in raising cattle, much as the von Thünen model would predict. Such a suggestion is less strong in southern New Jersey, except in the townships near Salem in Salem County, Greenwich and Stow Creek townships in Cumberland County, and northwestern Burlington County. But if one were to examine the density of cattle only in those Gloucester County townships opposite Philadelphia that

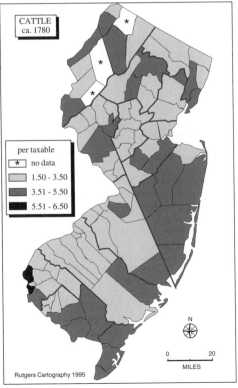

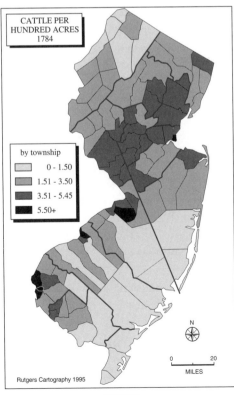

MAP 33   **MAP 34**

are entirely on the Inner Coastal Plain and in only those parts of other townships that lay within the Inner Coastal Plain, cattle densities would probably be greatest for this region. Per unit of area, both the northwest and the southeast, farther from the market, have fewer cattle. Thus in south Jersey, too, the von Thünen model appears to apply.

From the 1780s on, though tax lists separated horses and cattle, they did not differentiate between beef cattle and milch cows (for dairying) and beef cattle or oxen (used as draft animals). Maps derived from newspaper advertisements of real property, however, do help establish some notion of the distribution of these animals. Advertisements rarely mentioned the term "dairy" as a way of suggesting the possible value of land, but occasionally various terms denoting dairying appeared— "dairy in cellar," "dairy room," "milk cellar," and "milk room," for example, show that part of a dwelling functioned to support dairying (map 35). Most of these descriptors appeared in advertisements for northeastern New Jersey properties (especially in Dutch-settled areas) and thus suggest an orientation to the New York market.

On the other hand, advertisements that described separate structures for dairying—"dairy, dairy house, milk house, and spring house" (used for cool storage)— appeared much more often for West Jersey farms (map 36). Other newspaper articles document a concentration in this area on dairying for the Philadelphia market; one Burlington man murdered his wife in a jealous rage in 1769 just after she had prepared "a Quantity of Butter . . . to bring to the next Market at Philadelphia"; the woman also had managed "a Dairy of 40 Cows."[14] The relative absence of such terms for properties near Salem suggests that fattening may have been more important there. But taken together, these two maps certainly suggest a focus on dairying for the New York and Philadelphia markets. And the war damage claims indicate that dairying was a bit more important in some of the Dutch-settled areas such as Somerset County, where the percentage of milch cattle lost to marauding troops (and, indeed, of other cattle) was higher than in neighboring counties (table 25).

These damage claims may reflect the distribution of milch cattle most accurately because dairy cows required daily care and thus were not mobile in any practical sense. The data are probably less reliable for other stock. Farmers could easily drive ordinary cattle into distant available pasturage for an extended period when military activities threatened. Two documents from the period indicate that they probably did so. In an August 27, 1780, letter to Governor Livingston, George Washington stated that troops at his headquarters in Bergen County had had no meat for five days and that he had "moved down to this place with a view of stripping the lower parts of the Country of the remainder of its Cattle, which after a most rigorous exaction is found to afford between two and three days supply only, and those consisting of Milch Cows and Calves of one or two years old."[15] And one 1779 legislative act prohibited nonresident owners from moving livestock onto land left unfenced in Woodbridge and Piscataway townships because passing armies had destroyed fences. In the petition that must have provoked the legislation, resident landholders charged "that divers Persons from the interior Parts of the Country, taking Advantage of their difficult Circumstances, turn out and drive down to range upon the said Lands so lying uninclosed, great Numbers of neat

Table 25
Revolutionary War Damage Claims Pertaining to Livestock

County	Number of Claims	Percentage of Total Claims				
		Milch Cows	Cattle	Oxen	Sheep	Hogs
Bergen with Acquackanonk Twp. in Essex (Dutch)	436	40.6	18.6	4.6	28.4	31.9
Burlington (English)	230	38.7	14.3	5.6	35.7	46.1
Essex (New England)	234	46.2	16.2	13.2	47.4	40.6
Middlesex (Heterogeneous)	321	55.1	31.2	19.6	46.4	43.6
Somerset (Dutch)	114	68.4	40.4	9.6	37.7	51.8

Cattle, Horses and Sheep, to the great Detriment and Loss of the Owners and Possessors of such Lands."[16]

Given the importance of dairying at the time in southern and western portions of the Netherlands, the greater percentages of milch cattle in some Dutch-settled areas should be no surprise.[17] Other farmers must have been motivated to take up dairying by their proximity to the New York market, as advertisements and reports in the New York and Philadelphia newspapers indicate. For example, a property in Shrewsbury, a short voyage across Raritan Bay to New York, was advertised in 1747 as yielding enough hay to "Maintain 30 Milch Cows."[18] In 1760, one farm of seven

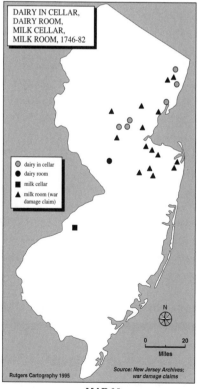

MAP 35

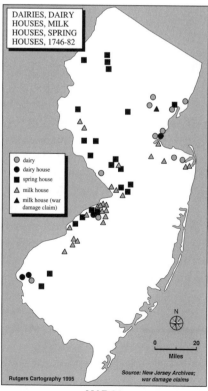

MAP 36

to eight hundred acres in "Hoobock," directly across the Hudson from New York, was advertised to include "the most commodious Dairy for at least thirty Cows," as well as abundant clover and salt hay, the right to run stock in the meadowlands of Bergen Commons, thirty-six head of cattle, one hundred sheep, twenty hogs, and a pair of oxen.[19]

Dairying was also important in southwestern New Jersey. From the 1760s on, Grant Gibbon's Salem store ledger credited customers for the butter, cheese, and milk they brought in; the butter and cheese, at least, were probably destined for the Philadelphia market.[20] In 1779, one of the rare advertisements that mentioned dairying directly offered for sale a farm at "Bridgetown" on the Cohansey in Cumberland County. It had "excellent meadow whereon may be grazed forty head of cattle yearly, besides keeping a large dairy."[21] And the farm account book of Robert Johnston indicates that Salem County supported large cattle operations after the Revolution. Johnston himself fatted cattle for the Philadelphia market—he listed the seventeen cows that calved between January and August 1785 and another twenty-nine between December 1785 and July 1786—and must also have carried on some dairying, judging by the large numbers of cows he kept. Johnston gave each one of them names, including "Brazen face," "Gentle," "Crumbely Horns," "Moon face Heffer," and "Young Frosty Face."[22]

Read noted that some of his Burlington County neighbors had dairy herds of from ten to twenty-three cows. Each herd, he calculated, brought their owners annual profits of £6-7. Each cow produced about 1,100 quarts of milk, which would make about 138 pounds of butter or 275 pounds of cheese. Most of these dairy products were destined for the Philadelphia market, but at least some of the milk appears to have fed the hogs.

From the relatively low profit margins Read recorded, though, farmers on the Inner Coastal Plain in southwestern New Jersey appear to have realized greater profits from fattening cattle and hogs than from dairying. In the 1790s, Thomas Newbold of Chesterfield Township, Burlington County, recorded agreements with butchers "for 25 head of fatten Cattle to be taken away and killed this fall [1795]." In December Newbold bought ten cows and sixteen steers from Barzilla Newbold in order to fatten them for market.[23] Of the fifty entries between April 5, 1805, and March 6, 1807, in the account book of cattle buyer Levi Webster, forty-five were for fatted cattle, obviously destined for the Philadelphia market.[24]

Charles Read noted that cattle were driven into Burlington County from North Carolina and Maryland to fatten, a practice von Thünen's model also suggested.[25] Cattle driven to pasture close to Philadelphia would make up the weight lost en route or even gain weight. They could then be slaughtered nearby and barreled for shipment. Read indicated that the area had sufficient feed and pasture to support these nonlocal herds, which tended to arrive "at any time from harvest till ye last of November."

Producers on New Jersey's Inner Coastal Plain made special efforts to satisfy the affluent of New York and Philadelphia with specially "fatted" cattle. Some of these specialized stockmen were widely known, such as John Forman, who in February 1763 advertised two six-year-old steers then at Freehold in Monmouth County. One was more than nine feet long and more than seventeen hands (5'8") high. "They have been fed in the best Manner they could have been fed ever since they were between 3 and 4 years old," Forman wrote; "they have had as much Indian Meal as they could eat, and the best Clover Hay, green Wheat, and the best Clover Pasture that could be had for them ever since the first beginning to feed them: Fatter nor larger Cattle has never been seen or raised in the said Country before."[26]

In Philadelphia in 1770, George and Benjamin Wilport advertised that they had killed "the large Steer, raised by John Tonkin of Springfield [Township] in Burlington County, New Jersey." To be sold on Saturday "at their Stall No. 45, in the Market," the steer weighed 1,745 pounds, 1,394 of it in the four quarters, 225 in tallow, and 126 in the hide.[27]

Northern New Jersey farmers were also raising cattle to sell on the New York market, partly because poor soils made livestock more promising. In 1796, Gavin Scott turned to cattle on his small farm near Elizabethtown because, he wrote, "Land is of Little value unless for feading Cattle if I was to plow and sow a field with corn and hire all the Labour the produce would Likely not pay. unless it was a rich spot. so that if you hire part and work part you only are paid Like a hired man."[28] Two years earlier, Theophile Cazenove noted that farmers on "very bad" soils in Chatham, Morris County, "try mostly the raising of cattle." In Hanover in the same county, he noted, "more and more the farmers are anxious to raise cattle" even though it involved the expense of stall feeding them from December to April. In the Kittatinny Valley, near present-day Washington, Cazenove observed that farmers were buying as much land as they could, "not so much, for cultivation" but rather to "send their cattle and horses to pasture in the uncultivated woods."[29]

Other observers agreed that in northern New Jersey, especially, farmers after the Revolution concentrated more effort on cattle than they had earlier. In 1787, New England attorney, cleric, and botanist Manasseh Cutler stopped two miles northeast of Morristown to visit the 126-acre farm of his uncle Uriah, who may have moved there in the late 1730s.[30] Uriah Cutler had "a large pair of oxen which he assured me were the only pair in town" and "a very pretty dairy of cows, having retained the idea of propagating neat cattle, which he brought from New England." The term "neat cattle" probably referred to bovines, as distinct from the traditional biblical use of the term "cattle" to refer to all quadruped livestock. Cutler's remarks make clear that raising cattle had not always been so widespread as it then was in New Jersey and that many farmers still could not be "prevailed upon to leave their old habits." His uncle also had "five fine horses," which Cutler noted was a custom more in keeping with "the style of Jersey farmers."[31]

As feed tended to be in great demand during the winter, livestock were slaughtered in the late fall or early winter, and some farmers could sell hay for enough money to make feeding it to their own livestock less sensible. "I do not know what to say about the Cattle," an unidentified correspondent in New York wrote to John Stevens in Hunterdon County on January 25, 1792. "I have considerable more hay than my stock can consume, but at the high price hay goes at think it would be more profitable to dispose of the Hay than to feed it out to stock. However if you cannot conveniently dispose of your Cattle for the winter elsewhere you're please to send them down."[32] Other farmers had the opposite experience: in 1800, Scott noted of one nearby recent English emigré, "Last sumer he had 24 Cows cost 12½ Dollars each besides he had a number of Steers all made an average Double there price for there summers grass."[33]

Official prices for beef cattle during the inflationary days of the Revolution reflected farmers' added expense of stall-feeding cattle during the winter in northern areas. Grass-fed beef brought £0.5.6 a pound, but beginning in January, after the animals had been confined for a month or so, the price rose to 0.6.6 and then a shilling per month higher through May, when pasturage again became available and prices dropped accordingly (table 26).[34] Veal was only valued at 0.5.0 at this time, although account book credits to local farmers show veal to have had the same value as beef (table 27).

As feed grew scarcer during the winter months, the price butchers paid graziers for meat also rose. In October and November 1756, butchers paid twenty to twenty-two shillings for a hundred pounds of beef, twenty-five to twenty-seven in late December, twenty-seven to twenty-eight by the middle of January 1757, thirty to thirty-five by the middle or end of February, and as much as thirty-eight to forty shillings per hundred pounds by March and April.[35] Late winter beef prices were also high because stall-fattened cattle would "tallow well"; tallow, used to make candles and soap, brought a higher price than meat.

Cazenove noted in 1794 that four-year-old cows could be sold for from twenty to thirty dollars in both the New York and Philadelphia markets. And Read recorded the results of several experiments around the state in fattening cattle. In December 1756, Robert Ogden of Elizabethtown slaughtered an eighteen-month-old heifer whose four quarters weighed 610 pounds, "Gutt fatt" 70 pounds, and kidneys 34 pounds each for a total value of £11. Woodward noted that Ogden was well known for his success in fattening cattle, and Jacob Spicer reported in 1755 that Ogden had slaughtered a three-year-old steer whose four quarters weighed

Table 26
Official Meat Prices, 1779

Beef		
	Best grass-fed beef	5.6 lb.
	Best stall-fed beef	
	January	6.6 lb.
	February	7.6 lb.
	March	8.6 lb.
	April	9.6 lb.
	May	10.6 lb.
	June	11.0 lb.
	Good merchantable beef	£95.0.0 barrel
	Best veal	5.0 lb.
	Rendered tallow	15.0 lb.
	Hides	
	Raw hides, green	6.8 lb.
	Calf-skins, green	10.0 lb.
Pork		
	Merchantable pork by the carcass	6.8 lb.
	Well cured pickled pork	13.6 lb.
	Gammons (hams) and other bacon well cured	15.0 lb.
	Good merchantable pork	£125.0.0 barrel
	Rendered hogs lard	11.6 lb.
Mutton		
	Best mutton or lamb	5.6 lb.
	Winter-fed mutton to be the same price as stall-fed beef from the first of January to the first of April	

1,001 pounds.[36] Ogden's successes even made the newspaper: in 1763, a New York paper reported that for nine months he had fattened a steer bred by Lewis Johnston of Perth Amboy; when he slaughtered it in early March, it weighed in at about 1,700 pounds.[37] But John Harriman of Elizabethtown had not been able to make a profit on an ox he purchased for £5 in the fall of 1698. During the winter he stall-fed the animal 16½ bushels of corn, 11 bushels of oats, 2¼ bushels of buckwheat, and £1.10.0 worth of hay. His total feed cost was £9.20.ll, but the labor costs and the expense of housing the animal were uncalculated. When Harriman slaughtered the ox the following March, he received only £9.11.4½ for its meat, tallow, and hide. Why Harriman lost money is not known, but most likely the cost of fodder was too high.[38]

Potentially more lucrative than raising cattle for market was raising swine. A barrel of "good merchantable pork" commanded £125 in 1779 (see table 26), and local account books also uniformly assign a higher value to pork in every form, whether smoked or salted (table 28). Not only was it the preferred meat of New Jersey inhabitants,[39] but corn-fed pork was also a major item of export to the West Indies, chiefly from Philadelphia. Indeed, before the Revolution, "Burlington pork" was famed as being the best in the West India market; in 1789, Jedediah Morse declared that New Jersey hams "are celebrated as being the best in the world."[40]

However, the distribution of hogs is even more difficult to determine than the distribution of cattle. Hogs were only taxed in one year, and wartime dislocations in their distribution may have been even more pronounced. Moreover, surviving

Table 27
Beef and Veal, Representative Prices Credited to Local Accounts,
Number of Pence Per Pound of Weight, 1762–1804

Year and Date		Location	Price
1762—Sept. 21	(veal)	Newark Township	3.50
1764—July 23	(veal)	Newark Township	3.50
1771—Dec. 10	(beef)	Newark Township	3.25
1775—October	(beef)	Newark Township	3.50
1775—December	(beef)	Newark Township	3.00
1776—November	(beef)	Newark Township	4.00
1791—April	(beef)	Warren Township	3.50
1791—Sept. 22	(beef)	Warren Township	3.50
1792—June 8	(veal)	Warren Township	3.50
1792—July 3	(veal)	Warren Township	3.50
1792—Aug. 5	(veal)	Warren Township	3.50
1793—Oct. 16	(beef)	Warren Township	3.50
1794—May 7	(veal)	Warren Township	4.00
1794—Oct. 14	(beef)	Warren Township	4.50
1795—Jan. 4	(beef)	Hunterdon County	4.00–5.00
1795—Apr. 9	(veal)	Warren Township	5.50
1796—September	(beef)	Warren Township	5.50
1797—Nov. 25	(beef)	Warren Township	5.00
1799—Jun. 25	(beef)	Warren Township	6.00
1799—Oct. 5	(beef)	Warren Township	5.00
1800—February	(veal)	Warren Township	5.00
1800—May 25	(veal)	Warren Township	5.50
1800—July 1	(veal)	Warren Township	6.00
1800—Oct. 30	(beef)	Warren Township	4.50
1803—June 3	(veal)	Warren Township	4.00
1803—Oct. 12	(veal)	Warren Township	5.00
1804—June 12	(veal)	Franklin Township	5.00

Table 28
Pork and Ham, Representative Prices Credited to Local Accounts,
Number of Pence or Cents Per Pound of Weight, 1764–1815

Year and Date		Location	Price
1764—Sept. 27	(hams)	Newark Township	8.00
1766—Mar. 7	(pork)	Newark Township	6.00
1791—Sept. 22	(pork)	Warren Township	8.00
1792—June 10	(pork)	Warren Township	7.00
1794—Mar. 8	(pork)	Warren Township	10.00
1794—Mar. 24	(pork)	Warren Township	9.00
1795—Jan. 4	(pork)	Hunterdon County	5.00–6.00
1795—Apr. 9	(pork)	Warren Township	12.00
1797—Oct. 13	(pork)	Warren Township	12.00
1799—Oct. 5	(pork)	Warren Township	12.00
1800—Oct. 25	(pork)	Warren Township	12.00
1801—Mar. 4	(pork)	Warren Township	12.00
1815—February	(pork–200 lb. barrel)	Kingwood Township	$0.09
1815—February	(hams–300 lb. cask)	Kingwood Township	$0.10

tax lists enumerating hogs exist for only two of the eleven contemporary townships in Sussex County. Nonetheless, the map of the distribution of hogs in about 1780 does suggest that some parts of southern New Jersey harbored relatively large numbers of hogs—particularly parts of Salem County, where hogs, like cattle, were probably fattened for the Philadelphia market (map 37). The practice of running hogs in the woods is implied by the relatively large numbers of the animals in sparsely settled Maurice River, Middle and Upper townships in the Outer Coastal Plain. Elsewhere, the pattern at this time looks a great deal as if both Philadelphia and New York had emptied New Jersey farms in their immediate hinterlands of their hogs.

Revolutionary damage claims suggest that hogs were among the favorite spoils of war on the part of marauding troops (see table 24). As would be expected, losses were large in Burlington County and in northeastern New Jersey as well, where Somerset County's claims were greatest. Scattered references to hogs indicate that they were ubiquitous in the farm economy of northern New Jersey but that farmers there did not specialize in them as farmers to the south appear to have done.

Just as references to dairying in property advertisements can help determine the density of milch cattle from place to place in New Jersey, the distribution of smokehouses—widely used to process hams ("gammons") for market—can serve as a surrogate indicator of the relative density of hogs (map 38).[41] Indeed, advertisements suggest a great focus on the smoking of hams in southern Hunterdon County and in Burlington County on the Inner Coastal Plain, which must have been a primary area for fattening hogs. On this part of the Inner Coastal Plain, where the soils were considered to be poor for wheat but good for corn, hogs had been allowed to range the woods early on; later, when Philadelphia merchants developed their market with the West Indies, farmers here grew corn on which to fatten hogs for market. In New Jersey, the Inner Coastal Plain and southern Piedmont were the best place to fatten hogs, for the area was close to the market and could produce corn in abundance. If a "Corn Belt" existed in New Jersey at this time, it was in southern Hunterdon County and the fertile Inner Coastal Plain running southward.

Local records corroborate this assumption. Between 1756 and 1760, Richard

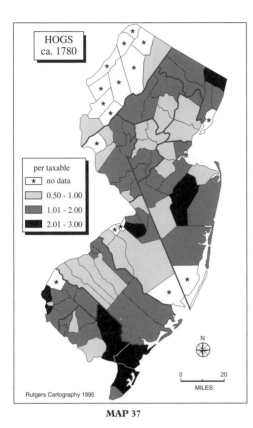

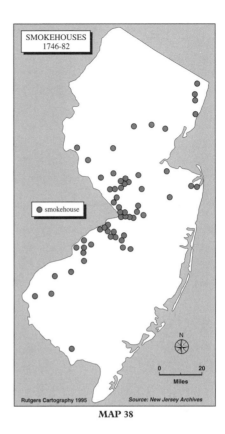

MAP 37   **MAP 38**

Reed recorded carting wheat, barrels of pork, and bushels of salt (for preserving the meat) from Amwell Township in southern Hunterdon County to New Brunswick and Trenton; the pork and most of the wheat were probably then shipped to either New York or Philadelphia.[42] In a 1772 sale notice, Richard Brown, living in Crosswick's Creek in Upper Freehold Township, Monmouth County, nine miles from Bordentown, noted that from his property "produce may be transported to Philadelphia, at a moderate expence"; the farm, he declared, was well situated "for collecting pork, which may be yearly had in large quantities in the neighborhood, as good in quality as any where in the province of New Jersey."[43]

Surely because of the reputation corn-fed pork had acquired, corn was the preferred feed for pigs. In 1800, Gavin Scott used his eight hundred bushels of corn and probably some of the milk from his dairy to fatten hogs.[44] Charles Read reported an experiment by Joshua Bispham of Morristown, in which he initially reduced the two quarts of feed farmers in southwestern New Jersey normally fed hogs each day. On September 11, 1756, Bispham began to feed two pigs weighing seventy pounds each one quart of raw corn and one pint in swill each day. By October 18, the pigs had gained about three-quarters of a pound per day, or a collective total of sixty-four pounds. From that point, Bispham fed them three quarts of corn a day. On this, they each gained about one and three-quarters pounds a day. When they were slaughtered January 11, their combined weight was 292 pounds; dressed, they weighed 230 pounds. Read calculated that the corn was worth two shillings a bushel and the pork three pence a pound, so the profit on the two hogs was twelve shillings each. It would have been higher, he thought, if they had not been kept too long in cold weather.[45]

Not all farmers could realize such profits, however. In 1756, Jacob Spicer attempted to fatten eight hogs on the Outer Coastal Plain in Cape May County but discovered that "the value of the hogs was totally sunk by feeding them, particularly when corn is worth 3s. per bushel, and pork 30s. per 100lbs." One "stunted pig," about six months old, weighed only 89½ pounds despite the fact that "she eat up almost all my crop of corn."[46] Clearly it did not pay to fatten hogs at Cape May, where corn yields were low and grain relatively expensive to acquire (three shillings per bushel as opposed to two on the Inner Coastal Plain).

Farmers elsewhere often fed grasses and produce other than corn to hogs. Edward Antill fed his hogs boiled potatoes and "Dutch" (or red) clover, which he mowed two or three times each day for this purpose. "The great Art of raising Hogs to advantage," he wrote, "is always to keep them thriving upon the cheapest food, if they are neglected and suffered to go back, they are Stunted in their growth and it takes a great deal more to bring them up again."[47] Charles Read noted that turnips, clover pasture, rye pasture, timothy pasture, and milk in swill were all used to advantage. Documents from a case before the New Jersey Supreme Court in 1749 also suggest that smaller, poorer farmers in northern New Jersey did not use corn for hog fodder. Abraham Phillips, a tenant of James Alexander and Robert Hunter Morris on a farm in Horse Neck, about twelve miles northwest of Newark, stated in a deposition to the court that he had fenced "a Hog-Pasture" on the property only to have another man claim the property and threaten him. According to Phillips, the claimant and five other men then destroyed his fencing, which "turned his Fattoning Hogs loose, who ran into the Woods, and it was three or four Days before he could find them again, when a Breeding Sow of this Deponent's was found dead." They had also torn down the fence around his "Stack-Yards" and burned "a Stack of Oats of between Twenty and Thirty Bushels, a Stack of Corn Stalks and Flax, some Buck-Wheat Straw, in short, all the Provision and Fodder which this Deponent had got to subsist his Creatures during the winter."[48]

For poorer farmers and for others who, like Spicer, lived in areas where corn was scarce and expensive and where the climate permitted, it made more sense to let hogs run in the woods and thus avert the cost of fattening them. In 1779, James Parker kept his hogs in outdoor pens that his farm laborers moved about as needed. Parker surely penned the animals to keep them from rooting in his meadows and oat fields.[49] Other farmers who did not pen hogs fitted them with a triangular yoke around the neck to keep them from moving through loose fences, a custom in Pennsylvania, northwestern New Jersey, and the New England-settled sections in the north. The Camps, for example, debited Jonah Conger for "yoaking piggs" in 1753.[50]

The volume of the pork trade may be judged from some of the entries in the ledgers of general stores and local producers. Thirty-four people brought 178 hogs to Grant Gibbon of Salem between November 6, 1765, and January 21, 1766.[51] He paid twenty-five shillings per hundred pounds for these hogs, or a not inconsiderable total of almost £272. Nine of these customers brought two hogs each, but others brought from nine to thirty-seven, which certainly indicates that some farmers specialized in raising these animals. That the weights of these hogs varied widely suggests that some farmers might have suffered feed shortages or simply were not good at raising them. The hogs of the five farmers with from nine to thirty-seven pigs weighed near the mean of 122.2 pounds. Jacob Scoggen's thirty-seven hogs had a mean weight of 120.9 pounds just before Christmas, while John Woodside's fifteen hogs had a mean weight of 123.3 pounds when he brought them in almost three weeks earlier. John Breeding's two hogs averaged 140.5 pounds on November 27, but James Mason's two, brought in three days later, only averaged 80.5 pounds each.

Gibbon also gave farmers store credit for packing pork for him and for smoking meat; in 1766, he recorded a credit of £1.7.4 to Thomas Goodwin "By Smoaking 328 Gamns [hams]." In Chesterfield Township, Burlington County, almost thirty years later, Thomas Newbold listed in his "farm accounts" the hogs he had slaughtered, some of them apparently his own or partly his on shares, others apparently belonging to neighbors. By December 31, 1793, he had slaughtered 108 hogs totaling 22,746 pounds, or 210.6 pounds on average. On December 27, 1796, Newbold recorded receiving 8,162 pounds of pork from David Thomson, "for rent between Michael Taylor & myself which we satt in partnership"; during the following December he recorded "David Thomsons pork 52 hogs wt 9304 lb to be put up and the proceeds divided between Michael Taylor and myself."[52]

Although most New Jersey hogs averaged about two hundred pounds, contemporary newspapers recorded larger ones. The *Boston Evening-Post* reported that one large hog, "bred in New Jersey" and kept "some Time for a Show" in Philadelphia, weighed 574 "when singed and dress'd" when it was slaughtered on January 24, 1738. The hog "was not near so fat as was expected," the newspaper noted, judging from its size: from its nose to the end of its tail it measured eight feet, four inches.[53] In early December 1767, a Philadelphia paper mentioned an even more impressive animal, "brought to Town, alive, from New Jersey," weighing about 850 pounds. "Those who have seen him think he is the largest Creature of the Kind ever raised in America," the newspaper stated, and added later that the hog would be sold the next market day "for the Gratification of the true lovers of fat Pork."[54]

Sheep were distributed quite differently throughout New Jersey in this period. These animals were not taxed systematically later than 1768, although some townships did tax them and especially distinguished merino sheep in 1815. However, sheep were enumerated by county in 1751 (table 29).[55] This listing indicates that northern New Jersey tended to favor sheep production more than southern New Jersey, with the notable exception of Cape May County. This anomaly is explained by the fact that sheep were especially prevalent in areas settled by New Englanders, Cape May among them. Comparing each county's proportion of the state's total number of sheep to each county's total and taxed land shows this concentration more plainly. Essex County, for example, contained almost 10 percent of New Jersey's sheep but less than 4 percent of its land and only a little more than 5 percent of its taxed land. Gloucester County, on the other hand, held only 5.5 percent of the provinces's sheep but more than 8 percent of the taxed land and more than 13 percent of total area. A petition summarizing taxable categories in Gloucester County in 1768 also revealed few sheep, while contemporary tax lists from New England-settled Lower Township, Cape May County, showed a relatively high number of these animals.[56]

From an early point, farmers in New England-settled sections of New Jersey

Table 29

Table 29
Acres of Land Taxed, Actual Area, and Sheep
as Percentage of Total for the Colony, by New Jersey County, 1751

County	Acres of Taxed Land	Actual Area	Sheep
Middlesex	8.4	4.9	10.5
Monmouth	12.3	14.7	11.1
Essex	5.4	3.7	9.9
Somerset	11.1	4.9	10.7
Bergen	6.3	6.8	5.9
Burlington	11.6	11.2	10.9
Gloucester	8.3	13.3	5.5
Salem	6.9	4.1	5.4
Cumberland	4.2	8.7	4.1
Cape May	2.9	3.0	3.4
Hunterdon	14.5	6.9	13.6
Morris	8.2	17.8	8.9
Province	100.1	100.0	99.9

showed more interest in sheep. In 1694, the General Assembly of East Jersey passed an act "for the Encouragement of the breeding Sheep" that made sheep tax free.[57] Revolutionary War damage claims also show that more sheep were taken by troops in these sections; Burlington County in the southwest and areas settled by the Dutch in northern Jersey lost fewer and presumably had fewer to lose, although the troops' preference for beef and pork may also account for the small losses.

Still, the records of the Camp family of Newark Township indicate that mutton was a common food in northern New Jersey, and many farmers in the northern sections raised sheep for their wool. In September 1770, one New Jersey farmer (probably in Hunterdon County) urged the production of wool and flax to provide the raw materials for an American textile industry and thus to reduce the nation's dependence on English exports.

The writer cited the case of one farmer whose forty-six sheep were valued at £0.8.0 a head, or £18.8.0 for the lot, in the fall of 1769. When the farmer sheared his sheep the next May, he recovered 136 pounds of wool valued at £13.12.0. By the following September he had sold or his family had eaten eight weathers (castrated males) at 0.15.0 each and four ewes at 0.8.0 each, valued together at £7.12.0. Despite the consumption or sale of twelve animals, the flock had increased by twenty and its corresponding value by £4. Thus, the correspondent pointed out, on an investment of £18.8.0, the farmer had realized a profit of £25.4.0 in just one year. He noted that the open winter that year had made it possible to graze the flock outdoors and that the only additional feed the farmer provided was "Corn Stalks, in February and March to the Heavy [pregnant] Ewes." In the summer, the writer noted, "a Fallow of about 45 Acres kept them till the first of Sept. except about three Weeks." The correspondent declared that an increase in the total number of sheep in Hunterdon County, then estimated at twenty thousand, would greatly benefit farmers, who would do better in general "if they kept fewer useless Horses and plowed fewer worn out Fields."[58]

At the annual town meeting on April 28, 1788, Newark Township officials offered a bounty to encourage wool production on the grounds that "the increase of Sheep and consequent production and increase of Wool [is] of the highest importance to the interest and prosperity of this Country, and the inhabitants of this Township."[59] The highest premium of £10 was to be awarded to the person shearing the greatest quantity of wool from his own sheep the following spring; bounties of from £8 to £2 were given to the farmers shearing the next five highest amounts. Crèvecoeur had also noted that despite the northeast's rapid urbanization "the inhabitants of New-ark, like those of Elizabethtown, have a community herd, which, under the care of one shepherd, wanders way off to graze."[60] By 1810, he noted, the "mania for home manufactures and fine wool" led farmers to expand their flocks by importing merino stock from Spain. A decade later when woolen imports from Great Britain were again allowed into the country, the craze for merinos had ended, and sheep farmers returned to their earlier emphasis on mutton production.[61]

Sheep were folded (penned to produce manure) in relatively large numbers in both Cape May and Essex counties by midcentury. In 1751, Jacob Spicer drove his large flock of thirty-nine sheep out to pasture and then folded them, which must have enhanced the poor soils of this region.[62] In Newark Township in May 1755, Joseph Camp credited "Mr. Cranstone" £0.2.6 for each of eleven nights Cranstone folded sheep on Camp's land. Through May 19, 1756, Camp paid 0.4.0 for the "Sheep 2 nights in the garden" and 0.15.0 "By the Sheep 5 nights on the planting ground."[63]

Two surviving township tax lists for 1751 permit an even closer look at the preference among New England-born settlers for raising sheep. These lists exist for Lower Precinct in Cape May County, settled by New Englanders, and Maurice River Precinct, Cumberland County, settled thirty years later largely by Swedes and Finns; in 1751, 40 percent of the precinct's population were Swedes, Finns, and their descendants.[64] These two precincts lay within fifteen miles of each other on the Outer Coastal Plain; their soils and terrain were basically the same. But land use in the two townships was markedly different (tables 30 and 31). Some of this difference may relate to the longer settlement and greater orientation to the sea at Cape May, but cultural differences account for some of it as well.

Much more land was taxed at Cape May, due no doubt to its earlier settlement, but at Maurice River, comparing the patterns of ownership of horses and cattle with landholding makes clear that most farmers were running their stock on land they did not hold and on which they paid no taxes. And by any measure, there was a much greater emphasis on raising sheep in Lower Precinct than in Maurice River. Even within Maurice River, Swedes tended to own fewer sheep than other settlers, largely English (table 31), even though they did not differ markedly from each other in the size of their landholdings or in their ownership of horses and cattle. Swedish and Finnish settlers in New Jersey tended to be woodsmen and thus less interested in farming than were others.

Mutton does not appear to have been nearly as popular a dish as beef in southern New Jersey. Charles Read had much less to say about sheep than about other livestock, which reflects the far greater tendency among Burlington County farmers to raise cattle and pork.[65] Only 10 percent of the livestock purchased by Levi Webster, a buyer for the Philadelphia market in Gloucester County, were sheep in

Table 30
Maurice River Precinct and Lower Precinct
Tax Ratables, 1751

	Maurice River		Lower Precinct	
Acres Taxes	3,090	(2.4%)	10,830	(51.6%)
Taxables	62		101	
Swedes	25	(40.3%)	2?	(1.9%)
Those holding improved land and horses and cattle	14	(22.6%)	64	(63.4%)
Those holding horses and cattle only	30	(48.4%)	13	(12.9%)
Horses and cattle	538		820	
Horses and cattle per taxable	8.7		8.1	
Sheep	74		942	
Sheep per taxable	1.2		9.3	
Livestock owners holding horses and cattle but no sheep	2	(56.8%)	10	(15.6%)
Mean holding of horses and cattle	11.6		10.9	
Median holding of horses and cattle	11.0		10.0	
Mean holding of sheep	8.1		14.6	
Median holding of sheep	7.0		13.0	
Horses and cattle to sheep ratio	3.5		0.9	

Table 31
Maurice River Precinct Tax Ratables, 1751

	Swedes		Others	
Taxables	25	(40.3%)	37	(59.7%)
Holders of improved land and horses and cattle	7	(50.0%)	7	(50.0%)
Holders of improved land not holding horses and cattle	3	(75.0%)	1	(25.0%)
Holders of horses and cattle only	11	(39.3%)	17	(50.7%)
Total holding of horses and cattle	18	(41.9%)	25	(58.1%)
Total holding sheep	5	(27.8%)	13	(72.2%)
Mean improved acreage	192.9		184.3	
Median improved acreage	180.0		150.0	

Table 32
Lamb and Mutton, Representative Prices Credited to Local Accounts,
In Pence per Pound of Weight, 1796–1811

Year and Date		Location	Price
1796—Aug. 19	(lamb)	Warren Township	6.00
1799—July 29	(lamb)	Warren Township	4.00
1800—July 1	(lamb)	Warren Township	4.00
1800—Aug. 15	(lamb)	Warren Township	5.00
1802—June 22	(lamb)	Warren Township	5.00
1802—July 28	(lamb)	Warren Township	5.00
1802—Sept. 15	(lamb)	Franklin Township	4.00
1811—July 5	(mutton)	Knowlton Township	5.00

1805; the rest were cattle.[66] Available methods of preserving meats did not work well for mutton, which made its market far more local than what existed for beef and pork, and its prices were also relatively low (table 32). Moreover, sheep needed a great deal more supervision than cattle or hogs: wolves and dogs preyed upon them, and they had to be kept away from the deadly mountain laurel.

Still, the Philadelphia market presented enough demand for good mutton to encourage some sheep husbandry in southwestern sections. As Carl Woodward has argued, "It is doubtful if in the eighteenth century the mutton of Gloucester, Burlington, and Salem Counties could be equalled anywhere in the colonies nor could it be greatly surpassed in England."[67] Read noted that farmers preferred to feed sheep corn, both green and kernel, along with "moist meadow." "Common" sheep fed this way would weigh in ten or twelve pounds per quarter, "if large & very fatt 20 lb."

Some farmers rented out sheep to others who received a share of the income from them, either in wool or in the value of the mutton. In May 1778, James Parker recorded renting twelve sheep for twelve pounds of wool. On May 23, he had shorn 166 pounds from thirty-three other sheep and twenty-five lambs, some of which had been sheared in August 1777.[68] On January 28, 1792, Thomas Newbold of Chesterfield Township, Burlington County, noted in a memorandum that "Abraham Peterson took 9 Sheep three of them lambs for himself to the Shares he is to return the old Stock good at the expiration of 3 years also every sixth lamb and one pound of wool of each old Sheep."[69] In 1794 Newbold agreed to let Asa Poinsett have seven ewes and one ram for three years in exchange for one pound of wool per year from each animal and every tenth lamb. These agreements appear to be very generous, perhaps because caring for sheep was labor-intensive, but clearly there were enough poorer farmers willing to work for shares to make the system work.

The threat to sheep presented by wolves and unsupervised dogs provoked numerous legislative acts at all levels of government in New Jersey. In March 1763 forty-eight inhabitants of Burlington County petitioned the legislature for relief against the depredations of dogs.

> Whereas Sundrey Losses and Damages, hath and doth frequently happen to the Inhabetance, by dogs killing, wounding, and destroying of Sheep Lambs &c which we Concive may in Some Measure be Ocassioned by people Keeping a needless number of Dogs, and Especially those who have the Least occasion for them, which gitting Together in the Night time often dos Great Damage and not found out or if by chance taken and killd, (which is the common Custom when Detected) is but poor Sattisfaction to the partie Agrived: And as we are daly Liable to Losses of this kind, and no fund or provision for Redress, as yet, in Such Case made and provided Therefore we Humbly pray the Honourable house will take this affare into Consideration, And make Such provision for the Redress of Sufferers in Manner aforesd.[70]

In 1765, the colony instituted a one-shilling tax on dogs to help control the danger to sheep, but many farmers felt it was too low to create a fund large enough to compensate owners who lost sheep in this way. In 1770, in a letter to a Philadelphia newspaper, "a Grazier" urged that the tax be increased to two shillings because "the

Sums raised did not pay all the Damage done."[71] But this, too, was inadequate. In 1806, a new law returned the authority to levy and collect dog taxes to annual town meetings, who were also permitted to "make such other regulations and bye laws to protect their sheep from the ravages of dogs, as a majority . . . may deem expedient."[72]

Then, in 1811, the state reasserted authority in "an Act of the preservation of Sheep" by placing a tax of fifty cents on the first dog owned and five dollars on every additional dog to pay the damages inflicted upon sheep when the offending dog or dogs could or would not be identified.[73] Each "slut" (bitch), even if it was the only dog owned, was assessed at five dollars. The act also permitted anyone to kill a dog "found chasing, worrying or wounding any sheep or lamb or that shall be at any time found running at large, beyond the owner's premises without a collar affixed around its neck having the christian and the whole surname of the owner legibly inscribed thereon." Owners refusing to kill dogs found to have abused sheep were liable for a fine of ten dollars for the first offense and treble damages for the second offense. The act inexplicably did not pertain to the counties of Sussex, Hunterdon, Bergen, and Morris, probably because dogs were used for hunting there to a greater extent than elsewhere.[74]

The tax on dogs must have been a controversial subject, because it was repealed and later replaced by new legislation in 1820 that reduced the tax to fifty cents for first dogs, male or female, and one dollar for every additional dog. Townships were authorized as well to lay additional taxes on dogs not to exceed five dollars.[75] Damages from wolves could also be compensated from each township's fund, and if these funds were not expended on these damages townships were permitted to spend them for other legitimate purposes. The 1820 law suggests that the dog problem may have become both localized and less severe, perhaps because more enclosures were adequately fenced.

Horses were of the utmost importance to New Jersey farmers, not only for transportation—it was considered demeaning to walk long distances—but for farm work as well. Horses were, however, expensive, and tax lists indicate many farmers could not afford to own one. Like other livestock, the distribution of horses was very much affected by the Revolution. And, like sheep, horses appear to have been more numerous in northern New Jersey than in the southern portion of the state in about 1780 (map 39). Moreover, foraging expeditions through the Inner Coastal Plain and the northern Piedmont probably decreased the number of horses in these regions. Still, 1784 township tax data show that northern New Jersey had a greater density of horses than did southern Jersey (map 40). Agglomerated places such as Perth Amboy and Trenton Township show higher densities, as might be expected. But New Brunswick does not, which suggests that the area had not yet fully recovered from the depredations of the Revolutionary armies. Horses were much less common on the Outer Coastal Plain and in the northern Highlands.

Among those who could afford them, horses were also a symbol of status. Horse racing was a popular pastime among the elite; wealthier farmers showed much interest in possessing horses of superior breed, and stud or "covering" horses were taxed at a special rate. The distribution of covering horses for 1784 (map 41)[76] suggests rural affluence more than anything else. The Outer Coastal Plain and the northern Highlands and Ridge and Valley sections had few or no stud animals,

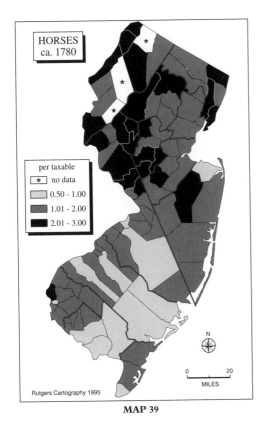

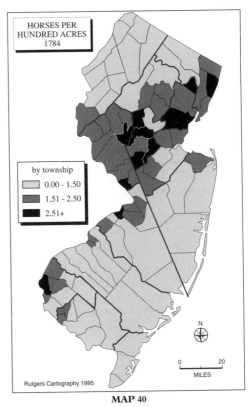

MAP 39   **MAP 40**

while the better soils of the Piedmont and Inner Coastal Plain harbored the greatest numbers. The keeping of stud horses appears to have been a lucrative land use.[77] The more celebrated animals, such as the "famous grey horse Northumberland," were advertised widely. Northumberland was kept at "John Hart's Esq." in Hunterdon County, where pasture for mares was available at "a moderate Price." Northumberland's stud fee was £0.45.0 for the season and 0.22.6 for "the single Leap." One 1773 advertisement described the horse's attributes and lineage.

> He is full Fifteen Hands Two Inches high, free from all Blemishes, and is allowed by all Judges, to be the best made Horse ever imported; he was bred by Lord MAZARINE, and got by the famous Horse, BUSTARD, to a Daughter of Old CRAB, Grand Dam by Old Babram; he is a Brother to FREEMASON, and Lord MONT EAGLE's famous Horse Botton, who kept the course of Kildare, in Ireland, for three Years successively; his performances in England, Ireland and America, are well known to all Sportsmen; he is very sure, and his Colts are allowed to be the best made of any in America.[78]

Another 1773 advertisement promoted an all-purpose horse called "The True Briton," formerly kept in Woodbridge, Middlesex County, but then in Woodbury, Gloucester County. The stud rate was four dollars for a single leap, about the same fee Northumberland commanded, £3 for the season, or £5.8.0 to ensure a foal. The notice stated that The True Briton, fifteen hands high and "a most beautiful lively brown," was "the strongest and best made horse on the continent to get colts for either gears, saddle or running, as he hath got a large number of the smartest colts of any half bloods in the Jerseys or Pennsylvania. . . . It would be needless to say anything of his pedigree or stock, as it hath been so well and so often ascertained heretofore."[79]

As the advertisement for The True Briton indicates, stud animals changed hands often, perhaps because familiarity bred contempt among local customers. The "Bellsize Arabian" sent from Philadelphia to northern Hunterdon County for the 1768 breeding season may have been a case in point. The agreement between Richard and Peter Footman of Philadelphia and land agent John Emley of Alexandria Township specified that the horse was to be kept for four months in Alexandria Township by Ralph Johnson, who was to house, care for, and feed it for £12. The stud fee was £3 and the fee for an attending groom 0.2.6.[80]

Abraham Williamson of Amwell Township, Hunterdon County, owned several stud horses in full or in part in the late 1790s and the first years of the nineteenth century.[81] For one, "Julius Caesar," Williamson kept fairly extensive records. In January 1801, he had obtained at least a share of Julius Caesar from Cornelius Hulick of Mansfield Township, Sussex County, who for $350 had bought a half-interest in the horse from Derrick Hulick a month earlier. During the 1796 breeding season in Mansfield Township, Julius Caesar served as stud to sixty-nine mares and earned £55.17.0 ($146.86). Another account, apparently for the 1797 breeding season, lists at least forty-three mares serviced and at least $223 in stud fees. By March 1802, Julius Caesar belonged entirely to Williamson, for he agreed to have James and Timothy Porter of Lebanon Township, Hunterdon County, maintain the horse and to retain for himself three-fifths of the stud fees, which amounted to $57. Williamson also owned part of at least two other stud horses at about the same time, "Bold Figure" and "Study." In Salem, Grant Gibbon's stud "Merry Tom" served thirty-one mares between April and August 1766 for an average fee of £1.7.0.[82]

By contrast, farmers in New Jersey's Dutch-settled areas, at least as late as the end of the eighteenth century, favored using heavy draft horses, a breed that had originated in Utrecht.[83] Horses, to a much greater extent than oxen, seem to have been the draft animals of choice throughout the eighteenth century.

Some evidence documents other farm animals in New Jersey. For example, one tantalizing reference from 1768 suggests that mules were bred in Morris County on a 2,000-acre tract about fifteen miles from Newark. In a notice offering the property for rent, William Kelly of New York noted that it "is deem'd one of the finest Places in America to breed Mules for the West Indies," though it does not state that mules were actually bred there.[84]

Other farm animals commonly mentioned are the various types of fowl and bees. Fowl were

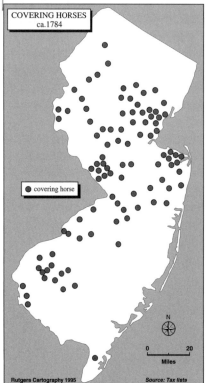

COVERING HORSES
ca. 1784

● covering horse

N

0   20
Miles

Rutgers Cartography 1995   Source: Tax lists

MAP 41

mostly consumed locally, and bees were kept for pollination, honey, and beeswax. Because these animals were among those for which farmers claimed damages after the Revolution, some idea of regional distribution may be discerned (table 33). Fowl, especially turkeys, were kept to a greater extent in Burlington County than elsewhere, to be eaten on special occasions.[85] But bees were apparently fewer in numbers there, which may be due to the fact that orchards (especially apple orchards) were not so prevalent; thus the need for pollinators was less.

Ordinary chickens were sometimes called "dunghill" fowl, undoubtedly because much of their food came from insects, worms, and other products of dung accumulation. Most likely, they were ubiquitous. In southwestern New Jersey, chickens roosted in trees at least during the warm weather, for, according to Kalm, "they had no henhouses."[86] They were thus prey for owls and other larger birds.[87] Elsewhere, chickens were probably kept in coops in the barn and fed buckwheat during the colder months.[88] At least one tavern kept large numbers of chickens on hand, most likely to feed travelers: when George Campbell advertised the sale of his well-known Hudibras Tavern in Princeton in 1765, he noted that it included "a large Hen-House, a Hog-House, and a new Hen Coop 2 Stories high which will contain 200 Fowls."[89]

By 1750, some farmers in northern Monmouth County appear to have specialized in keeping chickens for large-scale egg production. As von Thünen's model would predict, only farmers close to a major market—New York was only a short trip across Raritan Bay—could have concentrated on producing such a highly perishable product, and account books document that egg production became more prevalent as urban markets grew.[90] Farmers in Newark Township may also have been specializing in poultry at about that time. By 1800, according to Woodward, large numbers of poultry were being raised in the immediate vicinities of New York and Philadelphia.[91] Swain Ogden was credited 0.18.6 "by fethers" in Samuel Harrison's Newark Township account book.[92]

Apparently, ducks were not widely kept among New Jersey farmers, except possibly in Burlington County. Geese appear to have been more common, more so in the English and New England sections than in Dutch-settled areas. Peter Kalm described the geese near Elizabethtown to have worn yokes much like hogs wore at the time, and for the same reason. "The geese in some of the places by which we

Table 33
Revolutionary War Damage Claims Pertaining to Domestic Fowl and Bees

County	Total Claims	Percentage of Total Claims				
		Dunghill Fowl	Turkeys	Ducks	Geese	Beehives
Bergen with Acquackanonk Twp. (Dutch)	436	21.6	4.4	2.9	5.9	25.0
Burlington (English)	230	43.9	20.4	12.2	23.0	6.1
Essex without Acquackanonk (New England)	234	26.9	3.8	0.4	23.1	14.1
Middlesex (Heterogeneous)	321	21.2	9.9	4.4	14.3	13.1
Somerset (Dutch)	114	19.3	13.2	3.5	1.7	13.2

passed that day and the next wore three or four little sticks a foot in length about their necks," he wrote. "They were fastened crossways, to prevent them from creeping through half-broken fences. They looked extremely awkward, and it was very diverting to see them in this attire."[93] In 1774, Charles Read noted that nineteen geese, "well fed," yielded 4¼ ounces of down. The "large kind of Geese" at Elizabethtown, he noted, were "not so mischevious as ye Smaller sort - Nor are their Feathers or down so good by farr." Read's observation indicates that different geese were raised from place to place.

Both Kalm and Read mentioned guinea fowl. Kalm had seen them from the road between Princeton and New Brunswick.[94] Read stated that guinea fowl should be allowed to nest as they pleased as they would rear their young and "bring them home to you."[95]

Bees were distributed as extensively as were orchards in New Jersey. Read, who devoted little space to apiculture beyond copying a recipe for brewing of metheglin (or mead, a honey beer), noted that bees were kept on Cape May.[96] Read probably kept some himself. Metheglin was often listed in account books from around Newark Township in the 1740s[97] and was mentioned in accounts from other places through the early years of the nineteenth century.[98] Beeswax, too, was taken by local general stores in payment for other goods. Sometimes, the beeswax these stores took in was used to credit their accounts with large wholesale merchants. On November 12, 1763, Richard and John Samuel, wholesale merchants of Philadelphia, credited John Hatkinson of Mt. Holly in Burlington County with £2.5.11 for twenty-nine pounds of beeswax. On December 2, Samuel Tucker of Trenton received a credit of £18.4.2 for 230 pounds.[99]

Notes

1. Anne Capnerhurst to her sister, September 27, 1787, Capner-Exton-Hill Papers, NjR.

2. Gavin Scott to his brother, April 1799, Scott Family Papers, NjHi.

3. Smith, *History of the Colony,* 489–500. As a leading member of the Quaker community in Burlington County, the treasurer of West Jersey from 1751 to 1775, and a member of the Governor's Council in 1763, Smith was in a good position to evaluate regional differences in agricultural production. *See Docs. Rel. N.J.,* 1st. ser., 9:394–95.

4. Benson, *Peter Kalm's Travels,* 1:181.

5. Stevens Family Papers, NjHi.

6. Woodward, *Ploughs and Politicks,* 254–55, 267–78.

7. Read reported that red clover hay should be mowed and laid in a swath. In the afternoon it should be placed in divisions or cocks of about a bushel in size and turned upside down several times before being carted in. A "Dutch Wooden fork of Three prongs" served this effort best, he noted. See ibid.

8. Ibid., 272.

9. *Docs. Rel. N.J.,* 2d ser., 1:435.

10. Bidwell and Falconer, *History of Agriculture,* 103–4.

11. Martha Bland, "Life in Morristown in 1777," *Proc. N.J.H.S.* 51 (1933): 151.

12. Gavin Scott to his brother, April, 1799, Scott Family Papers, NjHi.

13. "Morris Township Tax Ratable List, 1787," County Tax Ratables, 1772–1822, Department of Education, Archives and History Microfilm and Records Unit, New Jersey State Library.

14. *Docs. Rel. N.J.,* 1st ser., 1769:526–27.

15. George Washington to Governor Livingston, August 27, 1780, Manuscripts Collection, Bureau of Archives and History, New Jersey State Library.

16. *Docs. Rel. N.J.*, 2d ser., 3:297–98.

17. David S. Cohen, *The Dutch-American Farm* (New York, 1992), 136.

18. *Docs. Rel. N.J.*, 1st ser., 12:381.

19. Ibid., 1760:509–11.

20. Grant Gibbon Store Ledger, Sinclair Collection, NjR.

21. *Docs. Rel. N.J.*, 2d ser., 3:51.

22. Robert Johnson Farm Account Book, 1788–1790, Sinclair Collection, NjR.

23. Thomas Newbold Farm Accounts, 1790–1827, Sinclair Collection, NjR.

24. Levi Webster Receipt Book, 1805–1817, Sinclair Collection, NjR.

25. Woodward, *Ploughs and Politicks*, 230–32, 332–40. See also the 1752 petition from Morris County charging that livestock was being driven there from neighboring counties. *Docs. Rel. N.J.*, 1st ser., 12:471.

26. *Docs. Rel. N.J.*, 1st ser., 24:140.

27. Ibid., 1770:120.

28. Gavin Scott to his brother, June 9, 1796, Scott Family Papers, NjHi.

29. Kelsey, *Cazenove Journal*, 2–3, 4, 15.

30. Tuttle, "Journals of Rev. Manasseh Cutler," 75–96.

31. Ibid., 94–95. The Morris Township tax list for 1787 indicates that Cutler's farm was a good-sized but by no means very large farm for the area at the time. He was taxed for two horses and six cattle; his son Jesse, who lived with him, was taxed for two horses and four cattle but no acreage.

32. John Stevens, "Correspondence re Family," January 25, 1792, Stevens Family Papers, NjHi.

33. Gavin Scott to his brother, April 21, 1800, Scott Family Papers, NjHi.

34. *Acts of the General Assembly of the State of New Jersey*, 4th Session, 27–28.

35. "Diary," 3, Spicer Papers.

36. Woodward, *Ploughs and Politicks*, 339; Ellis, "Diary of Jacob Spicer," 140.

37. *Docs. Rel. N.J.*, 1st ser., 24:155.

38. John Harriman Account Book, 1694–1730, Special Collections, Firestone Library, Princeton University.

39. See Gavin Scott's comment earlier in this chapter. Kalm noted that corn "was the best food for hogs, because it makes them very fat, and gives their flesh an agreeable flavor, preferable to all other meat." See Benson, *Peter Kalm's Travels*, 1:179. In 1763, New York merchant John Watts wrote to John Riddell in Virginia, "What Pork may be I dont know, but if you could meet with a little really Corn fed reasonable it would answer I believe best." "Letter Book of John Watts," 192, 322.

40. Smith, *History of the Colony*, 496; Morse, *American Geography*, 288.

41. Peter O. Wacker, "Cultural and Commercial Regional Associations of Traditional Smokehouses in New Jersey," *Pioneer America* 3 (July 1971): 25–34.

42. "Miscellaneous Memoranda," Reed Family Papers, NjHi.

43. *Docs. Rel. N.J.*, 1st. ser., 28:90–91.

44. Gavin Scott to his brother, April 21, 1800, Scott Family Papers, NjHi.

45. Woodward, *Ploughs and Politicks*, 350–63.

46. "Extracts from a Diary," 198.

47. Antill to Dr. Templeman, February 28, 1769, New Jersey Tercentenary Commission, Sinclair Collection, NjR.

48. *Docs. Rel. N.J.*, 1st ser., 7:370–75.

49. James Parker Diary, NjHi.

50. Benson, *Peter Kalm's Travels*, 1:115; Schmidt, *Rural Hunterdon*, 187; Camp Family Papers, NjHi. Hogs also continued to be run in the woods of the Outer Coastal Plain. David Brewer, a carpenter, was paid £0.5.10 for "Rafting timber & Pork" to the Job Point Store of Richard and Constant Somers in 1788, probably from around Great Egg Harbor River. Somers Ledger A, Job Point Store, Stewart Collection, Savitz Library, Glassboro State College.

51. Grant Gibbon General Store Ledger, 1764–1775, 174, Sinclair Collection, NjR.

52. Thomas Newbold Farm Accounts, 1790–1827, Sinclair Collection, NjR.

53. *Docs. Rel. N.J.*, 1st ser., 1738:522.

54. Ibid., 1769:497.

55. *Votes and Proceedings of the General Assembly of the Province of New Jersey* (Woodbridge, N.J.,

1769), 50. For the listing of merino sheep in 1815 see the existing tax ratable lists, by township. On the 1751 tax list, see Peter O. Wacker, "New Jersey Tax Ratable List."

56. "To the Honourable House of Representatives of the Colony of New Jersey in General Assembly Convened; The Petition of the freeholders Inhabitants of the county of Gloucester, in behalf of the said County [1768]," Stewart Collection, Savitz Library, Glassboro State College.

57. Leaming and Spicer, *Grants*, 345.

58. *Docs. Rel. N.J.*, 1st ser., 1770:244–46.

59. "Records of the Town of Newark, New Jersey from Its Settlement in 1666 to Its Incorporation as a City in 1836," *Collections of the New Jersey Historical Society* 6 (1966): 165.

60. Crèvecoeur, *Sketches*, 603.

61. Carl R. Woodward, "Sheep at $1,000 a Head," *New Jersey Agriculture* (October 1928): 14–15.

62. Ellis, "Diary of Jacob Spicer," 89, 178, 184.

63. Camp Family Record Book, NjHi.

64. "A List of the Names and Sirnames; and of the Estates Real and Personal of the Inhabitants and Householders of the Lower Precinct of the County of Cape May, 1751," and "Prince Maurice's River Precinct in Cumberland County, 1751," Stewart Collection, Savitz Library, Glassboro State College.

65. Woodward, *Ploughs and Politicks*, 361–63.

66. Levi Webster Receipt Book, 1805–1817, Sinclair Collection, NjR.

67. Woodward, "Sheep at $1,000 a Head," 14.

68. Parker Diary, NjHi.

69. Newbold Farm Accounts, Sinclair Collection, NjR.

70. "Petition of the Inhabitants of Burlington County to the Legislature Requesting Redress for the Damages Done to their Flocks by Dogs, March 8, 1763," Manuscripts Collection, New Jersey Archives, New Jersey State Library.

71. *Docs. Rel. N.J.*, 1st ser., 1770:262–63. One of the surviving dog tax lists, for Deptford Township in Gloucester County in 1773, lists 141 dogs and 133 owners. "Deptford Township Dog Owners of 1773," *Genealogical Magazine of New Jersey* 22 (1947): 17–18.

72. *N.J.S.L.* 30 (1806):689–90.

73. Ibid., 35 (1811):327–29.

74. Ibid., 36 (1812):24. That the exemptions were for hunting dogs is suggested by a supplement to the act of 1811 passed the next year, which extended it to cover Morris County and the townships of Trenton and Maidenhead in Hunterdon. It also exempted Cape May.

75. Ibid., 42 (1818):114–15; 44 (1820):160–62.

76. Department of Education, Division of State Library, Archives and History Microfilm and Records Unit, Trenton, New Jersey, County Tax Ratables, 1772–1822.

77. Charles Read discussed at length how to breed and raise horses; see Woodward, *Ploughs and Politicks*, 328–30. Read said colts should be weaned in the fall if a farmer had enough good green corn feed or excellent hay to feed them; if not, they should suckle for a year. Colts should be pastured during the summer and during the winter "run out on good days" and kept in the stable at night. Read advised feeding grain to horses only older than two as otherwise "it stiffens their Joints."

78. *Docs. Rel. N.J.*, 1st ser., 28:476–77.

79. Ibid., 477–78.

80. Richard and Peter Footman Agreement with John Emley, Philadelphia, February 10, 1768, Race-Emley Papers, Hunterdon County Historical Society.

81. Williamson Papers, Sinclair Collection, NjR.

82. Gibbon General Store Ledger, Sinclair Collection, NjR.

83. John Witherspoon, *A Description of the State of New Jersey* (Philadelphia, 1802), 405 (copy at Rutgers University Library); Woodward, *Agriculture in New Jersey*, 9.

84. *Docs. Rel. N.J.*, 1st ser., 26:88–90.

85. See, for example, the account with Ann Wetheral, 1766–67, Grant Gibbon Store Ledger, Salem, N.J., 1764–68, Sinclair Collection, NjR.

86. Benson, *Peter Kalm's Travels*, 1:236.

87. Ibid., 309.

88. Johnson, *Memoirs and Reminiscences*, 68.

89. *Docs. Rel. N.J.*, 1st ser., 29:532.

90. Joseph W. Hammond, "Man with a Basket of Eggs: Agricultural Symbolism in an Early Portrait from Monmouth County, New Jersey" (Unpublished paper, 1994). Hammond's thesis is based on a portrait of Pieter Luyster, which emphasizes a basket of eggs, and on numerous account entries indicating large shipments of eggs to New York by Luyster and others in northern Monmouth County.

91. Woodward, *Agriculture in New Jersey*, 27.

92. Samuel Harrison Account Book, NjHi.

93. Benson, *Peter Kalm's Travels*, 1:123.

94. Ibid., 122.

95. Woodward, *Ploughs and Politicks*, 365–67.

96. Ibid., 367.

97. Samuel Harrison Account Book, NjHi.

98. See, for example, the Isaac Vail Ledger, Warren Township, N.J., esp. 3, 78, Sinclair Collection, NjR. Vail was buying metheglin at two shillings per quart.

99. Richard and John Samuel Merchants Accounts, Philadelphia, 1759–1763, Sinclair Collection, NjR.

CHAPTER 6

REGIONAL DIVERSITY AND CHANGE THROUGH TIME: THE EVIDENCE FROM ACCOUNT BOOKS AND TAX LISTS

In March 1747 the *Pennsylvania Gazette* carried an advertisement for a "Pleasant country seat" on the "Rariton road" in present-day Bound Brook, where a store had been kept "upwards of twenty years."[1] The store was run by Jacob Janeway and John Broughton; Janeway lived on the property at the time but evidently no longer owned it. The store was not kept in the large main house but in a smaller structure twenty-four by twenty feet nearby. It featured a "lintel" (or lean-to) where "rum, melasses, salt &c" were stored. Because the account books for the store between 1735 and 1746 have survived, we know that this modest building served a very wide hinterland.[2]

Janeway and Broughton's accounts listed not only day-to-day transactions with a large number of people but also where they lived (many more than twenty miles distant), their occupations (unless they were farmers), and family relationships. What farmers in this region produced at the time is plainly indicated in what the store's proprietors credited them for. Even the occasions when customers largely settled accounts in cash reveal that market conditions were sufficiently favorable to put cash income in farmers' pockets. But the presence of cash also conceals those farm products taken not to local stores but to urban markets, a shortcoming of this type of data generally when it is mined for information about the agricultural economy.

The account books from Bound Brook document the overwhelming importance of wheat in the Raritan Valley economy before 1750. But at the same time animal skins were also an important product. Many of the customers of the Bound Brook store in these years appear to have lived to the north and west, probably in northern Hunterdon County, then in its initial wave of settlement. The accounts also show an early emphasis on butter, perhaps because the valley had filled rapidly with Dutch from Long Island. These settlers were already oriented to an urban market, and they were culturally inclined to dairying.[3] As farmers' records also attest, flax and flax seed were often mentioned in the Bound Brook accounts, probably because of Scots-Irish merchants in the area; indeed, the Raritan Valley was an early locus for the cultivation of flax, though the center of production shifted later to Hunterdon County. Flax and flax seed also show up regularly in store accounts from places both outside the Outer Coastal Plain and on very poor soils.

Janeway and Broughton kept daybooks, which record transactions on a daily basis. Store ledgers, by contrast, aggregate all of the dealings that a store proprietor transacted by individual. Taken together, these accounts can reveal a great deal about land use from place to place and from time to time, as well as a tremendous diversity of products and services changing hands, from quinces to a lawsuit. Tables 34–39 summarize data derived from random samples of separate transactions in thirty New Jersey account books from the 1740s to the 1820s (map 42). The evidence of account books is generally supported by the data of county and township tax lists covering the same areas of the state.

These records vary enormously in the detail they provide about transactions. In a day book, the number of transactions and the number of items credited would generally be about the same; customers usually brought in one product or provided one service at a time, though occasionally they might be credited for two or more products such as a quantity of grain and furs brought to the store on the same day. Ledgers, however, listed many different transactions under one customer, so that a sample of one hundred transactions would generally include much more than one hundred items; over several months, for example, a man might be credited with skins, beeswax, rye, and wheat.

Because quite disparate values and amounts of produce were recorded in these accounts, a random sample was made without regard to these variables. The tables list an item once for every entry. The items were aggregated and recorded on the tables in the order of the most to the least frequently mentioned.

Products or services that constituted 10 percent or more of the sample taken are shown in capital letters; items that made up more than 5 percent but less than 10 percent of the sample are shown in upper and lower case, and those in lower case only were less than 5 percent of the sample.

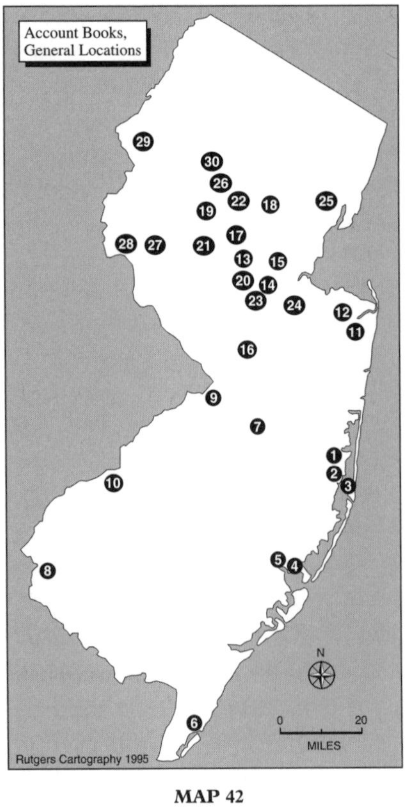

Table 34 aggregates the samples collected from account books of stores on the Outer Coastal Plain. The earliest account was compiled by a merchant dealing with residents of Toms River (1) and Forked River (2) on the coast in the 1750s.[4] These people were probably farming the better soils on the Cape May formation. The record suggests that both agricultural and forest products (mostly deerskins and cordwood) provided most income for inhabitants and that very little cash was changing hands. Corn and rye were often recorded, but wheat was not, a finding consistent with all other data from the Outer Coastal Plain.

An individual account book from Barnegat Bay (3) in the 1760s, though sparser, shows an even greater concentration on forest products in the form of fence rails and shingles. Again, very little cash changed hands in this economy.[5] At Somers Point (4) and Jobs Point (5), on the somewhat better soils of the Cape May forma-

Account Books, General Locations

Rutgers Cartography 1995

MAP 42

Table 34
Local Products as Entered in Accounts,
Outer Coastal Plain, 1751–1809

Year(s)	Location and Data Type	Sample	Products*
1751–60	Toms River, Forked River Merchant's Day Book	50	PORK & HAMS, RYE, DEERSKINS, CORDWOOD, CORN, Lumber, Work, Cooperage, Hides, flax seeds, butter, beef, wheat, eggs, leather, cheese, cash, hay, bricks, bark, goose feathers, bolts, flour
1766–67	Barnegat Bay Individual's Day Book	16	RAILS, SHINGLES, "rufage" boards of pine & cedar, cedar bolts, cranberries, cash
1773–81	Somers Point Store Ledger	91	CASH, WORK, SHINGLES, LUMBER, Skins (Deer, Mink, Muskrat), Pork & Hogs, Cattle, rails, shoemaking, fish, turkeys, tar, tailor work, hay, geese, cooperage, harness, fowl, carpentry, feathers, corn, rope, stockings, smith's work, wheat, carting, flax, oysters, salt
1778–90	Job's Point Store Ledger	100	CASH, LUMBER, SKINS (DEER, FOX, MUSKRAT), SHINGLES, WORK, CORN, Rye, Carpentry, Cordwood, Beef, Carting, Pork & Hogs, fish, tailor work, eggs, hides, butter, potatoes, corn, smith's work, tallow, apples, apple trees, shoes, clover seed, wheat, linen, flour, venison, cow, baskets, fowl, feathers, spinning, oats, scow hire
1805–8	Cape May Court House(?) Store Ledger	100	CASH, LUMBER, RAILS, Work, Carting, Cordwood, flour, shoes, bark, barley, scow hire
1807–9	New Hanover Township Burlington County Individual's Day Book	33	LUMBER, WORK, CASH, STEERS, Pork, Bark, corn, flax, rye

*All upper-case letters indicate ten or more entries for a sample size of one hundred. For smaller samples the entries are taken as a percentage of the total. Similarly, for the sample of one hundred entries, products with a capitalized first letter have five or more entries and those with all lower-case letters have fewer than five entries. All products, services, and cash payments are listed in descending order of magnitude.

tion, a cash economy prevailed in the 1770s and 1780s, but forest products were still more important than agricultural products.[6] The great diversity of agricultural products in store accounts here suggests, however, that some people may have concentrated on agriculture and were not primarily woodsmen. Here, too, corn and rye were recorded far more often than wheat; hogs and cattle were also often in the record, though mutton and sheep were not.

Two other, later records from the Outer Coastal Plain, from Cape May Court House (6) and New Hanover Township, Burlington County (7),[7] suggest many of the same things: lumbering was the most important activity, and wheat was scarcely grown. The first does not refer to livestock, especially to sheep, an oddity that may be explained by the fact that Spicer and other stock owners were selling sheep in large numbers to butchers in Philadelphia.

Store accounts from southwestern New Jersey (table 35) at once appear far different from those of the Outer Coastal Plain. The Salem (8) store ledgers, one from 1750 to 1752 and the other from 1760 to 1778,[8] appear far richer and thus probably indicate how thriving agriculture was on these excellent Inner Coastal Plain soils. Here corn was mentioned very often while wheat was not; the large amount of butter changing hands reflects the considerable importance of dairying, undoubtedly for the Philadelphia market. Accounts from Salem in 1810–11[9] show that dairying became even more important and that hogs continued to be a major product. Farther north on the Inner Coastal Plain, near Bordentown (9),[10] pork and beef production seem to have been more important than dairying.

An account book from Woodbury (10) covering from 1788 to 1829[11] may have been compiled by a farmer running a small store or trading on a very small scale. Chickens and especially eggs were the leading agricultural products, both suggesting orientation to an urban market. Eggs, which are highly perishable, had to have been produced for a relatively proximate non-agricultural population. Elsewhere in New Jersey, chickens and eggs assume economic importance only in places a very short distance from urban markets or later in time, when a substantial number of people no longer employed in purely agricultural activities began to constitute a market for eggs, so easily raised on a "dunghill" by a farmer.

The most extensive record for any part of New Jersey is from the central section, especially the Raritan Valley and northern Monmouth County (table 36). The 1730 store day book from Shrewsbury (11),[12] shows butter and eggs to have been the

Table 35
Local Products as Entered in Accounts,
Southwestern New Jersey, 1750–1811

Year(s)	Location and Data Type	Sample	Products*
1750–52	Salem Store Ledger	100	CASH, PORK & HAMS, BUTTER, Beef & Veal, Work, Mutton, wheat, cooperage, carting, tallow, deerskins & venison, vinegar, corn, weaving & spinning, tailoring, rye, eggs, turnips, cordwood, flax seed, turkeys, cranberries, oats, beans, potatoes, shoes, candles, butter molds, wheelbarrows, pasturage, quinces, cheese, stockings, woodworking, grass
1764–70	Salem Store Ledger	100	CASH, PORK & HAM, FLAX SEED, WORK, Butter, Beef, Corn, Fowl, eggs, sheep, rye, weaving, cooperage, lumber, leather work, cheese, cows, horses, turnips, tallow, bricks, hay, beans, sleigh, carpentry, wool, shoemaking, coffin, carting, cider, oats, fence, linen, cabbage, wheat, geese, vinegar, chairs, onions
1779–89	Woodbury Store Day Book	50	CASH, WORK, Dung, Tailoring, Chickens & Eggs, Straw, Shad, Lumber, honey, beef, cordwood, corn, potatoes, peaches, shoes, spinning, pork, leather, butter, hay
1790–97	Bordentown Area Farm Day Book	50	CASH, WORK, PORK, Beef, Buckwheat, corn, rye, sheep, timothy seed, tallow, hides, salt hay, vinegar, cooperage, venison, spinning, ketchel, scythe, rails, shingles, log
1810–11	Salem Store Day Book	113	BUTTER, CASH, Cheese, Hams, Flax Seed, wool, eggs, nails, vinegar, rags, leather, lard, skins, peaches, candles, stockings, corn, shoes, veal, carting, wheat, cordwood, potatoes, rye flour, honey, quills, pails & tubs, cows, oats, chairs

*All upper-case letters indicate ten or more entries for a sample size of one hundred. For smaller samples the entries are taken as a percentage of the total. Similarly, for the sample of one hundred entries, items with a capitalized first letter have five or more entries and those with all lower-case letters have fewer than five entries. All products, services, and cash payments are listed in descending order of magnitude.

main local products, certainly destined for New York markets; Shrewsbury was both on rich soils and only a few hours by sloop from this city. Shrewsbury store records of 1745 to 1750 show essentially the same emphasis on butter, eggs, pork, and beef; corn again was more important than wheat. A contemporary record from nearby Middletown (12), probably compiled by a tanner, is consistent with the Shrewsbury accounts.[13]

Yet at Bound Brook (13) in the 1730s and 1740s, wheat was a significant product; the merchant shipper's ledger from New Brunswick (14)[14] also shows wheat and butter to have been major products in the Raritan Valley between 1730 and 1760. By the time of the Revolution, other Raritan Valley accounts emphasize wheat and butter, which were probably more predominant west and south of the Raritan than in the New England-settled section to the north, where corn appears more often in account books.[15] The New Brunswick shipper's ledger also makes numerous references to hemp; here and in northern Morris County the crop was grown widely, probably especially in glaciated sections.

Similarly, other account books document specialized operations (which naturally skew the samples significantly). The Piscataway (15) store ledger of 1784–88,[16] for example, reflects a focus on the products of woodlands, particularly oak bark, used by tanners; internal evidence suggests that the source for this bark and wood was apparently the hinterland of South River (24), where poor sandy soils and swampy conditions mitigated against cultivating crops. The Hightstown (16) mill and store day book[17] shows a decided emphasis on ground wheat, not replicated in this central New Jersey area. The Middletown (12) distillery day book[18] shows that proprietors accepted products of weaving and spinning in exchange for other goods; these they accumulated for sale in bulk elsewhere, probably in New York. One Warren Township (17) farmer's ledger[19] also lists receipt of woven and spun goods, but unlike the Hightstown accounts mentioned corn and other grains far more often than wheat.

The Turkey (now Berkeley Heights) (18) store ledger from 1791 to 1798[20] well represents the produce of a relatively poor portion of the New England-settled section, the swampy upper Passaic basin and nearby Watchungs. Numerous exchanges involving butter reflect an emphasis on dairying, and farmers here were also producing eggs, most likely for the nearby expanding urban population in Newark (25). Flax seed was listed very often, as were animal skins probably trapped in the nearby Great Swamp; that inhabitants continued to rely on the bounty of the natural environment for their livelihood is also reflected in the number of quail and partridge accepted in lieu of cash. At Bedminster (19) in the 1790s, apples were clearly important—Cazenove had noted the continual advance of apple trees west of Newark—though the types of produce and grain changing hands here were not specified.[21]

A farmer's ledger from Franklin Township (20), compiled between 1800 and 1806, shows too that wheat was by then a very minor product; rye and corn eclipsed it in importance. Flax seed had also emerged as a major product.[22] Stores in New Brunswick (14),[23] which would have been the major immediate destination of commercial crops in this region, accepted corn and rye but not wheat from their customers between 1802 and 1816; even in more remote rural stores such as those at Pluckemin (21),[24] Basking Ridge (22),[25] and Ten Mile Run (23),[26] proprietors

Year(s)	Location and Data Type	Sample	Products*
1730	Shrewsbury Store Day Book	100	CASH BUTTER, EGGS, Hogs & Hams, Corn, Turkeys, fowl, shoemaking, tallow, skins, flax, cooperage, turnips, cider, wheat, cheese, venison, corn, carpentry, cranberries, beeswax, carting, rye
1735	Bound Brook Store Day Book	100	WHEAT, CASH, Butter, Beeswax, Skins, work, flour, carting, rye, flax seed, cooperage, oats, tailoring, salt, shoes
1738–39	Bound Brook Store Ledger	100	WHEAT, CASH, FLAX & FLAX SEED, Skins (Beaver, Fox, Raccoon), hogs, butter, beeswax, turkeys, starch, iron, carpentry, geese, carting, eggs, nuts, oats, spinning & weaving, fowl, corn
1742–44	Bound Brook Store Day Book	100	CASH, WHEAT, Iron, beef, pork, shirts, work, lawsuit, linen, mare & colt, carting, flax seed, wax, hat
1742–46	Bound Brook Store Ledger	100	CASH, WHEAT, Flax & Flax Seed, iron (bar iron), wax, cow & veal, work, smith's work, weaving, cooperage, metheglin, cheese, butter, leather, buckwheat, turnips, mare & colt, geese
1745–50	Shrewsbury Store Day Book	55	CASH, BUTTER, EGGS, CORN, Hams & Pork, Wool, Cordwood, Spinning & Knitting, wheat, boat construction, tallow, flour, work, cows, rye, wax, cooperage, mutton, potatoes, flax seed, ducks, turnip, cheese, veal
1730s–50s	New Brunswick Merchant Shipper's Ledger	100	CASH, WORK ON AND MATERIALS FOR SCHOONER, FLOUR & WHEAT, Cordwood, Lumber, Butter, hemp, corn, flax, shingles, beef & veal, fish, mutton, turnips, cheese, wool, cooperage, fowl, hogs, potatoes, parsnips
1749–51	Shrewsbury Store Day Book	27	CASH, BEEF & VEAL, Tallow, Corn, butter, eggs, baskets, hogs
1753–60	Middletown Store Day Book	100	CASH, LEATHER & HIDES, SHOES, WORK, spinning, bark, oats, (Tanner?), tailoring, corn, rye, buckwheat, flour, cooperage, carpentry, cider, tallow, flax seed
1772–75	Bedminster Farmer's Accounts	52	CASH, wheat, lumber, butter, sows
1772–90	Millstone Day Book	100	CASH, WHEAT & FLOUR, BUTTER, Corn, Flax Seed, Carting, Cooperage, beeswax, buckwheat, candles, veal, rye, hat, mittens, tallow, brooms, eggs, trays, axes (blacksmith)
1773–75	Bonhamtown Store Ledger	100	CASH, CORN, CORDWOOD, Work, Flax seed, Bark, butter, veal, rye, cooperage, weaving & spinning, lumber, wool, wheat, feathers, pork, leather work, oyster shells, eggs, beeswax, geese, fish, cider
1775–76	Millstone Store Ledger	100	CASH, Butter, flax seed, wheat & flour, carting, corn, eggs, beeswax, hats

*All upper-case letters indicate ten or more entries for a sample size of one hundred. For smaller samples the entries are taken as a percentage of the total. Similarly, for the sample of one hundred entries, items with a capitalized first letter have five or more entries, and those with all lower-case letters have fewer than five entries. All

Year(s)	Location and Data Type	Sample	Products*
1784–88	Piscataway Store Ledger	100	CASH, BARK, CORDWOOD, WORK, COOPERAGE, Flax, Flax Seed, butter, shoes, hogs, corn, veal, weaving, lumber, oats, brick, tailoring, leather, eggs, hay
1785–91	Hightstown Mill and Store Day Book	100	COOPERAGE, WHEAT, CASH, Corn, Rye, veal, butter
1788–1803	Middletown Distillery Day Book	96	CASH, WEAVING & SPINNING, Work, smith's work (on still), fish, mutton, rye, wheat, flax seed, carpentry, oats, wild fowl (ducks & geese), corn, shoes, cooperage, apples, boards, oysters, tallow, tailoring, veal, cattle hides
1789–1800	Warren Township, Somerset County Farmer's Ledger	100	FARM WORK, CASH, CARPENTRY & MASONRY, WEAVING & SPINNING, CORN, BEEF & VEAL, BUCKWHEAT, RYE, Potatoes, Flax & Flax Seed, Ashes, Shoes & Boots, wheat, hogs, smith's work, shad, cider, turnips
1791–98	Turkey Store Ledger	100	CASH, BUTTER, FLAX OR FLAX SEED, SKINS (RABBIT, MUSKRAT, RACCOON), WORK, EGGS, CORN, OATS, Ashes, Veal, Quail, Brooms, Fowl, Rye, Rags, hay, boards, wool, beeswax, partridges, candles, wheat, pork, buckwheat, tallow, beef, fat
1793–98	Bedminster Township Store Day Book	100	CASH, "PRODUCE," "GRAIN," APPLES, Rye, Work, flax seed, corn, lime, hogs, bulls, butter, cider, wheat, nails, buckwheat, horse hides, cordwood, quinces, oats, tallow, beeswax, straw, weaving, carpentry
1800–1806	Franklin Township Farmer's Ledger**	25	CASH, RYE & RYE FLOUR, VEAL, LINEN & TOW, FLAX SEED, CORN & CORN MEAL, BUCKWHEAT, WORK, Oats, Tobacco, Salt, Harness, Cash Skin, Mutton, Spirits, Eggs, Straw, nuts, flour, brooms, wool, butter, rags, coal, cider, cordwood, shingles, nails, vinegar, watermelons, potatoes
1802–7	New Brunswick Store Day Book	100	FILL & SCOW HIRE (PROBABLY DOCK CONSTRUCTION), CORN, CASH, Cooperage, rye, seed, flour, carting, cordwood, turkey (December 23)
1803–4	South River Bridge Store Day Book	100	CASH, Bark, Cordwood, Butter, Pork, carting, shoes, eggs, house frame & lumber, rye, skins, tallow, hides, calf, work, tailoring
1809	Pluckemin Store Ledger	100	CASH, PORK & HAMS, WORK, BUTTER, Bark, Oats, corn, flax seed, eggs, whisky, rags, rye, beeswax, tallow, skins, fencing, sheep, cedar ware, peaches, lime, veal, quills, tailoring, earthenware, chestnuts, linen, nails, cherry juice, wheat, cordwood, twine, hides, iron
1809–11	Basking Ridge Store Day Book	100	CASH, BUTTER, NAILS, Eggs, work, rags, flax seed, corn, hogs, cider & cider spirits, rails, weaving, cedar pail, lumber, lime, hay, iron
1810	South River Bridge Store Day Book	100	BARK, CASH, CORDWOOD, Carting, Hides, Shoes, butter, homespun thread, rye flour

**Debits. The keeper of the accounts delivered these goods and services to others rather than crediting others for delivery to him.

Year(s)	Location and Data Type	Sample	Products*
1816	New Brunswick Store Day Book	100	CASH, CORN, Rye, Work, shad, flax, lumber, rails, eggs, rags, oats, tailoring
1818–22	Ten Mile Run Store Day Book	100	CASH, BUTTER, EGGS, rags, cooperage, whiskey, candles, beef, flax, linen, spinning, hogs, brooms, earthenware, hats, rakes
1819–25	South River Bridge	100	CASH, CORDWOOD, CARTING, corn, rye, pork & hogs, butter, hides, shoes, whisk brooms, smoked beef, tailoring, muskrat skins, lambs, repair of pump, spirits

credited customers most for butter, eggs, pork products, and other grains between 1809 and 1822; transactions involving wheat were the least frequently mentioned of all involving grains.

The general area served by a store at South River Bridge (24)[27] (present-day Old Bridge) concentrated on oak bark and cordwood between 1803 and 1825. These poor, often swampy soils had clearly remained intractable to agriculture; woodland products prevailed through the 1820s, although more and more farmers were beginning to raise milch cattle, hogs, rye, and corn. But flax seed, so much favored elsewhere, was not one of the predominant crops in this region; it was obviously more at home on the better soils.

An analysis of the grains recorded in central New Jersey account books between 1730 and 1825 (table 37) shows clearly the decline of wheat and the rise of corn after the Revolution. Wheat, of course, functioned in a slightly different economy; it was a major commercial crop for export, while corn was also raised (and, many accounts suggest, principally raised) to feed stock. Still, corn was evidently a major commercial crop by the turn of the nineteenth century, and the total area devoted to it may have greatly surpassed that devoted to wheat during its heyday. Records from northern Monmouth County, south of Raritan Bay, emphasized corn over wheat early on. Rye also appears more frequently in the record after the Revolutionary War; it probably replaced wheat as the main winter grain crop in many areas, and on poor soils, such as those at South River Bridge on the Outer Coastal Plain, rye was probably always the dominant grain crop. Early on, the New York market attracted butter and egg production in northern Monmouth, and through time stores in central New Jersey were accepting such products in greater amounts as the number of non-farmers in clustered settlements increased.

Account books from northeastern New Jersey are far less plentiful and, for the Dutch-settled area, sadly lacking (table 38). Some central region ledgers covered areas of Dutch and New England settlement, however. The earliest accounts from Newark Township (25),[28] from the early 1750s and early 1760s, are the records of a sawmill and store and so naturally emphasize lumber and timber, but wheat and other grains are listed. Most significant, though, are apples, cider, hay, and salt hay. Dairying is suggested by transactions involving veal and cows, but butter does not appear in the record. The hay may have been largely for beef cattle, and farmers

Table 37
Grains Entered in Account Books, Central New Jersey 1730–1825

Year(s)	Location	Grains*
1730	Shrewsbury	Corn, Wheat
1735	Bound Brook	WHEAT, rye, oats
1738–39	Bound Brook	WHEAT, oats, corn
1742–44	Bound Brook	WHEAT
1742–46	Bound Brook	WHEAT, buckwheat
1745–50	Shrewsbury	CORN, wheat, rye
1730s–1750s	New Brunswick	WHEAT, corn
1749–51	Shrewsbury	Corn
1753–60	Middletown	oats, corn, rye, buckwheat
1772–75	Bedminster	wheat
1772–90	Millstone	WHEAT, Corn, buckwheat, rye
1773–75	Bonhamtown	CORN, rye
1775–76	Millstone	wheat, corn
1784–85	Piscataway	corn, oats
1785–91	Hightstown (mill and store)	WHEAT, Corn, Rye
1788–1803	Middletown	rye, wheat, oats, corn
1789–1800	Warren Township	CORN, RYE, BUCKWHEAT
1791–98	Turkey	CORN, OATS, Rye, wheat, buckwheat
1793–98	Bedminster Township	Rye, corn, wheat, oats, buckwheat
1800–1806	Franklin Township	RYE, CORN, BUCKWHEAT, Oats
1802–7	New Brunswick	CORN
1803–4	South River Bridge	rye
1809	Pluckemin	Oats, corn, rye, wheat
1809–11	Basking Ridge	corn
1810	South River Bridge	rye
1816	New Brunswick	CORN, Rye, oats
1819–25	South River Bridge	corn, rye

*All upper-case letters indicate ten percent or more of the sample. A capitalized first letter followed by lower-case letters indicates more than five percent but less than ten percent of the sample. All lower case indicates less than five percent of the sample. Refer to Table 36 for the sample size.

there might have fed milk and corn to hogs. Numerous entries for shad and clams document the continued importance of natural products even in this most densely developed section.

The Ralston store near Mendham (26)[29] provides a useful view over a long period, from 1787 to 1812, of the products of the western extent of New England settlement in Morris County. Entries for ashes (for potash production, most likely), nails, and iron attest the presence of the charcoal iron industry. Wheat, butter, corn, and flax seed were important early in this period, but by 1800 wheat appears to have much diminished, eclipsed by corn, butter, and flax seed; by 1810 flax seed had surpassed all other products listed. Also by 1810, the presence of industrial enterprise other than ironmaking—specifically, textile production—was evinced by references to payments in flannel.

Table 38
Local Products as Entered in Accounts,
Northeastern New Jersey, 1752–1812

Year(s)	Location and Data Type	Sample	Products*
1752	Newark Township Sawmill & Store Day Book	48	WORK, CARTING, APPLES, HAY & SALT HAY, Flax, corn, timber, wheat, pasturage, mutton, carpentry, hogs, buckwheat, cheese, turnips, clams, cows, rye, veal, leather, cordwood
1763	Newark Township Sawmill & Store Ledger	33	WORK, CASH, LUMBER, TIMBER, VEAL, CORN, APPLES & CIDER, CARTING, Wheat, Oats, Buckwheat, Carpentry, Spinning & Weaving, clams, beef, leather, rye, geese, mutton, oxen, hogs, turnips, colts, salt hay, pasturage
1772–94	Newark Township (Irvington) Personal Account Book	33	WORK, CORN, CARTING, CORDWOOD, HAY & SALT HAY, HOGS & PORK, BUCKWHEAT, CLAMS, FLAX & FLAX SEED, SHAD, APPLES & CIDER, Wheat, Oats, Carpentry, Bark, Pasturage, Timber, mutton, well curb, use of team, hides, metheglin, meslin, rye, beans, cash, potatoes
1787–89	Mendham Store Ledger	100	CASH, ASHES, NAILS & IRON, WHEAT, BUTTER, CARTING, CORN, Flax Seed & Tow, Rye, Beef, & Veal, Farm Tools, pork, leather work, cooperage, spirits, cloth, shoes, buckwheat, lumber, oats, cordwood, turnips, mutton, rails, feathers
1800–1801	Mendham Store Ledger	100	CASH, CORN, BUTTER, FLAX SEED & FLAX, CIDER & CIDER SPIRITS, Nails & Iron, Buckwheat, work, beeswax, carting, cooperage, quinces, honey, shingles, lime, rye, oats, candles, pork, oysters, carpentry, raccoon skins
1810–12	Mendham	100	CASH, FLAX SEED, CLOTH (FLANNEL) & WEAVING, Candles, Nails & Iron, carting, butter, whiskey, leather, eggs, corn, tallow, lumber, onions, work, sheep skins, shoes, bran, geese

*All upper-case letters indicate ten or more entries for a sample size of one hundred. For smaller samples the entries are taken as a percentage of the total. Similarly, for the sample of one hundred entries, items with a capitalized first letter have five or more entries, and those with all lower-case letters have fewer than five entries. All products, services, and cash payments are listed in descending order of magnitude.

Northwestern New Jersey, settled later, is also represented by only a few store accounts (table 39). One pre-Revolutionary account book, probably from the north central part of Hunterdon County (27),[30] the same general area covered by the Bound Brook store, stressed wheat, pork products, potash, and ashes, the latter undoubtedly related to the iron industry; butter, corn, and flax seed were also significant. And the records of the store at Greenwich Forge (28),[31] near the mouth of the Musconetcong, documents a community of ironworkers, an emerging local market for surrounding farmers. The store account often listed beef, veal, and mutton, undoubtedly food for the forge's laborers and their families; at no other rural store does mutton show so strongly in the record. Butter also was important, which suggests either dairying in the area or a very particular response on the part of some farmers to supply this community of industrial workers.

A store and farm ledger from Knowlton (29)[32] emphasizes that grains such as rye

Table 39
Local Products as Entered in Accounts,
Northwestern New Jersey, 1773–1819

Year(s)	Location and Data Type	Sample	Products*
1773–74	Hunterdon County (probably North Central) Day Book	50	CASH, WHEAT, PORK & HAM, POTASH & ASHES, COOPERAGE, CARTING, Butter, Corn, Flax Seed, Wax, Honey, rye, smith's work, buckwheat, logs, earthen ware, wool, hides, churns
1779–80	Greenwich Forge Day Book	100	BEEF & VEAL, BUTTER, MUTTON, Bread, Ham & Bacon, Cash, Cordwood, wheat, rye, corn, tallow, strawbaskets (for charcoal), apple whiskey, work, flour, potatoes, pigeons, milk pot, brooms, tow linen, shoes, hides, buckwheat
1805–15	Knowlton Store and Farm Ledger	50	WORK, CASH, RYE, CORN, WHISKEY, BUCKWHEAT, Wheat, Hogs, Lumber, Beef, Potatoes, mutton, apples, leather, clover, oats, geese, shoes, cooperage, carpentry, tar, plaster, baskets, loan of team, flax seed, tallow, turnips, spinning, shingles, shad, turkeys, tailoring, masonry, ashes, fulling, smith's work, honey
1805–19	Succasunna Farm Day Book	25	CORN RYE, POTATOES, Veal, Flax, Hay, vinegar, butter, pork, calf, skin, beef

*All upper-case letters indicate ten or more entries for a sample size of one hundred. For smaller samples the entries are taken as a percentage of the total. Similarly, for the sample of one hundred entries, items with a capitalized first letter have five or more entries and those with all lower-case letters have fewer than five entries. All products, services, and cash payments are listed in descending order of magnitude.

**Debits. The keeper of the accounts delivered these goods and services to others rather than crediting others for delivery to him.

and corn were more important than wheat by the early nineteenth century; so does a contemporaneous farmer's day book from Succasunna (30) mentioning corn, rye, and potatoes but not wheat.[33] Shad and pigeons were also mentioned in both accounts.

Another source of data on regional distinctions and on change through time is contemporary tax lists. These lists are available in the form of both abstracts for townships, which allow comparisons to be made between counties, and individual township lists, which record the names of residents. These records are especially valuable because they permit calculations of mean landholdings, landlessness, and other such phenomena. However, available tax data permit comparisons only between counties and townships representative of the several physiographic divisions of New Jersey, the areas of distinctive cultural background, and the typical zones proffered in the von Thünen model. Data for some townships and counties that might be invaluable to our understanding of land use simply do not exist. Also, as townships often became subdivided after the Revolution, especially in the northeastern part of the state, comparable data often do not exist for that general area. These data will be analyzed from south and east to north and west in New Jersey (map 43) and from the county to the township level.

The most relevant tax categories for comparison are those of land and livestock, and the nature of these categories changed somewhat through time. In 1751, when provincewide data are first available, land was taxed if there was any improvement

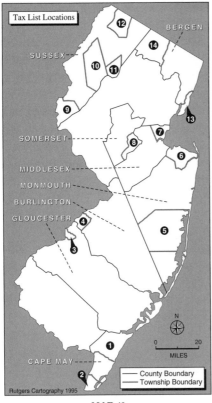

MAP 43

on it. This definition of taxable land was changed during the Revolution, when both improved and unimproved land were taxed. The legislation stipulated that "all Tracts of Land, held by Deed, Patent or Survey, whether improved or unimproved, shall be valued at the Discretion of the Assessors and Chosen Freeholders."[34] The meaning here, presumably, was that the large tracts still held in many places, especially in the areas of marginal soils and that had not been subdivided by the East and West Jersey Proprietors, were not to be taxed. Indeed, in the townships lying in the Outer Coastal Plain and in the glaciated Highlands especially, the amount of taxed acreage rose dramatically, presumably due to the proprietors' subdividing and selling off the land.

In 1784, the distinction between the two categories was spelled out: "all Lands whereon any Improvements are made, the whole Tract shall be considered as improved land."[35] Presumably, the "unimproved" land lay apart from the "improved" land, a situation that would especially have pertained to woodlots in the more densely settled areas. In areas of little agricultural development such land was probably also used for cordwood or lumber and to run livestock. Some of the tax lists show unimproved land separately, and some do not, especially in those areas where extensive improvement had taken place, such as on the Piedmont and the Inner Coastal Plain.

Another change in the way land was taxed occurred in 1781. The need for revenue during the Revolution stimulated many new tax categories, some of which were discontinued after the war. The new category of "houses and lots," however, long outlasted the conflict. The tax act specified that in the assessor's valuation of land "Houses and Lots of Land . . . shall not be included in the above Valuation, but such shall be valued by the respective Assessors and chosen Freeholders at their Discretion, having Regard to their yearly Rents and Value."[36] The act clearly recognized the significance of non-agricultural activities and especially the growth of clustered settlements. The "houses and lots" category may thus be used to some extent as a surrogate for "urban" growth and the expansion of non-agricultural activities.

The livestock category also changed through time. Cattle and horses of two years old and up were combined on the list of 1751. Sheep were dropped from the provincewide list of 1769, when cattle and horses were listed in separate categories. In 1790 the law was changed to cover cattle three years or older,[37] and by 1802 horses, too, were listed only if three years old or older.[38] In 1801 mules were added to the horse category, but it is probable that few were listed. Thus, presumably, a dip in the numbers of cattle in 1790 and horses in 1802 reflects the change in the way that the categories were defined rather than a real decline in numbers.

Between 1751 and 1822, the taxed area in Cape May County slightly more than doubled, from slightly more than 40,194 acres to 83,149 acres, but even compared to counties with larger amounts of poor soil, Cape May's expansion was quite modest (fig. 9). When improved and unimproved land were separated into different tax categories, the amount of improved acreage in Cape May changed very little, but the amount of unimproved acreage greatly expanded. Total acreage in improved land dipped slightly in the 1790s in Cape May as elsewhere, which suggests that something affected agriculture negatively during this decade. Upper Township (1) saw the greatest growth between 1783 and 1822; improved acreage rose from 13,801 to 17,134 acres; unimproved acreage rose even more dramatically, from 14,876 acres to 32,178 acres. These increases were typical of general trends between the end of the Revolution and the 1820s in places earlier bypassed for richer soils elsewhere. As New Jersey had run out of unexploited good land, the poorer, more marginal areas had began to be used to a much greater degree than before.

Although acreage expanded in Cape May, the numbers of cattle and horses ostensibly changed little (fig. 10). But in view of the fact that 1790 and 1802 tax lists excluded two-year-olds in each category, livestock holdings in general probably expanded slightly. In Lower Township (2), which saw the greatest gains in taxable land, the number of cattle dropped by almost one hundred animals between 1792 and 1822, but because of the change in tax law the number of cattle may actually have remained roughly constant. Elsewhere on Cape May the numbers of cattle and horses fluctuated much less, which in turn suggests some expansion; overall, however, modest expansion in the number of these animals cannot explain the significant expansion in total acreage. Most likely, these newly taxed lands were probably woodlands being used for cordwood to fuel industries and technologies just then beginning to grow—iron, glass, the steam engine. It is also possible that sheep herds had expanded: on

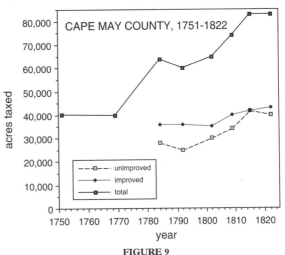

FIGURE 9

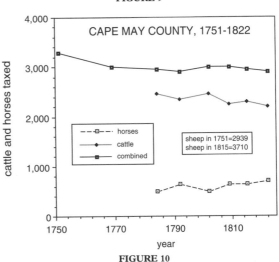

FIGURE 10

Cape May, 2,939 sheep were taxed in 1751 and 3,710 in 1815; the latter included 17 full-blooded merinos, 772 part merinos, and 2,921 "common or native" sheep.[39]

In Lower Township alone between 1751 and 1810, the number of people taxed almost doubled, rising from 101 to 198 (table 40).[40] The amount of improved acreage appears to have risen steadily, suggesting clearance and agricultural activity despite the poor soils. The number of individual landholdings rose from 63 in 1751 to 95 in 1785 and then held steady; the mean size of landholdings declined very gradually after the Revolution. The number of horses rose slightly through 1810, while the number of persons owning horses held fairly steady. More people held land than held horses, which suggests that some may have been too poor to afford them or, possibly, did not need them because they were largely involved in maritime activities. Landlessness also increased to embrace more than half of the taxables by 1810, which could signify either rising poverty or a greater emphasis on woodland and maritime employment. By themselves, these data indicate that little economic expansion took place in Lower Township for about six decades.

This lack of growth becomes more apparent when similar data are analyzed from Gloucester County to the north (figs. 11 and 12 and table 41). Taxed acreage there rose from 114,274 acres in 1751 to 386,105 acres in 1822—it more than tripled, in other words, while in Cape May it had slightly doubled over this time. Of taxed land in 1822, 169,990 acres were listed as improved and 216,115 as unimproved. Horse and cattle rose from 7,189 in 1751 to 11,960 in 1822; 7,849 were cattle and

Table 40
Taxables, Land Taxed, and Livestock in Lower Township,
Cape May County, 1751–1810

Year	1751	1768	1782	1802	1810
Taxables	101	121	145	177	198
Landholdings	63	84	95	96	98
Landless (%)	37.6	30.6	34.5	45.8	50.5
Acres Taxes	10,830	9,608	13,502	11,643	11,204
Improved (%)	*	*	69.1	76.4	78.9
Median Size (acres)	100	80	100	93	96
Mean Size (acres)	170.9	114.4	142.1	121.3	114.3
Houses and Lots	*	*	0	17	27
Horses	*	*	146	144	171
Horse Holders	*	*	88	84	89
Median Held	*	*	2	2	2
Mean Held	*	*	1.7	1.7	1.9
Cattle	*	*	536	569	502
Cattle Holders	*	*	96	110	123
Median held	*	*	4	3	2
Mean Held	*	*	5.6	5.2	4.1

*Not Listed

4,111 horses.

The amount of land taxed rose spectacularly between 1769 and the end of the Revolution as the ample room for clearance and improvement in Gloucester (even on the Inner Coastal Plain) came to filled up. Immediately after the Revolution, the amount of acreage taxed held steady because a decline in the amount of unimproved land was offset by a slight increase in the amount of improved land. After 1793, the amount of unimproved land taxed began to expand, spectacularly so after about 1811. The opposite trend affected improved land after 1801. The gains in unimproved land occurred in those townships lying entirely in the Outer Coastal Plain, as the pines were developed by such industries as ironworks and glassworks; the number of new townships subdivided from existing ones indicates the rapid growth in this area.[41]

The numbers of horses and cattle in Gloucester County rose gradually from 1751 to about 1800. At the time that improved

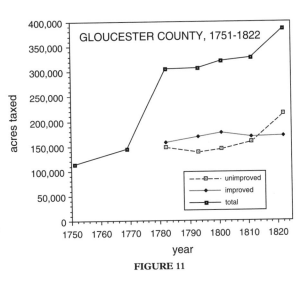

FIGURE 11

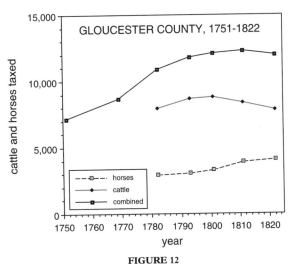

FIGURE 12

acreage began to decline, the numbers of cattle also began to fall while the number of horses continued to increase, trends that occurred in the townships experiencing great industrial activity, where human populations also rose. Cattle tended to increase slightly or to hold steady on the improved soils of the Inner Coastal Plain, suggesting the continued viabilty of dairying or of fattening cattle for the Philadelphia market.

Surviving tax lists from 1779 to 1802 for Newton Township (3), just opposite Philadelphia, permit a closer examination of change in Gloucester County. Newton Township, unlike most of the other townships fronting the Delaware, lay entirely on the Inner Coastal Plain. The intensity of development is suggested by the fact that all the land taxed was listed as improved, a fact von Thünen's model might have anticipated in an area on good soils so close to a major market (table 41). But the diminution in acreage through time suggests that land was being taken out of agriculture, most likely for residential purposes. This possibility is corroborated by the increases in houses and lots, and by the decrease in the average size of properties.

Table 41
Taxables, Land Taxed, and Livestock in Newton Township, Gloucester County, 1779–1802

Year	1779	1790	1802
Taxables	157	220	298
Landholdings	67	84	92
Landless (%)	57.3	61.8	69.1
Acres Taxes	9,426	9,528	9,285
Improved (%)	*	100	100
Median Size (acres)	100	110	67
Mean Size (acres)	140.7	113.4	100.9
Houses and Lots	*	41	65
Horses	190	274	318
Horse Holders	54	99	112
Median Held	3	2	2
Mean Held	3.5	2.8	2.8
Cattle	400	705	670
Cattle Holders	56	133	140
Median Held	7	3	3
Mean Held	7.1	5.3	4.8

*Not Listed

The numbers of cattle especially rose significantly. Salem County owners showed a greater tendency to hold cattle (for dairying or fattening, both in keeping with the von Thünen model) than those in Lower Township, as well a tendency toward much more clustered settlement, more rapidly diminishing sizes of holdings, and much greater landlessness.

Burlington County, lying astride the inner and outer portions of the Atlantic Coastal Plain, showed growth similar to that which occurred in Gloucester County, though increases in the amount of unimproved land taxed were not so spectacular. In Chester Township (4), lying just a few miles north of Newton Township on the Inner Coastal Plain, tax lists from 1763 to 1813 (table 42) show that while all taxed land was also listed as improved there, less subdivision of agricultural land for residential purposes was taking place.[42] In Newton, for example, there were 65 houses and lots for 298 taxables in 1802; in Chester there were only 27 houses and lots for 308 taxables in 1797. Chester was within the Quaker sphere of South Jersey and was also near the Philadelphia market, but it was evidently far enough from Philadelphia not to experience as much non-agricultural growth. Acreage taxed in Chester actually rose, an imponderable feature of the tax data that can only be accounted for by the slight boundary adjustment with neighboring Evesham Township in 1801 or more accurate survey methods.[43] In any case, the Chester tax lists depict a township where the number of landholdings was rapidly increasing, perhaps because of inheritance, and the sizes of holdings rapidly declining as a consequence. By 1813 the median size of farms was less than a third of those in the

Table 42
Taxables, Land Taxed, and Livestock in Chester Township,
Burlington County, 1763–1813

Year	1763	1774	1780	1797	1813
Taxables	145	168	228	308	440
Landholdings	67	82	101	164	215
Landless (%)	53.8	51.2	55.7	46.8	51.1
Acres Taxes	17,847	18,230	18,264	19,939	20,624
Improved (%)	★	★	★	100	100
Median Size (acres)	250	200	157	101	76
Mean Size (acres)	266.4	222.3	180.8	121.6	95.9
Houses and Lots	★	★	15	27	46
Horses	★	★	182	372	474
Horse Holders	★	★	58	139	200
Median Held	★	★	3	2	2
Mean Held	★	★	3.1	2.7	2.4
Cattle	★	★	591	833	883
Cattle Holders	★	★	100	183	235
Median Held	★	★	5	3	2
Mean Held	★	★	5.9	4.6	3.8

*Not listed separately

1760s; average size declined nearly in the same proportion. Obviously, the large farms so characteristic of Quaker-settled southern New Jersey were beginning to disappear. Cattle numbers were on the increase and cattle were owned by more people, as in Newton Township.

Monmouth County straddled the Inner and Outer Coastal Plains, and tax data exist that document trends from the end of the Revolution until 1822. Further, enough data exist at the township level to allow some comparisons between Dover Township (5)[44] in the Outer Coastal Plain between 1773 and 1797 and Middletown Township (6), which not only lay on the fertile Inner Coastal Plain but had a direct and longstanding relationship with New York across easily navigated Raritan Bay.

Monmouth's taxed acreage expanded after 1751, with the amount in improved land reaching a plateau shortly after 1800 and then dropping while unimproved acreage greatly expanded (fig. 13). The number of cattle held fluctuated greatly between the end of the Revolution and 1822; after 1790, even taking into account the exclusion of two-year-old cattle, a large increase in overall numbers of cattle took place, and then a decline became apparent after 1801 (fig. 14). The same trends appear in both Middletown and Dover until 1810, when the number of cattle in Dover continued to diminish and the number in Middletown grew modestly.

In Dover, taxed area more than doubled between 1773 and 1797, indicating a significant increase in the population (table 43). Property sizes fell, but because there must have been plenty of unoccupied land on which to run stock, the decline

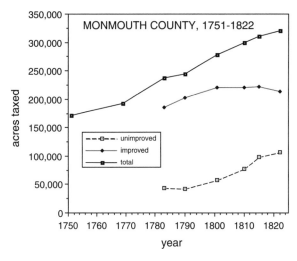

FIGURE 13

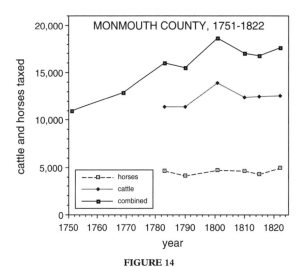

FIGURE 14

was not nearly as severe as on the Inner Coastal Plain. Like many other places, the amount of land taxed and the number of cattle in Dover actually declined between 1779 and 1789 and then rose over the next few years, which in this area may indicate that farmers a bit farther north, who had lost large numbers of cattle during the war, were driving cattle from Dover to market. The rise in the number of taxables and of land taxed in the relatively brief period between 1789 and 1797 probably indicates that Dover, on the poor land on the Outer Coastal Plain, was receiving a substantial influx of population who were creating "improvements." The steady decline in the percentage of landless taxables from 1773 to 1797 also attests this process, and the extreme dispersion of population is shown in the fact that there were only three houses and lots in 1797.

It is more difficult to explain the great drop in the number of horses and those taxed for holding horses in Dover, especially when taxables and acres taxed had risen greatly by 1797 and cattle increased greatly as well. An influx of non-mobile industrial workers might explain some of the decline in horses, but perhaps more to the point is the fact that most of the people then taking up marginal lands in Dover could not afford horses.

In Middletown[45] tax data from 1779 and 1808 show that almost all of the land was improved, but even in this more fertile region areas of poorer soil were populated and subdivided after the Revolution, probably for cordwood production as the increase in total land used, from 33,969 to 41,106 acres, cannot be explained by the less pronounced increase in the number of cattle from 1,725 to 1,815. Cattle remained important, although mean holdings fell from 6.5 to 4.5, and farm sizes were shrinking from a mean of 147.1 to 110.5 acres.

Most of the land in the Middlesex County area lay in the Piedmont and the remainder on the Inner Coastal Plain, but the accessibility offered by the Raritan River brought about its early settlement and improvement (figs. 15 and 16). Before the Revolution, for example, it ranked third in the entire colony in percentage of improved land (see table 4). The area taxed appears to have expanded significantly until about 1800; afterward only modest expansion took place. Unlike the counties such as Monmouth straddling the coastal plain, unimproved acreage remained almost constant in Middlesex from the 1790s on; these areas were probably used to harvest cordwood and tan bark, as the South River Bridge store's day book revealed.

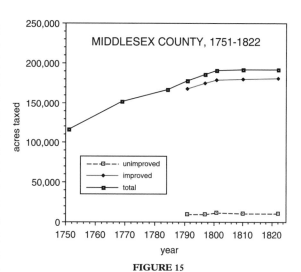

FIGURE 15

The great devastation Middlesex County suffered during the Revolution is reflected in the decline in the numbers of cattle and horses between 1769 and 1784. As in many other places, cattle increased greatly between the end of the war and about 1800, when numbers declined for a decade and then began to rise again. The numbers of horses fluctuated much less; the decline in their numbers by 1810 probably reflects the exclusion of two-year-olds rather than a real decline.

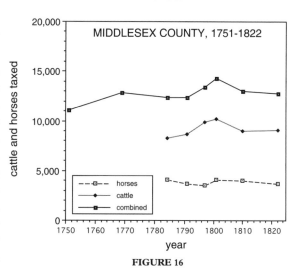

FIGURE 16

Within Middlesex County, tax data exist for Woodbridge Township (7) from 1779 to 1822, during which time it remained undivided (table 44). New Englanders settled Woodbridge early, and apparently none of the land in the township, which lay entirely on the Piedmont, was unimproved; surely some land lay untilled, but it must have been within existing improved tracts. Here, too, the extensively utilized salt and fresh meadows must have been considered improved land. The small fluctuations in the amount of land taxed after 1779 show that almost all the land had been subdivided from the original proprietary holdings. The decline in size of parcels is consistent with what took place elsewhere, but it must have held far greater consequences in these New England-settled regions, where farms were small from the start. After 1800, the decline in the size of acreage held per person slowed significantly, however, suggesting that parcels could not be smaller and still be viable. Moreover, the number of landholders in Woodbridge dropped, probably as people left or were forced to leave the land, while houses and lots greatly expanded in number as settlement density increased and the economy turned toward non-agricultural land uses.

Table 43
Taxables, Land Taxed, and Livestock in Dover Township, Monmouth County, 1773–1797

Year	1773	1779	1789	1797
Taxables	147	142	184	258
Landholdings	64	75	121	174
Landless (%)	56.5	47.2	34.2	32.6
Acres Taxes	12,092	20,173	19,783	27,174
Improved (%)	*	*	76.1	70.5
Median Size (acres)	150	150	100	90
Mean Size (acres)	188.9	243.4	163.5	156.2
Houses and Lots	*	*	6	3
Horses	*	130	138	89
Horse Holders	*	70	74	49
Median Held	*	2	2	2
Mean Held	*	1.9	1.9	1.8
Cattle	*	823	546	833
Cattle Holders	*	103	109	172
Median Held	*	5	3	4
Mean Held	*	7.9	5.0	4.8

*Not Listed

As in the county as a whole, the number of horses in Woodbridge varied slightly, but cattle numbers rose significantly after the Revolution, declined after 1802, and then began to rise again, though very slightly, after 1810. Even though mean and median holdings were far smaller than in areas farther south, cattle were obviously important here.

Woodbridge may be contrasted with Franklin Township, Somerset County (8), which lay nearby and entirely on the Piedmont. Franklin was also settled fairly early, but it was settled several decades after Woodbridge and overwhelmingly by the Dutch. For Franklin, tax data began to be compiled about 1735 and ended in 1815 (table 45). The entire tax list of about 1735 was reprinted, and in 1745 names not on the earlier list were added. The lists were published largely for genealogical reasons (and the names certainly underscore the population's Dutch origins), but the acreage and livestock attributed to individuals were probably accurate.[46]

If no deaths are assumed to have taken place between 1735 and 1745, which is hardly likely, and if the acreage associated with the new names on the 1745 list is added to the acreage of 1735, the total acreage for Franklin would be 28,035. In 1779, 28,104 acres were taxed, and there was little change after that time. Undoubtedly, deaths between about 1735 and 1745 would overstate the acreage total of 1745, but the data still make quite clear that by about midcentury the land in Franklin had been parceled out. Here again, there was little unimproved land, but wood lots did remain as integral parts of properties such as the Van Lieuw farm.

Dutch holdings were generally much larger than those of New Englanders in the

Table 44
Taxables, Land Taxed, and Livestock in Woodbridge Township,
Middlesex County, 1779–1822

Year	1779	1788	1802	1810	1822
Taxables	502	481	701	769	942
Land Holdings	286	254	362	378	406
Landless (%)	43.0	47.2	48.4	50.9	56.9
Acres Taxed	23,019	22,592	23,781	24,246	24,421
Improved (%)	100	100	100	100	100
Median Size (acres)	64	45	50	48	44
Mean Size (acres)	80.5	88.9	65.7	64.1	60.2
Houses and Lots	*	58	107	184	202
Horses	693	744	753	709	626
Horse Holders	291	350	344	301	341
Median Held	2	2	2	2	2
Mean Held	2.4	2.1	2.2	2.4	1.8
Cattle	1,458	2,196	2,040	1,637	1,740
Cattle Holders	341	388	468	460	436
Median Held	3	4	3	3	2
Mean Held	4.3	3.7	4.4	3.0	5.7

* Not Listed

area, and comparisons between Woodbridge and Franklin bear out this fact. Even with substantial subdivision, the farms in Franklin were still much larger than those in Woodbridge in 1815. And the Dutch held more horses and, especially, far more cattle than did the New Englanders. Thus, the contrasts in land use established by these two groups had lasted more than a century. Interestingly, the fluctuations in the total numbers of cattle in Franklin parallel those for Woodbridge, suggesting perhaps some general external stimuli.

About 1735, three-quarters of the taxables in Franklin Township held land, but by 1815 that figure had fallen to little more than half. In Franklin as elsewhere in central New Jersey (unlike parts of southern New Jersey), subdivision of land included increasingly the houses and lots category.

Although the rapid development of central New Jersey resulted in a great deal of subdivision of existing townships, these areas cannot be compared through time because the abstracts that exist for other counties do not exist for these central areas. However, good abstracts exist for Sussex and Bergen counties, as well as for some of the townships. Sussex County represents areas that lay in the Highlands and Ridge and Valley physiographic areas. The region was settled relatively late and was fairly remote from both the Philadelphia and New York markets. The relative lateness of settlement is evident in the fact that the tax record began in 1769 rather than in 1751 (fig. 17). Sussex was divided from Morris County only in 1753.[47]

The area's late settlement is also evident in the great expansion of the area taxed between 1769 and 1784. Significantly, there is a decline in the amount of improved

Table 45
Taxables, Land Taxed, and Livestock in Franklin Township,
Somerset County, ca. 1735–1815

Year	ca. 1735	1745*	1779	1789	1808	1815
Taxables	125	99	303	291	425	568
Land Holdings	94	61	179	174	243	257
Landless (%)	24.8	38.4	40.9	40.2	42.8	54.8
Acres Taxed	16,451	11,584	28,104	28,099	28,088	27,978
Improved (%)	★	★	★	98.4	★	★
Median Size (acres)	150	200	143	125	100	100
Mean Size (acres)	175.0	189.0	157.0	161.5	115.6	108.9
Houses and Lots	★	★	★	20	96	148
Horses	★	★	714	673	705	728
Horse Holders	★	★	172	192	232	260
Median Held	★	★	4	3	3	3
Mean Held	★	★	4.2	3.5	3.0	2.8
Cattle	1,206	1,069	1,149	1,302	1,082	1,239
Cattle Holders	119	97	177	211	264	291
Median Held	9	9	6	5	3	4
Mean Held	10.1	11.0	6.5	6.2	4.1	4.3

*Not listed

land taxed between 1784 and 1796 and then only modest growth before the amount of improved land taxed reached a plateau after the War of 1812. On the other hand, the amount of unimproved land taxed constantly increased, with an especially rapid rise from 1796 to 1806. In contrast, the numbers of cattle constantly expanded, with an especially rapid rise after 1815 (fig. 18). The numbers of horses appear to have been related to changes in the amounts of improved land.

Greenwich Township (19) in the southwestern part of Sussex County was settled in the 1730s, relatively early, because it lay partly in the fertile valley of the Musconetcong (in the Highlands) and partly in the Ridge and Valley section. It largely escaped glaciation during the Pleistocene Era. Still, despite its location on some of the better soils in the region and its access to the Delaware, Greenwich's improved land continuously fell between 1796 and 1822, from 26,536 acres to 23,591 acres in 1822. Improved land was obviously being abandoned. On the other hand, unimproved land rose from 2,312 acres to 7,531 during the period, and the rise in cattle numbers from 778 to 997 between 1796 and 1812 and then to 1,289 during the War of 1812 suggest that farmers were actively raising stock on these lands. By 1822, the number of cattle dropped to 932. Similarly, the horse population rose from 719 to 970 during the three years of the War of 1812.

The northern, largely glaciated sections of Sussex County, Hardwick Township (10), within which lay the small village of Hackettstown, saw a slight increase in improved land between 1796 and 1806, from 23,279 to 24,700 acres, but no growth through 1822, which suggests that nearly all of the land viable for agrictural activity had already been developed by 1806. The decline in unimproved land taxed from 13,246 acres to 7,325 acres between 1796 and 1806 also suggests as much. Nearby Andover Furnace ceased operation after the Revolution, and forest began to reappear in the cut-over areas, but bloomeries (forges that produced iron directly from the ore) established at the end of the century may have been taxed for the woodlands they used in 1796.[48] The numbers of cattle fluctuated during the period and showed no great change during the war as they did in Greenwich, but their numbers rose slightly from 1,377 in 1796 to 1,461 in 1822. The horse population grew at a similar rate, from 642 in 1796 to 687 in 1822.

Subdivided from Newton Township in 1798, Byram Township (11) lay on poor glaciated soils in the Highlands. It included the ironworking community of Stanhope, and if any New Jersey township could be characterized as having "rock farms" it was Byram. The township's total of 3,066 improved acres in 1806 had expanded to 3,631 acres in 1815 and then declined to 3,190 acres by 1822. Unimproved land rose from 3,489 acres in 1806 to 7,715 acres in 1822. Cattle also increased during these years, from 318 to 422, and horses increased modestly from 92 to 105. However, an increase in horses during the war years from 106 to 143 must have reflected the increased activity of the iron industry. The increase in unimproved land probably reflects both the activity of the iron industry and the custom of running stock in the woods.

In one of the remotest parts of New Jersey, the glaciated Ridge and Valley section encompassing part of the "Drowned Lands," Wantage Township (12) was settled relatively late. In 1796, Wantage had 14,951 improved acres; as additional land was settled, improved acreage rose to 26,438 in 1815. But by 1822, only 24,630 acres of improved land were recorded while unimproved land almost continuously increased, from 1,064 acres in 1796 to 13,708 acres in 1822. The increase in cattle mirrored the increase in unimproved land, from 1,600 in 1796 to 2,658 in 1822. Undoubtedly, a large part of the unimproved land must have been used as wood-

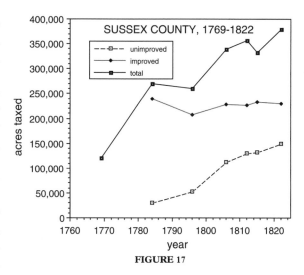

FIGURE 17

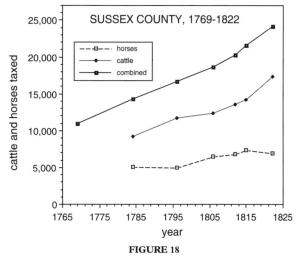

FIGURE 18

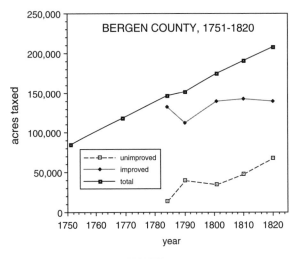

FIGURE 19

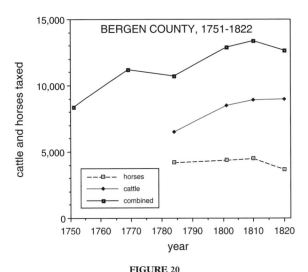

FIGURE 20

land pasture.

Total acreage in Bergen County, which straddled the Piedmont and the glaciated Highlands, rose between 1751 and 1820, but improved acreage dipped in the 1790s, increased until about 1800, and declined slowly thereafter. Unimproved acreage increased until 1790, dipped slightly by 1801, and then began to grow again through 1820 (fig. 19). Bergen's cattle and horses expanded vigorously before the Revolution and, as in Middlesex County, declined during the conflict; from the end of the Revolution to about 1801, cattle expanded swiftly until their numbers leveled off by 1810. Horses must have reached a plateau by the years after the war, and then their numbers began a sharp decline in 1810 (fig. 20).

A brief analysis of two of Bergen's townships helps to explain what was going on. Bergen Township (13), immediately opposite Manhattan (table 46), had large areas of unimproved land due to the existence of undrained marshes—unlike Newton Township opposite Philadelphia, where the marshes had been diked. Acres taxed in Bergen expanded rapidly after the Revolution, perhaps because of diking in these marshes, and then declined after 1802 as more and more land was taken up for residential use; still part of the township, Jersey City was incorporated in 1820.[49] Here, as opposite Philadelphia on the Inner Coastal Plain, mean and median sizes of properties declined rapidly while numbers of taxables and property holders had more than tripled between 1784 and 1822. However, the numbers of horses increased very slightly during the period, suggesting again the decline in farming as the number of landholders owning horses declined. At the same time, though, more people in Bergen held cattle. The relatively high mean suggests a commercial orientation to markets in both Jersey City and New York City. Dairying and fattening animals for the market both were probably carried on.

In the county's Pompton Township (14), which lay in the interior, entirely in the glaciated Highlands, the primary economic activity was the iron industry, not com-

Table 46
Taxables, Land Taxed, and Livestock in Bergen Township,
Bergen County, 1784–1822

Year	1784	1794	1802	1814	1822
Taxables	188	253	316	550	602
Land Holdings	101	197	229	217	231
Landless (%)	46.3	25.1	27.5	60.5	61.6
Acres Taxed	11,153*	14,136	14,452	14,042	13,672
Improved (5)	*	81.3	83.6	85.2	81.3
Median Size (acres)	104	43	38	40	37
Mean Size (acres)	101	58.3	63.1	64.7	59.2
Houses and Lots	(2)**	(13)**	(2)**	67	133
Horses	354	379	406	466	396
Horse Holders	113	141	154	184	186
Median Held	3	2	2	2	2
Mean Held	3.1	2.7	2.7	2.5	2.1
Cattle	454	1,084	935	1,153	1,053
Cattle Holders	117	193	209	290	244
Median Held	4	4	4	3	2
Mean held	3.9	5.6	4.5	3.9	4.2

*only "improved" taxed in 1784.
**properties less than ten acres, but no houses and lots category used.

mercial agriculture (table 47).[50] Formed from the western portions of Franklin and Saddle River townships in 1797, Pompton's population grew from 327 to 610 between 1797 and 1821, but its amount of improved land dropped, suggesting that some agricultural land may have been abandoned in this poor-soil area. In 1797, for example, John Old's four thousand improved acres were probably being cut to produce charcoal for the iron industry, because he was taxed as well for a furnace. The diminution in amount of improved land, then, may reflect a more realistic local method of assessing these woodlands.

Judging by the names on Pompton tax lists, by 1797 a large number of iron-workers were Irish immigrants who held no land or rather small parcels. Mean and median property sizes show the relatively small size of holdings, though the mean is skewed by a few relatively large properties such as that of Olds, who owned eight thousand acres overall. Despite the presence of industrial workers who generally did not hold land, landlessness actually fell during the period as people took up small parcels of poor, rocky, cut-over woodland, probably to graze cattle, as the marked increase in their numbers over twenty-five years of tax data reveals.

Both county and township tax lists document that the period of expansion in New Jersey agriculture after the Revolution was followed by some sort of decline, which in turn was followed by expansion in the early years of the nineteenth century. These data support what Carl Woodward suggested earlier—that an agricultural depression afflicted the state after the war. This depression combined with the

Table 47
Taxables, Land Taxed, and Livestock in Pompton Township,
Bergen County, 1797–1821

Year	1797	1821
Taxables	327	610
Land Holdings	192	315
Landless (%)	47.7	48.4
Acres Taxed	24,221	33,466
Improved (%)	76.1	28.4
Median Size (acres)	42	65
Mean Size (acres)	126.2	106.2
Houses and Lots	12	20
Horses	266	432
Horse Holders	130	210
Median Held	2	2
Mean held	2.1	2.1
Cattle	1,164	1,544
Cattle Holders	250	413
Median Held	4	2
Mean Held	4.6	3.7

opening of western lands to settlement to stimulate the outmigration of many Jersey farmers and the accompanying abandonment of improved lands.[51] But the growing demand for timber in urban places, especially New York and Philadelphia, and the growth of such local industries as iron and glass caused the exploitation of—and tax levies on—unimproved land to increase. And there appears to have been a greater emphasis placed on cattle almost everywhere after the Revolutionary War. These events did not occur at the same time in all places, certainly, but they occurred throughout the state roughly from the last years of the eighteenth century into the early years of the nineteenth.

The effect of the War of 1812 is also reflected well in the tax lists. The drop in cattle numbers before 1810 in some places probably reflects the embargo on foreign trade in effect from December 1807 to March 1809. Immediately afterward, the Nonintercourse Act prohibited trade only with England and France through May 1810.[52] Then the war stimulated expansion in the agricultural economy, as cattle ownership data makes manifest.

Tax lists also show that the limits of the good soils had been reached in New Jersey after the Revolution and that people began to try to establish a living on the very poor soils of the Outer coastal Plain and the glaciated Highlands, where the greatest growth in taxed lands took place in these postwar years.

Farmers did attempt to grow crops, as account books and other evidence document, but their major emphasis was evidently on cattle production and the clearance of land to serve as pasture for them. Even on increasingly smaller parcels of land, some as small as ten acres, large numbers of cattle were raised in the townships directly opposite Philadelphia and New York. Generally, except in places immediately around Philadelphia, there were fewer small parcels in South Jersey than in the north, but farm sizes began to fall drastically in many places on the Inner Coastal Plain, perhaps reflecting more intense uses such as market gardening.

Finally, tax lists make evident long-standing cultural contrasts in land use and rapid change in response to market conditions in central and in northwestern New Jersey. Variation in the size of landholdings and in livestock ownership in central New Jersey lasting into the third decade of the nineteenth century appear to have been a function of whether a township was settled by New Englanders or Dutch, for example. And farmers in Sussex County appear to have expanded especially their holdings in cattle in response to greatly enlarged needs stimulated by the War of 1812.

Notes

1. *Docs. Rel. N.J.*, 1st ser., 12:339–41.

2. Jacob Janeway, Daybook of Janeway and Broughton General Store, Bound Brook, 1735–1747, 3 vols., Sinclair Collection, Alexander Library, NjR. See also Kenn Stryker-Rodda, "The Janeway Account Books, 1735–1746," *The Genealogical Magazine of New Jersey* 33 (1958): 1–3.

3. Cohen, *Dutch-American Farm*, 136.

4. Account Book, Monmouth County, N.J., 1751–1778, New-York Historical Society, New York, N.Y.

5. Barnegat Accounts, April 1766–September 1767, Hendrickson Papers, Sinclair Collection, NjR.

6. Richard Somers, Ledger Book E., Somers Point, May 31, 1773–March 10, 1781, and Richard and Constant Somers, Ledgers Book A, Job Point Store, 1788–1790, Stewart Collection, Savitz Library, Glassboro State College.

7. Nathaniel Holmes General Store Accounts, Ledger A, Cape May Court House, 1805–8, and John Earl, Account Book, New Hanover Township, Burlington County, 1786, Sinclair Collection, NjR.

8. Ledger of . . ., General Store Keeper, Salem, N.J., 1750–1752, and Grant Gibbon, General Store Ledger, Salem, N.J., 1764–1778, Sinclair Collection, NjR.

9. Burt Family Account Book A, Pittsgrove Township, Salem County, 1801–7, Sinclair Collection, NjR.

10. Thomas Newbold Farm Accounts [Bordentown vicinity], 1790–1822, Sinclair Collection, NjR.

11. Samuel Mickle Daybook or Journal, Book B, October 13, 1788–October 8, 1829, Stewart Collection, Savitz Library, Glassboro State College.

12. Account Book of Thomas Holmes, General Merchant, Shrewsbury, N.J., 1728–1730, Sinclair Collection, NjR.

13. Holmes Account Book, 1745-1750; . . . . Fletcher, Account Book of a General Store at Shrewsbury, 1749-1751; General Store Accounts [Middletown], 1753–1763, Hendrickson Family Papers, Sinclair Collection, NjR.

14. New Brunswick (N.J.) Merchant Shipper's Ledger, 1730s–1750s, NjR.

15. Van Neste and Van Liew, Book A, Millstone, 1772–90, Sinclair Collection, NjR.

16. John Ross Store Accounts, Ledger C, Piscataway [Bonhamtown], 1772–86, Sinclair Collection, NjR.

17. William Smith Mill Accounts [including general store], Hightstown, May 25, 1785–March 31, 1791, Sinclair Collection, NjR.

18. Ledger of Sales of Distilled Liquors, Middletown, 1788-1803, Hendrickson Family Papers, Sinclair Collection, NjR.

19. Edward F. Randolph Ledger, Warren Township, 1789–1800, Sinclair Collection, NjR.

20. Jonathan Valentine Account Book, Turkey [New Providence], 1791–98, NjHi.

21. John Bryan General Store Ledger C, Bedminster Township, 1793–98, Sinclair Collection, NjR.

22. Benjamin Smith Farm Ledger, Franklin Township, 1800–6, Sinclair Collection, NjR.

23. James Richmond Account Book, New Brunswick, N.J., 1802–7, and Bennet and Bishop General Store Daybook, New Brunswick, N.J., February 3, 1816–July 28, 1818, Sinclair Collection, NjR.

24. Jacob Kline and Son General Store Ledger Book Accounts, Pluckemin, 1809–12, Sinclair Collection, NjR.

25. Doty and Southard General Store Daybook, Basking Ridge, 1809–11, Sinclair Collection, NjR.

26. Elmendorf and Cortelyou General Store Ledger, Ten Mile Run[?], April 1818–March 1822, Sinclair Collection, NjR.

27. Day Books, General Store [South River Bridge], 1803–25, Herbert Family Papers, Sinclair Collection, NjR.

28. Joseph Camp Day Book, 1752, and Caleb Camp Book A, 1763, Camp Family Record Books, NjHi; Nathan Tichenor, His Book, 1772–1819, Irvington Free Public Library, Irvington, N.J.

29. John Ralston Record Books, Ledger, Record Book A, Journal, Mendham, 1787–1812, Sinclair Collection, NjR.

30. Mehelm and Berry Account Book, Hunterdon County, 1773–74, Sinclair Collection, NjR.

31. Richard Backhouse and Co., Daybook, Greenwich Forge, 1779–80, Forge Books, Historical Society of Pennsylvania, Philadelphia.

32. Jesses Knowles Account Book, 1805–21, Knowles Family Record Books, NjHi.

33. Aaron Kitchell Farmer's Accounts, Succasunna, 1805–19, Sinclair Collection, NjR.

34. *Acts of the General Assembly of the State of New Jersey* (Trenton, 1779), 10.

35. Ibid., 1784, 159.

36. Ibid., 1782, 84.

37. *N.J. Laws,* 4:550; *Acts of the General Assembly,* 1790, 614.

38. *Acts of the General Assembly,* 1801, 107.

39. All sheep were listed for Lower and Middle townships and none for Upper Township, which does not seem logical. If Upper Township harbored as many sheep as the other two townships per unit area, Cape May's sheep population had greatly expanded since 1751. Of course, we must also recognize that illogical data do exist in the tax records and too much cannot be made of one tax list without supporting evidence elsewhere.

40. Frank H. Stewart, "Cape May County Ratables, 1751," *Genealogical Magazine of New Jersey* 14 (1939): 32–35; "Cape May County Ratables, 1768," ibid., 59–65. Despite the titles, both of these lists cover only Lower Precinct (Township).

41. In 1774, Galloway was subdivided from Egg Harbor; in 1798, Weymouth was also subdivided from Egg Harbor; in 1813, Hamilton Township was created from adjacent portions of Egg Harbor and Weymouth townships; in 1820 Franklin Township was created from the eastern (Outer Coastal Plain) portions of Greenwich and Woolwich townships. See Snyder, *New Jersey's Civil Boundaries,* 68–69, 71, 138.

42. "The Account of all that is Taxable in the Township of Chester this present Year–1763," Frederick Paulding Papers, Sinclair Collection, NjR.

43. Snyder, *New Jersey's Civil Boundaries,* 96.

44. The Dover Township list for 1773 is in the holdings of the Monmouth County Historical Association, Freehold. See David J. Fowler, "Dover Township 1773 Rateable," *Genealogical Magazine of New Jersey* 58 (1983): 115–18.

45. No table is provided for Middletown.

46. The original manuscript tax lists have disappeared.

47. Snyder, *New Jersey's Civil Boundaries,* 229.

48. County Tax Ratables, 1772–1822.

49. Snyder, *New Jersey's Civil Boundaries,* 147.

50. Ibid., 211.

51. Woodward, *Ploughs and Politicks,* 42.

52. Bernard Bailyn, et al., *The Great Republic: A History of the American People* (Lexington, Mass., 1981), 298.

Ninth Month, September, 1819.

CHAPTER 7

THE SEASONAL ROUND OF AGRICULTURAL LAND USE

In 1751, Jacob Spicer of Cape May County owned at least 2,342 acres in the county's Lower Precinct, as well as fifty cattle and horses, thirty-nine sheep, and one slave. Spicer owned more than one-fifth of the precinct's taxed land, but because tax lists of the time recorded the names of land occupants, not owners, he probably owned even more land and livestock than official records credited to him. He certainly owned tenanted farms in nearby Maurice River Precinct in Cumberland County, and he probably hired tenants to farm properties elsewhere, perhaps in Lower Precinct itself; his tenants probably raised cattle, sheep, and horses for him on shares.[1] Finally, he ran a general store.

Spicer owned a huge amount of land for one person, even by the standards of the sparsely populated Outer Coastal Plain.[2] Fortunately, he kept a remarkably complete diary of his activities, especially for 1755 and 1756, that describes in detail his agricultural efforts and the diligence with which he raised livestock.[3] Even though he was by any measure unusually wealthy, knowledgeable, and articulate, Spicer's seasonal round probably differed only in scale from the routines other farmers in his region followed. Records left by New Jersey farmers—both prosperous and not so prosperous—in other parts of the state suggest not only a common train of activity but significant regional and cultural variation in agricultural practice that more general records have indicated.

Fourteen farmers' accounts, beginning with Spicer's in the extreme southeast (1), and ending with Jesse Knowles's in the northwest, add flesh to the bones of more statistical information about New Jersey agriculture (map 44). In many instances, several years of these accounts have been analyzed and combined to present a year as completely as possible. Collectively, these accounts document that the milder climate of southern New Jersey permitted farmers to leave livestock outdoors longer, to mow for a greater part of the year, and to harvest earlier. In the north, harvest and planting were about two weeks later, and the mowing season was considerably shorter. On the small farms and scattered holdings in Essex County, apples were of paramount importance; on Cape May, livestock was preeminent. From central Hunterdon County south, corn production, largely to feed hogs, was a highly significant activity among most farmers. And almost everywhere, hay and flax commanded a great deal of attention and effort. In New Jersey, the nearly universal significance of mowing testifies to the importance of livestock, especially cattle, in the economy; in Cape May, where mowing was not a critical activity, stock

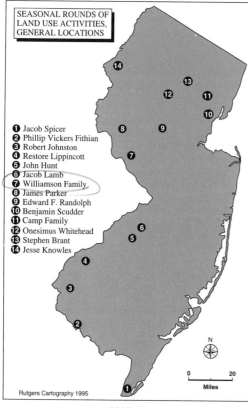

MAP 44

were pastured outdoors throughout the year. Flax, a labor-intensive crop, was another universal; cultivating its seed and fibers may in fact have grown more important with time. And all of these accounts document continued trapping, lumbering, hunting, and fishing.

In January 1756 Spicer made the first of his many negotiations that year with tenants who would lease his lands and raise his stock on shares. In January, he leased land he owned in the Maurice River area of Cumberland County to a "Swede," which suggests that this cultural group retained its identity in the eyes of other inhabitants a full century after the fall of the New Sweden colony on the Delaware. Although Spicer was an absentee owner, his other holdings were not so distant that he could not keep tabs on his tenants; he frequently did. Early in the month, too, Spicer went to the "beach," by which he meant to indicate one of the barrier islands where he kept livestock. He saw there thirteen hogs and later retrieved three of them, presumably for slaughter. And at about the same time, he took in at his store seven mink skins, eight raccoon skins, and one fox skin from John Erickson, Jr. of the Maurice River area; clearly some inhabitants, perhaps especially descendants of Swedish settlers, still earned part of their livelihood from trapping.

By mid-January Spicer and his "Boys" (hired hands) were driving "below" four horses and fifty-four sheep, the horses to a "neck" or narrow peninsula and the sheep to an island where they apparently intermingled with the flocks of other stock owners. Spicer complained that month that neighbors' hogs had rooted in his cleared area and destroyed hay, but free-ranging was clearly not a concept that disturbed him in principle: later that month he put sixty of his cattle and five belonging to neighbors on one of the nearby islands.

In February and early March (better recorded in 1755 than in 1756) Spicer was largely involved in "public service"—he was both a legislator and purchasing agent for the colony's complement of troops for the French and Indian War.[4] At the end of March, he continued negotiating with others to purchase, sell, and lease land, and he lent one man cattle to raise on shares. At the end of the month he visited Maurice River, presumably to check on his holdings there. He recorded contributing £0.7.6 (more than two days' wages for a common laborer) to a fund to provide a more direct road to "Gloucester" and thus to improve overland transport to Philadelphia markets. In the beginning of April 1756 Spicer negotiated to lease a farm he had just purchased; he agreed to supply cows and calves, presumably for the tenant to raise on shares. On April 4, he recorded receiving the rent from another of his leased farms. He spent the rest of the month in public service, though he recorded receiving cedar tops (from the white cedar swamps of northern Cape May) as cordwood.

In early May, Spicer endorsed another land lease and collected rent for a fishery, both presumably on Cape May. He agreed as well to abate his leaseholder Jacob Bennett's rent by twenty shillings for each head of stock taken off an island and five shillings for each cleared acre not tilled that year.[5] Also in early May, Spicer drove his cattle again and negotiated more agreements for raising cattle on shares. In the middle of the month, he settled the course of the line fences with neighbors of a farm he had purchased, and he built and repaired existing fences on the property. By that time, Spicer noted that the "most affecting Dearth [drought] I ever knew" had struck the region. He dug for water for the cattle, probably an easy chore given the sandy soils and the high water table, and then drove some of his cattle to this place. Later he dug more watering holes in other places to try to counteract the dry weather.

On May 17, Spicer "went . . . for Sheep." Although he did not record why, his strategy evidently was to maintain his flock on the relatively poor pastures of the barrier islands and other nearby places and then to place them on better pasture and fatten them on corn to prepare them for market. On May 19, he discussed with others the estimated costs of building a sawmill that could cut a "stick" (presumably length) of thirty-five feet. Early in June, Spicer attended to the gelding of some of his stock and then spent two days establishing the bounds in a white cedar swamp he jointly owned. On June 5, 7, and 8, rain finally fell. On the thirteenth, he visited one of his tenanted properties only to find it "entirely Devoured by Trespassing Creatures." The house on the farm was in serious disrepair, he noted, and needed new shingles and clapboard. For the rest of the month, when he was not busy with the deed and plans for a recently purchased farm, he negotiated agreements for others to raise sheep on shares, leased one of his farms, and went "to the Beach," where he found "41 head of Cattle & 17 fine calves in a Company together—along the strand." Presumably these were his, as were the thirteen horses and the single colt he later visited there.

Early in July, Spicer worked in his store, at which time he took in 409 muskrat skins, 15 raccoon skins, 10 mink skins, 8 fox skins, and 3 deer skins. In the middle of the month, he finished his harvest of wheat, only a little more than four bushels per acre on sixteen acres of land. Such meager harvests, certainly due at least partly to drought that year, must have encouraged Spicer to concentrate instead on livestock, with which he was busy for much of the rest of July. He also made more agreements to have sheep raised on shares, and, at the end of the month, had ninety-three of his flock sheared. At that time, he also stated that he had twenty-five lambs and eighty-nine cattle, only twenty-five of which were "home."

Spicer spent most of August in public service and was hunting up stock wandering freely through the woodlands early in September. He and two other men discussed the possibility of buying Stipson's Island, presumably for their stock, but they agreed to conceal their interest (undoubtedly to keep the price down) in order to conduct "a private previous Inspection" of the island. That month, too, Spicer agreed to rent his plantation on Maurice River for only £4, which suggests either that the place was not very productive or that an additional unrecorded agreement contained an exchange of services on the part of the tenant that lowered the rent. On September 19, he sold four oxen, eighteen steers, and eight cows for £115, indicating clearly how much more lucrative livestock was than property rental.

Early in October, Spicer went to Philadelphia, in part to arrange the sale to a butcher of sixty of his sheep "fatted the latter part of the season & kept upon Corn" until the middle of January. The butcher offered him twelve shillings a piece. Later that month, he began to make note of lumbering activity. He indicated that he would purchase barrel staves at twenty shillings per thousand on site and sell them for forty shillings, probably in Philadelphia. At the end of the month, he hired a hand to pursue the "Cedar Swamp Business this winter" and recorded that his father-in-law had begun to cut and cart cordwood. Spicer also arranged to sell more cattle, or, failing that, to kill and dry them.

In December Spicer spent the first part of the month at home "Imployed about my Trade," presumably as a storekeeper. On December 12, he "went below" to drive thirty sheep of his own and some belonging to neighbors from Cape Island back to Lower Precinct. Three days later, he sold twenty-one wethers (castrated male sheep) for seven shillings each and twenty-seven ewes at six shillings each.

Jacob Spicer's record contains little about growing crops, not surprising given the poor soils on Cape May; raising cattle and sheep and exploiting the woodlands for wood, pasture land, and furs were primary. His account also indicates that many residents in this region were tenants, not freeholders, who leased land from him and raised his livestock on shares. Elsewhere in southern New Jersey, there were probably fewer sheep; in the interior, there was a greater devotion to lumbering; along the coast, the fishery and shellfishery were critical.

The even more detailed records of Philip Vickers Fithian, residing near Greenwich in Cumberland County (2), allow a fairly complete reconstruction of his daily activities on the family farm for part of 1766 and 1767, about a decade after Spicer's account was written.[6] Fithian was a young man when he kept his journals—he had just turned nineteen on December 29, 1766—and he was much more directly and extensively involved in agricultural work than Spicer was. His journal describes both his activity and, at least occasionally, that of at least one other member of his immediate family.

Because of the relative mildness of the climate in southwestern New Jersey, Fithian could work outdoors in January. For about ten days that month, he cut, carted, and "sleded" wood both for his own family and for an aunt. One day he "drove our cattle to the other place" and returned with oats that had evidently been stored there. About two weeks that month he devoted to cleaning flax and threshing wheat; over another four days, he killed nine hogs (together weighing 1,363 pounds, or an average of only a little more than 151 pounds each), cleaned out the stables, and took care "of the creatures." Clearly Fithian had a barn, though whether the family owned it or not is unknown.

In February, Fithian spent five days outdoors cutting and sledding wood. He spent about half a day putting one of the hay stacks stored outside in the barn. Over fourteen days he threshed and dressed flax; it took him three days to thresh rye and another half a day to clean wheat. On February 27, he recorded that two men working for a neighbor "dressing flax, and kiln drying it, . . set fire to the Barn and burn'd it down, together with abundance of flax and fodder." In March, Fithian spent another nine days on his own flax.

On March 6, Fithian was able to begin to work the ground to "plant a nursery of Peach and Apple trees." On warm days, he manured and planted a peach nursery and began to sow some lettuce and parsnip seeds in another garden. But "stormy" weather inhibited the family's normal agricultural routine often that month. On one such day, Fithian shelled a bushel of corn and killed hogs; another he spent "bottoming some chairs." And on the afternoon of March 12, he noted, "we did nothing by reason of the extreme cold." But later that month, he continued to cut and haul wood and began to attend to the fencing. On March 27, he and his uncle were splitting rails when Fithian's ax "sliping unluckily struck my uncle" but "not so bad as I expected by the stroke." On March 31, he wrote, "our folks carted some posts I holed some in the afternoon and we put them up with the old pales round the yard."

In early April, Fithian continued to split rails, put up pales, and enclose a meadow. On April 6, he and other family members began in earnest to plant the just-fenced kitchen garden with beans, peas, parsnips, parsley, onions, lettuce, carrots, cabbage, radishes, "and the like." They also planted peach scions in the nursery. On April 8, they began to plant potatoes and five days later began to plow for flax. When they had finished their own flax field the next day, they sowed and harrowed two acres of flax at a neighbor's farm.

On at least six days from April 15 to May 6, the Fithians plowed to prepare a field for corn, and they spent at least another ten days carting dung and mud to this field. On odd days during the rest of the month of April, they worked on banking the meadow, carting wood, and hiring a blacksmith to repair plowshares, coulters, hoes, and other farm tools. During April, Fithian's father went fishing four times. On his first outing he caught a dozen small fish and a number of "very large tarepoins [terrapins]." He then fished with a seine, without much luck until April 20, when he caught three dozen "fine fish," probably shad.

Corn continued to take up most of the family's time in May. From May 6 to 14, they planted their own crop and then spent a day planting for a neighbor. At least four more days were spent cultivating the corn before the end of the month. On other May days, they were planting potatoes, "sticking" string beans, planting peas and beans, and, toward the end of the month, plowing the "pumpkin patch," carting mud to it, and planting the pumpkins. In May, too, they fished again using a seine, worked on the meadow banks, mowed, fenced the hog pasture and mended other fences, and washed and sheared their sheep.

At the end of May and the beginning of June, drought hit the region. On Tuesday, June 9, the Fithians spent the day fasting, an old religious custom during times of trouble (Fithian was later educated as a Presbyterian minister). Finally, in the afternoon on June 12, the first rain in almost three weeks fell. The drought forced the family to replant some of the corn and pumpkins; the year before, terrible winds and rains in late June and early July threatened to destroy their flax, wheat, and corn harvests. After replanting in 1767, the Fithians spent at least nine days in June harrowing, howing, and plowing the corn crop. Six days in June were taken up with mowing and making hay and a day or so with hilling the potatoes and hoeing the beans, pumpkins, and other smaller crops. Over several days, Fithian burned brush, perhaps to expand pasture for cattle. He built a new sluice to allow water to drain from the diked meadow during low tide. Mending fences continued, and Fithian built a new one around a "turnip patch." The only recreation he mentioned in June was a trip "to the Beach fishing &c." on the thirteenth.

At the end of June, Fithian began to reap rye; in early July, he started to pull flax. He worked in the kitchen garden one afternoon, "reap'd at our bearded Wheat" one Monday morning, and turned and bound "some of our Rye" that afternoon. Reaping and loading wheat took up the next eleven days (except Sunday, when Fithian customarily did not work). On July 14, he and his family "finished reaping for ourselves and got in all our grain" and then spent six days reaping "for uncle Sam'l Fithian" and other neighbors. By about the 20th, the area grain harvest was apparently over. Through most of the beginning of August, Fithian worked at odd chores: he "turned 2 & 20 dozen butter moulds," "helped frame sluice," "cut hoop poles" used to bind casks, and carried mud in a wheelbarrow and canoe to the meadow bank. He also spent one day hoeing corn.

On August 2, Fithian "planted out turnip patch," apparently for the second time, and two days later he began to mow and make hay. On August 10, he wrote, "the Melons and the Cucumbers with their native excellency . . . yield us a noble repast." He harvested the kitchen garden and mowed, raked, and carted hay throughout the rest of the month, although by August 23, he noted, intermittent fevers and chills kept many of his neighbors from working. "It is at present a remarkable sickly unhealthy time," he wrote on September 11; "it is said there is hardly one family in the place but what some of them are sick; and some families not able to help one another &c." Four days later, he observed that "the Fever and Ague is universal & very bad." On October 7, Fithian recorded that many were still sick with fever though "few have been carried off by death"; it was his last reference that year to the sickness. Two days earlier, he had recorded a frost, which had presumably killed the mosquitoes in surrounding marshes that served as the vector for the disease. Clearly, as Kalm had noted almost twenty years earlier, malaria was a major problem in relatively mild and marshy southern New Jersey; Fithian himself had been incapacitated by "fits" of malaria for at least six days in late August and early September the year before.[7]

With the largest part of the harvest behind them, the Fithians spent September on more diverse tasks. Early in the month, they plowed and harrowed for the winter grain crop, picked apples, topped corn and bound the tops, took up broom corn, and mowed in the nearby salt marsh. By the middle of the month, Fithian began making cider and threshing and sowing wheat. This last chore was completed by October 4, and in these early October days he also spread dung, pulled beans and calavance peas, threshed and cleaned them, gathered potatoes (eighteen bushels, probably only enough for the family to use), and then went out into the marsh to retrieve the cattle. In the second week of October he began to thresh rye and flax seed; from October 10 to 14 he plowed, sowed, and harrowed in the rye. Then he began to spread the flax to rot, to pick winter apples, to thresh hemp seed, and to make more cider. By the third week of October Fithian had begun to gather in the corn crop and to pen the family's hogs "to fat." Over the rest of the month he finished the corn harvest, brought in the corn tops, and carted fifteen loads of corn on the cob.

Early in November, Fithian was mowing again on the bank of the meadow. He carted wood, cleaned flax seed, worked on repairing the bank, "killed our beef," and finished threshing and cleaning the flax seed. On November 8, he finally found himself with time to go "guning & fishing & etc." and to help his uncle cart and spread flax, thresh rye, and cart wood. After midmonth he continued to thresh rye, put up apples for the winter, cart wood, and pull turnips, a two-day chore that suggests the family had planted quite a large crop.

On December 1, the Fithians' bull was slaughtered, and afterward cold and stormy weather kept him indoors for days. He did "nothing but look after creatures" one day and spent others killing the hogs for an aunt and then for an uncle, threshing, and turning and dressing flax. On a few days he was able to work outdoors sawing and splitting wood and carting sand and gravel for a neighbor.

The better soils of the lower Cohansey region in which Fithian lived allowed a mixed and much more varied pattern of agricultural land use than Spicer could pursue at Cape May. His family raised hogs, cattle, and sheep, but their numbers were not great and the weights of their hogs at slaughter were not impressive. Fithian had horses, because he was frequently engaged in "hauling" and at least once had his horse hardware and a plow repaired. But he never mentioned horses, which suggests he kept them for nothing but farm work, and the few references to livestock, especially when compared to Spicer's frequent discussion of them, suggest that crops were far more important in this region. The Fithians spent most of their time on corn, wheat, and rye, perhaps in that order, although the actual acreage in wheat may have been greatest. For the Fithians, wheat and rye, and perhaps flax, were probably commercial crops; they probably did not grow oats or barley. Yet apparently for their own use, they grew an extremely wide variety of other crops, including hemp and broom corn, and they were sufficiently concerned about maintaining soil fertility to spend time hauling and spreading dung and mud. They also spent much time repairing and building fences, probably a post-and-rail fence around the kitchen garden but worm or zig-zag rail fences elsewhere; rarely did Fithian mention cutting posts. And the fact that he spent so much time working on dikes and sluices on the family's meadows attests the importance of hay in maintaining what stock they had over the winter.

The picture of land use that emerges from the 1782-83 farm account book of Robert Johnson or Johnston, living near Salem (3), is quite different from Spicer's and Fithian's; although there is no direct indication of it, his account may also show some lingering effect in the area of the Revolution.[8] Salem lay on the quite good soils of the Inner Coastal Plain, far better soil than Spicer and Fithian owned. The account book states that Johnston owned a house in Salem Town, and the August 1782 tax list shows a Robert Johnston, Esq. as the holder of fifty acres of improved land, thirty acres of unimproved land (presumably marsh), and no livestock in Salem Town.[9] The extant 1783 tax records for nearby Mannington Township also list a Robert Johnston, Esq. as holding 216 acres, eleven horses, fifty cattle, two slaves, and two "chairs" (wheeled vehicles). The people mentioned in the account book also appear on these two tax lists but not elsewhere. It seems logical to suppose, then, that Johnston was the compiler of the account book; his name is shown as "Johnston" only in the front and back of the book, but probably in a different hand.

The seasonal round of agricultural work on Johnston's farm was carried on for the most part by several local landless men whose labor Johnson credited in his account book. Statistical evidence about the agricultural labor force suggests a relatively higher quotient of such men in southwestern New Jersey than in other parts of the colony. Johnston's hired men were married, for they are shown as householders on the Mannington tax list, and one of them owned a horse and two cattle and was taxed for a shop or tavern. But because this man did farm work for Johnston, the shop was probably a marginal enterprise.

In January, Johnston's hired men threshed and cleaned wheat and oats (the Fithians, directly south, did not grow oats at all) and dressed flax. Johnston also had them dig a well on a property he owned in Salem and sent a hog weighing 190 pounds to be slaughtered in the same town. One of his workers split posts and rails for fencing; another made cider. In February, they concentrated mostly on wheat. Johnston declared that the 295 bushels he raised in a field next to his barn "a poor crop," though it would have seemed monumental by Cape May standards. Johnston also sold hay and wheat locally and sent wheat and corn to a local mill.

In early March, Johnston's men pruned apple trees and hauled hay to a shallop bound for Wilmington. Between March 8 and 15, they sowed timothy seed. During the rest of the month, they hauled fence rails to the property, drove cattle in to feed, hauled dung, and began to plow the fields. They continued to plow in early April and sowed oats, flax, and corn. One man worked at Tuilbury Meadow, presumably ditching or repairing the bank. They continued to plow and prepare the cornfield toward the end of the month and then drove cattle onto the "wild marsh," presumably a natural, unbanked meadow.

As with the Fithians, corn occupied the workers on Johnston's farm through much of May. The field was furrowed at the beginning of the month; then planting began on May 6 and continued through the month. Even the orchard was plowed for corn, which indicates that intertillage was practiced. At the end of the month Johnston put two hundred bushels of corn on board a shallop and received £0.2.2 per bushel, or a total of £21.13.4; he then emptied the corn cribs next to the stable of 235 more bushels. His men hayed the "Tuilbury Banks" and delivered cedar rails for fencing that month, and Johnston sold veal and weaned seven calves.

June was taken up with harrowing and plowing corn and mowing hay. The men drove cattle to the embanked marsh early in the month, and one of them spent a day and a quarter painting the "cheas house," indicating that Johnston kept a dairy. At the end of June, Johnston began to reap his winter grain, most likely wheat. During the ensuing two weeks of the wheat harvest, the men continued to mow and began to cradle the oats, which took about a week. During August, Johnston's men continued to mow and cart hay, and he again sent small quantities of wheat and corn to the local mill.

In September, the men began to plow for another wheat crop and continued to mow. That month, Johnston cleaned forty and a half bushels of wheat for sowing, indicating that he probably planted as many acres. Wheat clearly was a major enterprise. He kept sending wheat to the mill and then, after the apples had been picked, began to make cider; toward the end of the month, he sent cider to the still. On September 14, Johnston paid the manager of the embanked Tuilbury Marsh £0.21.8 for each of the thirity-one acres he owned there; in all, he recorded, he had spent £17.9.8 in cash and work on the bank that year. His total costs were

£33.11.0, so Johnston owed £16.1.8. Unfortunately, he kept no account of the value of the hay his men mowed continuously on this marsh, though it was probably a vast quantity.

At the beginning of October Johnston sold nine "fat" cattle for £77.10.0 and credited a neighbor who had apparently joined him in shipping cheese. By October 5, his men were pulling corn, carting cider to the still, and plowing and sowing wheat. One of his workers removed the three cows Johnston had allowed him to pasture. His hands were also put to work at Tuilbury "at muskrat holes and dams" and spent several days building a hog pen, which must have been fairly large judging by the time it took to construct it.

At the beginning of November, Johnston's men began to plow the fallow land. They sowed rye for more than a week and continued to pull corn and carry cider to the still. At the end of the month, they began to draw out the flax, and early in December they slaughtered and prepared the hogs for market.

Johnston had them kill twenty-one hogs, and they "salted up" twenty, collectively weighing 2,543 pounds—far more than Fithian's hogs weighed. Johnston sold nine others. By December 9, the men began to slaughter cows and "beevs." The rest of the month was devoted to shipping corn and carting more wheat to the local mill.

At the end of 1782, Johnston recorded "What I Sold in One Year" to total £300.9.8, though clearly this sum does not include the profit he realized from selling his hogs and from many other smaller transactions. Cheese was responsible for more than a quarter of his income, but he infrequently discussed the commodity in his daily record; still, other data confirm that dairying was important in Salem County.

Clearly, Johnston was quite prosperous. Corn was his major crop, and he probably used most of it to fatten stock, especially hogs. But wheat also took up a good deal of his and his laborers' time, as did hay from the banked marsh which was probably used mostly as fodder for the beef and dairy cattle. Undoubtedly, most of Johnston's wheat, pork, beef, and dairy products were sent to the Philadelphia market; his cider, oats, rye, and flax may also have been commercial crops, at least in part, and he might have sold whatever corn and hay his own livestock did not consume. Johnston also sold mutton, but the relatively few entries about sheep indicate that these animals were not among his most important livestock. And, unlike Fithian, Johnston did not mention producing butter.

Farther north on the relatively unimproved Inner Coastal Plain near Philadelphia, in Greenwich Township, Gloucester County (4), Restore Lippincott worked as a contractor building entire dwellings and as a farmer on 250 acres valued at a somewhat higher rate than the land of his neighbors.[10] Township tax lists for 1787 show that Lippincott owned eight cattle, three horses, five hogs, and a riding chair. He was also taxed on the money he had loaned out ("money at interest"), fully £1,890.

Although his holdings were not as vast as Spicer's, Fithian's, or Johnston's, Lippincott clearly had above-average income; he surely made far more than ordinary carpenters made in day labor (see tables 13 and 14), and his loans were significant. Because his diary is not nearly as extensive for any one year as some, records from three years—1769, 1770, and 1771—were examined to develop an understanding of his seasonal activity.

Although Lippincott's land was probably more improved than that of some of his neighbors, he still had much unimproved land: in January and February, he cut wood and cleared swampland for pasture. He burned charcoal from the wood, probably for the Philadelphia market, and made fence rails. On January 14 his cow calved, and on February 3 his sow bore four pigs. At the end of March he planted peas and plowed for flax.

It snowed at the beginning of April in Greenwich Township, so Lippincott threshed winter grain while the snow still lay on the ground. He also cut and hauled logs for one of the houses he had contracted to build. On April 6, he began to plow for corn; on April 14, he sowed flax and planted turnips. He began to spread dung on the fields, planted potatoes, made a fence around his cabbage garden, and continued to plow for corn through the middle of the month. He also fixed a hole in the bank of his meadow, hauled rails, and caught and cleaned two hundred shad. At the end of the month, he sowed red clover among the flax, plowed, continued to make fences, and recorded the birth of three additional pigs. In early May, another cow calved.

Like other farmers in the southern region, Lippincott planted corn and potatoes in May. At midmonth he was furrowing for and began to plant pumpkins, as well as watermelons, peas, and more potatoes. Toward the end of the month he built a cow pen. In the first week of June he was harrowing corn and then turned to mowing clover and plowing the weeds in his cornfield. He also plowed his turnip patch. In June, Lippincott mowed on his home place and on a banked meadow on Mantua Creek; he then spent the rest of the month mowing, making, and hauling hay. Toward the end of the month he bought a pair of steers (apparently to fatten) and began to reap rye. On June 23, he, unlike most other New Jersey farmers, planted tobacco.

In July the rye harvest continued and the wheat harvest began. The wheat harvest lasted two weeks, and then Lippincott returned to mowing hay; then, in the third week of July, the oat harvest began. With the harvest at its height, he engaged both black and white day laborers. Lippincott also began to pull flax during this month. At the beginning of August he began to mow what he called the "second crop," which was probably clover; a few days later he mentioned "racking up" clover. He also sowed his turnip patch and began plowing his "flax ground" for wheat. By midmonth he was plowing the fallow in the orchard for wheat; intertillage was apparently customary here as in Salem. On August 18 Lippincott began to sow rye; on August 26 he began to sow wheat. He mended the sluice on one of the banked meadows, and he continued to mow.

In September and October, Lippincott sowed wheat, killed a cow for "a beef," and worked "about hay." Early in November he began to dig potatoes and to sow rye in the orchard. Toward the end of the month he killed his brown cow for "good beef," slaughtered two hogs, and pulled turnips. On November 28 he was "shipping tobacco." In December Lippincott did mostly indoor work—winnowing flax seed, breaking flax, threshing rye, and slaughtering hogs. He also worked outdoors clearing the swamp, hauling dung out to his fields, and fixing the floodgate on his banked meadow.

Even if Lippincott spent as much time building houses as he did farming, he clearly spent a great deal of time in agricultural work. As elsewhere in southwestern New Jersey, banked meadows were central to his enterprise, and he devoted much effort to keeping his in good repair and to mowing and making hay. But, unlike Johnston, Lippincott could only hire day laborers for the harvest, and he still had land to clear and drain; one might have expected as much on that part of the Inner Coastal Plain (see map 11). Yet Lippincott's farming was more mixed than Johnston's, more like the farm the Fithians worked; like Fithian, he was less engaged in livestock than in general farming. He apparently had no dairy, but he may have produced some crops, especially cabbage and watermelon, for garden truck. Whether he grew pumpkins and potatoes for his stock is not clear, but Lippincott seems to have produced enough hay to feed the few animals he owned. For him, rye and corn were more important than wheat. But he kept no sheep, in keeping with the relatively low numbers of the animals shown in other sources of data for Gloucester County.

In Evesham Township, near Moorestown in Burlington County (5), the Quaker preacher John Hunt also worked as an occasional carpenter and farmer in 1774. He farmed on sixty-five acres valued at £19, below the mean assessed acreage in his township and well below the mean value of property holding in Evesham. In that year, he was listed to own nine cattle and a horse, and he was also taxed for a "shop" of an unidentified sort. In 1779, Hunt held the same amount of land he had five years earlier, but he then had three horses and only four cattle. He no longer had a shop, but he did have a servant.

Between 1770 and 1777, Hunt recorded his agricultural work on this part of the Inner Coastal Plain.[11] One January and February he killed and dressed a calf; at the end of March he pruned his apple trees and the "nursery" of trees he intended to transplant. He also leveled the area where his hogs had been "ruteing." In early April he made a bark mill for tan bark and helped lay out a road. He hauled dung toward the end of the month and then, in early May, went to the Delaware to get shad. Toward the end of that month Hunt planted "punkins."

In May and June Hunt recorded fixing two cheese presses, making one, and selling some stray sheep; some of his flock were killed by dogs in the middle of the month. At the end of June he hoed his corn; in early July he mowed, reaped, and made hay for the rest of the month while helping neighbors with similar chores. He did not indicate whether he sowed wheat or rye. Later in July he harrowed his corn, and toward the end of the month in two years he traveled, probably to the nearby Outer Coastal Plain, to "get hiccleberries of which there was great plenty." In August he made a fence through his meadow.

In early September Hunt was threshing, but again he did not state the type of grain. On September 10, 1774, he "went up in the barrens to get cranberries . . . we kild a deer and got cranberries enough tho I thought it seemd los time to me." Through much of September in several years Hunt built and repaired apple mills. In October he hauled and husked corn, picked apples, and made cider. During this month in 1770, he made a hog pen, turned flax, and fenced his haystacks. He rarely recorded his activities in December, but in one November he built a cow house for another farmer and a "meet tub" for another, killed and butchered his hogs, and salted the pork.

John Hunt's relatively meager record does document the importance of corn and pork to the economy of southwestern New Jersey. He kept sheep, more a northern

Jersey custom than a southern one. Also, Hunt apparently hoed his corn rather than just plowing it, as was the custom generally in southern New Jersey. He may have had much less in cultivation than other farmers did, as the relatively small size of his farm would indicate. Hunt made a surprising number of references to cider mills, but because he was a carpenter the construction and repair of all such mills in his region may well have devolved upon him.

Jacob Lamb's even less detailed farm ledger adds some detail about seasonal work in this area during the next decade, from 1788 to 1796.[12] In 1779, Lamb held 438 acres in Northampton Township (6) valued at £66 per hundred acres, considerably above the mean for the township. Northampton lay largely on the Outer Coastal Plain, but Lamb probably farmed on the better soils of the Inner Coastal Plain; the twenty acres of unimproved land he owned may have been on the Outer Coastal Plain. In 1779, Lamb owned six horses and seventeen cattle; in 1796 he had the same number of horses and three more cattle. His land and livestock holdings were respectable, certainly greater than Hunt's, but his ledger makes no reference to a specialty in raising cattle or in dairying.

Like Hunt, Lamb killed hogs in January; in February he dressed flax, and in March he threshed rye. In April Lamb usually made fence rails and worked in a cedar swamp. With some regularity over the years, Lamb planted corn by mid-May. In one May he sheared sheep (perhaps not his own). Through the rest of May, June, and early July, Lamb typically mowed hay and probably cultivated corn, as later, abundant mentions of husking corn suggest. On July 17, 1788, Lamb was reaping, though he did not say what; he then mowed through the rest of July and August and plowed, perhaps to prepare for a winter grain crop, in late September one year. He thus apparently focused on corn and hogs, grew some rye but probably no wheat, and worked in the off-season cutting lumber on the Outer Coastal Plain.

The early nineteenth-century record left by the Williamson family on the fertile soils of the southwestern Piedmont in Amwell Township, Hunterdon County (7), is far more extensive than Hunt's or Lamb's.[13] Like Johnston, the Williamsons were affluent enough to employ numerous day laborers, so the record they kept of seasonal land use reflects the activity of these hired people. The 1803 Amwell tax list shows two William Williamsons and two Abraham Williamsons, but it was probably the Abraham who owned 292 improved acres and 22 unimproved acres who generated the family employment records. This Abraham Williamson also owned another tract of 138 acres, one slave, six horses, thirteen cattle, a riding chair, and a dog. His land was valued at £58 and £52 per hundred acres, a little above the township's mean. The other Abraham Williamson was listed as a "weaver" who also held eighty-seven acres, no horses, three cattle, and a dog; one William Williamson was a tanner who owned a tan yard, a five-acre lot, one horse, one head of cattle (most likely a cow), and a riding chair; the other owned 124 acres, three horses, and six cattle. Probably more than one of these men kept these papers, though it is not known whether all were related.

The men the Williamsons employed appear on the tax list largely as householders who owned small lots of land but not farms. Several owned horses and cows, some only a cow, and some no livestock at all, which suggests that they were relatively poor. Still others were single men with no land and no livestock; several of these men probably lived on one of the Williamson farms.

The more severe winters of the northwestern interior of New Jersey kept the family's laborers indoors for all of January and most of February. They slaughtered cattle, threshed wheat and, to a lesser extent, oats, broke flax, and cleaned wheat after it had been threshed. At the end of February, they ventured outdoors to sow clover, and early the next month they transplanted young apple trees; then they returned indoors for much of the rest of March to dress and break flax.

By the middle of March, the Williamsons' workers could spend most of their time on outdoor work. They pruned the mature apple trees, sowed grass seed by mid-month, and sowed flax slightly later. They mended fencing and pounded plaster to be used on the fields. In April, they mended more fence, cultivated flax, and hauled dung and plaster out to the fields. But they could not plant the kitchen garden until the beginning of May, when it was also possible to begin to plant corn. This latter task took three weeks; so did drawing earth to place on the corn. In May, workers also castrated hogs and cattle, dunged the fields, plowed, and peeled bark, perhaps for William Williamson's tannery. Sheep were shorn at the end of the month.

Workers made fencing and built a "hog house" at the beginning of June and then began to mow in the second week. By June 15, they began to hoe, and throughout the rest of the month they continued to mow hay and hoe the corn crop. By July 6, they were able to begin to pull the flax crop; by July 9, the rye harvest had begun; a few days after that, the wheat harvest commenced. By the end of the month workers were cradling oats, "hauling in" the rye and wheat, pulling more flax, and mowing more hay. On July 20, workers spent three and a half days plowing the apparently substantial buckwheat crop. Throughout August, they mowed and threshed both flax and rye.

The Williamsons' account never mentions planting corn, but they must have grown it, for in early September in two years workers spent three full days carting corn to New Brunswick. The crop thus must have been not only sizeable but also raised with an eye to the market. Workers threshed rye, set out flax to ret, mowed more hay, and began to make cider in early September as well. By midmonth plowing and harrowing began for the winter grain crop, though which one is not indicated; workers also continued to mow, haul dung, and cart corn to market.

In October corn continued to be husked, flax retted, and grass seed sown. By midmonth workers harvested the buckwheat, threshed the oats, and continued to pick apples. Early in November they threshed the buckwheat and continued to husk corn; they also dug potatoes, possibly from the kitchen garden. Corn husking continued into November, when workers also began to haul corn stalks (presumably for fodder), transplant apple trees, cut wood, make cider, and repair fences. Workers returned indoors in December to slaughter hogs and to break and dress flax; outdoors, they cut and hauled cordwood.

The Williamson accounts do not directly state it, but they imply that by 1800 rye had overshadowed wheat in importance and that corn was preeminent over both. Unlike most farmers to the south, the Williamsons grew corn not only to fatten stock (most likely hogs, as no Williamson owned many cattle) but to sell on the commercial market; by this time, New Brunswick merchants were taking in far more corn than wheat. Corn may indeed have been the most important product of the Williamson farm, though flax was plainly quite significant as well.

Another record of agricultural activity in the Piedmont's Hunterdon County was left by James Parker, whose diary of daily events at Shipley, his estate covering parts of both Bethlehem and Kingwood townships (8), is one of the richest extant.[14] Parker was a wealthy proprietor, and his practices were widely regarded as good farm management. He was certainly no ordinary farmer, but in many respects his seasonal round differed little from that of more typical farmers. Parker lived at Shipley, which included about 650 acres of fertile land just south of the Highlands, from 1774 until 1787, but tax lists for both townships record him to have owned only 250 acres in each, valued at about the mean or slightly higher. Shipley was either smaller than descendants recalled it to be, or Parker understated the acreage to keep his taxes down, as he admitted doing with other properties. In 1780, Bethlehem Township tax lists show Parker to have owned nine horses, ten cattle, five hogs, two slaves, a riding chair, and a covered wagon, one of only two in the entire township. Unlike Lippincott, Parker was not taxed in either township for money he had loaned out in 1780, although some other residents were. Parker must have had "money at interest," but he may have persuaded assessors that his real residence was elsewhere and thus that this tax should be levied there.

Parker, like the Williamsons and Johnston, hired agricultural laborers, and many of them appear on the two townships' tax lists in 1778. They were all householders or single men without property; one was listed as owning eleven acres, one horse, and one cow, but he was exceptionally well off for the lot. Parker began the year with only "my own people," meaning to indicate the slaves he owned and the white laborers he had under contract as opposed to ordinary day laborers. These men killed a calf and an ox in January and undertook "different works" such as cutting and hauling cordwood, threshing oats, breaking flax, and hauling home buckwheat straw. Parker provided wood and two bushels of buckwheat to the wife of a neighbor who was away, probably due to the war, and two bushels of turnips to another neighbor. He sent a "parcell" of flax off to a man to dress on shares; he was, Parker wrote, to "break & swingle it and to have every third pound." Parker must have had so much flax that it made sense to farm some of it out to others. Like Spicer far to his south, Parker spent much of January visiting his tenants, some as far afield as New Brunswick.

At the beginning of February Parker's men killed a calf, of which he kept half for his "own use" and distributed half to neighbors. At the same time, he recorded hanging in another man's smokehouse twenty of his hams, "16 of them very large," sixteen large shoulders, sixteen fletches (or sides), and eight "P Chops." Just as men on less thriving farms did, Parker's men spent the first two weeks of February doing what he often called "foul weather work," dressing and breaking flax, threshing and cleaning wheat, and cutting wood as the weather permitted. They threshed twenty-nine bushels of wheat, placed five of those "in one of the bins," bagged the rest, and sent it to Philip Grandin, the local miller and merchant who also sold Parker his sugar, coffee, and snuff. During February, too, Parker sold turnips and potatoes and put his men to work cleaning rye and wheat. By February 18, they had cleaned thirty-one bushels of rye and sent twenty-seven of them to Grandin. Parker's men also began to cut fence rails in a wood lot in the nearby Highlands.

Like Spicer, too, Parker spent a good deal of time negotiating with tenants. On February 20, Parker recorded that one Sussex County tenant, Christopher Longstreet, objected to Parker's proposal that his rent be paid in grain. Longstreet told him that "it was unsuitable to lease for a Share of the summer grain [presumably corn or buckwheat] as they seldom raised more of that than was necessary for their own use but offered me 100 bus wheat certain." Thus wheat continued to be the major grain of Sussex County at the time.

Also in February, Parker's men continued to work with the flax and to split fence rails, to pack flour from Grandin, to thresh fifty-one bushels of wheat, to place lime on the potato ground (probably not a large area, as workers spent only a half a day on the chore), and to begin to cultivate the kitchen garden. By the beginning of March, they were cutting wood and hauling limestone, later to be converted to lime for field fertilizer. They continued to prepare flax, shod horses, and killed another ox. Parker continued to sell small amounts of wheat and corn to neighbors. On March 6, one man was "making rails round the raspberries"; peach trees also grew in the garden.

Work on the flax continued into March. In one day, Parker recorded, one of his men cleaned 212 pounds; on the next, he cleaned 312. Other workers swingling the flax were producing 22 to 25 pounds per day. By mid-March, workers were cutting wood, preparing the kiln to burn lime, and threshing rye and wheat. They were using horses for the latter job, which suggests that much wheat remained to be threshed; perhaps some of this wheat had been rent in kind paid to Parker. On March 17, Parker wrote, one of his bull calves died in the woods, which suggests that even affluent farmers ran stock in the woodlands. During the rest of the month, his men kept at the jobs of threshing wheat and swingling flax. They also helped the lime burner Parker hired and began by the end of the month to bring up hay that had been stored in the meadow. Parker sent a neighbor some turnips, carrots, and parsnips, one of his men continued "railing in raspberries," and another spent part of a day "sporting at pidgeons."

Procuring limestone and buying lime continued into the beginning of April, when workers transplanted Parker's grafted apple trees to the orchard and began to plow for flax in the "potato ground." On April 10, they began to prepare the cornfield. Parker sent his "large spotted sow" off to market in return for two hundred pounds of smoked meat, and on April 11 he noted that "a waggon came with shad of which I bought for myself 10" and another ten for his fellow proprietor John Rutherfurd; five days later a neighbor brought him another fifty of the fish.

Amid more routine activities, Parker set out thirteen white mulberry trees next to his English walnut trees to provide a "back avenue" on April 13. He hired another farm worker as he began to harrow and sow flax the next day; he spent several days planting, which suggests that he grew a considerable amount.

His men began to plant potatoes on April 17 in the garden and then to clear brush from "new ground" on which he intended to sow oats. Even as a severe frost the next day damaged his fruit trees, Parker hired two more new workers; by April 26, he had eight men in his employ, five at work sowing oats, harrowing, and putting up staked rail fences, one beginning to plow for corn, one working in the kitchen garden, and one sent to retrieve Parker's son away at school. At the end of April, the men had sown twenty-five bushels of oats. They plowed and hauled burnt lime to the cornfield, sowed more flax and harrowed it, "sprouted" (perhaps weeded) the oat ground, and threshed last year's oats.

In May, Parker's men emptied the lime kiln and slacked the contents, and two men took twelve young cattle to pasture on, apparently, a tenant's land. Parker had his eighteen ram lambs castrated, and his men began to plant corn on May 17. Through May 24, the men spread lime, plowed, built and mended fence, replanted seed washed away by the rain, and cut up two heaps of potatoes for seed. Parker again sent 482 pounds of "ruff" flax to a man to swingle on fifths, and on May 24 four of his men washed his flock of sheep and sheared sixty-three of them the next day.

In May 1778, when Parker began his Shipley diary, he was receiving rents for tenanted land in Peapack, Somerset County, and in Sussex County. His men planted forty bushels of potatoes on three and a half acres; Parker probably never planted a larger crop in later years. In early June, the workers began to plow a field for buckwheat and to plant pumpkins on land that had earlier received a great deal of dung. Parker's plans to plow weeds out of his cornfield were thwarted by wet ground, so some of his men were "grubbing"—removing roots, stones, and other material—from newly cleared land he proposed to use for buckwheat. On June 9, he killed a wether for his own use. Like farmers elsewhere, Parker slaughtered sheep whenever he wanted fresh meat, but cattle and hogs were customarily slaughtered in the fall and put up for later use.

While most of his men plowed the buckwheat ground, cleaned the cow house, and did other work in mid-June, Parker sent one hand down to New Brunswick with his wagon "for Clams or oysters"; the man returned the same night with one hundred clams, which indicates that the road between the farm and the town was quite good. Parker also negotiated fees and duties with his lime burner, planted more pumpkins, began to harrow the corn, and rounded up two stray sheep. Later that same month, his men harrowed and dressed the corn with hoes, and then they began to sharpen their scythes for the beginning of the mowing season. Also in June, Parker watched the surveyors of the highways plot a new road right-of-way to "the Corner of my new cornfield." This must have pleased him, because roads that ran along property lines improved a farmer's ability to carry farm products to buyers.

In general, as farmers to the south spent a great deal of effort maintaining and improving their banked meadows, pasture land appears to have been in short supply on Shipley. On June 23, Parker failed to secure "Pasture for fatting cattle"; perhaps he used his better cleared lands for such cash crops as wheat, rye, flax, and corn. Two men thatched the cow house at about this time, and on the next day Parker noted that "Bees swarmed took a Hive large." Then, on June 25, mowing began and absorbed much of the next two weeks. Hands carted some hay to the horse stable, some to the barn, and some to the cow house; they stacked still more. Parker's hay crop was apparently large, probably because his meadow was irrigated.

On July 10 the rye harvest began as mowing continued apace; the buckwheat ground was also harrowed. Some men then cradled the rye and raked and sheaved it, while others planted the potato ground and mowed; by July 13, when the last of the hay had been removed from the meadow, Parker had harvested forty-nine loads and as many tons. Seventeen loads of the best hay had been placed in the barn, twelve "very good" loads went to the cow house, three were stored in a barrack (an open structure with a moveable roof used to store hay and grain), and seventeen were left in stacks. On July 15, the wheat harvest began to occupy almost all of the work force on Shipley, as well as additional local hands hired by the day. Ground was also plowed for buckwheat, sown on July 16. The first wheat harvest was over three days after it began, and on July 18 Parker dismissed the day laborers. Later in July, men cut clover for seed in the orchard, carted dung to the heap by the barn, planted cabbages, plowed the buckwheat ground, cultivated pumpkins, and began to pull the flax crop.

For the flax, Parker used two of his own men, two local boys, two local white women, and a black woman and her son, who were most likely slaves. Tax records suggest that the white laborers were the sons, brothers, wives, or daughters of local householders who did not have viable farms; apparently, neighbors with paying farms were using all their relatives on their own properties at this time of year. Later in the month, Parker hired four more local men and three women, again apparently landless people, to pull the flax. On the day they were hired, they pulled flax until dinner time, by which time they had harvested all of the flax in the orchard—$2^3/4$ acres. But Parker's men clearly had not finished getting in his large crop. On July 25, he recorded that "a Number of the Neighbours that I had invited to the frolick came & pulled and finished the whole by night." He offered two of the men who helped, both householders, an acre of flax, probably on half-shares.

When the workers were not harvesting flax, they were put "into New wheat" and continued mowing, dressing pumpkins, raking cut clover, working in the garden, harrowing the corn crop, coopering, and carting poles for barrel hoops from newly cleared land. At the end of July, the oat harvest began and continued into early August. They worked continually to prepare and fence new ground. Parker made a point of noting that his workers girdled the trees instead of cutting them down immediately; just as he let his livestock run in the woods, he also took the expedient course of girdling. His men threshed the flax and prepared it to ret, sowed turnips, and threshed wheat and rye; rye straw was used as thatch on the barrack. On August 7 Parker bought a sow and seven pigs.

By August 21, 3,863 sheaves of oats had been harvested, or a little more than 515 bushels. Parker had a calf slaughtered, and for more than two days four men continued to dung four acres of fields; they plowed the dung in as they spread it, he wrote, so that none of the "strength of it is evaporated and I expect great produce from it." They also laid lime down in heaps on the fallow ground and spread it by throwing it in shovelfuls. By September 5, the men were threshing seed wheat, and by September 8 they began to sow $42^1/2$ bushels of it. Meanwhile, Parker sold more wheat to neighbors at this time, so the men must have been harvesting the grain as well. Limited by his poor "fatting pasture," Parker sent two oxen and two cows to fatten on another farm; he also killed two of his seventy-one sheep for his own use. Through September, men continued to plow and to top corn and put the tops up for winter fodder. They also threshed the rye for seed and plowed the former oat and flax fields to plant rye. The men threshed and dressed the flax and mowed the second growth of grass.

In October, as mowing continued, the men threshed oats and rye and cleaned flax seed. They also began to cross-plow stony ground, shifted wheat into a barrack, harrowed, cut the buckwheat (by October 28, 243 bushels had been threshed), and planted twenty-seven acres of rye, which took four days. On October 13, the apple harvest began, and workers started carrying apples to a cider mill, where they were turned into five barrels of "good Cyder" and two and a half barrels of "water Cyder." Apples were thus a minor product at Shipley. By October 20 five wagon-loads of "small and not ripe" pumpkins had been harvested; Parker thought they "were hurt in the last Harrowing which was after the vines began to run and they were unavoidably much bruised in that operation."

At the beginning of November Parker began to let some of his workers go. By this time of year, most of them worked at odd jobs around Shipley, digging potatoes and gathering in corn and turnips. The potato harvest amounted to 294 bushels. Parker's yield in "good corn" was about the same as of "hog corn" that year, he noted; by December 4, the workers had harvested 270 bushels of "white corn in the Ear" and 262 of the "yellow." Parker calculated that two bushels of ears made one of shelled corn. The turnip harvest totaled sixty bushels.

Early in December Parker went to New Brunswick, Raritan Landing, and Perth Amboy on business. In New Brunswick, he traded raw hides for leather with tanner Henry Guest. Despite his obvious affluence, Parker bartered as often as he could. He paid Philip Grandin with seed potatoes for a hogshead of sweet apple cider, for example, but his Shipley diary was written in wartime, when paper money was rapidly depreciating. Troops passing through the area kept his workers from doing very much while Parker was away; Parker must have instructed them to guard against thievery on the part of the troops, for he wrote on December 10, "my three blacks taking care and looking about them for there is little to be done when any troops here." That month, one of Parker's tenants brought him two "small Hogs they weighd 88 & 84 lb" as part of his rent. His work force of five kept busy in the cow house, probably removing dung, which they also undertook to do in the sheep yard in the middle of December. They gathered more turnips, killed eight hogs weighing between 164 and 222 pounds, butchered them, and salted the pork. From December 18 to 26, Parker was away from the farm, and when he returned he wrote that the work his men had ostensibly done "made little appearance. . . . While the cat's away. . ." On his travels, he mentioned that one of his Sussex County tenants paid more than half of his £25 rent by wintering and caring for some of Parker's cattle.

James Parker had an extremely large holding of land, even for that period, and he employed a large labor force. His diary indicates that he engaged in mixed farming, raising both livestock and grains. Wheat seems to have been especially important, not only for Parker but for his tenants to the north in Sussex County. Corn was also important, as was flax; both crops required much labor. But meadowland was evidently scarce, so Parker ran some livestock in the woods and devoted a great deal of attention to hay.

The ledger book of Edward F. Randolph, a farmer in Warren Township (9), provides some idea of seasonal activities in northern Somerset County at a later time, between about 1790 and 1804.[15] In 1807, Randolph owned two farms, one 162 acres and the other 140 acres. These were relatively large parcels for the township, where holdings of thirty to fifty acres were far more common. Although his ledgers indicate that he carried on a substantial trade with his neighbors, Randolph was not listed as a merchant. But he was taxed for a wagon, relatively rare in that area.

Randolph's ledger is generally mute about his activity during the winter, though it does occasionally note that he hauled cordwood in February, probably from the rocky slopes of the Watchung Mountains. Early in March he received hives of bees, heifers, veal, mutton, and apple trees from neighbors; by the end of that month and in early April shad began to appear in his record. The book's frequent mentions of veal suggest that dairying was a major enterprise in the area. In May Randolph plowed and carted corn to Perth Amboy; in June he mowed hay and washed sheep. In July he credited one neighbor for hoeing his potatoes and "halling in wheat" and another for supplying him with one hundred clams. Also in July, he mowed again and began to pull flax; he also credited neighbors for lamb.

Randolph harvested his rye early in August and began to make cider at the end of that month. He credited neighbors for veal, lamb, and a pig. After the middle of September he began to top his corn and husk it; then, in the third week, he harvested his buckwheat. Early in October Randolph dug potatoes, slaughtered hogs, and credited a man for a dozen bluefish. He threshed buckwheat throughout the month; judging from the number of ledger entries, it was an important crop. In November Randolph continued to husk corn and haul corn tops, work on flax, kill hogs, and haul cordwood. His year closed with slaughtering hogs (one of 287 pounds and one of 238 pounds), bringing in turnips, corn, and buckwheat, and working "over the mountains."

The records of the Scudder family—miscellaneous notes kept in the margins of almanacs—document seasonal activity in the New England-settled section of northeastern New Jersey. The Scudders came from Huntington, Long Island, also settled by New Englanders, to Rahway in Elizabeth Township, Essex County, in 1740. Benjamin Scudder, to whom the earlier notations are attributed, was born on Long Island in 1732 and erected a mill and a house on the east branch of the Rahway River on the border between Springfield and Connecticut Farms (10), divisions of Elizabeth Township, before 1761. He later built a sawmill and a distillery in the same area.[16] The tax list for the Springfield portion of Elizabeth Township in 1779 lists a Benjamin Scudder as owning a mill, one hundred acres listed at £20 (about the mean for the township), four horses, and eight cattle. In the New England-settled section, these holdings were well above the average.

The Scudders' marginal notes span from 1780 to 1813, but they are most abundant in the 1790s and early 1800s. The January activities of the Scudders involved mostly carting hay cut earlier from the salt meadows to their farm. They also drew cordwood from a local swamp and cleaned wheat. In February, they continued to bring in hay from the meadows and began to carry cordwood from "the mountains," probably the Watchungs, which lay at some distance; that they traveled so far for wood probably signifies how deforested this part of the Piedmont was. In February of one year, Scudder hired a man and his slave to thresh rye in his barn in exchange for every twentieth bushel.

In March, the Scudders slaughtered an ox one year and sold part of the meat to neighbors. They also made cider, an unusual activity in late winter; they probably used apples they had stored. On March 11, 1813, Scudder noted that two men "Drawd at my fishing place below the house near 500 suckers at one haul." Suckers were not often mentioned in other accounts, and it may be that then, as now, they were regarded as something of a trash species; their deliberate netting may indicate the relative poverty of at least some in this region.

Notations became more plentiful in April, when the Scudders began to plant flax seed and to distribute some of it to neighbors in return for double the amount each borrowed. Scudder also lent neighbors buckwheat seed. In April, too, he planted timothy and clover "on the Sandy ridge west of the mill." And when the shad runs began around the middle of the month, Scudder and others devoted several days to netting the fish. In April 1780, Scudder recorded, "Mr. Thief" stole his seven-week-old pigs and sixty pounds of meat out of his smokehouse, a symptom of the dislocation the Revolution caused in this part of New Jersey. In later years, Scudder bought shoats in April to fatten. One April, he drove six "creatures" (cattle) out of the barn to pasture at Canoe Brook, which may indicate either that he had little or no pasture land on his property or that, in the New England fashion of land distribution, he owned a separate parcel of pasture land.

In May, the Scudders began to plant potatoes and broom corn and turned out more stock on local meadows. They sheared sheep: in 1810, twenty-four sheep were shorn, but in 1806 Scudder did not wash the sheep until near the end of the month and did not shear them until early June. In the second week of May, he lent seed oats to neighbors. The long winters put the apple trees, which came into bloom in May, at risk; in several years killing frosts damaged some trees. In one May, Scudder attempted to breed his mare to Moses Austin's horse for £0.30.0; in another, he paid five dollars to take the animal to Nathan Squire's stud twice, with no success; and in still another May he paid £20.0.0 in stud fees to Samuel Richards. In early June 1800 he tried to breed the mare with Joseph Denman's stud and paid five dollars in fees; he was unsuccessful again, and it seems likely that the mare was infertile.

By the end of May, the Scudders generally were able to begin to plant corn. One May, they sponsored a "stone frolic" to get neighbors' help in removing the abundant erratics and glacial till from the fields. They also hived bees this month. Early in June, Scudder moved his sheep into land in the Watchungs and began to cut posts and rails for fencing, some at "ye mountain." He also spent part of the first two weeks of June working on the roads. One June, Scudder's sons went clamming, and in the latter part of the month the family began to hoe corn. Scudder's hoe was stolen on June 15, 1782, by three locals "with the help of a dog," another indication of the desperate circumstances of at least some people in the vicinity.

In the beginning of July, the corn was plowed, and neighbors often borrowed buckwheat for planting. On July 4, 1814, Scudder remarked that the day's celebration interfered with needed chores. "At Springfield I Heard that Ben Scudder Junr & Enoch Scudder got warm or Stue Eyed & Tuesday they Did no work but Set and Drinked at my house," he wrote. "I had to hire David Crane . . . for about one hours work to help carry Hay in the Barn that Sd Ben Scudder had Cut." Scudder also drove more stock to pasture at Orange in the Watchungs. By mid-July, they were harvesting rye, wheat, and oats, and by the end of the month they began to pull flax. At frolics, such as the one Mrs. Tomkins held in 1810, they helped neighbors with their flax crops.

In August, the Scudders were occupied largely with mowing, mostly on the salt meadows in Newark and Rahway. They also brought some hay in from the Watchungs. Scudder moved his cattle in from Orange and Canoe Brook. He cut timothy for seed and continued to mow and cut wood; the family also made cider again at the end of August. In early September Scudder began to plow for his winter wheat and rye, which he sowed generally in the third week of the month. At about the same time he moved some of his stock back to the Watchungs; perhaps the cooler weather had revived the pasturage there. The Scudders picked apples, made cider, and clammed, sometimes as far away as Long Island. In 1789, one man provided Scudder with eight hundred clams, for which he paid a shilling per hundred.

In October, the Scudders began to concentrate on the apple crop in earnest, picking, making cider, and distilling the cider. Local children and wives joined in the picking, so the crop was probably substantial. Scudder sowed some winter grain at the beginning of the month and brought the stock home from the Watchungs. He dug potatoes early in the month and began to bring in the corn crop toward the end. The apple harvest and cider making continued into November, but the Scudders' focus turned this month to wood. Many notes document wood cutting and frolics. Because Scudder ran a sawmill, he was especially busy during this time, when the streams remained ice-free.

Like many other New Jersey farmers, Scudder slaughtered hogs in December, and he brought more cattle back from the Watchungs. The family drew hay off the salt meadows and continued to cut wood and make cider. Scudder kept at work in his sawmill. But the winter weather was severe, making outdoor work sometimes hazardous: on December 21, 1798, one almanac note reads, "att night Isaac Scudder froze his feet in Newark meadow."

Despite Scudder's above-average landholdings in this northern area, he still had to go relatively far afield for many of his agricultural activities, such as pasturing stock, gathering wood, and haying. Just as the banked meadows were critical to southwestern New Jersey farmers, salt hay was of great importance to Scudder. Scudder grew wheat, but his almanacs contain more references to corn and flax. He probably fed corn to his cattle, hogs, and sheep. Apples and cider assumed great significance in this regional economy, which also seems to have been relatively poor: the Scudders, more affluent than most, frequently lent seed to other farmers in the area, and frolics appear to have been a common way of amassing labor enough to do large jobs at minimal expense.

Like the Scudders, the Camp family in this New England-settled region ran a sawmill and undertook various tasks for their neighbors. They also had a store in Newark Township (11), a bit north of the Scudder farm, and their record books date from a period extant tax lists do not cover—the mid-1750s to the mid-1760s.[17]

In January the Camps usually carted salt hay from the Newark Meadow for people who owned parcels there but who apparently did not own wagons or sleds, the latter commonly used to transport heavy materials while snow was on the ground. The Camps also cut and transported wood for people such as Mary Wheeler, who must have been a widow. They spent much of February on these tasks, as well as on "fanning" wheat—removing or cleaning the chaff from the grain.

Early in March, the Camps pruned their apple trees and then transplanted them later in the month and during the first two weeks of April. In March and April, they also made and repaired fences. Here, the Camps made both the traditional New England post-and-rail fence and fences of stone, from glacial till and erratics. In the third week of April, they began to plow with oxen and to harrow, and early in May they started to plant corn. Hoeing and other work on the cornfields continued through June and into July, as did work on fencing: one local farmer was credited for damages the Camps' pigs had caused on his property. By the end of the month, mowing became a primary activity, and some plowing, though of what is not stated, also took place.

Early in July, the Camps were mowing both fresh and salt hay. Wheat began to be cradled toward the end of the month, but the account books made no reference to rye. At the beginning of August oats began to be harvested. Mowing and plowing continued through August into early September, when cider making began. Making cider seemed to dominate this month and October, though, apparently, seed wheat was planted, mowing continued apace, and the family began to thresh and clean the first crop of wheat. By mid-October, the Camps began to take in the corn crop and to thresh buckwheat; they also brought in pumpkins.

Picking apples and cider making also dominated November. The rest of the corn crop was brought in, wheat was threshed, wood was cut and carted, fences were repaired, and butchering began at the end of the month. The year ended with cider making, butchering, cutting cordwood, carting in hay from the meadows, removing stones from the fields, and taking up flax.

The Camp records testify to the importance of cider in the economy, and they make clear that many residents of this area could not afford to own carts and wagons because they had to hire others, including the Camps, to cart hay in from scattered meadows. The Camps also plowed for people who must not have had oxen, horses, or a plow. For the Camps, corn was the most important grain crop; wheat and buckwheat were also grown, but rye evidently was not. Livestock were not often mentioned, though it is likely that the hay and much of the corn were probably grown for these animals.

The ledger book of Onesimus Whitehead, covering from 1790 to 1814, probably reflects the activity of a more ordinary farmer in this New England-settled section (12).[18] In 1787 Whitehead owned seventy acres, three horses, and four cattle; by 1794 he had acquired seven more acres and four more cattle, but he no longer had horses. Whitehead also appears to have been a butcher. Like the Camps and the Scudders, Whitehead provided services for people in his area and recorded them with some care, so it is possible to develop some understanding of the common activities in the area.

In January, Whitehead cleaned rye and oats and butchered hogs; in February he drew wood out of a swamp, perhaps the Great Swamp, although in March he specifically mentioned Ford's Swamp. In April and May he built and mended fences. Throughout May he gathered bark, probably also from a swamp, and at the end of the month he sheared sheep and covered his corn, though he did not record planting it. In June he hoed his cornfield, and in July he sowed buckwheat, drew hay, and helped reap oats. He may have helped to mow hay for neighbors in August and certainly did so in September. In September and October he cleaned his rye; in October and November he butchered beef and hogs. He cradled buckwheat and harrowed rye in October and threshed and cleaned his buckwheat in November, when he also carted cordwood from a swamp. Butchering also dominated December. Whitehead recorded cleaning rye and wheat in that month, though he mentioned wheat far less often than other grains. He spent one December day at a "coal pit," where charcoal was probably being produced for the local iron industry.

Stephen Brant kept an even sparser record, a slim ledger noting many of the seasonal employments for people between 1773 and 1794 in Hanover Township,

Morris County (13).[19] Brant appears to have been worked largely as a carpenter, but he also did agricultural day labor. In 1778 he possessed only forty acres, two horses, three cattle, and one hog, but he used some of his livestock to haul hay and goods at a fee for other farmers. Ten years later he had increased his holdings to sixty acres, of which fifteen were unimproved, two horses, and eight cattle.

In January, Brant cut timber, drew logs, and made a "slead"; he also sledded hay to Newark one January for £0.10.6, which suggests that demand for hay was great there at the time. In January 1791 he recorded drawing hay with "4 Creatures Below" and charging 0.10.0; the prices he could command suggest that Brant was moving the hay over fairly long distances. His regular fee for house carpentry in January appears to have been only 0.5.0 per day. He also recorded cleaning hemp in January and threshing oats.

In February Brant drew hay from the meadow for 0.3.6 per day and sledded an unidentified product to Newark for 0.10.0. He made sleds and did other wood-working jobs, and on his farm he threshed rye and worked on flax. Brant was also supplying veal, corn, and hemp seed to his neighbors. In March he continued to cut and draw wood, work on flax, and provide other farmers corn, flax seed, rye, and hemp seed. In April he mended fences, drew dung, plowed, and sold hay.

In May and June, though he continued to hire himself and his team out for plow-ing, Brant worked mostly at building houses and barns. For July Brant recorded only the days he spent mowing and plowing for others. In August he mended a wagon; in September he hauled apples to the cider mill, dug ditches, and did some butchering. In October, Brant built a hog pen, cut and drew fence rails, mowed, gathered and husked corn, threshed flax, and cut buckwheat. He worked at a cider mill for 0.5.0 a day, probably doing carpentry. He continued to draw rails in November, to work at threshing and to bring in corn and corn stalks; he also began to turn and dress flax. He sold beef and pork, built and fixed stables, and "weighed" hemp. In December Brant continued to sell small quantities of beef, butchered hogs, carted wood, rented out his wagon, threshed, worked at "brakeing hemp," and dressed flax. Over several December days, he carried dung to the orchard.

As in the accounts kept by others in northeastern New Jersey, Brant did not mention wheat. He appeared to spend more time carting wood and digging ditches, which suggests that most of the swamps were still forested; at the same time in the Piedmont much of the land was cleared. Brant's frequent references to hemp indi-cate the prevalence of this crop in the glaciated section; the only other references to hemp were in the accounts kept by the Fithians in Cumberland County.

The ledger of Jesse Knowles of Knowleton Township, Sussex County (14), cov-ered the years from 1808 to 1822.[20] Knowles ran a store and also farmed in this northwestern section, but because no tax lists survive from this period his precise holdings are not known. However, Knowles was able to hire laborers to do agri-cultural work for him; he recorded people working at dressing flax (apparently the most significant activity) and processing oats and corn in January.

In February, people in his area spent much time drawing and threshing rye, but again dressing flax took up most of their time. They also cut wood "at the moun-tain." In March Knowles's customers cut wood and made fences for him. Clover seed was being planted at the same time, and Knowles bought shoats to fatten. As in February, farmers devoted some time in March and April to threshing rye, and some trapping still took place in this region: in 1813 one customer brought Knowles a muskrat skin worth as much as the prevailing daily wage.

The beginning of April was devoted to making post-and-rail, worm, and stone wall fences. In the third week, his workers began to harrow oats and flax and to place plaster on the fields. Corn was planted in the third week of May. Fence building continued through May and June, and Knowles recorded his work on the roads. But June's most important activity was mowing; Knowles mentioned clover several times. He also recorded one and a half days' work in a tobacco patch in 1822; Restore Lippincott had recorded planting tobacco in June a quarter century earlier in Gloucester County.

Like other farmers, Knowles needed to hire more labor in July than in other months. Mowing, especially of clover, continued early in the month, but in the second week the rye harvest began. Depending on the length of the growing season from year to year, harvesting winter grains probably continued through the end of the month. In the third and fourth weeks Knowles mentioned pulling flax, hoeing potatoes, harvesting oats, and mowing; mowing and cutting and threshing oats continued into August. By midmonth flax was being threshed and dung drawn out to the fields. In the third week buckwheat began to be cradled. At the end of August and into September Knowles's laborers were busy picking the abundant stones from the fields. In September they also mowed clover, hauled dung, and threshed rye; by midmonth the apple harvest began.

The first part of October was devoted to husking corn and the latter part to harvesting buckwheat and picking apples. In November, the hired day labor continued harvesting buckwheat and hauling and husking corn; they also turned to threshing rye and slaughtering hogs. In December, slaughtering, husking corn, and dressing flax appeared to occupy most of his workers' time. Knowles's accounts attest, as do those of other north Jersey farmers, the paramount importance of rye over wheat among the winter grains into the nineteenth century. Growing hay and corn for livestock stock was also important.

Certainly, differences in physical circumstances, the duration of settlement, farm size, land distribution, and cultural background affected both land use and regional economies. Generally, though, the seasonal round on the well-settled and better soils in New Jersey during the latter part of the eighteenth century is well reflected in a series of illustrations that appeared in one unidentified early nineteenth-century publication (see chapter heads).[21]

In January and February, the weather kept most farmers at indoor tasks such as threshing, preparing flax, and slaughtering or butchering livestock. Depending too on the weather, stock were usually kept indoors; despite Kalm's statements about the prevalence of running livestock outdoors in the winter in southwestern New Jersey, these account books, generally kept by farmers perhaps more affluent than the ones Kalm talked to, suggest that not many farmers did so later in the century. Some outdoor work, such as cutting wood and hauling hay, was possible and necessary in January and February even in the coldest sections. And in more temperate areas, farmers also began to mend and build fences, a perennial and continuous chore, and even as far north as Hunterdon County some sowed clover and limed land.

March combined indoor and outdoor work. In the southwest cattle could be pastured outdoors early in the month; plowing could begin, and both timothy and peas could be planted. Apple trees were transplanted and pruned at this time in almost every place where they were grown. In southern Hunterdon County, it was possible to sow grass seed and flax by the end of March.

By April farmers all over the state were outdoors nearly all the time, plowing, planting oats and flax, banking marshes; in South Jersey they could plant corn, turnips, and potatoes in April, while farmers elsewhere could not plant these crops until May. North Jersey farmers such as Benjamin Scudder planted buckwheat, timothy, and clover in April, however, and everyone near waters in which the shad ran fished for or bought them during this month.

In May, planting corn occupied almost every farmer, and those who kept sheep usually sheared them during this month. In South Jersey, mowing could begin in May, and farmers in the north could plant potatoes. In June, farmers spent a great deal of time cultivating, usually harrowing and hoeing corn, and mowing was universally pursued during this month. Harvest season began toward the end of the month, often beginning in South Jersey with rye.

July was taken up with the various harvests, generally two weeks later in the north, and demanded the greatest amount of additional labor. After rye came the wheat and then the oat harvest. Farmers also continued mowing and began to pull flax, sometimes before the winter grain harvests. Some farmers in the north planted buckwheat while wheat was being harvested, and they cultivated kitchen gardens and other crops.

In August mowing was universal, and in the south farmers began to plow for their winter grain crops; they sowed rye and then wheat by the end of the month. The oat harvest continued into August in many places, and the rapidly growing buckwheat was also harvested on some farms. Lippincott and Parker, much farther north, also planted turnips in August. In September farmers all over the state continued to plow for and plant winter grains and began to harvest corn and, in some places, buckwheat. Mowing continued everywhere. In Essex County, apples and cider making began to command a great deal of attention in September and through much of October, as did the corn harvest.

And as the harvest season began to pass in South Jersey in October, farmers began to sell livestock. Slaughtering began. By November, most New Jersey farmers had retreated indoors for the most part, though they continued to bring in the corn and buckwheat harvests, to plant rye, and to dig potatoes and turnips until the ground froze. Additional workers were let go in November, if not earlier. The livestock were brought indoors, and farmers continued slaughtering, butchering, and putting up meats; they threshed and broke and dressed flax.

Evidence of the seasonal pace of agricultural life and how it changed regionally and over time is too scant to do more than tentatively suggest other conclusions. The emphasis on wheat, for example, seems to have declined while corn and rye grew more important. The number of cattle may also have increased. Other accounts hint at but do not discuss deforestation in such areas as the Piedmont and the relative abundance of unimproved land in Gloucester County. And there are many suggestions of poverty. Large landholders employed landless men and their families largely on a seasonal or daily basis. One wonders what their off-season lives were like. Many other workers did agricultural labor on "shares"; still other small farmers in New England-settled places borrowed seed and paid it back with interest. The evidence of massive tenancy is abundant, and in all places farmers continued to exploit the woodlands, animal populations, and other features of the environment to supplement their income from agriculture.

★ ★ ★ ★ ★ ★ ★

Broadly speaking, this study has examined three major influences on land use patterns in New Jersey up to about 1820—the effects of the physical environment, those generated by cultural diversity and settlement history (including different perceptions of the environment by disparate cultural groups), and whether distance from markets affected the ways in which land was used. Other factors—length of settlement, density of population, motivations toward wise or strictly exploitative use, and such external factors as wars—have also been assessed for their effects on land use.

First, physical variations clearly affected how land was used. The poor soils of the Outer Coastal Plain largely remained the domain of those involved in an extractive economy, whether it was hunting, fishing, or lumbering. Cattle were also run in the woods. On poorer soils elsewhere or in poorly drained places, exploitation of the natural environment for hunting and gathering continued, especially on a seasonal basis. Everywhere, local streams and rivers were fished, especially for shad in the spring, to provide a source of protein.

On the better soils, hunting and lumbering gave way in most places to permanent agricultural clearance, although a need for firewood and lumber encouraged the preservation of some wooded land on farms or the acquisition of wood lots on poorer land close by. In the Raritan Valley especially, trees such as the white oak essentially paid the cost of clearance for permanent agricultural use.

New Jersey's climate allowed the production of northwestern European crops and the raising of European livestock. Yet the longer, warmer, American summer allowed as well the maturation of an important New World crop, maize or Indian corn, which yielded heavily and could be fed to livestock. The longer growing season and relatively mild winter of southwestern New Jersey encouraged farmers to turn out their stock early, and even in many places to vouchsafe completely bringing them inside during the winter.

Early on, local farmers attempted to "improve" the natural environment for agricultural purposes (to the detriment of native plants and animals) by cooperating in drainage projects and, in the southwest, by diking and draining meadows along the Delaware and its tributaries. Farmers used these low, drained places largely to produce hay to carry horses, cattle, and sheep through the cold months. Especially in the northwest, streams and springs were diverted to irrigate low meadowland, also for hay production. Soil was altered as well. Manure was used widely, especially near agglomerated settlements where it was most abundant. Marl was used by about the mid-eighteenth century in Burlington County, and lime was burned before the Revolution in the northwest.

The fact that distinct cultural groups settled in distinct regions also clearly affected how New Jersey land was used. Those places settled first were readily accessible to transportation by water and were also on the better soils. All cultural groups demonstrated a commercial motive toward the land, to use it for agriculture and in other ways that would yield a profit. The Swedes and Finns in the southwest used the woodlands for lumber, for hunting wildlife, or for running hogs (which they also hunted when needed). They began moving from the west bank of the Delaware to establish permanent settlements in New Jersey just a few years before the English Quakers began arriving in the mid-1670s. These Swedes and Finns apparently left no record of their earliest agricultural land use in New Jersey, but by about the middle of the eighteenth century personal narratives and tax data permit some estimation of their activity. Peter Kalm observed that the sandy soils on the east bank of the Delaware were poor for European grain crops such as wheat and rye, but he was amazed that maize grew so well in them. He described the landscape from Gloucester County south as mostly wooded, the population to have been engaged as much in lumbering as in agriculture, and what he judged to be a general lack of good husbandry in regard to livestock, especially sheep.

The data on sheep permit a comparably rare opportunity to gauge directly the response of two different European groups (the Swedes and Finns, later just called "Swedes," and the English) to the same environment. Gloucester County, where most of the Swedes lived, had fewer sheep per unit area in the 1760s than did counties occupied by New Englanders. In 1761 in the Lower Precinct of Cape May on the Outer Coastal Plain, almost all if not all of the names on the tax list are English, many of them emigrants from New England; there were probably no Swedes. Here, there were many sheep both by unit area and by taxable resident. At the same time (1761), there were much fewer sheep by both area and taxable in Maurice River Precinct in Cumberland County, on exactly the same soils as prevailed on the Outer Coastal Plain. Even within Maurice River Precinct, Swedes unquestionably held fewer sheep, both individually and as a group, than non-Swedes living there at the time. Sheep require supervision, and it is likely that the Swedes were much more accustomed to the patterns of lumbering and hunting.

The Quaker perception of the productivity of the local soils may well have been influenced by the earlier Swedish population. Kalm's equation of sandiness with poor soil quality was reiterated within a generation by Samuel Smith, whose Quaker family had pioneered on Burlington County's Inner Coastal Plain. But by 1800 John Witherspoon declared these same soils to be very productive.[22] There is a good chance that the beginning of the "corn belt" economy in Burlington and Gloucester counties—an agricultural economy that revolved around growing corn to use as food for hogs—relied at least in part on the perception among early Swedish settlers that local soils were poor. Availability of labor may also have played a role, as corn demands more care than wheat during its growing season.

English and Irish Quakers had followed closely on the heels of the Swedes in southwestern New Jersey, and, with the establishment of their colony of West New Jersey, they soon dominated the area. The Quakers established a system of large landholdings on the Inner Coastal Plain's excellent soils, worked by a landless white labor force. They were willing and able to invest in such improvements as diking.[23]

But despite the fact that they inhabited a similar environment, the New Englanders in the northeastern part of New Jersey long delayed making such alterations in drainage patterns. These New Englanders entered New Jersey after having spent a generation or more as a cultural group in New England or on Long Island. Unlike the Quakers, they came not as proprietors of a new colony but as groups collectively taking up large tracts under the auspices of the colony of East

New Jersey. They tended to create nucleated settlements more than did others, even such other Englishmen as the Quakers, and their practice of periodic distribution of land in their large "towns" into relatively small landholdings may well have created parcels too small to be economically viable in the mixed agricultural economy of the Revolutionary period. Their principal solution to this problem was to emphasize apple production; the return from apples produced to make cider and applejack per unit area was much higher than they could have realized from raising any other general crop or livestock.

New Englanders in northeastern New Jersey also tended to keep more sheep than did others and often grazed them on the common land (as yet undivided) set aside for the use of the town. Near the coast, the salt and freshwater marshes were divided into small holdings of generally just a few acres, from which hay was made to feed stock through the winter. Perhaps the small size of these plots and the general lack of capital on the part of most people kept New Englanders from diking these lands; perhaps, too, New Englanders perceived marshes in a very different way than did Quakers. New Englanders' culture certainly appeared to be much more traditional and conservative than Quaker culture.

The Dutch, in possession of New Jersey before the coming of the English and settled under the auspices of the English and Scot proprietors, also demonstrated distinct attitudes toward and uses of the land. Opposite Manhattan the Dutch farms were relatively small, while landholdings much above the mean for the entire colony of New Jersey were the rule in the fertile Raritan Valley. Long after others had subdivided their lands, the Dutch held on to fairly large farms, especially in this region. The evidence suggests clearly that the Dutch were focused in somewhat greater degree than other cultural groups on dairying and that larger landowners relied more heavily on slave labor. As a group, the Dutch appear to have been quite successful economically, and a keen instinct for profit may explain their tendency to concentrate on commercial agricultural production. Their land use is best explained by the location of their farms with respect to the market. Other cultural groups also show distinct differences in land use. By the mid-eighteenth century, for example, the Scots and Scots-Irish in the Raritan Valley may have engaged in a large production of flax, both for linen and seed.

The labor of African Americans, most of whom were slaves and most of whom were owned by the Dutch, probably added to Dutch prosperity. Free blacks were paid less than whites, and it would have been difficult for them to have acquired a farm. And in the northwest, settled relatively late by a mixture of groups (primarily people from East New Jersey but also Pennsylvanians of German and Scots-Irish origin), residents tended to be tenants of large landholders, and their leases determined how they would use land: most leases required tenants to preserve woodland, to clear only part of their leasehold for agriculture, and to establish meadows for hay and apple orchards. In general, they were to pay their rent in wheat, the major commercial crop in the middle colonies.

From the first days of settlement, commercial production of agricultural goods was the goal of many if not most farmers.[24] Within the first decade of settlement, agricultural products were being exported either directly abroad or through the rising ports of Philadelphia and New York. "Subsistence" was of course a major factor in new settlements, but the requirement to pay taxes and the need and desire for goods that could not be produced locally had to be met by the production of a surplus to be sold. Given this motivation, land use in New Jersey might have varied as von Thünen's model suggested—by the distance of farms from the market center and the cost of transportation to that market.

But, like southeastern Pennsylvania, New Jersey had not one but two major market centers. And, rather than being isolated centers, as von Thünen's model had assumed, these markets were also entrepôts, shipping goods abroad. Thus, as James Lemon found in testing von Thünen's model in southeastern Pennsylvania, the market system in New Jersey was not closed.[25] Yet Philadelphia and New York had no serious rivals; New Jersey towns, unlike those in southeastern Pennsylvania, remained very small until the nineteenth century, and no large county towns provided competing local markets. In this respect, New Jersey's situation mirrors the von Thünen model more closely.

With Philadelphia and New York as its market centers, all of New Jersey fit within the first three rings von Thünen's model postulated. Transportation by water was even more important in New Jersey than in Pennsylvania, a fact that forces another modification of the model. Von Thünen had assumed that transportation to market would be overland. But the use of boats as well as wagons in both New Jersey and Pennsylvania would in effect expand these rings outward where water transportation was readily available, because water transport was less expensive than land. Finally, within a very few miles of the Philadelphia market, New Jersey's Outer Coastal Plain introduced a most important variable—generally very poor soils.

Still, evidence for the existence of an innermost ring—an area of intensive use emphasizing the production of fluid milk and garden truck (including fresh fruit), the fattening of livestock, and growing hay for local use—appears to be much better in New Jersey than in Pennsylvania, where tax records did not list milch cattle separately or indicate truck crop production. Certainly, more cattle were to be found per unit area near the two major market centers than elsewhere, especially as the eighteenth century progresssed. Fattening of cattle took place there or close by, especially when transportation by water is taken into account: witness the banked marshes in such places as Salem County. If Crèvecoeur's statements were accurate, such land use was also prevalent near New York. New Jersey's "corn belt," where hogs were fattened, butchered, and smoked to produce the "Burlington pork" so desired in the West Indies, was within the first ring and close to Philadelphia, again taking into account the ready access by water.

According to the tax lists, the incidence of improved land appears to have been very high on good soils near the market. Truck crops were certainly produced in the first ring or near navigable water offering quick transport to market; such land use became increasingly important as the demand for produce rose with the burgeoning populations of New York and Philadelphia. Eggs, logical for the first ring because they were so perishable, appear to have been a specialty of some farmers in northern Monmouth County, a short sail to New York, by 1750.

But tax data do not permit an assessment of fluid milk production in New Jersey. Dairying was widespread and generally oriented to the two cities, but the "milch cattle" listed in the Revolutionary War damage claims could just as well have been used for butter and cheese production as for milk. In any case, skim milk was widely used to feed the ubiquitous hogs. In New Jersey as in Pennsylvania, butter and cheese were produced much nearer to the market, not fully ninety miles away as von Thünen's had suggested based on his German example. Yet the model does fit the production of hay, which was probably significant within the first ring because of the cost involved in transporting it and the need to fatten animals locally on it. John Stevens banked his marshland in Hoboken, immediately opposite New York, and his statement about the local value of his hay suggests that the von Thünen model probably applied in this case.

The second ring of land around the market center, von Thünen hypothesized, was devoted to forestry, and there is abundant evidence of land relatively close to the market in New Jersey being used to produce wood, especially on the fertile Inner Coastal Plain in southern Gloucester County and on the relatively poor soils of northern Monmouth and southern Middlesex counties. Much of Gloucester's wood production was exactly within the second ring. Kalm's statement about the environs of Philadelphia at midcentury supports the notion that people had in mind the value of timbered land close to the market center. And wood could be transported much less expensively from New Jersey to Philadelphia and New York by water than over land. This fact would tend to extend the forestry zone to New Jersey's Outer Coastal Plain, which without question continually supplied the two cities with wood for various uses. Commercial grain production in New Jersey also seems to have followed von Thünen's model, which placed it in the third ring. The third rings from New York and Philadelphia overlap in the Raritan Valley, which was New Jersey's premier commercial wheat-growing area until about the time of the Revolutionary War and the arrival of the Hessian fly.

New Jersey is too small to fall within more than three of von Thünen's theoretical rings, but if time is factored in with distance the further reaches of his model also seem to fit. Von Thünen analyzed an area that had long been settled. In New Jersey, many areas had not been settled even by 1750. Land use in the newly settled areas tended to correspond with uses in the area beyond von Thünen's third ring. Land was used very extensively in these sections; hunting predominated, and cattle and hogs were run largely unsupervised in the woodlands. Such activity, von Thünen held, would occur far from the market center. In New Jersey, such land uses persisted in areas of marginal soils and steep slopes well into the nineteenth century.

Population density, related both to length of settlement and cultural predilections, would also affect how intensively land was used; the arboriculture of New Englanders and their greater devotion to sheep certainly suggest as much. And increased population density also heightened the demand of the local population for the products of local agriculture. As the numbers of inhabitants grew in Philadelphia and New York and later in such New Jersey places as Newark, demand grew for the typical products of von Thünen's inner ring—truck crops, liquid milk, eggs, and fattened livestock. Serving the needs of local consumers probably accounts at least partially for the facts that farm sizes decreased (because the vast acreage necessary to produce grain for export was no longer necessary) and land use became more intensive in northeastern and southwestern New Jersey in the early nineteenth century.

External factors also affected the way New Jersey residents used the land. Bounties and prizes encouraged hemp and grapes, for example. Abundant, cheaper land to the west and south encouraged the abandonment of farms from the 1790s on. On the other hand, population pressure encouraged expansion on to poor-soil "rock farms" in the glaciated northern Highlands, and local tax returns suggest that the coming of the War of 1812, with its embargo, at first discouraged and then stimulated cattle production. In general, wheat gave way to corn and to a greater emphasis on cattle by the end of the eighteenth and into the early nineteenth century.

Finally, New Jerseyans' approaches to land varied widely according to socio-economic variables as well, factors that may help explain the differing evaluations of New Jersey agriculturists during this period. Kalm and others criticized New Jersey farmers for their methods of husbandry, but such visitors as Andrew Burnaby called New Jersey the "Garden of America." Burnaby was inspired by the holdings of the wealthy gentlemen farmers he visited in or near the Raritan Valley, whose homes had Van Dycks on the walls and whose farms were most likely worked by slaves. Had he ventured off the beaten track and visited the tenant farmers of the northwest, who had no stake in preserving (much less enhancing) the fertility of their farms, or the part-time agriculturists of the Outer Coastal Plain, he might have come to a very different conclusion.

The township tax lists indicate that there were an enormous number of very poor people. They left few records, perhaps only a name on a tax list, a transaction in a store ledger, or an entry of wages paid them in a farmer's account book. The records that have survived, of a Jacob Spicer, an Edward Antill, a James Parker, and a Charles Read, were compiled by people wealthy according to the standards of the day, farmers who were continually calculating how to get the most out of their holdings without degrading them. They could afford, and had, plenty of hired labor. Perhaps the closest to an "ordinary" farmer among those who left substantial written records was the Scott family of Elizabethtown. They were recent immigrants from Britain in the 1790s and were in many ways atypical; they ran, for example, a tobacco business on the side. But they were not wealthy. The letters they sent home indicate a constant interest in optimizing their returns without ruining their lands. As did their long-settled New England neighbors, they came to the conclusion that apple orchards brought the best return.

By 1820, New Jersey had been occupied for perhaps eight to ten thousand years, but the intense transformation of its largely wooded environment into a cleared and farmed landscape in most places had only begun 160 years before. By 1820 the change was nearly complete. Yet much work remains to be done to understand how this transformation took place. Tax lists might be analyzed at the county and township level, for example, for information on economic activities not addressed here. How did the distribution of grist mills relate to grain production? Where were the tanneries, and how were they related to the raising of cattle? How did extractive industries such as the mining of iron and copper affect other kinds of land use? And, certainly, New Jersey's remarkable diversity warrants that environmental circumstances, culture and ethnicity, and market factors receive more intensive scrutiny at all levels. This study has attempted to sketch the broad, major patterns of land use that contributed to the transformation of New Jersey, but certainly much of the fine detail remains to be drawn.

Notes

1. Frank H. Stewart, contributor, "Cumberland County Ratables," *Genealogical Magazine of New Jersey* 14 (April 1939): 36–37. Only Maurice River Precinct (later Township) is included here. Spicer was not enumerated on this list in 1751. It does not appear in the record, but it would be reasonable to suppose that, as with land, the possessor and not necessarily the owner paid taxes on livestock.

2. Frank H. Stewart, contributor, "Cape May County Ratables, 1751," Ibid., 32–35. Only Lower Precinct (Township) is included here.

3. Jacob Spicer Diary, NjHi.

4. Spicer was well known throughout the province for his legislative work and for his compilation, with Cape May's Aaron Leaming, of the laws of New Jersey; see Leaming and Spicer, *Grants*. Spicer's broad knowledge of the economy of the entire province is reflected by the fact that his colleagues chose him to amass the data required for the provincewide tax ratable list of 1751. See Wacker, "New Jersey Tax Ratable List," 23–47.

5. Bennett's name does not appear on either the Lower Precinct or Maurice River township tax lists for 1751; he may have resided further north on Cape May.

6. Philip Vickers Fithian, "Journal and Letters, 1766–1767," Special Collections, Firestone Library, Princeton University. Fithian's journal, workbook, and letters, along with some additional material referring to life on the Cohansey, have recently appeared in F. Alan Palmer, ed., *The Beloved Cohansie of Philip Vickers Fithian* (Greenwich, N.J., 1990). I am indebted to Robert Burnett for loaning me a copy of this work. See also Philip Vickers Fithian, *Journal and Letters of Philip Vickers Fithian, 1773–1774*, ed. Hunter D. Farrish (Williamsburg, Va., 1957).

7. Benson, *Peter Kalm's Travels*, 1:91, 127–28, 191–94.

8. Farm Account Book of Robert Johnson [Johnston], Salem, New Jersey, 1782–1790, Sinclair Collection, NjR.

9. Ronald V. Jackson, ed., *New Jersey Tax Lists, 1772–1822* (Salt Lake City, Utah, 1981), 4:1859, 1867. Tax ratable lists by township can be found in "County Tax Ratables, 1772–1822," Division of Archives and Records Management, New Jersey Department of State, Trenton. No "Robert Johnson" or "Robert Johnston" appears in the finding aid for the tax lists of Salem County during this period, but because these aids have been shown to be occasionally inaccurate, the extant tax lists for Salem Town and the surrounding rural townships were analyzed.

10. Restore Lippincott Diary, Gloucester County Historical Society, Woodbury, N.J. Lippincott's 250 acres were valued at £3,000, while John Hooton's 455 acres were only valued at £1,500.

11. Edward Fuhlbruegge, intro., "John Hunt's Diary," *Proc. N.J.H.S.* 52 (1934): 177–93.

12. Jacob Lamb Farm Ledger, Northampton Township, Burlington County, 1788–(1792)1802, Sinclair Collection, NjR.

13. Abraham Williamson, Bills, Receipts, Checks, etc., 1768–99 along with the papers of John Williamson, John S. Williamson, Jacob Williamson and Richard Williamson, Sinclair Collection, NjR. The Williamson records were generated by several family members. The "Memorandum Books" which list payments for seasonal activities and employment records are in the William Williamson Papers, but documents in the same handwriting containing references to local laborers and the amount of payments to them also appear contemporaneously in the Abraham Williamson Papers.

14. James Parker Diary, NjHi. Parker sold off most of the property at Shipley in 1787; the rest was sold shortly after his death in 1797. The homestead on the property was gone by 1931. See Parker, "Shipley," 117–38.

15. Edward F. Randolph Ledger, Warren Township, Somerset County, N.J., 1789–1800, Sinclair Collection, NjR.

16. Burnett and Hutchinson, "Marginal Jottings," *Proc. N.J.H.S.* 63 (1945): 150–75, 219–36; 64 (1946): 20–31, 100–109, 168–71, 219–25; 65 (1947): 47–50, 152–59, 198–209. A Richard Scudder was also listed in the township as owning 174 acres, four horses, ten cattle, and a slave. He may or may not have been a relative and, indeed, it would be difficult, if not impossible, to sort out all of the Scudders listed.

17. Camp Family Record Books, 1752–1833, NjHi.

18. Onesimus Whitehead, Ledger Book C, 1784–1811, Whitehead Papers, Joint Free Public Library of Morristown and Morris Township, Morristown, N.J.

19. Stephen Brant Account Book, 1773–94, NjHi.

20. Jesse Knowles Account Book, 1805–21, Knowles Family Record Books, NjHi.

21. This illustration series can be found in the papers of Carl Woodward, Sinclair Collection, NjR.

22. John Witherspoon, *A Description of the State of New Jersey, Answers in Part to Mr. Marbois's Questions Respecting New Jersey* (Philadelphia, 1802), 409.

23. In his analysis of southeastern Pennsylvania, James Lemon determined that "differences in customs and practices associated with national groups have . . . been mistated or exaggerated out of proportion to their significance." In his view, a much more important distinction existed between "church" and "sect" groups. Sects such as Quakers and Mennonites favored cooperation and discipline, and the evidence from such sources as estate inventories indicates that they experienced greater economic success than members of such "church" groups as Presbyterians.

However, as this study has attempted to demonstrate, cultural differences do appear to have been very real in New Jersey and to have had significant influences on land use. See Lemon, *Best Poor Man's Country*, 15–23.

24. Meinig, *The Shaping of America*, 129–44.

25. Lemon declared that because of such variables as the use of boats, the presence of two market centers, the competition of county towns, and the fact that much produce was exported, von Thünen's model generally failed to apply to southeastern Pennsylvania. But the records left by "imprecise tax collectors" and the paucity of other data" might have accounted, he felt, for the seeming absence of such regional trends. Lemon might have been happier with his findings if his study had considered the relationship of south and central New Jersey to Philadelphia, but such an effort would have meant using sets of data very different from those available for Pennsylvania and very difficult to compare. See Lemon, *Best Poor Man's Country*, 185.

Tenth Month, October, 1819.

AFTERWORD

MATERIAL CULTURE AND THE RURAL ECONOMY: BURLINGTON COUNTY, NEW JERSEY, 1760–1820

O n April 27, 1791, anticipating a death that came two years later, Samuel Stevenson made out his will. Stevenson lived in Nottingham Township, in the northwest corner of Burlington County, near the Delaware River. His will makes clear that he was a grandfather, with a married daughter and a young grandson but no other immediate heirs; that he lived not with his daughter but on his own "plantation"; and that he had a living brother, whom he asked to be executor of the will.[1]

The inventory of Stevenson's estate, which two of his neighbors recorded in March of 1793, adds detail to these sketchy personal traces of his life. Stevenson died with £1691.16.9 in personal property (that is, the sum of his wealth, excluding land, which was not then appraised in New Jersey), of which some £1424 was in bonds and book accounts and the remaining £268 in movable property:

	£	%
Livestock	100	37
Farm Tools	23	9
Produce	69	26
Household Goods	63	24
Cash	13	5
Total:	268	101 (excluding assets)
Financial Assets	1,424	84 (of total wealth)

For those who live in an America of almost limitless household commodities and who consider consumer spending a pastime, Stevenson's world, with so much invested in production and so little allotted to consumption, is truly foreign. Yet the late eighteenth century was an age when personal wealth increasingly took on a "modern" character, as consumption goods and liquid assets came to define the quality and comfort of material life. Probate records such as Stevenson's permit us to reenter this world and to reconstruct the household economy in one rural New Jersey county in the late eighteenth and early nineteenth centuries.[2]

Stevenson's probate inventory establishes that he died a modestly prosperous farmer, whose livestock holdings suggested a pattern that is best called general husbandry. He owned a bull, four cows, a heifer, and two yearling cattle; five horses (one a highly valued gelding); a sow and five pigs; and fourteen shoats (young hogs). A mix of animals assured food throughout the year; it also created more opportunities to sell small quantities of meat, leather, wool, and other such products to neighbors. Stevenson's livestock holdings indicated a substantial investment, relative to the remainder of his estate, but no specialization. Notably, he had no oxen (horse power was a more common and less expensive way to plow a field) and no sheep. The small number of swine seems unusual; as Peter Wacker has indicated, western Burlington County supplied pork and beef for the Caribbean commerce of Philadelphia merchants. But in March, when the inventory was taken, Stevenson's hogs had already been slaughtered: at the time of his death, he was storing in the house a significant quantity of beef and bacon.[3]

An inventory, of course, can provide at best only an indication—dependent on the season in which the inventory was recorded—of a farmer's store of perishable commodities. Stevenson had died after he had sold his crops and after his household had used his reserves of food and fodder, but well before the harvest season. Still, what remained at the time of the inventory provides evidence of the diversified grain-livestock agriculture that was common throughout the mid-Atlantic region. Stevenson's primary field crop was corn. He had some "in ears" (presumably to fatten livestock) stored in the garret and more growing in the field, but he also had rye stacked and waiting to be threshed and a stack of hay (which again suggests his emphasis on raising livestock). In the yard were four thousand oak shingles and one thousand feet of board; he may have purchased these for his own use, but it is more likely that they were farm products awaiting sale. Like most New Jersey farmers, Stevenson grew some flax, but so little was listed in the inventory that some had probably already been sold or spun. Missing is any indication that he planted winter wheat; also absent were by-products from winter butchering, such as tallow, leather, or hides; vegetables (although, again, we know that virtually every farmer kept a garden); and apples or cider, which would indicate he had planted an orchard. Nor did the appraisers list a gun, seine, or canoe, which might have indicated that he complemented his food supply with hunting and fishing.[4]

What did Stevenson need, other than land, to cultivate his crops and manage his livestock? The Indians of the Delaware River region had grown corn with only wooden hoes to help them; to the south, in the Chesapeake, the first English settlers planted tobacco and corn with only slightly more efficient tools. More than a century later, Stevenson's farm was comparatively "mechanized." He owned a cart, to bring crops from the field, and two wagons, to take them to market; two plows, perhaps one for breaking the soil and one for weeding (both presumably wooden; iron plows were not available from local blacksmiths until the late 1790s); a harrow; a cutting box (used to cut the chaff after the grains had been threshed); an assortment of "dung forks" and other hand-held implements; and various gears and chains for field work. There was also a spinning wheel; possibly his wife or daughter had once used it in making flax linen. In sum, mixed husbandry on the scale of Stevenson's required a considerable number of tools but a fairly modest investment, and once a farmer had built up a stock of implements, replacing them periodically absorbed little additional capital.[5]

The adjective "modest" best captures the essence of Stevenson's farming endeavors. Without wife and children to assist him or to require his support, Stevenson had probably scaled back his husbandry to point where he could live comfortably with minimum effort. What had his earlier effort allowed him to accumulate? What, in material terms, did living comfortably mean? Some of his personal property had surely already gone to his married daughter, but even allowing for this possibility, his household furnishings and personal effects seemed few and mostly rudimentary. We know Stevenson owned a two-story house big enough to offer hospitality and a modicum of privacy: it had a "front" room and two side rooms on the lower floor, two bedrooms above, and a separate kitchen with a garret above and cellar below. He owned very few expensive household furnishings: only a tea table (in the front room, which may have served as a parlor) and teaware (but stored away in a closet) connoted luxury. In the "North East Room," he had his bed, a looking glass (common enough to be found in perhaps two out of every three households), and a dresser (by this time, most households had at least one piece of furniture specifically for storing clothing). His other household possessions were few and ordinary—some pewterware (but no silverware, which had begun to replace other tableware in more fashionable households), an old bookcase and desk (but only a few shillings worth of books, not the "library" that might be itemized in the estate of a lawyer or wealthier farmer); a walnut table (but no mahogany pieces—walnut was used for functional furniture, mahogany for elegant); a teakettle (but no coffeepot) and no spices in the kitchen; no clock or watch (despite the increasing attention farm households paid to time); and no table linen or other indications of refinement or color. By the standards of the 1790s, when both European imports and locally fashioned clothing and household goods were readily available, Stevenson died with little that suggested the influence of new standards of comfort and convenience.[6]

Yet this ordinary farmer was owed a considerable amount of money. His credits totaled more than five times the amount of his other personal property. The appraisal listed a judgment bond, two additional bonds (with eight years and five months of accumulated interest), three book accounts for small sums, a note, and several other obligations. Without a final account, there is no way to determine the debts that Stevenson may have incurred, but with land as well as movable property to borrow against, he may well have owed even more than others owed him. Nevertheless, his substantial credits indicate how the accelerated private and public borrowing and lending of money in the Revolutionary era had affected rural life.[7]

Stevenson was an "average" farmer, an older landowner who was neither extremely wealthy nor on the margins of poverty. Without arguing that Stevenson was "representative," the inventories of such farmers can still reveal much about late eighteenth-century rural life in New Jersey. Specifically, probate inventories from Burlington County can be used to explore three sets of questions about rural life in the late colonial and early statehood period: (1) did rural life improve over time, did the economy grow, did the stock of productive assets and consumption goods increase? (2) were there significant regional variations within Burlington County in wealth holding and the growth of the rural economy? and (3) how did the rural economy of New Jersey compare with other areas in the mid-Atlantic?

In answering the first two sets of questions, this study elaborates some of Peter Wacker's findings about the regional dimensions of New Jersey's agricultural development, and it attempts to build a fuller context for understanding diaries and account books such as Erkuries Beatty's and James Ten Eyck's. Probate inventories provide sensitive indices of regional variation, of change over time, and of distinctions within communities in the accumulation of material possessions. New patterns in what people needed, wanted, and owned appeared slowly, almost imperceptibly, and diaries, letters, travel journals, and even account books provide brief glimpses of a virtually unchanging rural tradition of household self-sufficiency. It is precisely at this point that a systematic study of probate inventories can help. If the account books and diaries of men and women like Ten Eyck, Beatty, and Crane offer evidence of persistent patterns in rural society, probate records document more sensitively the balance between persistence and change. Used carefully, probate records can pinpoint small shifts in how much people owned, in what they owned, in how they farmed, in the comforts and conveniences of everyday life.[8]

Exploring the third question not only helps determine New Jersey's place in the mid-Atlantic economy but also permits an exploration of the long-held notion that New Jersey was something of a backwater among early American colonies. The northern Chesapeake and southeastern Pennsylvania, both of which lay in the orbit of Philadelphia's growing urban market, were among the most economically complex and prosperous rural regions in early America. Western New Jersey was also ideally situated to share in the economic development of the Philadelphia hinterland and, more generally, the mid-Atlantic. Did it? And if so, did it to the same extent as other areas?[9]

More generally, this study seeks a fuller understanding of the material lives of New Jersey's rural inhabitants during the bewildering but invigorating years between the 1760s and 1820s. The French and Indian War, the Revolution itself, the financial uncertainty of the Confederation Period, the long and commercially disruptive period of war between England and France in the 1790s and early 1800s, the War of 1812, and finally the Panic of 1819 each affected export markets and crop prices and thus shaped early American agriculture. Ordinary people as well as their wealthier neighbors had, moreover, to rethink or defend traditional notions about politics, religion, and family as they went about their farming, and such rethinking was not entirely separate from how they managed and ordered their agricultural work. Did, in fact, the farming life of the revolutionary generation change in a significant way?[10]

On the whole, the thoroughness of the recording of material possessions in New Jersey inventories was considerably less than a modern researcher would hope for (and less thorough than in neighboring Maryland, Pennsylvania, and Connecticut during the same period), and thus extracting data from such records has required several methodological strategies. This analysis draws on every complete probate inventory recorded in Burlington County during the years 1762–70, 1791–96, and 1817–23. Burlington County inventory values given in the text and tables have been standardized to reflect 1791–96 Burlington prices; values used to compare Burlington with other counties have been standardized to reflect Kent County, Maryland, prices from the 1790s (see appendix).[11]

Burlington County lies northeast across the Delaware River from Philadelphia and just south of where farmer and diarist Erkuries Beatty lived. Burlington transected what became New Jersey; it stretched from the Delaware River to the

Atlantic Ocean and included some of the more densely populated and intensively farmed lands in the state as well as some of the region's most sparsely settled towns. Across the whole county, however, the population grew continuously between 1760 and 1820, from perhaps 10,000 black and white inhabitants to more than 28,000.[12]

The course of the early American economy, historians now believe, is best described as one of extensive economic growth. As population grew, the economy was able to support an ever greater number of people at the same standard of living as those who were already there. From the perspective of early modern Europe, where population increases generally foreshadowed starvation and epidemic diseases, the extensive growth of the New World economy was a remarkable achievement and the major factor in the continuous stream of immigration to North America. This pattern of economic growth can be distinguished from intensive economic growth, or an increase in per capita wealth over time. It is much less certain if such growth—the hallmark of modern, industrial economies—occurred during the seventeenth and eighteenth centuries. Studies of Massachusetts towns as well as northern urban centers have argued that poverty increased and economic life became far less secure in the eighteenth century; though most of these studies have not attempted to measure economic growth directly, they imply that the New England and urban economies stagnated and wealth was redistributed toward those who already were well off. Studies of the rural economy in the middle colonies and the South provide a somewhat more optimistic picture of the economic prospects of white inhabitants. There is general agreement that there was some, though limited, per capita economic growth during the colonial period. This growth was associated with the initial period of settlement and farm building as well as with the decades before the American Revolution, when better grain prices and agricultural diversification stimulated agricultural endeavor. The postwar period of strong agricultural prices presumably continued this growth, which must have been especially marked in the Raritan River corridor between New York City and Philadelphia where the expansion of nearby urban markets augmented overseas demand for foodstuffs. While historians have not addressed questions about economic growth in early New Jersey, the inventories suggest two hypotheses: between the 1760s and 1820s the Burlington County economy grew intensively (measured in terms of average wealth per decedent), and this growth was disrupted but not stopped by the effects of the American Revolution on farming and markets.[13]

The years from the 1760s to the 1820s were quiet ones economically in Burlington County. As elsewhere, in southern New England, the mid-Atlantic, and the northern Chesapeake, the grain market brought growing prosperity, but in a rural economy such prosperity was registered more in terms of extensive than intensive economic growth. In the 1760s, the average value of the 108 inventories recorded in Burlington County was £231.8.0; for the 201 inventories recorded between late 1817 and early 1823, the average was £298.3.0. Average inventory value does not compare readily to such modern measures of economic well-being as per capita gross national product; rather, it is a crude measure of only one thing, the growth in the average accumulation of material possessions. Thus it is a rough index of intensive growth, which, while small, was nonetheless significant, the equivalent of a large herd of cows or of a very substantial collection of luxury goods, perhaps a riding chair, a clock, a mahogany desk and bookcase, a watch, and several high-quality feather beds. Moreover, this growth occurred as the population of Burlington County increased steadily.[14]

The inventories also confirm the disruptive effect of the American Revolution. In the wake of the war, average estate value dropped substantially from its average in the 1760s. Between 1790 and 1796, the average value of the 74 inventories recorded in the county was £193.6.0. From 1797 to 1800, inventory wealth averaged a surprising £381.7.0 (142 inventories), considerably higher than in the 1820s. As the Federalist Party liked to claim, the 1790s were extremely good times economically, at least in central New Jersey.[15]

In one way, the long-term pattern of wealth-holding changed dramatically: wealth became more liquid. Financial assets—bonds, bills, notes, and book accounts—are not included in the measure of wealth (on the assumption that one person's credits are balanced by their debts to others), and unfortunately individual records of debts (listed in administrative accounts) were very rarely saved in New Jersey. Assets (as opposed to debts) were usually noted in the inventories, and between 1760 and 1820 their absolute and relative significance grew enormously. In the 1760s, 63 percent of inventories included financial assets, and the average value of these assets was £238.5 (this is in addition to the £231.8 in personal wealth); in the 1790s, 58 percent of the wealth holders had assets, worth on average £376.2. Between 1817 and 1823, slightly more than 70 percent of the inventories contained financial assets, and their average value was £837.4. If personal wealth and financial assets are added together, then financial assets accounted for an ever growing percentage of total wealth—51 percent (1760s), 66 percent (1790s), and 74 percent (1820s). Unlike the increase in material wealth, the growth in liquid assets was spectacular. Clearly the late eighteenth-century circulation of paper money by the colonies (including New Jersey), the heavy borrowing by both the state and national governments during the Revolution, and the funding of state and national debts by the new federal government created a far more liquid currency and helped accelerate private borrowing and lending. While the inventories reveal nothing about land ownership, the decrease in the average size of holdings makes it seem probable that financial assets replaced land as the primary form of investment and inheritance for rural families.[16]

Wacker's analysis suggests significant regional variations in the pattern of economic change within Burlington County. The rural economy of the Inner Coastal Plain (along the Delaware River) ought to have differed sharply from that of the more isolated, later-settled, and less fertile interior regions and from that of townships on the Atlantic seaboard. Probate and tax records confirm this expectation. Chester Township, situated in the southwestern corner of the county, was fairly representative of the more heavily settled areas along the Delaware River (map 45). The township was one of modest-sized farms, its population distributed among the households of landowners, lot owners, and tenants. While virtually every family worked the land it occupied, there were also slaves (though their small numbers dwindled over time) and laborers, not yet married, who worked for others. Between the late colonial period and the early nineteenth century in Chester, as in so many small, early American communities, population grew, the size of landholdings diminished, and the number of tenants and agricultural laborers increased (table 48). To take perhaps the most striking statistic, the proportion of landowners with fewer than fifty acres was 3.8 percent in 1774, 35.7 percent in 1796, and 41.6 percent by 1813. At the same time, the number of residents with lots or tenancies grew from 61 in 1774 to 80 by 1796 and then to 136 in 1813.[17]

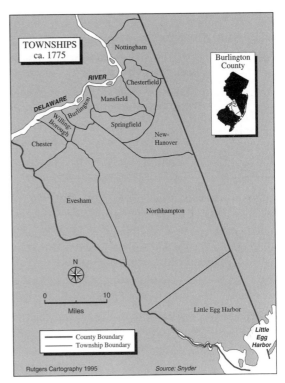

MAP 45

As the township became more densely packed, its population supported more local industry and farmed more intensively. In 1774, there had been three grist and saw mills in Chester; in 1813, there were eleven mills or shops, including tanneries, distilleries, and a fulling mill. In both years, a typical grist mill served approximately twenty to thirty families, but the geographical size of the neighborhood from which a mill drew its customers shrank from about nine square miles in 1774 to three square miles in 1813. Tax lists indicate that as farms became smaller, landowners maintained the size of their herds by pasturing more cattle per acre. Presumably, this shift required more systematic attention to fodder crops, or a move from wheat to hay.[18]

At the other extreme, in the east, were the townships that sprawled across the Pine Barrens. They were larger, supported far fewer people relative to their area, and had more land waiting to be improved than in the west. When the Reverend Carl Mangus Wrangel, dean of the Swedish Lutheran congregations in America, toured the Jersey coast in 1764, he described in some detail Egg Harbor Township, directly south of Burlington County:

> The country hereabouts has been inhabited only during the last twenty years. Previously there had been only wild, barren ground between Philadelphia and Egg Harbor, so that travelers had to provide themselves with food for both their horses and themselves when they came this way. The land sells for $10 a hundred acres and the soil consists mainly of drift sand, which, however, produces reasonably good crops of maize and rye; but wheat does not grow especially fast. There are no meadows, but good wooded pasturage is available for the cattle throughout the summer. In the winter they bring their herds to the seaside in Egg Harbor, where they pay ten shillings a head for the winter; they fetch hay for the horses from the same place. They have to depend principally on the woods, which consist here of spruce, pine, and cedar, for a livelihood; several sawmills are therefore located here, where boards and building lumber are sawed and shipped partly by the river and partly by wagon, to Philadelphia.

Table 48
Taxable Population of Chester Township,
Burlington County, 1774, 1796, 1813

	1774	1796	1813
Number in Each Taxable Category			
Landowners	78	151	233
House and Lot Owners	—	26	46
Non-Landed Householders	61	54	90
Single Men	28	48	68
Slaves	20	3	0
Total	187	282	437
Average Acres Owned	228.9	116.0	88.9
Percent Owning			
Less than 50 Acres	3.8	35.7	41.6
200 Acres or More	50.0	23.8	11.1
Number of			
Grist and Saw Mills	3	3	11
Tanneries	0	2	4
Distilleries	0	0	4
Fulling Mills	0	0	1
Fisheries	0	3	4

Note: Householders included "all married Men living with their Parents, and not supporting a separate Table, the estimated Value of whose ratable estate does not amount to Twenty-five Pounds." *Acts of the General Assembly of the State of New Jersey, 1787,* chap. 208, 431. Householders could be landowners, albeit poor, but most were probably tenants or cottagers; householders and house and lot owners that held land are here included among the landowners.

Source: New Jersey Tax Ratables, New Jersey State Archives, Trenton.

Wrangel traveled north, stopping at Little Egg Harbor in Burlington County, where he had heard Swedes lived "like savage heathens" with "no other homes than hovels in the woods." He was told that these men "live by hunting and what they earned they were said to turn into rum." Yet in this sparely inhabited township Wrangel found a prosperous saw and grist mill operator, who employed most of his neighbors in cutting and sawing wood and collecting grain for shipment to the West Indies.[19]

More than thirty years later, when Julian Ursyn Niemcewicz recorded in detail his trip to the Pine Barrens, he wrote after visiting Egg Harbor that "all the seashore for three of four miles does not have a single dwelling place and there is very little farming. Apart from the poor quality of the land a reason for the lack of habitation is the holding of large acreage in one hand." Yet the steady commerce with Philadelphia and the West Indies in lumber and provisions and the iron foundry at Batsto made this "uncultivated, uninhabited country, covered in forests" a more profitable place for trade "than many fertile and well-populated provinces in Europe."[20]

The Little Egg Harbor tax returns accentuate the structural differences between east and west. Farms were not only larger (164 acres, on average, in 1796, compared with 116 in Chester), but they grew proportionately larger over time, from

152 acres in 1773 to 164 in 1796 and then to 227 in 1813. But the average holding of improved acreage was considerably less than along the Delaware. The number of people taxed almost doubled between 1773 and 1796 but then actually decreased slightly by 1813. And where in 1796 there had been seven mills, a tannery, and an iron furnace, in 1813 there were only four mills listed in the tax records. The rate of tenancy did not increase, which suggests that those who owned land had less opportunity or incentive than they would have had in the west to develop their holdings. Most striking is a comparison of western and eastern population densities: in 1784 in Chester Township there were thirty-four people per square mile, while there were only five per square mile in Little Egg Harbor. By 1820, both east and west had become more densely populated, but the disparity remained: Chester now had sixty-six people per square mile and Little Egg Harbor but nine.[21]

Analysis of the probate inventories reinforces and adds nuance to this picture of differential regional development. The west (the Inner Coastal Plain) was clearly more prosperous than the east (the Outer Coastal Plain), prosperity reflected not simply in personal wealth but in the accumulation of financial obligations as well. Put differently, the interior and seaboard townships fared less well economically than those more directly linked to the Philadelphia market. Along the Delaware River, the northern townships were initially better off than those to the south, but over time the southwestern townships caught up. To the east, the picture was one of stagnation through the 1820s (table 49). In the east, a greater percentage of pro-

Table 49
Average Inventoried Wealth and Financial Assets by Region,
Burlington County, New Jersey, 1762–70, 1791–96, 1817–23
(values in pounds of local currency and adjusted to 1790s values)

Wealth by Period	North	South	Region Central	East	Unidentified
1762–63	314.8	187.2	236.8	184.8	131.2
1791–96	250.6	167.6	154.9	168.9	168.7
1817–23	342.1	382.0	203.7	176.1	306.4
Assets by Period					
1762–73	666.7	97.4	96.1	33.4	139.7
1791–96	423.1	726.2	58.8	48.5	288.6
1817–23	778.5	1,964.8	258.1	269.4	243.9
Number	100	105	138	13	26

Note: Because of the small sample size (13), one inventory, valued at £1,844.3, with £231.6 in assets, is excluded from the east averages. Including it would raise average inventory wealth to £593.1 and lower the average asset figure to £260.0.

Regions
North: Chesterfield, Mansfield, Nottingham, Springfield
South: Burlington, Chester, Willingboro
Central: Evesham, New Hanover, Northampton
East: Little Egg Harbor

Source: Inventory Sample B, Burlington County Probate Records, NJSA.

bated wealth was tied up in livestock, cattle herds were larger, and corn was the dominant crop; along the Delaware, oats, hay, and rye were often as important as corn, apple cider production was more common, and swine, rather than cattle, were the primary market animals. Throughout Burlington County, farmers raised little wheat (table 50). In the ongoing debate about the role of the market in early America, the Burlington evidence strongly suggests the crucial roles that circumstance and opportunity played in shaping the rural economy; location and soil conditions defined the range of choices farmers had and set limits on what they could and could not expect to achieve through agriculture.[22] Changes over time in accumulated wealth and regional variations in wealth-holding provide one picture of Burlington's rural economy. But to appreciate how such figures translated in human terms the analysis must turn to individual inventories that can each in some way be taken as representative of material life in Burlington County. Thomas Gill died during the winter of 1764–65 in Chester Township on the Delaware River. He was a self-styled yeoman, with young children and a small family, a farm of his own, and an estate worth £221 when he died. He had two oxen, five head of cattle, and four young horses; two plows, part ownership of a wagon (sharing expensive farming equipment was common practice), some carpenter's tools, and few other agricultural implements; and few household possessions beyond some candlesticks, a looking glass, pewterware, and a teakettle.

Table 50
Farming Assets in the Inventories from
Four Burlington County Townships, 1760s–1820s

	Nottingham *Inner Coastal North*	Chester *Inner Coastal South*	Northampton *Outer Coastal Central*	Little Egg Harbor *Outer Coastal East*
Inventory Value	434.9	148.1	114.1	179.9
Livestock	73.7	34.4	26.0	58.3
Farm Equipment*	21.9	9.8	9.1	20.3
Crop	61.2	21.1	22.5	38.5
Percent Value in				
Livestock	15.3	17.0	13.1	33.6
Farm Equipment*	7.7	5.1	9.3	11.1
Crop	9.2	9.5	12.0	13.8
Index of Farm Equipment*	3.9	2.6	1.7	7.2
Number of Cattle	4.3	4.5	3.1	8.7
Number of Sheep	3.8	4.1	4.6	3.2
Number of Swine	6.7	6.7	3.8	7.5
Percent of Crop Value in				
Wheat	.9	2.2	2.9	1.0
Corn	15.8	8.6	7.2	26.7
Non-Grain Crops	22.5	42.4	35.1	43.0
Percent of Households with				
Apples, Cider, or Cider Mills	15.4	25.9	16.7	10.0
Carpenter Tools	15.4	18.5	16.7	30.0
Oats or Rye	38.5	33.3	27.8	30.0
Potatoes	30.8	7.4	27.8	30.0
Wheels or Looms	46.2	40.7	44.4	80.0
Number of Cases:	13	27	18	10

*Farm Equipment: sum of the number of plows, carts, wheat fans, and four times the number of wagons.
Source: Inventory Sample A, Burlington County Probate Records, NJSA.

Four beds worth £16.15, a chest of drawers worth 0.90, a few crude chairs, and a tea table were not only his most valuable furniture; they were his only furniture. Left for the family were small amounts of hay, corn, rum, and meat remaining from the harvest. Only the fact that he owned a teenage slave girl, a riding chair (a two-wheeled chair pulled by a horse), a barrel of rum, and a bateau distinguished Gill from the common lot of smallholders in Burlington County.[23]

William Arden of neighboring Evesham Township left an inventory in 1794 worth £193.4. Arden was older than Gill, a grandfather outlived by his wife, three sons, and at least two grandchildren. His home had only three beds (for at least two of his sons had already left home), a few chairs, a stove, and almost no household goods other than earthenware and pewterware. As a farm, however, Arden's household seemed a bit more substantial than Gill's: he had livestock worth £76 (Gill's were worth £43), a wagon valued at £7.10, two plows, a scythe, a harrow, a cider mill, a spinning wheel, two looms, and a butter churn. Thus, in addition to taking care of the grain crop, Arden's family was probably running a diary farm, tending an orchard, spinning flax, and perhaps weaving for neighbors. What is most striking, then, is how crudely Arden lived on a farm that seems quite productive. In contrast, David Middleton of Nottingham, in the northwest corner of the county, left an inventory when he died in 1818 that suggested how standards of material comfort were changing. Middleton, like Gill, was a small farmer with a small family. In an inventory appraised at £260.8, there were only two cows, a calf, some hogs, and four horses, and no farm equipment except plows, harrows, and hand tools. But in Middleton's home were six beds (worth £75), a costly bureau, a dresser, china for the family table, a watch, and a looking glass.[24]

Bracketing the estates of men like Gill, Arden, and Middleton were the inventories of the very poor and very rich. At the low end of the scale were men with only clothing and tools to their names (presumably transient laborers) and widows with meager household possessions. Joseph Aaronson, for example, died in 1792 with only £8.7.9; by the time his estate was probated, his widow had remarried and turned the administration of her husband's estate over to one of his kin. As he had had only a cheese press, a linen wheel, a bed, his clothing, and some pewter, she probably feared that debts would consume the estate. Cato Bound, probably a free black, left even less when he died in 1823—a hoe and ax and some carpenter tools, all willed to his young daughter. Ruth Heritage, a widow, had only a bed and bedding, a case of drawers, and £1.4.0 in cash when she died in 1793. But her impoverishment may have been more apparent than real, for she was survived by a married daughter and left her grandchildren a note worth £42.[25]

At the other end of the spectrum were the prosperous farmers, slaveowners, merchants, and entrepreneurial artisans. Of them all, James Robson was the wealthiest. Robson was a Moorestown tanner, who when he died in 1820 had an estate worth more than £6,100 (virtually all of it in cash and leather), and bonds, bills, mortgages, and notes worth an additional £8,034. The only other items noted by the appraisers were his beds, clothing, books, two horses, and trade tools. In the 1760s, the richest was Edward Tonklin, a Springfield township slaveowner with some seventy head of cattle and land in Burlington City, Mansfield Township, and Gloucester County as well in Springfield; along with an estate of £1,588, Tonklin had £5,714 in financial assets. The estate of Edward Brooke, a well-to-do Mansfield

Township farmer who died in 1795, gives some indication of how wealth could translate into luxury. Brooke's £1,368 in property included ornamental "Greenbone" knives and forks, silverware, and queensware. One of several thin-bodied, cream-colored earthenwares popular in England in the mid-eighteenth century, queensware was gradually replacing delftware as a luxury import. He also had a small library (with a thirteen-volume encyclopedia, a copy of *Jersey Laws,* an edition of the *Practical Farmer,* and a Greek translation) as well as a share in the Philadelphia Library, mahogany and walnut tables, a desk-bookcase, and a watch. He too had several thousand pounds in notes and bonds—the most consistent signal of the changing configuration of rural society.[26]

Analysis of the composition of probated estates—both in terms of general categories of wealth (livestock, producer goods, consumer goods, crop, labor, cash, and trading stock) and in terms of specific items (plows or teakettles, for example)— helps trace such changes in the pattern of wealth-holding in Burlington County. While the late eighteenth and early nineteenth centuries remain something of an economic "dark ages" (historians have had little to say about the pattern of long-term economic development in this era), there is a general sense that these were prosperous years punctuated by financial uncertainty and hindered by war in Europe and America. By extrapolating from such impressionistic findings several trends become apparent in the probate inventories—greater capitalization of farms, more consumer goods, heavier investment in financial securities, and more loans. Yet the sum of these changes cannot have been too great, as per capita economic growth was quite limited between 1760 and 1820. In what ways, then, did the material life of Burlington County residents change during this period?

Surprisingly, there was very little change between the 1760s and 1820s in the average value of household goods, livestock, and farm tools held by Burlington County decedents. And when things changed, it was because people held less. For example, the average value of livestock was £57 in the 1760s but only £42 in the 1790s and, despite an improvement in estate values, just £34.9 in the early 1820s (see appendix and tables 48–50). This change may have reflected the fact that landholdings were decreasing in size, but a more direct cause was the decreasing proportion of farmers in the population. The most abrupt change was in the labor component of wealth, from a little more than £20 per estate in the 1760s to virtually nothing thereafter, as religious benevolence and wage labor brought a gradual end to slavery and the Revolutionary War ended the trade in indentured servants. If, then, over time people held no more or even less in livestock, consumer goods, farm tools, and labor, why did average estate value rebound after the early 1790s? Offsetting the uniform decline in the value of production and consumption components of wealth in Burlington inventories was a steady increase in cash reserves, more than tripling from about £22 in the 1760s to about £80 in the 1820s. This growth was due almost entirely to the fact that the cash holdings of the wealthiest residents multiplied substantially. When added to the multiplication of bonds, bills, and notes in the inventories, this increase in cash reserves points to a fundamental transformation of wealth-holding patterns in Burlington County.[27]

The fortunes of the Burlington County farming population followed a slightly different course. Of the county's people, farmers were the most numerous group and the most significant economically; they were also considerably more wealthy than the population in general. Unlike what prevailed among the general population, their average wealth increased steadily throughout the era, from £317.4 in the 1760s to £351.2 in the 1790s and then to £590.7 in the early 1820s. The value of farm livestock, recalling the steady decline for the general population, jumped from £85.3 in the 1760s to £103.1 in the 1790s and then leveled off at £112.1 in the early 1820s (probably because of shrinking farm size), while the value of consumer goods in the farm household increased steadily and cash reserves went up sharply among both middling and wealthy farmers. The pattern for farmers, then, was somewhat different than for the general population: farming prospered during the Revolutionary era and the early years of the young republic; in the new century, farmers cut back on agricultural activity, but the wealth of the agricultural population continued to grow; and this wealth increasingly took the form of cash, credits, and consumer goods rather than additions to livestock and farm equipment.[28]

Table 51
Livestock, Farm Equipment, and Credit Holdings of
Burlington County Farmers, 1762–70, 1791–96, 1817–23

A. Ownership of Cows

| | Percent Owning during: | | |
Number Owned	1760s	1790s	1820s
0	9.4	3.8	4.8
1–3	25.0	30.8	52.4
4–9	50.0	50.0	28.6
10 or more	15.6	15.4	14.3
Average:	5.4	5.7	4.7

B. Ownership of Plows

| | Percent Owning during: | | |
Number Owned	1760s	1790s	1820
0	25.0	15.4	14.3
1	34.4	15.4	57.1
2 or more	40.6	69.2	28.6
Average:	1.5	1.8	1.4

C. Ownership of Wagons

| | Percent Owning during: | | |
Number Owned	1760s	1790s	1820s
0	37.5	3.8	9.5
1	43.8	19.2	38.1
2 or more	18.8	76.9	52.4
Average:	.8	1.9	1.7

D: Holding of Credit

| | Percent Owning during: | | |
Type of Credit	1760s	1790s	1820s
Bonds	37.5	26.9	19.1
Book Accounts	15.6	46.2	14.3
Notes	21.9	34.6	52.4
Number of Cases:	32	26	21

Note: Farmers were defined as men holding more than £15 in livestock and £5 in farm equipment. Merchants and women were excluded, but artisans were included.
Source: Inventory Sample A, Burlington County Probate Records, NJSA.

Table 52

Table 52
Ownership of Selected Household Goods
by Burlington County Farmers,
1762–70, 1791–96, 1817–23

Household Item	*Percent Owning during:*		
	1760s	1790s	1820s
Earthenware	62.5	65.4	76.2
Pewterware	87.5	84.6	28.6
Fine Earthenware	40.6	42.3	47.6
Silverware	25.0	23.1	23.8
Knives and Forks	65.6	53.9	57.1
Coffeepots/Kettles	12.5	38.5	42.9
Teapots/Kettles	53.1	65.4	33.3
Pepper and Spice Boxes	25.0	7.7	0.0
Candlesticks	37.5	38.5	42.9
Bed/Table Linen	56.3	76.9	81.0
Watches	21.9	15.4	38.1
Clocks	34.4	26.9	47.6
Books	68.8	46.2	57.1
Desk	25.0	61.5	61.9
Dresser	62.5	69.2	52.4
Bureau	0.0	11.5	47.6
Cupboard	28.1	34.6	61.9
Number of Cases:	32	26	21

Note: See Table 51 for the definition of "farmers."

Source: Inventory Sample A, Burlington County Probate Records, NJSA.

For the farming population itself, changes in material wealth were measured not only in pounds, shillings, and pence but in livestock, tools, and household possessions. Tables 51 and 52 suggest what was happening on the typical Burlington County farm between the 1760s and 1820s. Both large farms and poorly equipped farms were disappearing, and small holdings, adequately supplied with farm implements, were taking their place. This trend again parallels the tax record evidence of declining farm size in the more densely settled western half of the county. The typical farmer of the 1820s had few more animals and no more farm equipment than farmers thirty or sixty years earlier, but farms without cows, horses, swine, and such tools as plows, carts, wagons, sickles, scythes, crosscut saws, or wheelbarrows were now rare. Nor were there unambiguous signs of improvement in the accumulation of household necessities and comforts. While the average value of consumer goods increased over time (see appendix), there was little change in the frequency at which many representative and common manufactured goods—candlesticks, earthenware, bed and table linens, knives and forks—were found in farm households. Other items were noticeably less common in the 1820s than before—pepper and spice mills (perhaps a carryover of the Revolutionary-era boycotts of East India products), teapots and kettles (being replaced by coffeepots), and pewterware (copper, brass, and silver were substitutes). In contrast, certain relatively expensive goods became more popular—watches, clocks, and large furniture pieces such as desks, bureaus, and corner cupboards.[29]

Not only did an increasing number of farmers own such luxuries as clocks and bureaus, but the products themselves changed. The "clock" noted in the inventories of the 1760s became in subsequent decades an "eight-day" or "twenty-hour" clock; listings for watches increasingly noted if the watch was gold or silver; general-purpose chests of drawers gave way to dressers for clothing; "desks" occasionally became "desks and bookcases"; and with increasing frequency maple, oak, or mahogany was specified when tables or other pieces of furniture were listed. In part, tangible changes had occurred that the inventory itemization recorded: what was new was an awareness among appraisers that distinctions in form, style, and material among functionally similar items mattered to those who might buy or inherit them. Rural demand for such goods, many produced locally, and a growing sense of taste and style provided much of the impetus for what some historians have called the "consumer revolution" in early America.[30]

Independent women, mostly widows, were part of this consumer revolution. Women, in fact, fared surprisingly well relative to men in terms of household possessions; the difficulties they faced derived chiefly from being denied access to land, labor, and livestock, not from a lack of household goods (table 53). Women were more likely than men to have replaced pewter with silver, more likely to own dressers and bureaus for their bedroom and linens for their bed, and as likely to own clocks. The wills make clear that in many cases these possessions were crowded into a single room in a house owned by one of these women's older children, and only four of the thirty-seven who left an inventory managed a farm. More than half of all widows, however, held cash and about two-thirds left notes, bonds, or (rarely) book accounts. Elizabeth Emlez, of New Hanover, who died in early 1820, was the most prosperous widow of the era. A landowner, she rented part of her property and owned two horses, two cows, six hogs, and assorted poultry. Her household possessions included four beds and elaborate bedding, silverware, a clock, a cupboard, a desk and bookcase, and a bureau; she had an assortment of farm equipment, including two wagons; and she held more than £270 in bills and notes. More typical was Anna Hooton, who died in neighboring Evesham about the same time:

Table 53
**Comparison of the Ownership of Selected Household Goods
by Men and Women in Burlington County, 1762–1823**

	Percent Owning among:	
Household Items	*Men*	*Women*
Earthenware	57.6	43.6
Pewterware	58.8	38.5
Fine Earthenware	33.3	25.7
Silverware	21.2	51.3
Knives and Forks	46.1	41.0
Pepper and Spice Boxes	10.3	10.3
Watch	26.1	2.6
Clock	23.0	20.5
Books	44.2	33.3
Desk	41.8	25.6
Dresser	43.6	69.2
Bureau	18.2	30.8
Number of Cases:	166	39

Source: Inventory Sample A, Burlington County Probate Records, NJSA.

she had only her clothing, a bed, some earthenware, a bureau, a linen wheel, and a looking glass.[31]

For men as well as women, economic well-being correlated with access to productive resources. If the inventories of men are divided into three groups—poor (those worth £50 or less); middling (those worth more than £50 and less than £225); and prosperous (those worth more than £225)—it is possible to develop some sense of the relationship between wealth and the standard of living in Burlington County (table 54). Of course, those who died with £50 or less in inventoried wealth may well not fully represent Burlington County's poorer male residents, but as a group those who died with such small estates were clearly impoverished. To be poor generally meant a person had at most a cow or horse, a table and perhaps a bed, hand tools, clothing, and a small assortment of household goods. While prosperous residents devoted only 30.4 percent of their wealth to consumer items and middling residents 50.3 percent, household goods accounted for

Table 54
Ownership of Selected Household Goods by Level of Wealth,
Burlington County, 1762–70, 1791–96, 1817–23

| Household Item | Percent Owning during: | | |
Wealth Level	1760s	1790s	1820s
Candlesticks			
Poor	20.0	26.7	14.3
Middling	44.4	25.0	26.3
Prosperous	60.0	40.9	40.0
Earthenware			
Poor	50.0	40.0	47.6
Middling	50.0	55.0	63.2
Prosperous	80.0	54.5	70.0
Fine Earthenware			
Poor	20.0	20.0	0.0
Middling	27.8	45.0	26.3
Prosperous	60.0	45.5	45.0
Pewterware			
Poor	50.0	53.3	14.3
Middling	94.4	66.7	35.0
Prosperous	95.0	81.8	30.0
Looking Glasses			
Poor	20.0	33.3	28.6
Middling	72.2	40.0	68.4
Prosperous	90.0	54.5	75.0
Bibles			
Poor	20.0	6.7	0.0
Middling	27.8	10.0	15.8
Prosperous	20.0	13.6	30.0
Number of Cases			
Poor	10	15	21
Middling	18	20	19
Prosperous	20	22	20

Note: "Poor" indicates estates of less than £50; "middling" estates of £50 to £225; "prosperous" estates of more than £225. Financial assets have been excluded and estates evaluated in 1790–96 prices.

Source: Inventory Sample A, Burlington County Probate Records, NJSA.

65.1 percent of wealth among the poor (grain, livestock, and trade implements amounted to correspondingly less). In terms of the small comforts to which some eighteenth-century folk were accustomed, table 53 provides a measure of how poverty translated into deprivation. Most of the wealth poor people possessed was tied up in basic household necessities, yet they still did not usually have candlesticks, a looking glass, a Bible, or even pewterware as many of their neighbors did; and they had little beyond a hoe and ax to help them acquire more. Throughout early America, to be sure, the poor were often also young, and it may be that if these men had lived longer they would have acquired the wealth or inherited the land that the middling sort had. One historian has recently reached this conclusion in a thorough study of colonial Connecticut inventories, but even there the suspicion remains that a disproportionate number of poor inhabitants either died and left no inventory or left Connecticut without escaping their economic predicament. Even when inventories exist for itinerant workers or for those who were infirm and without family, such records tell us only so much, more what the poor did not have than what they did have and nothing about their expectations and opportunities. Whatever the limitations of using probate records to discuss poverty, the Burlington records at least indicate that approximately one decedent in three died with less than £50 in material possessions.[32]

The crucial factor in the gradual improvement of Burlington's economy, in the accumulation of financial assets, in the persistence of substantial inequality, in the reworking of luxuries into everyday articles of consumption, and in the shifting mix of crops was the area's relationship to urban and overseas markets. Burlington was centrally located in the mid-Atlantic, which in economic terms stretched from the northern Chesapeake to southern New England. The economy was defined by commitment to diversified, grain-livestock agriculture, by marketing networks spiraling out from the region's principal ports—Baltimore, Philadelphia, and New York—and by dependence for market income on both the Caribbean meat-corn trade and, initially, at least, the European wheat trade. Wheat, which in the mid-eighteenth century was as close to a "staple crop" as anything produced in the mid-Atlantic, ceased to play a central role in the Revolutionary era, while local, urban demand for farm produce opened up new marketing possibilities within the region and led to an increasingly variegated agricultural regime.[33]

A broad comparison between Burlington County and three other counties that collectively define the range of possibilities for mid-Atlantic agriculture helps fix New Jersey's place in the region's economy. Fairfield County, Connecticut, was on the northern boundary of the mid-Atlantic economy and tied to the New York market. Chester County, Pennsylvania, like Burlington, lay in the immediate hinterland of Philadelphia; Kent County, Maryland, was on the southern fringe of the region and linked by the Chesapeake Bay to both Baltimore and (with a land passage) Philadelphia. Three characteristics of Burlington County's economy invite specific comparison: (1) the decline in average estate value between the 1760s and the 1790s and the modest improvement of that index by the 1820s; (2) the substantial, sustained economic improvement in the fortunes of the farming population relative to the general population; and (3) the shift in consumption choices toward more costly and stylish items.

At first glance Kent County seems fundamentally different economically from its northern neighbors. Kent was settled in the mid-seventeenth century, about the same time as Fairfield but significantly earlier than either Chester or Burlington. Its tobacco economy no longer had the same growth potential as the economies of more recently settled northern places. Despite a gradual shift in the mid-eighteenth century from tobacco to grain, Kent planters, in contrast to the farmers of Burlington and Chester, still produced more for Atlantic rather than local markets, still relied far more heavily on slave labor than family members and wage workers, and still purchased imported rather than locally made household goods. Unlike in the Delaware Valley, in the northern Chesapeake rural industry had made little headway in providing alternative employment for the agricultural population, and there was nothing in Kent to match the seventy-five saw and grist mills, twenty-five tanneries, sixty-eight merchant shops, fifty-seven taverns, seven fulling mills, and three iron works that Burlington's tax assessors counted in 1784.[34]

All four counties, however, also had much in common, beginning with a similar Revolutionary War heritage. Each was the site of confrontations between British and Patriot regular troops and the local forces that aided them, and in all four counties property damage was extensive. Pitched battles were fought in Chester County in 1777 and in western Burlington in December of 1776 and June of 1778; British excursions were directed against Maryland's Eastern Shore in 1777–78 and 1780-81; the Fairfield coast was the scene of constant British forays, and the town of Fairfield was assaulted during the summer of 1779. The loss of crops, mills, cattle, and farmhouses during the fighting is well documented, but the overall cost of the war to the economy is far more difficult to assess. Balanced against burnt buildings, commandeered cattle, runaway slaves, and prohibitive wage rates were the speculative gains to be made in the provisions trade in food, clothing, and firewood for the troops.[35]

Other less impressionistic similarities are easier to relate to economic welfare. In the mid-eighteenth century Kent planters had shifted from tobacco toward wheat and corn, and the four counties increasingly shared a diversified grain and livestock economy. Moreover, despite the different settlement dates, each county was heavily populated by the 1780s when the first comparative statistics are available: Kent, with some 11,701 inhabitants in 1783, averaged 41 people per square mile; Chester had 28,541 inhabitants in the same year, or about 39 people per square mile; Burlington in 1784 had 15,801 people, or about 52 people per square mile in the settled area (although only 18 people per square mile if unclaimed land in the eastern part of the county is included); and Fairfield in 1782 had some 30,856 inhabitants and a population density of 44 people per square mile. Kent's economy was, of course, particularly dependent on coerced, unfree labor, not the norm for the mid-Atlantic; farming in New Jersey, Connecticut, and Pennsylvania relied on wage workers to supplement family help. But in each county, market production meant the systematic use of other people's labor by the householding population. In Chester, for example, the adult male population was approximately evenly divided in 1783 between landholders (owners and tenants) and free but dependent agricultural workers (cottagers and single men); in Kent, the ratio of the number of householders to the number of unfree or dependent workers was about three to one.[36]

One direct consequence of the linkage between slavery and market agriculture in Kent was that the county's planters were significantly more wealthy than other mid-

Table 55
Average Inventoried Wealth,
Burlington County, New Jersey; Chester County, Pennsylvania;
Fairfield County, Connecticut; and Kent County, Maryland,
1760–1820

A. *Inventoried Wealth* (excluding land and financial assets)

Period	Burlington	Chester	Fairfield	Kent
1760s	198.1	117.6	93.2	489.4
1790s	150.1	146.2	110.0	382.5
1820s	230.3	172.5	121.4	558.0

B. *Financial Assets* (excluded from wealth figures above)

Period	Burlington	Chester	Fairfield	Kent
1760s	172.8	106.6	14.9	69.3
1790s	291.6	188.0	49.3	89.4
1820s	336.2	299.1	92.6	123.1

Note: all figures in Kent County 1790 prices.

Sources: Probate Sample B, Burlington Probate Records, NJSA; Chester County Probate Records, Chester County Archives, West Chester, Pennsylvania; Fairfield Probate District Probate Records, Connecticut State Library, Hartford; Kent County Inventories and Accounts, Maryland State Archives, Annapolis.

Table 56
Average Inventoried Wealth of Farmers and Planters,
Burlington County, New Jersey; Chester County, Pennsylvania;
Fairfield County, Connecticut; and Kent County, Maryland,
1760–1820

A. *Inventoried Wealth* (excluding land and financial assets)

Period	Burlington	Chester	Fairfield	Kent
1760s	223.9	169.3	204.2	724.7
1790s	287.8	220.1	224.5	608.3
1820s	487.2	269.6	218.7	1,042.4

B. *Financial Assets* (excluded from wealth figures above)

Period	Burlington	Chester	Fairfield	Kent
1760s	82.7	118.6	31.6	94.7
1790s	334.3	231.4	87.0	155.1
1820s	553.2	390.8	129.6	158.7

Note: all figures in Kent County 1790 prices. Farmers were defined as men holding more than £15 in livestock and £5 in farm equipment. Merchants and women were excluded, but artisans were included.

Sources: Probate Sample B, Burlington Probate Records, NJSA; Chester County Probate Records, Chester County Archives, West Chester, Pennsylvania; Fairfield Probate District Probate Records, Connecticut State Library, Hartford; Kent County Inventories and Accounts, Maryland State Archives, Annapolis.

Atlantic farmers (tables 55 and 56). When William Hanson died in Kent in the spring of 1789, appraisers evaluated his estate in May and came back in August after the summer harvest. They recorded the estate of a planter as "representative" of his own society as Samuel Stevenson was of Burlington County. Hanson died without wife or children, a comfortably situated farmer with at least eight hundred acres of land and an inventory valued at £900 (in Maryland currency, land and financial assets excluded). He probably felt himself a step, though a small one, above the norm in Kent County: his accumulation of farmland and ownership of eight slaves, five of whom were field hands, marked him as a man of some means.

Other possessions set him apart from men like Stevenson: he owned silver-handled knives and forks and queensware plates and cups; seventy-six ounces of silver plate, a symbol of status as well as a form of savings; a riding chaise and harness; sixteen horses, used with the chaise as well as his plows; a crop of more than 500 bushels of corn and 122 bushels of wheat (at a time when wheat had virtually vanished from New Jersey fields). Such material possessions could, of course, be found in Burlington County, too, but either in smaller quantity or only among the very wealthy; by Kent standards, Hanson was not even among the very wealthy. In other ways, however, his possessions were strikingly ordinary and not much different from Stevenson's—a horse cart, two plows, and a few other farm implements; earthenware and cooking utensils; eight cows, fourteen younger cattle, two steers, and several dozen swine (but no sheep); and three spinning wheels (presumably used by the slaves). Measurable differences in accumulated wealth, then, did not directly or necessarily translate into qualitative distinctions between Kent planters and northern farmers. In Kent, an earlier period of tobacco planting, the continuous involvement in Atlantic commerce, and the widespread ownership of slaves all contributed to a greater accumulation of wealth than in the northern counties, but these differences did not, in and of themselves, define a different economic world.[37]

Almost as striking as the difference between Kent and the three northern counties is the fact that average estate value in Burlington County was significantly greater than in either Fairfield or Chester counties. Burlington was a somewhat older settlement than Chester, but it was not as old as Fairfield. Moreover, the eastern third of the county was relatively poor, while the development of rural industry in Burlington lagged considerably behind that of Chester. Chester and Fairfield may have been less wealthy because their economies supported a much larger population of middling farmer-artisans and cottage laborers; population density figures provide some support for this suggestion. The persistence of this wealth differential over time, however, suggests that in some way Burlington was a more prosperous place to live than was Fairfield or Chester.[38]

The Revolutionary era seems to have had a greater impact in Kent and Burlington than in Chester and Fairfield. Burlington rebounded more strongly than Kent, and in the Delaware Valley and southern New England wealth was considerably greater by the 1820s than it had been in the 1760s. Even more striking is the continuous growth throughout the region and over time in the accumulation of financial assets. Here, Kent lagged well behind Burlington and Chester; Fairfield trailed even further behind, though it caught up with Kent over time. In Kent, in all probability, investment in slave labor substituted for the mortgages, bonds, and notes in which Delaware Valley and southern Connecticut farmers put their money.

The general improvement of the regional economy is not unexpected. Despite the Revolutionary War, the recession of the mid-1780s, and the War of 1812, landowners found these to be profitable years for commercial agriculture. Urban growth and Atlantic markets gave farmers choices, and the consequence should have been economic growth and intraregional specialization. The upswing in cereal prices that stimulated the American grain economy in the mid-eighteenth century clearly was still making itself felt through the Panic of 1819. With land and livestock, it was possible to ride out the bad years comfortably and improve one's position in better times. Kent's somewhat anomalous situation may have stemmed from the fact that its economy peaked earlier. In the mid-eighteenth century, Kent planters had reaped the benefits of both high tobacco and grain prices; thereafter, they gradually abandoned tobacco for wheat, corn, and livestock farming. Growth continued, but at a much reduced rate.[39]

Changes in average estate values may also reflect changes in the occupational structure and sex ratio of those whose estates were inventoried. To take the most noticeable example, in Burlington in the 1790s, male non-farmers who died with considerably less personal wealth than was typical of other inventoried residents were a larger group proportionally than they had been in the 1760s. Even more strikingly, between 1760 and 1820 the relative number of women in the decedent population increased. As the accumulation of cash and interest-bearing securities became more common, the rural economy supported an increasing number of people who had "retired" from farming, had transferred their land, livestock, and farm tools to their children (or to a tenant), and lived with a minimum of household goods (and, thus, with little personal wealth for an appraiser to inventory). The growing number of non-farmers who lived in the farming economy testifies to the dramatic change in the definition of wealth and security in rural society. At the same time, it is possible that changing average wealth figures may reflect not simply the shifting composition of rural society but absolute gains or losses in welfare by particular groups. It is probable that the 1790s figures also reflect the ill fortunes of people squeezed off the land and buffeted both by the wartime disruption of the economy and the postwar commercial recession.[40]

While Kent and Burlington may have been harder hit by the economic disruptions of the Revolutionary era, they were also the counties with the most prosperous agricultural regimes (tables 57–59). Kent County farms were distinguished by their large cattle herds, their concentration on market crops (tobacco, corn, and wheat), and the relative lack of importance of secondary crops (oats, rye, potatoes). Kent planters had considerably more farm equipment than farmers in the Delaware Valley or southern New England, although equipment constituted a smaller percentage in value of their inventories. Relative to farmers in Chester and Fairfield, Burlington farmers had larger swine herds, harvested smaller wheat crops and larger corn crops, and paid more attention to produce other than grain. Fairfield stands out among all the counties because there alone average farm wealth dropped between the 1790s and the 1820s—perhaps because plant diseases and the infestation of the Hessian fly forced farmers to abandon wheat.[41]

Even if Fairfield agriculture stagnated, surely the central aspects of rural life for the landed farmers of the mid-Atlantic were stability and prosperity. This basic economic security must be evaluated in the context of an eighteenth-century social order in which traditional notions of status were under challenge politically and in which the traditional stability of rural society was being eroded by both poverty and resettlement. While farming life had always involved the uncertainties of nature and had long depended on the vicissitudes of the market, the multiplication of marketing opportunities in the late eighteenth century meant not only new ways to profit but also new chances to fail. Rural industry, wage labor, diversified production, and new investment possibilities brought with them risk and uncertainty as well as improvement. In this context, the landed farming population—more so than its urban counterpart—balanced stability and change and was able to keep market dis-

Table 57
Farming Economies in the Rural Mid-Atlantic:
Farm Inventories from Burlington County, New Jersey; Chester County,
Pennsylvania; Fairfield County, Connecticut; and Kent County, Maryland, 1760s

	Burlington	Chester	Fairfield	Kent
Inventory Value	223.9	169.3	204.2	724.7
Livestock	60.8	57.1	64.0	120.8
Farm Equipment*	18.5	13.6	13.0	26.7
Crop	50.7	24.8	34.8	157.1
Percent Value in				
Livestock	27.9	33.7	33.5	18.4
Farm Equipment*	8.1	8.8	7.9	4.2
Crop	19.0	16.5	17.6	23.6
Index of Farm Equipment*	5.8	2.7	2.6	4.4
Number of Cattle	10.4	9.9	14.0	20.2
Number of Sheet	9.9	10.3	16.3	29.8
Number of Swine	14.1	6.6	7.0	36.2
Percent of Crop Value in				
Wheat	7.6	29.0	28.2	50.9
Corn	18.1	5.7	9.7	14.7
Other Grains	29.8	45.4	18.4	2.2
Non-Grain Crops	41.1	17.3	39.6	21.9
Percent of Households with				
Apples, Cider, or Cider Mills	51.7	39.5	42.6	34.4
Carpenter Tools	27.6	29.0	42.6	72.1
Oats or Rye	65.5	63.2	76.6	44.3
Potatoes	17.2	5.3	0.0	13.1
Wheels or Looms	65.5	81.6	85.1	96.7
Number	29	38	47	61

Note: in Kent, "non-grain crops" excludes tobacco, which constituted 10.2 percent of crop value. See Table 51 for the definition of farmers.

*Farm Equipment: sum of the number of plows, carts, wheat fans, and four times the number of wagons.

Sources: Probate Sample A, Burlington County Probate Records, NJSA; Chester County Probate Records, Chester County Archives, West Chester, Pennsylvania; Fairfield Probate District Probate Records, Connecticut State Library, Hartford; Kent County Inventories and Accounts, Maryland State Archives, Annapolis.

ruptions at bay even as it exploited new opportunities the market provided.

In all four counties, the general improvement in the economic fortunes of the farm population led to only modest, selective changes in the pattern of consumption, something less than a "consumer revolution" (tables 60 and 61). Consider the important example of tableware. Before the Revolution, most farm households used both pewterware and earthenware; the ceramics were for everyday use and the pewter presumably for more elegant occasions. Pewter was, in fact, generally valued in inventories by weight and was probably accumulated not merely for functional purposes but as a financial reserve that the family could draw on in a tight situation. By the early nineteenth century, however, the use of pewter had become far less common everywhere except in Connecticut, where local production rather than foreign trade supplied households with pewter plates and cups. To replace pewter, families substituted silverware (which also functioned as an investment) and, to a lesser extent, finer varieties of ceramic tableware. In the early nineteenth century, just as in the mid-eighteenth century, however, to eat in a farm household generally meant being served on basic earthenware plates.[42]

Table 58
Farming Economies in the Rural Mid-Atlantic:
Farm Inventories from Burlington County, New Jersey; Chester County,
Pennsylvania; Fairfield County, Connecticut; and Kent County, Maryland, 1790s

	Burlington	Chester	Fairfield	Kent
Inventory Value	287.8	220.1	224.5	608.3
Livestock	85.1	67.1	69.0	140.0
Farm Equipment*	27.7	23.8	15.9	23.8
Crop	64.2	37.5	37.0	156.5
Percent Value in				
Livestock	33.8	34.5	34.9	26.5
Farm Equipment*	11.2	12.9	8.8	5.4
Crop	21.2	17.2	15.5	25.6
Index of Farm Equipment*	10.3	4.6	2.5	5.0
Number of Cattle	11.8	9.0	12.1	21.3
Number of Sheep	7.0	11.6	16.7	24.7
Number of Swine	16.9	7.0	7.4	27.8
Percent of Crop Value if				
Wheat	3.5	28.9	7.2	38.1
Corn	25.2	8.1	10.1	23.9
Other Grains	40.2	31.7	29.3	4.7
Non-Grain Crops	26.7	21.0	49.2	30.4
Percent of Households with				
Apples, Cider, or Cider Mills	62.5	46.9	45.8	19.7
Carpenter Tools	16.7	40.8	45.8	32.4
Oats or Rye	83.3	79.6	65.3	15.5
Potatoes	50.0	44.9	5.6	22.5
Wheels or Looms	79.2	81.6	91.7	90.1
Number	24	49	72	71

Note: in Kent, "non-grain crops" excludes tobacco, which constituted 2.9 percent of crop value. See Table 51 for the definition of farmers.

**Farm Equipment*: sum of the number of plows, carts, wheat fans, and four times the number of wagons.

Sources: Probate Sample A, Burlington County Probate Records, NJSA; Chester County Probate Records, Chester County Archives, West Chester, Pennsylvania; Fairfield Probate District Probate Records, Connecticut State Library, Hartford; Kent County Inventories and Accounts, Maryland State Archives, Annapolis.

The growing sense that it was important to measure time precisely and the status that owning timepieces brought to rural inhabitants also played out differently in the four counties. In Kent, the likelihood that a farmer had a watch improved from about one in four in the 1760s to one in two by the 1820s; in Chester, the poorest county, few farmers had watches in the 1760s, the 1790s, or the 1820s; in Burlington, the ratio went from not quite one in four in the 1760s to one in three in the 1820s; while in Fairfield a small minority had watches by the 1790s. Clocks became everywhere more common over the period, but while they could be found in the 1820s in 47 percent of the Burlington, 53 percent of the Chester, and 60 percent of the Fairfield farm inventories, they appeared in only 33 percent of the Kent inventories despite the fact that Kent farmers were considerably wealthier. The difference probably reflects the fact that Kent residents had readier access to European watches and other mid-Atlantic residents to clocks fashioned by local artisans.[43]

The inventories also establish that not simply in Burlington but throughout the region larger, more expensive pieces of furniture—desks, cupboards, and bureaus

Table 59
Farming Economies in the Rural Mid-Atlantic:
Farm Inventories from Burlington County, New Jersey; Chester County,
Pennsylvania; Fairfield County, Connecticut; and Kent County, Maryland, 1820s

	Burlington	Chester	Fairfield	Kent
Inventory Value	487.2	269.6	218.7	1,042.4
Livestock	93.2	77.9	68.5	216.6
Farm Equipment*	35.1	34.5	24.6	47.3
Crop	78.0	46.0	39.7	242.1
Percent Value in				
Livestock	26.9	29.4	32.6	26.5
Farm Equipment*	10.3	14.4	12.2	5.6
Crop	17.1	16.2	17.7	23.5
Index of Farm Equipment*	9.3	5.4	5.2	10.1
Number of Cattle	9.5	8.2	9.2	20.0
Number of Sheep	8.6	7.2	8.2	25.2
Number of Swine	12.7	8.7	4.7	32.5
Percent of Crop Value in				
Wheat	1.7	12.9	0.4	34.4
Corn	19.5	12.0	10.6	31.2
Other Grains	37.4	38.4	41.1	11.4
Non-Grain Crops	36.1	34.1	46.7	21.3
Percent of Households with				
Apples, Cider, or Cider Mills	42.1	47.5	56.7	34.9
Carpenter Tools	15.8	32.5	70.0	25.8
Oats or Rye	68.4	70.0	74.4	34.9
Potatoes	47.4	42.5	46.7	28.8
Wheels or Looms	63.2	85.0	94.4	83.3
Number	19	40	90	66

Note: in Kent, "non-grain crops" excludes tobacco, which constituted 4.6 percent of crop value. See Table 51 for the definition of farmers.

Farm Equipment: sum of the number of plows, carts, wheat fans, and four times the number of wagons.

Sources: Probate Sample A, Burlington County Probate Records, NJSA; Chester County Probate Records, Chester County Archives, West Chester, Pennsylvania; Fairfield Probate District Probate Records, Connecticut State Library, Hartford; Kent County Inventories and Accounts, Maryland State Archives, Annapolis.

in particular—increasingly could be found in farm homes. Such purchases presumably helped the local economy at the same time that they soaked up reserves that had previously been spent on European imports. More generally, they reflected a culture that was increasingly concerned with the use of private space and the orderly arrangement of possessions. Perhaps the farmers that bought cupboards and desks were attempting to order and control their private lives in a way that paralleled how Beatty and Ten Eyck used account books and diaries to impose routine and system on their agricultural endeavors.[44]

But if new material comforts can be "read" as providing privacy, security, and order, they also can be understood as disruptive in the same way that the new opportunities for investment were. Both upset the traditional relationship between possessions and status; both signified a more fluid, less secure ordering of human relationships. Luxury items had long been the possessions of the elite, and their ownership had reflected both the wealth and the leisure traditionally reserved to families of genteel origin. The spread of cheaply fashioned consumer goods to the homes of the middling sort in early America (as well as in eighteenth-century

Table 60
Comparison of Consumption Components of Farm Inventories,
Burlington County, New Jersey; Chester County, Pennsylvania;
Fairfield County, Conecticut; and Kent County Maryland, 1760–1820

	Burlington	Chester	Fairfield	Kent
Wealth	314.7	220.5	217.5	788.9
Value Consumer Goods	78.7	52.5	72.6	118.6
Percent in Consumer Goods	29.7	28.0	34.3	17.0
Value Beds and Bedding	27.2	16.5	25.7	37.1
Value Clothing	5.5	5.6	7.6	6.2
Index of Consumption 1	4.4	4.3	6.0	7.0
Index of Consumption 2	2.5	2.2	3.0	3.8
Furniture Index	6.4	5.7	6.9	8.5
Percent Owning Specified Items				
Books	59.7	64.6	80.9	78.3
Candlesticks	38.9	48.0	75.6	76.3
Clocks	34.7	37.0	32.5	20.7
Earthenware, Fine	41.7	34.7	42.6	62.6
Guns	62.5	44.1	58.4	71.2
Looking Glasses	63.9	52.8	79.9	84.3
Pewterware	70.8	69.3	86.6	77.3
Silverware	22.2	16.5	52.2	59.6
Teapots	52.8	46.5	85.2	68.2
Watches	20.8	18.1	11.0	34.9
Number	72	127	79	198

Index of Consumption 1: Presence of each of the following items adds one to the index: candlesticks, Dutch oven, earthenware, bed linen, knives and forks, fine earthenware, spices, books, watches, clocks, pictures, and silverware. Maximum score = 12.

Index of Consumption 2: same as above, but counts teapots, coffeepots, pewterware, coach, riding coach, looking glass, and imported cloth. Maximum score = 7.

Furniture Index: sum of number of beds and tables.

Note: See Table 51 for the definition of farmers.

Sources: Probate Sample A, Burlington County Probate Records, NJSA; Chester County Probate Records, Chester County Archives, West Chester, Pennsylvania; Fairfield Probate District Probate Records, Connecticut State Library, Hartford; Kent County Inventories and Accounts, Maryland State Archives, Annapolis.

England) did not invalidate the equation of wealth with luxury, but it did help blur the distinctions between "necessities" and "comforts" and between "comforts" and "luxuries." These distinctions were even further blurred as rural incomes increased, local artisans competed more vigorously with the import market, and refinements of styles multiplied the available variations in basic consumer items. The wealthy, of course, continued to have more and better household furnishings, but all but the poor and the dependent were likely to have a looking glass, a watch, or some such item that several generations before was either unavailable or exclusively found in the homes of genteel families.

This changing pattern of consumer purchasing might be termed a "democratization of wants," and it paralleled the ever greater circulation of financial obligations and paper money. As liquid assets replaced land as the primary form of investment and inheritance, the social order lost another of its defining institutions. Land was itself, of course, a speculative commodity, but for the individual farm family it retained a productive function that provided a hedge against the uncer-

Table 61
Frequency with which Specified Items were Found in Farm Inventories, Burlington County, New Jersey; Chester County, Pennsylvania; Fairfield County, Connecticut; and Kent County, Maryland, 1760s, 1790s, 1820s

	1760s	1790s	1820s
		Percent Holding	
Burlington			
Earthenware	65.6	66.7	79.0
Fine Earthenware	41.4	38.5	47.4
Clocks	34.5	25.0	47.4
Watches	20.7	12.5	31.6
Pewterware	86.2	87.5	26.3
Silverware	20.7	20.8	26.3
Chester			
Earthenware	63.1	53.0	67.5
Fine Earthenware	18.4	32.7	52.5
Clocks	21.1	36.7	52.5
Watches	18.4	18.4	17.5
Pewterware	81.6	73.5	52.5
Silverware	7.9	14.3	27.5
Fairfield			
Earthenware	78.7	73.6	90.0
Fine Earthenware	23.4	37.5	56.7
Clocks	6.4	15.3	60.0
Watches	0.0	15.3	13.3
Pewterware	89.4	93.1	80.0
Silverware	53.2	44.4	57.8
Kent			
Earthenware	88.5	84.5	84.9
Fine Earthenware	72.1	63.4	53.0
Clocks	14.8	16.9	30.3
Watches	27.9	28.2	48.5
Pewterware	100.0	87.3	45.5
Silverware	55.7	56.3	66.7

Note: See Table 51 for the definition of farmers.
Sources: Probate Sample A, Burlington County Probate Records, NJSA; Chester County Probate Records, Chester County Archives, West Chester, Pennsylvania; Fairfield Probate District Probate Records, Connecticut State Library, Hartford, Kent County Inventories and Accounts, Maryland State Archives, Annapolis.

tainties of economic life. New forms of investment, and the depreciation and inflation that went with them, undercut this certainty even as they opened opportunity to those closed out of the land market by high prices or traditional inheritance practices. One indication of this change was that women, who infrequently inherited land, increasingly received financial assets in estate settlements and, in turn, might die with considerable liquid wealth to their name.

Based on the Burlington County inventories alone it would be idle to speculate further on the precise timing of these changes and on their complex relationship to political ideology and cultural values. The emphasis here has been on the two sides of the story—the indications of order, prosperity, and security on the one hand, and the potential for disruption and democratization on the other. Despite the era's unsettling political events, Burlington County inventories reveal the gradual emergence of new patterns of consumer spending and financial investment amid a basic stability in rural life for farming households. They also reveal the persistence of poverty, or at least the continued existence of a significant number of people with few material possessions to their names. To be poor and male in the 1820s, in these terms, was very much like being poor and male in the 1760s—the "democratization of wants" did not transform the lives of agricultural laborers and others without the health or youth to fend for themselves. Nor did the democratization of wants reach an increasing number of women for whom independence and economic insecurity went together, even if some were left inheritances of bonds, notes, and other financial assets.

In none of this was Burlington County unique. New Jersey was not the economic backwater that it has occasionally been depicted to have been; rather, the economic trends in Burlington paralleled those in other parts of the Mid-Atlantic, and, in fact, Burlington farmers were somewhat more prosperous than their Pennsylvania and Connecticut counterparts. More likely than not, the variations in grain-livestock husbandry that probate records reveal in Burlington County and that Peter Wacker's work documents to have existed in the colony and state as a whole reflect the way that soil conditions, settlement date, and proximity to urban markets shaped agricultural life and household decision making throughout the region from southern New England to the northern Chesapeake.

To understand the transformation of Mid-Atlantic rural life in the late eighteenth century, we must settle for small changes. There may well not have been a "consumer revolution," but there was a new breadth of awareness of the power of the market to alter material life and of the opportunities, not always welcome, to define status, place, and power—not as birthrights, but through the risky business of commercial intercourse.

Notes

1. The basic source for this study is the Burlington County Probate Records (hereafter cited as BCPR), NJSA. The Genealogical Society of Utah holds microfilm copies of these records. Individual probate records are cited by the last name of the decedent and the sequential record number (in this case, Stevenson, #11519). Virtually all records contain inventories; some contain wills. When both will and inventory are mentioned, the reader should assume they are both to be found under the same record number.

2. For a general survey of the American economy during this era, see John J. McCusker and Russell R. Menard, *The Economy of British America, 1607–1789* (Chapel Hill, N.C., 1985).

3. On early American agriculture, see Paul G. E. Clemens, "Farming, Planting, and Ranching: The British Colonies," in *The Encyclopedia of the North American Colonies,* ed. Jacob Ernest Cooke (New York, 1993), 1: 677–97. In addition to Peter Wacker's discussion of agriculture in this work, see his earlier study, *Land and People, A Cultural Geography of Preindustrial New Jersey: Origins and Settlement Patterns* (New Brunswick, N.J., 1975),

4. Ibid.

5. On Indian agriculture, see Ives Goddard, "Delaware," in *Northeast,* ed. Bruce G. Trigger (Washington, D.C., 1978), 213–39, vol. 15 of *Handbook of North American Indians,* ed. William C. Sturtevant (Washington, D.C., 1978–), and Herbert C. Kraft, *The Lenape: Archaeology, History, and Ethnography* (Newark, N.J., 1986), 115–59.

6. Of the many works on early American household consumption patterns, see in particular Lois Green Carr and Lorena S. Walsh, "Changing Lifestyles and Consumer Behavior in the Colonial Chesapeake," in *Of Consuming Interests: The Style of Life in the Eighteenth Century*, eds. Cary Carson et al. (Charlottesville, Va., 1994), and Carole Shammas, *The Pre-industrial Consumer in England and America* (Oxford, Eng., 1990).

7. In *From Market-Place to Market Economy: The Transformation of Rural Massachusetts, 1750–1850* (Chicago, Ill., 1992), Winifred Barr Rothenberg analyzes the development of capital markets in early Massachusetts; her work is suggestive for the mid-Atlantic as well. For the impact of the Revolution on the money supply, see E. James Ferguson et al., eds., *The Papers of Robert Morris, 1781–1784*, 6 vols. (Pittsburg, Pa., 1973–84) and Ferguson's earlier study, *The Power of the Purse: A History of American Public Finance, 1776–1790* (Chapel Hill, N.C., 1961).

8. See Carr and Walsh, "Changing Lifestyles."

9. The economy of the mid-Atlantic is described in McCusker and Menard, *Economy of British America*, 189–298. Among other studies that deal with the mid-Atlantic, I used James T. Lemon, *The Best Poor Man's Country: A Geographical Study of Early Southeastern Pennsylvania* (Baltimore, Md., 1972); Paul G. E. Clemens, *The Atlantic Economy and Colonial Maryland's Eastern Shore: From Tobacco to Grain* (Ithaca, N.Y., 1980); Jackson Turner Main, *Society and Economy in Colonial Connecticut* (Princeton, N.J., 1985); and Thomas M. Doerflinger, *A Vigorous Spirit of Enterprise, Merchants and Economic Development in Revolutionary Philadelphia* (Chapel Hill, N.C., 1986). On the early national economy, see Douglass C. North, *The Economic Growth of the United States, 1790–1860* (Englewood Cliffs, N.J., 1961); Curtis P. Nettles, *The Emergence of a National Economy, 1775–1815* (New York, 1962); and Paul W. Gates, *The Farmer's Age: Agriculture, 1815–1860* (New York, 1960).

10. Ibid. For disruptions in the pre-Revolutionary urban economy, see Gary B. Nash, *The Urban Crucible, Social Change, Political Consciousness, and the Origins of the American Revolution* (Cambridge, Mass., 1979).

11. Unless otherwise noted, the following discussion relies on BCPR. For the years noted in the text, I have used two overlapping groupings of probate records, one that includes only completely itemized inventories (sample A) and a larger set that includes all the inventories (sample B). In both cases, I have used the full sample and a smaller set of inventories that includes only farmers. Footnotes indicate which group of inventories is being discussed. Each grouping is more carefully defined in the appendix, and the methodological problems associated with the use of New Jersey inventories are discussed there as well. It should be kept in mind that New Jersey inventories did not include real property (land and buildings).

New Jersey probate records have been abstracted in *New Jersey State Archives*, 1st ser., vols. 23, 30, and 32–42 (1880–1949). For other uses of these records, see Harry B. Weiss, *The Personal Estates of Early Farmers and Tradesmen of Colonial New Jersey, 1670–1750* (Trenton, N.J., 1971).

On the analysis of probate records, see Gloria L. Main, *Tobacco Colony: Life in Early Maryland, 1650–1720* (Princeton, N.J., 1982); Main, *Society and Economy in Colonial Connecticut*; Alice Hanson Jones, *Wealth of a Nation to Be: The American Colonies on the Eve of Revolution* (New York, 1980); Daniel Scott Smith, "Under-registration and Bias in Probate Records: An Analysis of Data from Eighteenth-Century Hingham, Massachusetts," *William and Mary Quarterly*, 3rd ser., 32 (1975): 100-110; and Gloria L. Main, "The Correction of Biases in Colonial American Probate Records," *Historical Methods Newsletter* 8 (1974): 10–28.

12. For New Jersey population figures, see Peter O. Wacker, *Land and People*, 413–17; and State of New Jersey, Department of State, Census Bureau, *Compendium of Censuses, 1726–1905, Together with the Tabulated Returns of 1905* (Trenton, N.J., 1906), 15–16. The 1760 figure is an estimate based on earlier and later censuses. Population figures by township for 1784 are available in Box 22, New Jersey Tax Ratables, NJSA, and, by county, in Jedidiah Morse, *The American Geography; or, A View of the Present Situation of the United States* (Elizabethtown, N.J., 1789), 284–85. Township figures for 1810 and 1820 are published in Thomas Gordon, *Gazetteer of the State of New Jersey* (Trenton, N.J., 1834), 112.

13. On economic growth in early America, the place to begin is Paul David, "The Growth of Real Product in the United States before 1840: New Evidence, Controlled Conjectures," *Journal of Economic History* 27 (1967): 151–95. See also Stanley Engerman and Robert E. Gallman, "U.S. Economic Growth, 1783–1860," *Research in Economic History* 8 (1983): 1–46. For a general discus-

sion of economic growth in the colonial era, see McCusker and Menard, *Economy of British America,* 258–76. Main, in *Society and Economy in Colonial Connecticut,* the most comprehensive probate inventory study yet undertaken, finds little indication of per capita economic growth in pre-Revolutionary Connecticut; see especially 115–51.

14. Sample B, BCPR. Such a measure of long-term growth is obviously sensitive to the "benchmark" periods selected for analysis. In this case, the selection was based primarily on the quality of the records, but it is important to note that using the 1760s and the years before 1820 biases the results against finding evidence of economic growth. The 1760s, because of the demand for wheat, were unusually prosperous, while the last years of the second decade of the eighteenth century were a time of falling prices, leading to the panic of 1819.

15. Sample B, BCPR, and Burlington County Probate Records, 1797–1800, NJSA.

16. Sample B, BCPR. Because there are no administrative accounts to match the Burlington inventories, it is impossible to determine the relationship between debts, obligations, and financial assets. In Chester County, Pennsylvania; Fairfield County, Connecticut; and Kent County, Maryland, on average, debts amounted to more than assets.

On New Jersey currency issues, see Thomas L. Purvis, *Proprietors, Patronage and Paper Money: Legislative Politics in New Jersey, 1703–1776* (New Brunswick, N.J., 1986), 144–75; Richard P. McCormick, *Experiment in Independence: New Jersey in the Critical Period, 1781–1789* (New Brunswick, N.J., 1950), 186–206; and Joseph Albert Ernst, *Money and Politics in America, 1755–1775: A Study in the Currency Act of 1764 and the Political Economy of Revolution* (Chapel Hill, N.C., 1973), 260–64, 316–18, 367. For a discussion of the relationship of land to financial assets in inheritances, see Toby L. Ditz, *Property and Kinship: Inheritance in Early Connecticut, 1750–1820* (Princeton, N.J., 1986).

17. Box 14, New Jersey Tax Ratables, NJSA. Chester Township tax lists survive for 1774, 1780, 1796, 1797, 1802, 1806, and 1813. For tax laws, see "An Act to Settle the Quota of the Several Counties in this Colony, for the levying Taxes," [1769] in *Laws of the Royal Colony of New Jersey, 1760–1769, New Jersey Archives,* comp. Bernard Bush (Trenton, N.J., 1982), 3d. ser., 3: 547–64; and Acts of 1781, chap. 12; Acts of 1782, chap. 31; Acts of 1783, chap. 19; Acts of 1787, chap. 208; Library of Congress, Early State Record Series (microfilm). The best discussion of early New Jersey agriculture is Hubert G. Schmidt, *Rural Hunterdon: An Agricultural History* (New Brunswick, N.J., 1945).

18. Ibid.

19. Carl Magnus Anderson, "Pastor Wrangel's Trip to the Shore," *Proc. N.J.H.S.* 58 (1940): 5–31; quotations are found on 11–12, 22, and 24.

20. Mitchie J. E. Budka, *Under Their Vine and Fig Tree: Travels through America in 1797–1799, 1805, with Some Further Account of Life in New Jersey by Julian Ursyn Niemcewicz,* vol. 14 of *Collections of the New Jersey Historical Society* (Newark, N.J., 1965), 222, 219.

21. Box 17, New Jersey Tax Ratables, NJSA. Tax figures survive for 1773, 1795–97, 1802, 1805–9, 1811–13. Population figures for density calculations come from the 1784 Burlington tax abstract, Box 22, New Jersey Tax Ratables, NJSA, and the *Compendium of Censuses,* 16. Area figures for density estimates can be calculated in two ways, based only on land actually settled or on the total area of a township. These figures use the total area as given in Gordon, *Gazetteer of the State of New Jersey,* 112. For Little Egg Harbor, the population rose between 1784 and 1820 from 602 to 1102; for Chester, from 1170 to 2253. Little Egg Harbor contained 76,800 acres; Chester, 22,000. In 1784, taxes were levied on 18,946 acres in Chester and 20,265 in Little Egg Harbor.

22. Wealth comparisons from sample B, BCPR; comparison of inventories from sample A, BCPR. The small sample size for the east region (Little Egg Harbor) means that these figures must be used with caution; I have excluded a particularly highly valued inventory from the sample in calculating the values in table 2.

23. Gill, #7809.

24. Arden, #11422; Middleton, #13003.

25. Aaronson, #11418; Bound, #13322; Heritage, #11497. Appraisers excluded a surviving husband's or wife's clothing; they may have excluded other personal property as well, but there was no statutory requirement to do so.

26. Robson, #13147; Tonklin, #8453; Brooke, #11585.

27. Sample A, BCPR. On slaveholding, see Jean R. Soderlund, *Quakers and Slavery: A Divided Spirit*

(Princeton, N.J., 1985).

28. Sample A, BCPR. See also, Main, *Society and Economy in Colonial Connecticut*, 200–240, and Schmidt, *Rural Hunterdon*, 90–111.

29. Sample A, BCPR.

30. T. H. Breen has imaginatively discussed changing attitudes toward consumption; see in particular "An Empire of Goods: The Anglicization of Colonial America, 1690–1776," *Journal of British Studies* 25 (October 1986): 467–99, and " 'Baubles of Britain': The American and Consumer Revolutions of the Eighteenth Century," *Past and Present* 119 (1988): 73–104. James Deetz, *In Small Things Forgotten: The Archeology of Early American Life* (Garden City, N.Y., 1977), provides a fascinating introduction to efforts to understand the meaning that colonial Americans assigned to material objects. For a more general introduction to work on material culture, see Kenneth L. Ames and Gerald W. R. Ward, eds., *Decorative Arts and Household Furnishings in America, 1650–1920: An Annotated Bibliography* (Winterthur, Del., 1989).

31. Sample A, BCPR; Emlez, #13115; Hooton, #13123.

32. In defining this aspect of the study, I relied heavily on Carr and Walsh, "Changing Lifestyles and Consumer Behavior." Main, *Society and Economy in Colonial Connecticut*, 109–10, 137–39, analyzes the relationship between age and wealth and argues that many poor decedents were young. On the rural poor, see Robert E. Cray, Jr., *Paupers and Poor Relief in New York City and Its Rural Environs, 1700–1830* (Philadelphia, 1988). The approximation that one decedent in three was poor is based on average estate values, financial assets excluded. In the 1820s many of these poor decedents who left inventories had a substantial amount in financial assets.

33. See note 9 above.

34. Clemens, *From Tobacco to Grain*. The 1784 Burlington County figures come from the Burlington County Tax Abstracts, Box 22, New Jersey Tax Ratables, NJSA.

35. On the Revolution, see "Inventories of the Damages Sustained by the Inhabitants of the County of Burlington in the State of New Jersey from the Wonton Ravage and Spoil of the Troops of the British Army and Their Adherents from December 1776 to August 1781," NJSA. The file contains 335 damage claims (some made as well because of damage done by the Continental Army), most of which date from December 1776 or June 1778. Descriptions of the fighting and occasionally of the damages can be found in Francis B. Lee, ed., *Documents Relating to the Revolutionary History of the State of New Jersey, Extracts from American Newspapers*, in *New Jersey Archives*, 2d ser. See, for example, vol. 2 (1778), 208, 279–80, 373, 375, 481–483 (fighting and property damage at Bordentown), and vol. 3 (1779), 100, 158–59 (coastal raids). More general treatments are Lloyd Griscom, *Burlington County and the American Revolution* (Burlington, N.J., 1976). For Maryland's eastern shore, see Ronald Hoffman, *A Spirit of Dissension: Economics, Politics, and the Revolution in Maryland* (Baltimore, Md., 1973), 197–203, 224–33, and J. Thomas Scharf, *History of Maryland from the Earliest Period to the Present Day* (Baltimore, Md., 1879), 2:317–19, 385–87, 429–31. On Chester County see J. Smith Futhey and Gilbert Cope, *History of Chester County, Pennsylvania* (Philadelphia, Pa., 1881), 59–116, which includes a summary of damage claims (110) similar to those for Burlington County. The war in Fairfield is discussed in Thomas J. Farnham, *Fairfield: The Biography of a Community, 1639–1989* (West Kennebunk, Maine, 1988), 78–97; and Joy Day Buel and Richard Buel, Jr., *The Way of Duty: A Woman and Her Family in Revolutionary America* (New York, 1984). For markets during the era, see Anne Bezanson, *Prices and Inflation during the American Revolution: Pennsylvania, 1770–1790* (Philadelphia, Pa., 1951).

36. For Kent County, the basic source is the 1783 State Tax (and census). The original is in the Scharf Collection, Ms. 1999, Maryland Historical Society, Baltimore, and a photostatic copy is available at the Maryland State Archives, Annapolis. For Chester County, the 1783 tax returns (with census) contain similar information, and the 1789 returns provide convenient summary data on mills and other artisan establishments in the county. The returns are at the Chester County Archives, West Chester, Pennsylvania, and are also available on microfilm from the Pennsylvania State Library, Harrisburg. For a discussion of the 1783 census, see Lucy Simler and Paul G. E. Clemens, "The 'Best Poor Man's Country' in 1783: The Population Structure of Rural Society in Late-Eighteenth-Century Southeastern Pennsylvania," *Proceedings of the American Philosophical Society* 133 (1989): 234–61. For Burlington County, the Burlington tax abstracts from 1773, 1774, 1784, 1801, and 1811, Box 14 and Box 22, New Jersey Tax Ratables, NJSA, are particularly useful, but there are no township returns for

1784 to go with the 1784 abstract. Fairfield population figures come from Evarts B. Greene and Virginia D. Harrington, *American Population before the Federal Census of 1790* (New York, 1932), 61, and the population density figure comes from Bruce C. Daniels, *The Connecticut Town: Growth and Development, 1635–1790* (Middletown, Conn., 1979), 52 (table 3).

On contrasting labor systems, see Paul G.E. Clemens and Lucy Simler, "Rural Labor and the Farm Household in Chester County, Pennsylvania, 1760–1820," in *Work and Labor in Early America*, ed. Steven Innes (Chapel Hill, N.C., 1988), 106–43; and Clemens, *From Tobacco to Grain.*

37. Kent County Inventories, IX, 65–67; Kent County Wills, VII, 234; Maryland State Archives.

38. These comparisons are based on the tables in the text. The Burlington source material came from both Sample A, BCPR, and Sample B, BCPR. Chester County data come from 243 Chester County inventories at the Chester County Archives, West Chester, Pennsylvania. Fairfield County data are derived from 621 inventories, most of which are available at the Connecticut State Library, Hartford. Kent County data come from 448 Kent County inventories at the Maryland State Archives, Annapolis.

Each of the three sets of inventories was evaluated in the local money of account, and price differences among the three counties were substantial. To take one example, the average value of a cow in Burlington County in the 1790s was 94 shillings; in Chester 89 shillings; in Fairfield 81 shillings; and in Kent 69 shillings (the value of a cow was used in the price index constructed for each county). The procedure used to create a price index and adjust estate values is discussed briefly in the appendix. While the four sets of inventories are not directly comparable, price differences do not affect a comparison of the trend in estate values over time.

One possible explanation for the difference between Chester and Burlington is the growth potential of the relatively unsettled central and eastern parts of Burlington County. As the comparison of Chester and Little Egg Harbor townships made clear, eastern Burlington had numerous entrepreneurial concerns before the Revolution, but these were not sustained, and the area remained thinly settled and not noticeably prosperous. In Chester there was no similar frontier area, although the western part of the county was less heavily settled.

39. On long-term trends in the economy, see North, *Economic Growth;* and Nettles, *Emergence of a National Economy.*

40. Analysis based on Sample B, BCPR. The percentage of decedents classified as poor males, non-farmers, or women in Burlington County went from 36 (1760s) to 58 (1790s) to 59 (1820). Women made up 13 percent of the sample in the 1760s, 22 percent in the 1790s, and 37 percent in the 1820s. In Kent, however, approximately two out of five decedents were poor males, non-farmers, or women in each time period, but their average wealth dropped considerably in the 1790s. This drop was largely responsible for the drop in average estate value of the entire inventory sample.

41. Livestock comparisons can also be made from the tax list, but they are at best rough estimates because the definition of taxable cattle was not the same in Burlington, Chester, and Kent counties. In Chester, individuals were taxed on horned cattle above three years of age (Acts of 1783, chap. 6); in Kent, black cattle (Acts of 1782, chap. 6, section 17); in Burlington, horned cattle two years old and upwards (Acts of 1783, chap. 19, section 2). The laws are in the Early State Records microfilm series. Alternatively, one can compare the number of cows and cattle per farm in the probate inventories. For Burlington, in the 1790s, there were 6.1 cows per farmer and 11.5 cattle per farmer; in Chester, 4.2 and 9.1; and in Kent, 9.6 and 21.2. Kent farms were on average, however, somewhat larger than Burlington and Chester farms. In 1784, Kent holdings averaged 258 acres per owner (excluding non-resident holdings) and 145 acres per occupier (including tenants); in Chester in 1784, occupiers averaged 135 acres (including tenants but excluding cottagers). Burlington figures are not available for 1783–84. For the definition of farmers applied to the probate inventories, see the appendix.

42. See note 38 above.

43. One can speculate on two other distinctions between watches and clocks: watches were more suitable for public rather than private display; and watches were more useful in regulating field work. While the former might favor the use of watches in the Chesapeake, the latter fits better with the wage labor system developing in Burlington and Chester.

44. Among recent studies that use probate inventories to study consumption, see the forum "Toward a History of the Standard of Living in British North America," *William and Mary Quarterly,* 3d ser., 45 (January 1988): 116–70; Jack Michel, "'In a Manner and Fashion Suitable to Their

Degree:' A Preliminary Investigation of the Material Culture of Early Rural Pennsylvania," *Working Papers from the Regional Economic History Research Center* 5, 1 (1981).

See also Cary Carson, "The Consumer Revolution in Colonial British America. Why Demand?"; Hoffman, *Of Consuming Interests*; Neil McKendrick, John Brewer, and J.H. Plumb, *The Birth of a Consumer Society: The Commercialization of Eighteenth-Century England* (Bloomington, Ind., 1982); Lorna Weatherill, *Consumer Behavior and Material Culture in Britain, 1660–1760* (London, 1988); and Kevin M. Sweeney, "Mansion People: Kinship, Class, and Architecture in Western Massachusetts in the Mid-Eighteenth Century," *Winterthur Portfolio* 19, 4 (Winter 1984): 231–55.

Probate studies are more useful in tracking durable goods than clothing, food, and alcohol, all of which were bought in quantity in Early America. Fine cloth and clothing were major import items, but outside New England, clothing was generally not itemized in inventories.

Eleventh Month, November, 1819.

APPENDIX

There are two methodological problems common to most work with probate inventories: (1) the estates of all decedents should have entered probate, but it is probable that some estates were not probated and that others were but the records no longer survive; (2) even if all decedents were probated, their inventories do not necessarily reflect the wealth distribution among the living population. In general, probate inventories may be biased toward an older, somewhat wealthier population, and in newly settled regions the extent of this bias may change markedly over time as the demographic structure of the population changes.

In the case of Burlington County, a third methodological problem arises. Except for the brief period after the American Revolution, approximately half of the probate inventories were taken down in summary form, not fully itemized. Thus an inventory might list values only for general categories such as "livestock," "household goods," or "implements of husbandry," to pick three common examples. In the post-Revolutionary period, most inventories were complete (fully itemized).

Finally, when comparisons are made across time, prices must be normalized to eliminate the effects of inflation or deflation. Or, when comparisons are made between regions, prices must be adjusted to provide similar units of account between regions.

This appendix describes the methods used to analyze the inventories and notes some of the remaining problems.

A. Constant Prices

Inventory prices were normalized in relationship to the prices in the 1790–96 probate records (expressed in pounds). Adjusting prices required dividing inventory values from the 1760s (expressed in pounds) by .88 and dividing inventory values from 1817–22 (expressed in dollars) by 2.61.

These indexes were constructed by comparing the prices of seven items in four categories—watches, teakettles, beds (consumption goods); plows and carts (producer goods); cows (livestock); and corn (produce).

	1762–69 (shillings)	1790–96 (shillings)	1817–23 (dollars)
Watch	100	78	11.00
Teakettle	8.95	8.06	.58
Bed	138	171	23.52
Plow	21	24	3.90
Cart	47	55	12.00
Cow	76	94	14.00
Corn	2.42	5.31	.53

To convert 1760 prices into 1790s values, (1) price ratios (1760/1790) were created for each item in the index; (2) these ratios were then averaged for each category of item; (3) and category averages were themselves averaged. In the last step, each category average was "weighted" to reflect the average percentage of value any given category of goods had in all the inventories.

For example, (1) the ratio for plows was .88 (21/24) and for carts .85 (47/55); (2) the average for producer goods was thus .865 ([.88 + .85]/2); (3) producer goods constituted 9 percent in value of all goods held in all inventories, so producer goods contributed .07785 (.09 x .865) to the final conversion index. Similar calculations were made for the other categories and to convert 1820 prices to 1790 prices.

The comparisons among the four counties required a creation of a second set of conversion indexes. These were constructed the same way for each county. Then each county index was converted to Kent 1790 prices. This two-step process created the following set of conversion indexes:

	Burlington	Chester	Fairfield	Kent
1760s	1.14	1.17	.98	.79
1790s	1.29	1.07	.88	1.00
1820s	3.37	3.61	3.69	2.97

That is, values given in the original inventories were divided by the above indexes to create equivalent values expressed in Kent 1790 prices.

B. Definition of Farmers

In the absence of adequate tax and demographic records, there is no completely satisfactory way to determine the relationship of the probated population to the living population. One could correlate tax records, inventories, and wills for the periods from 1773–76, 1796–1800, and 1802–15 but only at the sacrifice of the chronological scope of this essay. For the purposes of this essay, I have treated in detail a group whose estates probably reflect closely the wealth of a similar group among the living population—farmers. This group has been defined as men having at least (in 1790–96 prices) £15 in livestock and at least £5 in farm tools. I have added artisans who also meet these two requirements, and for Kent County I have included decedents whose farm tools were worth less than £10 but whose crop was valued at £20 or more. So defined, these farmers were almost exclusively landowners and, as the essay notes, were clearly more wealthy than the general probate population. The relationship of probated farmers to other probated decedents provides a very crude index of the general health of the economy.

C. Completely and Incompletely Itemized Inventories

This study was based primarily on a group of 205 inventories, 50 from 1762–69, 74 from 1790–96, and 81 from 1817–23. Almost all inventories from 1790–96 were complete, but the 50 used from 1760-69 and the 81 used from 1817–23 represented less than half of the inventories taken during those years; ones not included in the study were those that were incompletely itemized. To check the relationship between the complete and incomplete inventories, I recorded the data that was available from 58 additional inventories from 1762–69 and 120 additional inventories from 1817–23. These additional inventories provided information about the components of wealth-holding (crop, livestock, farm and artisan tools, consumption goods, store goods and artisan stock, cash, and financial assets), but not about specific items (for example, plows, cows, or desks). The two sets of inventories in both periods were very similar, with the important exception that the incompletely itemized inventories averaged much more in financial assets (bonds, bills, notes, and book accounts). Throughout the study, conclusions based on complete inventories are noted as coming from Sample A. Conclusions based on both sets of inventories are noted as coming from Sample B.

The tables that follow provide basic comparative figures for the completely and incompletely itemized inventories:

Table A.1
Comparison of Completely and Incompletely Itemized Inventories, Burlington County, 1762–69
(values in 1790–96 pounds)

	Complete	Incomplete	Average
All Inventories			
Average Wealth	256.6	210.5	231.8
Livestock	57.0	55.9	56.4
Crop	43.7	27.4	34.9
Tools	17.9	22.7	20.5
Labor	20.8	14.2	17.3
Consumption	81.2	73.4	77.0
Cash	21.8	12.3	16.7
Stock and Store	14.2	4.6	9.0
Assets[a]	223.8	251.1	238.3
Number	50	58	108
Farm Inventories Only			
Average Wealth	317.4	353.3	334.5
Livestock	85.3	103.7	94.0
Crop	65.6	50.9	58.6
Tools	22.6	39.5	30.6
Labor	32.2	22.6	27.6
Consumption	88.0	109.0	98.0
Cash	21.6	19.8	20.7
Stock and Store	2.2	7.8	4.9
Assets[a]	263.9	401.5	329.3
Number	32	29	61

[a]Assets not included in wealth figure.

D. Comparison of Inventories and Tax List Data

It is possible to provide some sense of how much the probate inventories over-represent wealthier (and older) Burlington County residents by comparing the inventory sample with county tax lists from the 1790s. Approximately two-thirds of the decedents from the 1790s could be located on a tax list and their landowner-ship and tax status determined. Table A.3 compares the tax status of Burlington decedents with the tax status of taxable inhabitants of Chester Township in 1796. While Chester Township is not representative of the entire county, it is typical of the more densely populated Delaware River region of Burlington. Not surprisingly, the table indicates that the probate inventories overrepresent the landed population and underrepresent tenants and cottagers (householders) and agricultural workers (single men).

Tax list figures can be used to adjust the average wealth estimate for Burlington County. To do this, it is necessary to calculate the average inventoried wealth for each tax classification and then construct a "weighted" average from these figures (using the percent representation of each tax classification on the tax list to weight the inventory figures). The result, using the Chester Township tax figures, is to

Table A.2
Comparison of Itemized Inventories,
Burlington County, 1790–96 and 1797–1800
(values from inventories)

	1790–96	1797–1800
All Inventories		
Average Wealth	193.6	381.7
Livestock	42.0	98.9
Crop	31.3	60.9
Tools	13.9	27.2
Labor	.6	.6
Consumption	71.5	148.8
Cash	31.0	22.4
Stock and Store	3.3	23.0
Assets[a]	376.2	331.3
Number	74	142
Farm Inventories Only		
Average Wealth	351.2	555.7
Livestock	103.1	173.8
Crop	76.4	100.1
Tools	33.4	49.7
Labor	1.8	1.0
Consumption	95.7	175.1
Cash	42.5	28.7
Stock and Store	.1	27.2
Assets[a]	398.1	343.7
Number	26	67

[a]Assets not included in wealth figure.*

Table A.3
Comparison of Completely and Incompletely Itemized Inventories,
Burlington County, 1817–23
(values in 1790–96 pounds)

	Complete	Incomplete	Average
All Inventories			
Average Wealth	297.4	299.0	298.3
Livestock	34.9	50.6	44.3
Crop	29.5	39.5	35.5
Tools	14.9	25.6	21.3
Labor	0.0	0.0	0.0
Consumption	73.2	101.4	90.0
Cash	68.2	46.1	55.0
Stock and Store	80.0	31.1	50.8
Assets[a]	434.1	1,109.7	837.4
Number	81	120	201
Farm Inventories Only			
Average Wealth	590.7	539.2	555.6
Livestock	112.1	127.4	122.6
Crop	95.1	99.1	97.8
Tools	41.9	57.3	52.4
Labor	0.0	0.0	0.0
Consumption	142.1	153.2	149.6
Cash	199.5	85.7	121.9
Stock and Goods	3.6	5.5	4.9
Assets[a]	648.1	1,974.7	1,552.6
Number	21	45	66

[a]Assets not included in wealth figure.

Table A.4
Comparison of the Tax Status of Burlington County Decedents in the 1790s
and Chester Township Taxables in 1796

Tax Status	Chester Township Tax List, 1796		Burlington County Decedents, 1790s		
	#	%	#	%	Wealth
Landed					
Landowners	104	37	45	47	584.5
Landed Householders	43	15	17	18	262.8
Other	4	1	4	4	372.1
House and Lot Owners					
Householders	23	8	12	13	303.0
House and Lot only	3	1	3	3	200.2
Householders	54	19	11	12	170.2
Singlemen	48	17	3	3	197.9
Total	279	98	95	100	358.8
Not on Tax List	n.a.		47		

Note: Percentages do not add up to one hundred because of round-off error. The wealth figures come from the probate inventories. The "total" wealth figure (column 5) is the weighted average; the weighting was done using the percentages in the tax list figures (column 2). See Table 1 for the definition of "householder."

decrease average inventoried wealth from 381.7 to 358.8 (see Tables A.2 and A.4). The more crucial problem, however, is not to correct the bias in the 1790 figures but to determine if the bias changes significantly between 1760 and 1820. Only if the degree of overrepresentation of landed (or of older, wealthier) residents is approximately the same in each time period do the probate inventories provide a reliable measure of economic trends in Burlington County.

E. Life-Cycle Analysis of the Probate Inventories

The problems suggested by the tax list analysis presented above can be addressed in part by life-cycle analysis. Table A.5 provides average wealth figures for several stages in the life cycle of Burlington County decedents in the 1760s, 1790s, and 1820s. In the case of men, the life-cycle stage was determined from wills; if there was no will, the individual's estate is in the "no information" category. In the case of women, widows were frequently identified as widows and occasionally identified as spinsters even when there was no will. Women about whom there was no information are in the "not married" category. As the categories are based on the wills, they are likely to overlap considerably. For example, the category, "Married, Children of Age," undoubtedly includes numerous decedents who had grandchildren but did not mention them in their wills, while the category, "Married, No Children," may include some decedents who had children but did not mention them.

The changing distribution of probate records in the various life-cycle categories between the 1760s and 1820s suggests a gradual aging of the probate population. As the proportion of immigrants in the population probably decreased from the 1770s on, the population may have aged; if so, this aging could account for the changing distribution. Alternatively, the change may simply reflect greater concern on the part of older residents to write wills; such a change might have accompanied the shift from land toward money and credits as the most important form of inheritance. An even more significant trend was the growing proportion of independent women among decedents. As these women remained poor relative to male decedents, including women in the calculations increasingly pulled down average wealth figures.

One measure of the impact of these changes is to ask what average wealth would have been in the early 1820s if the life-cycle distribution was the same as it had been in the 1760s. In the 1820s, average inventory wealth was 298.3. For those with life-cycle information (122 inventories), the average inventory wealth was 314.0. If the 1760s life-cycle distribution were used, average wealth would increase to 352.3. This reinforces the conclusion that 1760-1820 was an era of economic growth.

Table A.5
Average Wealth by Life-Cycle Stage of Decedents, Burlington County,
1760s, 1790s,1820s

Life-Cycle Stage	Average Wealth (pounds in 1790–96 values)		
	1760s	1790s	1820s
No Information	158.3	153.6	274.1
Young	18.4	85.9	81.4
Married, No Children	244.1	—	237.0
Married, Young Children	174.1	230.9	402.3
Married, Children of Age	375.4	290.8	195.7
Married, Grandchildren	437.8	272.6	392.8
Older, Not Married	308.8	580.6	2100.2
Women, Never Married	16.8	485.8	77.1
Women, Formerly Married	106.9	86.8	122.4
Women, Not Married	—	114.3	96.9

Number of Cases (and Percentage of Inventories)

Life-Cycle Stage	1760s		1790s		1820s	
	#	(%)	#	(%)	#	(%)
No Information	35	n.a.	30	n.a.	79	n.a.
Young	2	(3)	3	(7)	5	(4)
Married, No Children	3	(4)	—	—	6	(5)
Married, Young Children	17	(23)	4	(9)	14	(11)
Married, Children of Age	15	(21)	13	(30)	16	(13)
Married, Grandchildren	18	(25)	4	(9)	33	(27)
Older, Not Married	3	(4)	3	(7)	5	(4)
Women, Never Married	3	(4)	1	(2)	16	(13)
Women, Formerly Married	12	(16)	14	(32)	16	(13)
Women, Not Married	—	—	2	(5)	11	(9)
Total with Information	73	(100)	44	(101)	122	(99)
Total	108		74		201	

Note: percentages based on the number of decedents about which there is life-cycle information. Not all percentages sum to one hundred because of round-off error. See the text for definitions of life-cycle stages.
Source: Inventory Sample B.

A Note on Sources

This essay is designed to complement the extensive bibliography on land use, agriculture, and population in early New Jersey found in Peter O. Wacker, *Land and People: A Cultural Geography of Preindustrial New Jersey: Origins and Settlement Patterns* (New Brunswick, N.J., 1975).

In *The Best Poor Man's Country: A Geographical Study of Early Southeastern Pennsylvania* (Baltimore, Md., 1972), James T. Lemon accomplished three things that are of significance to this study. In a field dominated by work on New England and the Chesapeake, Lemon focused attention on the Mid-Atlantic and the prosperity of its mixed livestock-grain farm economy. Second, he stressed the "liberal values" of the farming population, their willingness to improvise and improve and their desire to profit. In arguing that most farmers were "liberal," Lemon broke with historians who contended that ordinary farmers were custom-bound and that only a small elite had the inclination or entrepreneurial skill to pursue market agriculture vigorously. He also broke with scholars who looked to cultural differences (in this case, British and German) for the primary explanation of regional variations in agricultural practices and development. In offering an alternative way of understanding the geography of agricultural development Lemon made his third major contribution. He related contrasting patterns of land use to soil conditions and location. Lemon argued that circumstance and opportunity, rather than differences in values and customs, explained why the inhabitants of some regions specialized in certain types of agriculture and inhabitants of other regions did not.

The Best Poor Man's Country and *Land and People* were not alone in opening up new geographical perspectives on eighteenth-century British North America. Andrew Hill Clark's *Acadia: The Geography of Early Nova Scotia to 1760* (Madison, Wisc., 1968); Harry Roy Merrens, *Colonial North Carolina in the Eighteenth Century: A Historical Geography* (Chapel Hill, N.C., 1964); and Peter Wacker, *The Musconetcong Valley of New Jersey: A Historical Geography* (New Brunswick, N.J., 1968) were among a number of extremely significant studies of land use and the growth and distribution of population. More recently, works such as John R. Stilgoe, *The Common Landscape of America, 1580 to 1845* (New Haven, Conn., 1982); William Cronon, *Changes in the Land: Indians, Colonists, and the Ecology of New England* (New York, 1983); and Donald William Meinig, *The Shaping of America: A Geographical Perspective on Five Hundred Years of History*, vol. 1, *Atlantic America, 1492–1800* (New Haven, Conn., 1986) have challenged colonial scholars to reconsider how they think about the land and landscape of early America. For New Jersey, A. Philip Muntz, "The Changing Geography of the New Jersey Woodlands, 1600–1900," (Ph.D. diss., University of Wisconsin, 1959), and Emily W. Russell, "Vegetational Change in Northern New Jersey Since 1500 A.D.: A Palynological, Vegetational and Historical Synthesis" (Ph.D. diss., Rutgers University, 1979) are useful sources.

The challenge to Lemon's work set off a fruitful debate. James A. Henretta focused specifically on *The Best Poor Man's Country* in "Families and Farms:

Mentalité in Pre-industrial America," *William and Mary Quarterly*, 3d ser., 35 (1978): 3–32, and asked if much of the behavior that Lemon attributed to market-oriented, liberal values could not be explained as family strategies to assure long-term household stability. That debate has enormously enriched our understanding of early American agriculture, as demonstrated in such recent works as Christopher Clark, *The Roots of Rural Capitalism: Western Massachusetts, 1780–1860* (Ithaca, N.Y., 1990)—which follows Henretta's work in focusing on household strategies—and Winifred Barr Rothenberg, *From Market-Places to a Market Economy: The Transformation of Rural Massachusetts* (Chicago, 1992)—which provides ample evidence that late eighteenth-century Massachusetts farmers responded enthusiastically to ever "thickening" market opportunities. Recently, the debate has led historians away from production to questions about consumption; the current state of the analysis can be seen in Cary Carson et al., eds., *Of Consuming Interests: The Style of Life in the Eighteenth Century* (Charlottesville, Va., 1994).

In light of Lemon's work, historians have done surprisingly little with Mid-Atlantic agriculture compared to what historical geographers have produced. The best two studies for New Jersey, both extremely useful despite their age, are Carl Raymond Woodward, *Ploughs and Politicks: Charles Read of New Jersey and his Notes on Agriculture, 1715–1774* (New Brunswick, N.J., 1941); and Herbert G. Schmidt, *Rural Hunterdon: An Agricultural History* (New Brunswick, N.J., 1945). Andrew D. Mellick, Jr., *Story of an Old Farm; Life in New Jersey in the Eighteenth Century* (Somerville, N.J., 1889), reprinted in an edition edited by Hubert G. Schmidt as *The Old Farm* (New Brunswick, N.J., 1961), also provides valuable insights.

Research into the primary sources on colonial New Jersey should begin with Mary R. Murrin, comp., *New Jersey Historical Manuscripts: A Guide to Collections in the State* (Trenton, N.J., 1987) and Don C. Skemer and Robert C. Morris, comps., *Guide to the Manuscript Collections of the New Jersey Historical Society*, vol. 15 of *Collections of the New Jersey Historical Society* (Trenton, N.J., 1979). For this work, the major repositories have been the New Jersey Historical Society, Newark; Rutgers University Library, New Brunswick; and the Department of State, New Jersey State Archives, Trenton. To survey New Jersey records comprehensively, it is necessary to check New York and Pennsylvania archives as well; both the New-York Historical Society, New York City, and the Historical Society of Pennsylvania, Philadelphia, have significant holdings of New Jersey diaries, letters, and account books.

Of the primary sources used for this study, diaries and account books were among the most important. While these are detailed in the text, two in particular stand out—the James Parker diaries, 1778–83, 3 vols., of Shipley Farm in Hunterdon County; and the Jacob Spicer diary, 1755–56, extracts, 1756–62. Both are in the collections of the New Jersey Historical Society. Spicer's has been published in *Proceedings of the New Jersey Historical Society*, 1st ser., 3 (1848–49): 103–4, 192–98; 63 (1945): 37–50, 82–117, 175–88. These diaries ought to be read in conjunction with *Ploughs and Politicks* and R.O. Bausman and J.A. Monroe, eds., "James Tilton's Notes on the Agriculture of Delaware in 1788," *Agricultural History* 20 (1946): 176–87. Many local archives, listed in Murrin's guide, have individual account books or diaries of great value as well.

Several record collections at the New Jersey State Archives were used extensively.

The New Jersey Tax Ratables, 1772–1822, provide information on holdings of land and farm animals and on the ownership of mills, taverns, and the like. In some cases, tax lists from 1781 or 1782 also contain population data. They are organized by county, township, and year. Because the legislature occasionally changed the definition of taxable property, the tax laws should be checked when using these records. While most of the pre-1770 tax lists have been lost, see Peter O. Wacker, "The New Jersey Tax Ratable List of 1751," *New Jersey History* 107 (1989): 23–47. The Wills series contains probate inventories and wills organized by county and year. Through 1800, New Jersey wills have been abstracted in volumes 23, 30, and 32–42 of the *New Jersey State Archives*, 1st ser. (1880–1949). A good introduction to the use of such records can be found in Alice Hanson Jones, *Wealth of a Nation to Be: The American Colonies on the Eve of Revolution* (New York, 1980). Finally, the Revolutionary War damage claims series contains information that complements that found in the probate inventories.

Extensive use has also been made of travel accounts. These accounts, as historians now point out, often tell us as much about the sensibilities and values of the travelers as they do about the people and landscape of early America. Of the many accounts of travel in New Jersey, among the most useful are Adolph B. Benson, ed. and trans., *Peter Kalm's Travels in North America: The English Version of 1770* (1937; reprint, New York, 1987); Carl Magnus Anderson, "Pastor Wrangel's Trip to the Shore," *Proceedings of the New Jersey Historical Society* 58 (1940): 5–31; Metchie J. E. Budka, ed., *Under Their Vine and Fig Tree: Travels through America in 1797–1799, 1805, with Some Further Account of Life in New Jersey by Julian Ursyn Niemcewicz*, vol. 14 of *Collections of the New Jersey Historical Society* (1965); and Johann David Schoepf, *Travels in the Confederation, 1783–1784*, ed. and trans. Alfred J. Morrison, 2 vols. (Philadelphia, 1911).

INDEX

Note: place names for counties, rivers, and townships are from New Jersey unless otherwise noted. Abbreviations: county: cty., township: twp. Figures, maps, notes, and tables are referenced by the first letter of the word and their number (example, 48 (M.9) for Map 9 on page 48).